Arata
THE LEGEND

16

We are Man, born of Heaven and Earth,
Moon and Sun and everything under them.

Eyes, Ears, Nose, Tongue, Body, Mind...

Purity will pierce evil and
open up the world of darkness.

All life will be reborn and invigorated.

Appear now.

STORY & ART BY
Yuu Watase

Arata
THE LEGEND

CHARACTERS

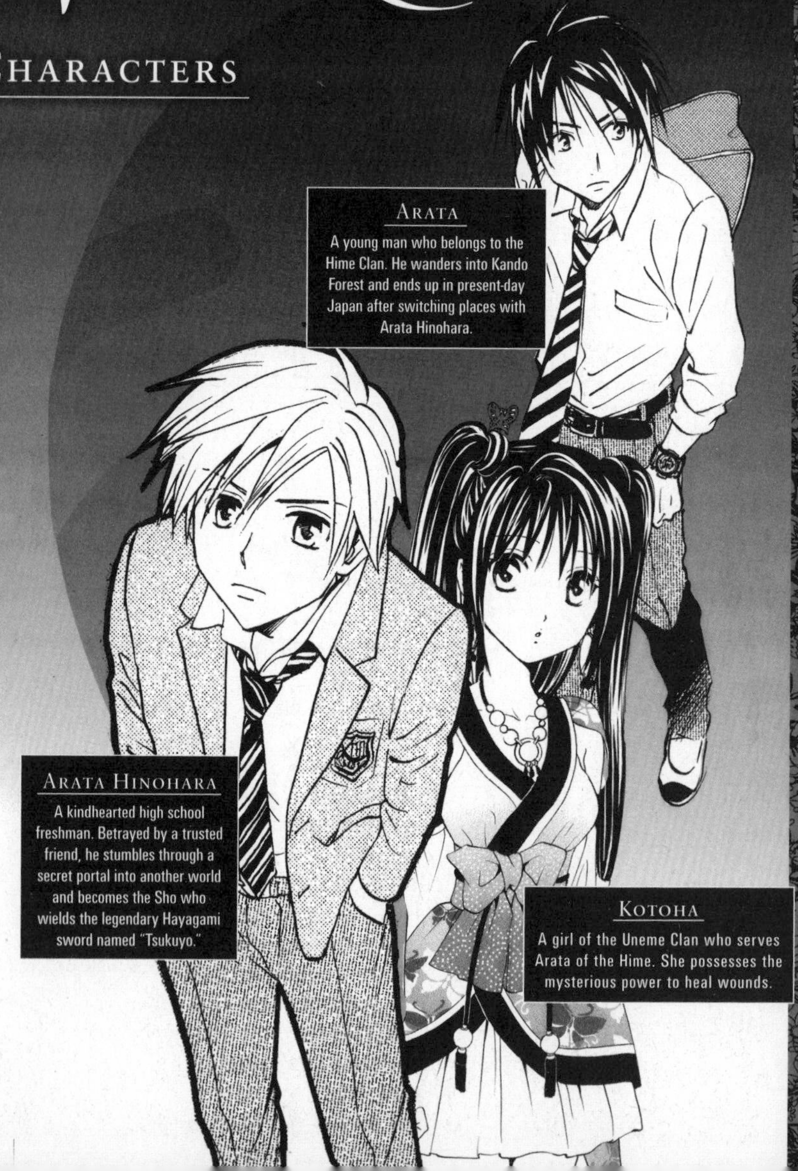
ARATA
A young man who belongs to the Hime Clan. He wanders into Kando Forest and ends up in present-day Japan after switching places with Arata Hinohara.
ARATA HINOHARA
A kindhearted high school freshman. Betrayed by a trusted friend, he stumbles through a secret portal into another world and becomes the Sho who wields the legendary Hayagami sword named "Tsukuyo."
KOTOHA
A girl of the Uneme Clan who serves Arata of the Hime. She possesses the mysterious power to heal wounds.

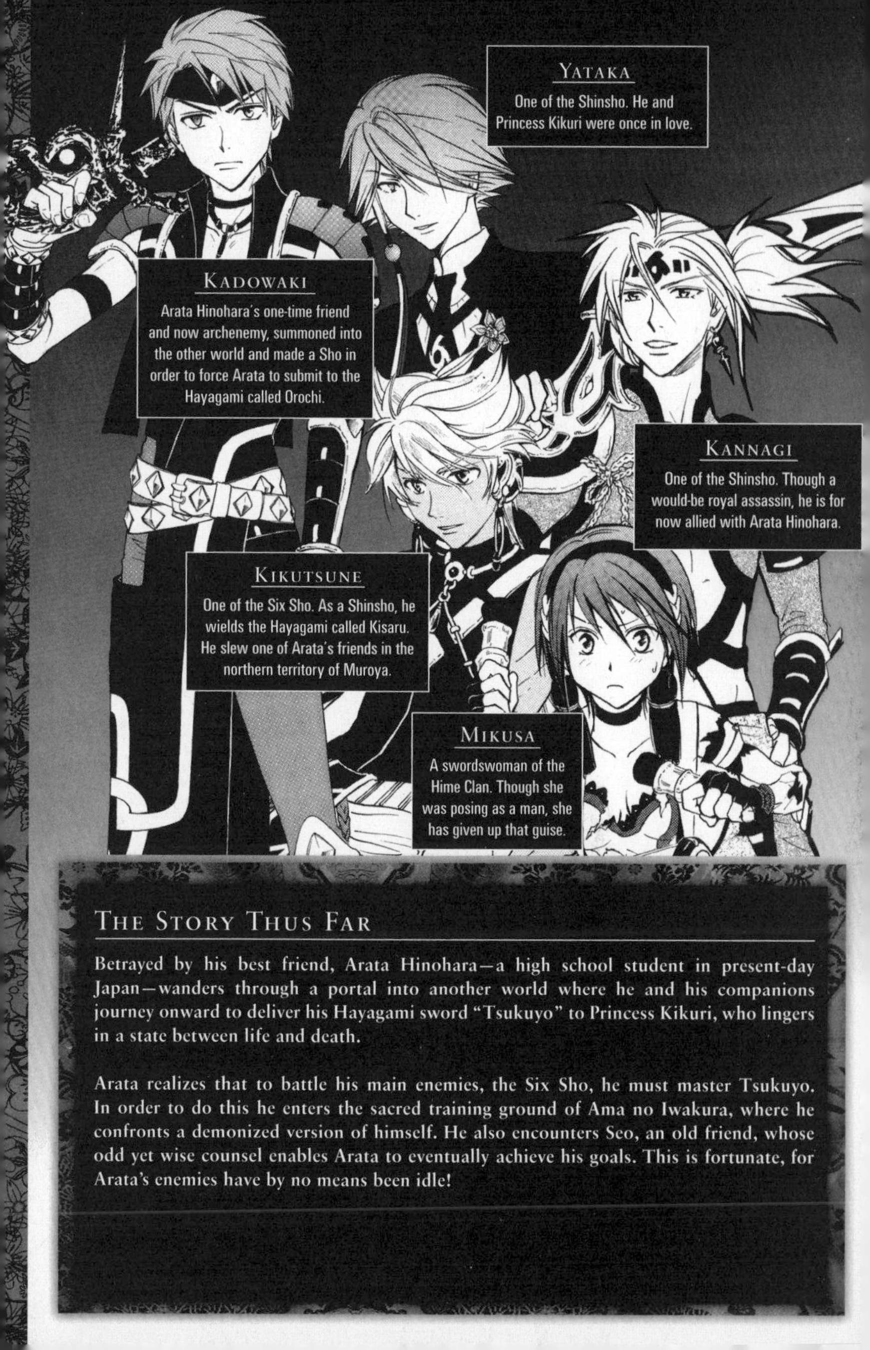
YATAKA
One of the Shinsho. He and Princess Kikuri were once in love.
KADOWAKI
Arata Hinohara's one-time friend and now archenemy, summoned into the other world and made a Sho in order to force Arata to submit to the Hayagami called Orochi.
KANNAGI
One of the Shinsho. Though a would-be royal assassin, he is for now allied with Arata Hinohara.
KIKUTSUNE
One of the Six Sho. As a Shinsho, he wields the Hayagami called Kisaru. He slew one of Arata's friends in the northern territory of Muroya.
MIKUSA
A swordswoman of the Hime Clan. Though she was posing as a man, she has given up that guise.

The Story Thus Far

Betrayed by his best friend, Arata Hinohara—a high school student in present-day Japan—wanders through a portal into another world where he and his companions journey onward to deliver his Hayagami sword "Tsukuyo" to Princess Kikuri, who lingers in a state between life and death.

Arata realizes that to battle his main enemies, the Six Sho, he must master Tsukuyo. In order to do this he enters the sacred training ground of Ama no Iwakura, where he confronts a demonized version of himself. He also encounters Seo, an old friend, whose odd yet wise counsel enables Arata to eventually achieve his goals. This is fortunate, for Arata's enemies have by no means been idle!

16
ARATA
THE LEGEND

CONTENTS

CHAPTER 148

STRANGE SOUND

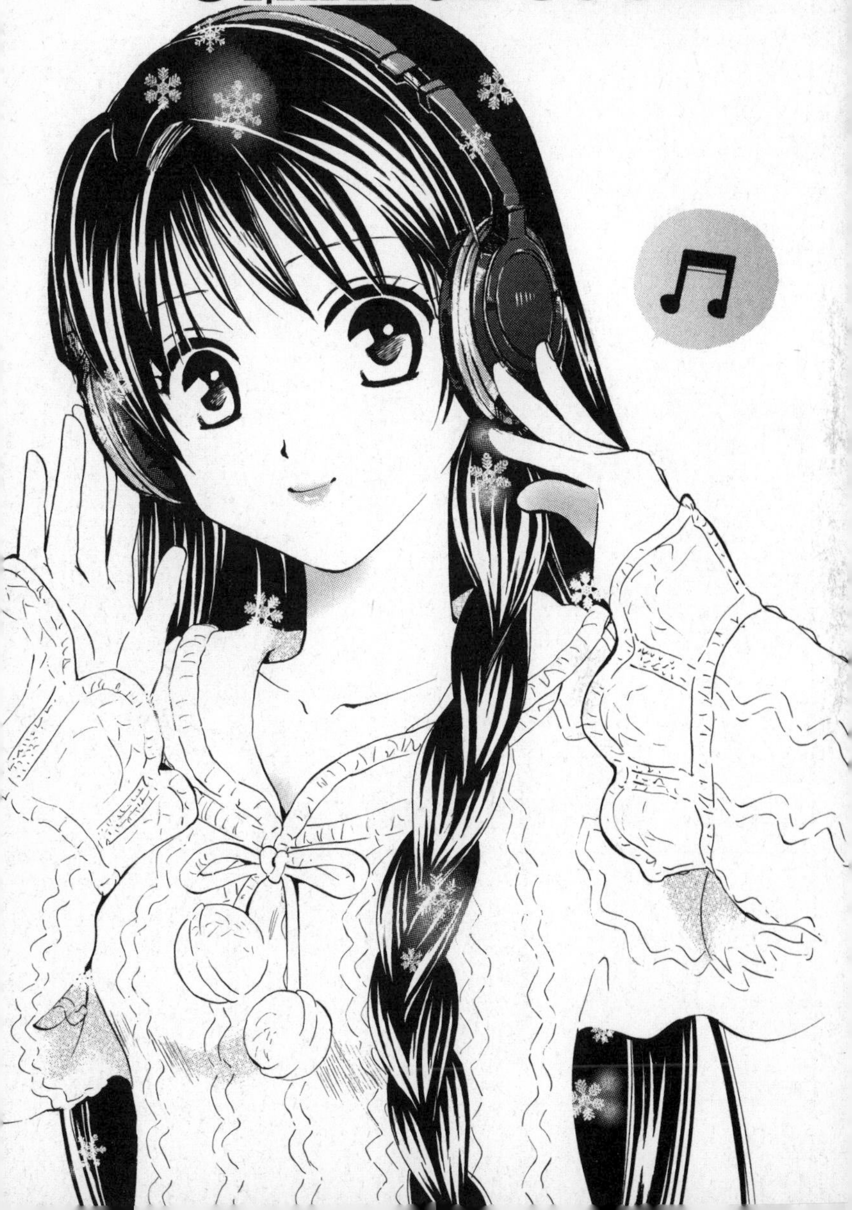

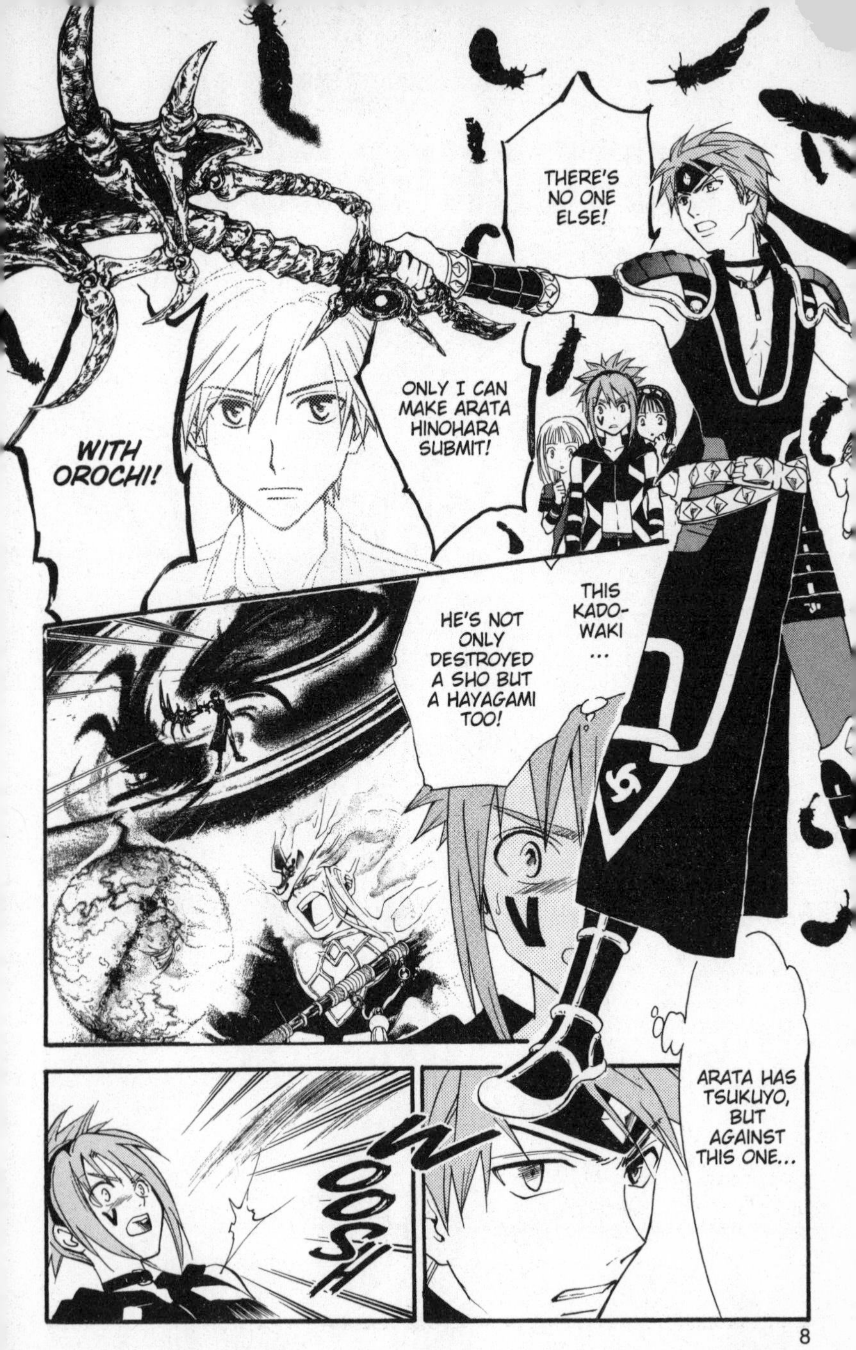
THERE'S NO ONE ELSE!
ONLY I CAN MAKE ARATA HINOHARA SUBMIT!
WITH OROCHI!
THIS KADO-WAKI ...
HE'S NOT ONLY DESTROYED A SHO BUT A HAYAGAMI TOO!
ARATA HAS TSUKUYO, BUT AGAINST THIS ONE...
WOOSH

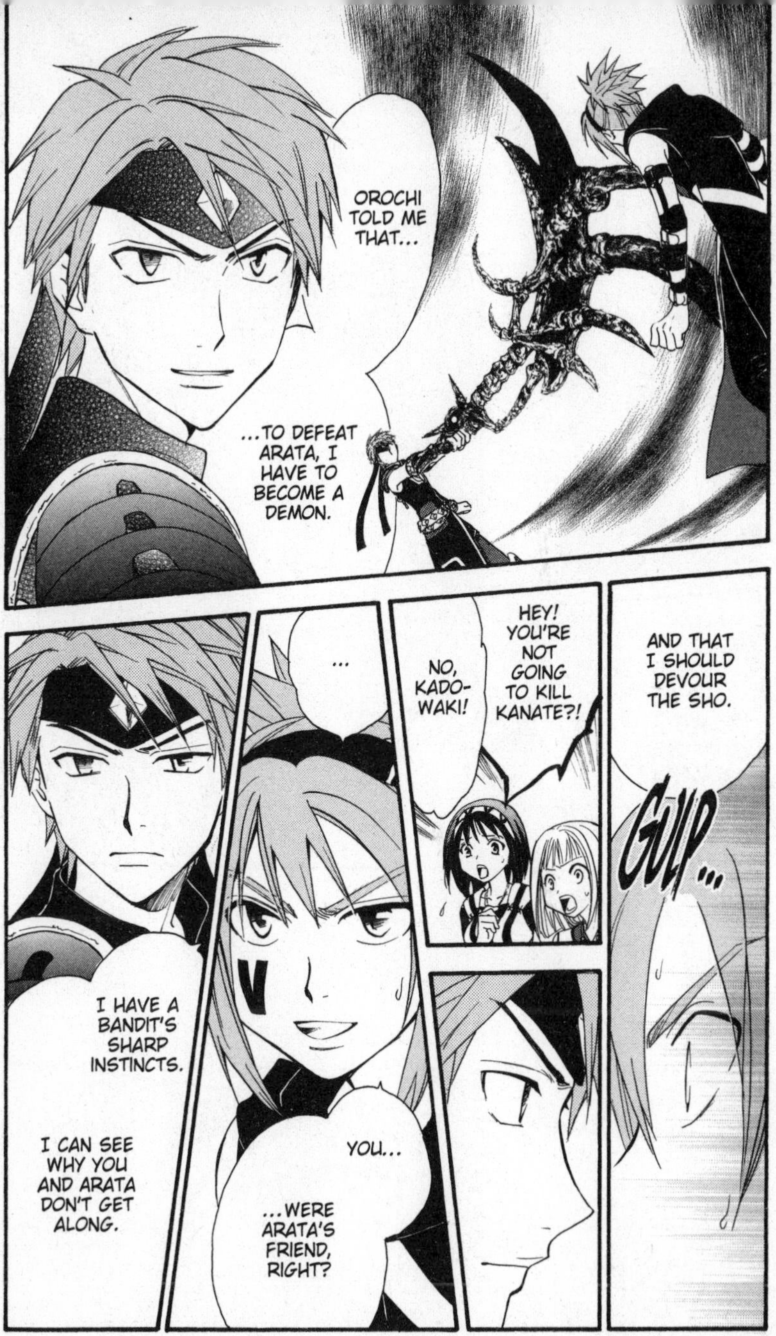
OROCHI TOLD ME THAT...
...TO DEFEAT ARATA, I HAVE TO BECOME A DEMON.
AND THAT I SHOULD DEVOUR THE SHO.
GULP...
HEY! YOU'RE NOT GOING TO KILL KANATE?!
NO, KADO-WAKI!
...
YOU...
...WERE ARATA'S FRIEND, RIGHT?
I HAVE A BANDIT'S SHARP INSTINCTS.
I CAN SEE WHY YOU AND ARATA DON'T GET ALONG.

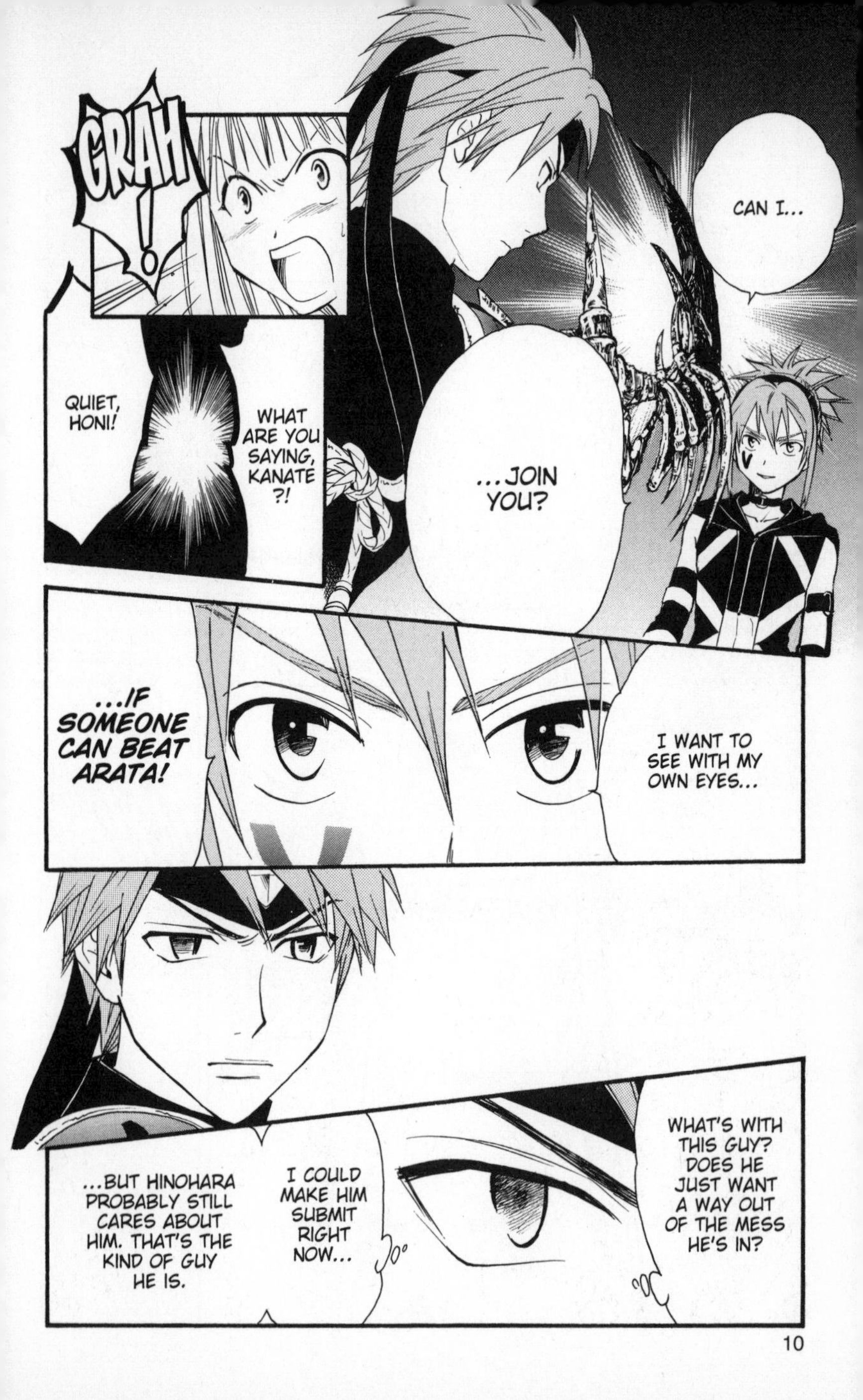
CAN I...
...JOIN YOU?
GRAH!
WHAT ARE YOU SAYING, KANATE?!
QUIET, HONI!
I WANT TO SEE WITH MY OWN EYES...
...IF SOMEONE CAN BEAT ARATA!
WHAT'S WITH THIS GUY? DOES HE JUST WANT A WAY OUT OF THE MESS HE'S IN?
I COULD MAKE HIM SUBMIT RIGHT NOW...
...BUT HINOHARA PROBABLY STILL CARES ABOUT HIM. THAT'S THE KIND OF GUY HE IS.

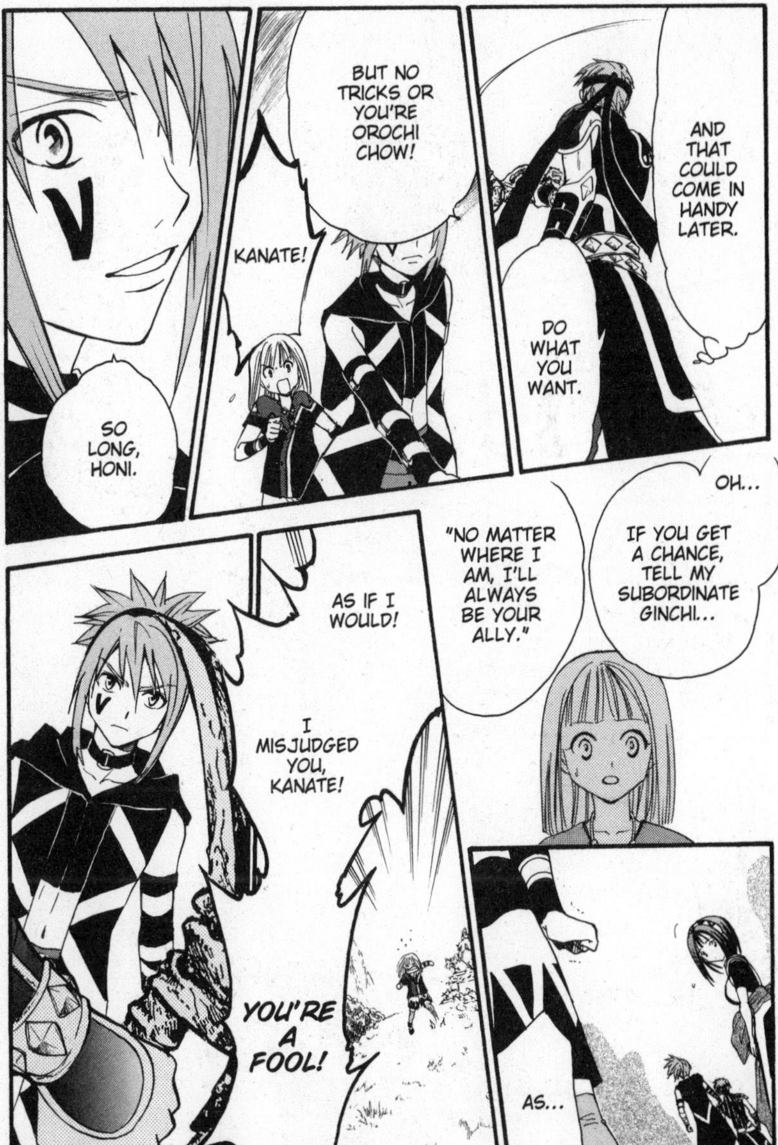
AND THAT COULD COME IN HANDY LATER.
DO WHAT YOU WANT.
BUT NO TRICKS OR YOU'RE OROCHI CHOW!
KANATE!
SO LONG, HONI.
OH...
IF YOU GET A CHANCE, TELL MY SUBORDINATE GINCHI...
"NO MATTER WHERE I AM, I'LL ALWAYS BE YOUR ALLY."
AS...
AS IF I WOULD!
I MISJUDGED YOU, KANATE!
YOU'RE A FOOL!

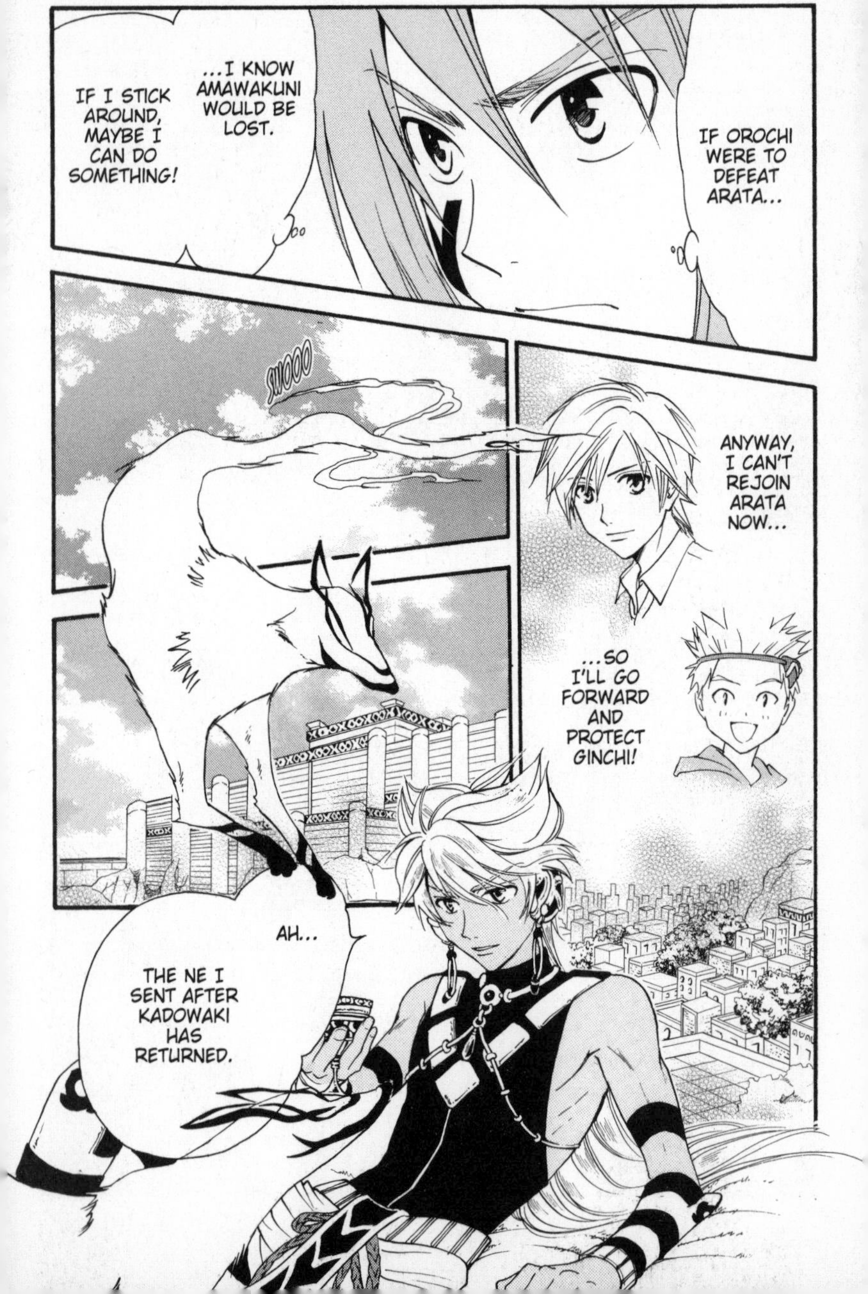
IF OROCHI WERE TO DEFEAT ARATA...
...I KNOW AMAWAKUNI WOULD BE LOST.
IF I STICK AROUND, MAYBE I CAN DO SOMETHING!
ANYWAY, I CAN'T REJOIN ARATA NOW...
...SO I'LL GO FORWARD AND PROTECT GINCHI!
SWOOO
AH...
THE NE I SENT AFTER KADOWAKI HAS RETURNED.

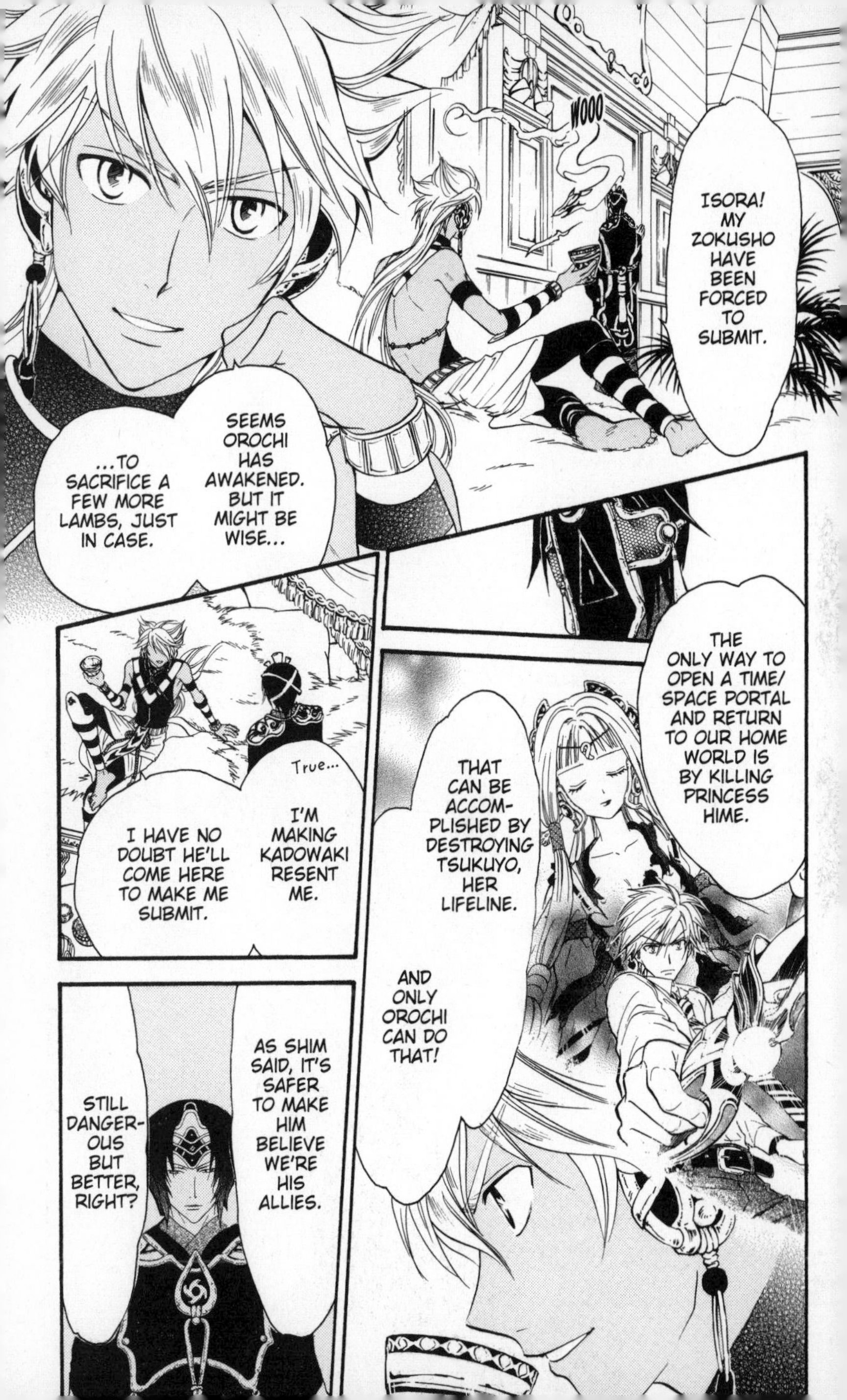

ISORA! MY ZOKUSHO HAVE BEEN FORCED TO SUBMIT.
WOOO
SEEMS OROCHI HAS AWAKENED. BUT IT MIGHT BE WISE...
...TO SACRIFICE A FEW MORE LAMBS, JUST IN CASE.
THE ONLY WAY TO OPEN A TIME/SPACE PORTAL AND RETURN TO OUR HOME WORLD IS BY KILLING PRINCESS HIME.
THAT CAN BE ACCOMPLISHED BY DESTROYING TSUKUYO, HER LIFELINE.
AND ONLY OROCHI CAN DO THAT!
True...
I'M MAKING KADOWAKI RESENT ME.
I HAVE NO DOUBT HE'LL COME HERE TO MAKE ME SUBMIT.
AS SHIM SAID, IT'S SAFER TO MAKE HIM BELIEVE WE'RE HIS ALLIES.
STILL DANGEROUS BUT BETTER, RIGHT?

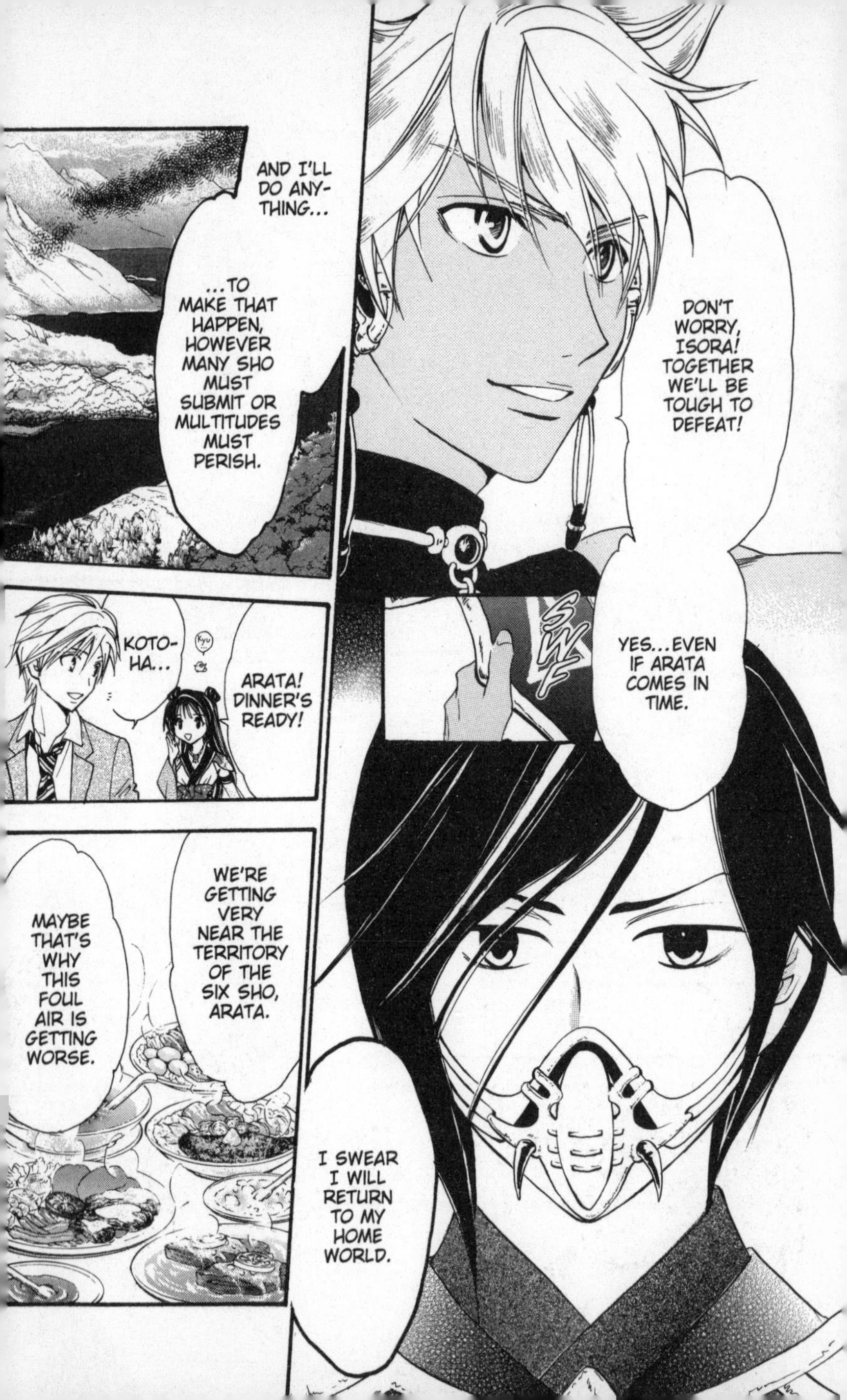
DON'T WORRY, ISORA! TOGETHER WE'LL BE TOUGH TO DEFEAT!
SWF
YES...EVEN IF ARATA COMES IN TIME.
I SWEAR I WILL RETURN TO MY HOME WORLD.
AND I'LL DO ANY-THING...
...TO MAKE THAT HAPPEN, HOWEVER MANY SHO MUST SUBMIT OR MULTITUDES MUST PERISH.
ARATA! DINNER'S READY!
Kyu
KOTO-HA...
WE'RE GETTING VERY NEAR THE TERRITORY OF THE SIX SHO, ARATA.
MAYBE THAT'S WHY THIS FOUL AIR IS GETTING WORSE.

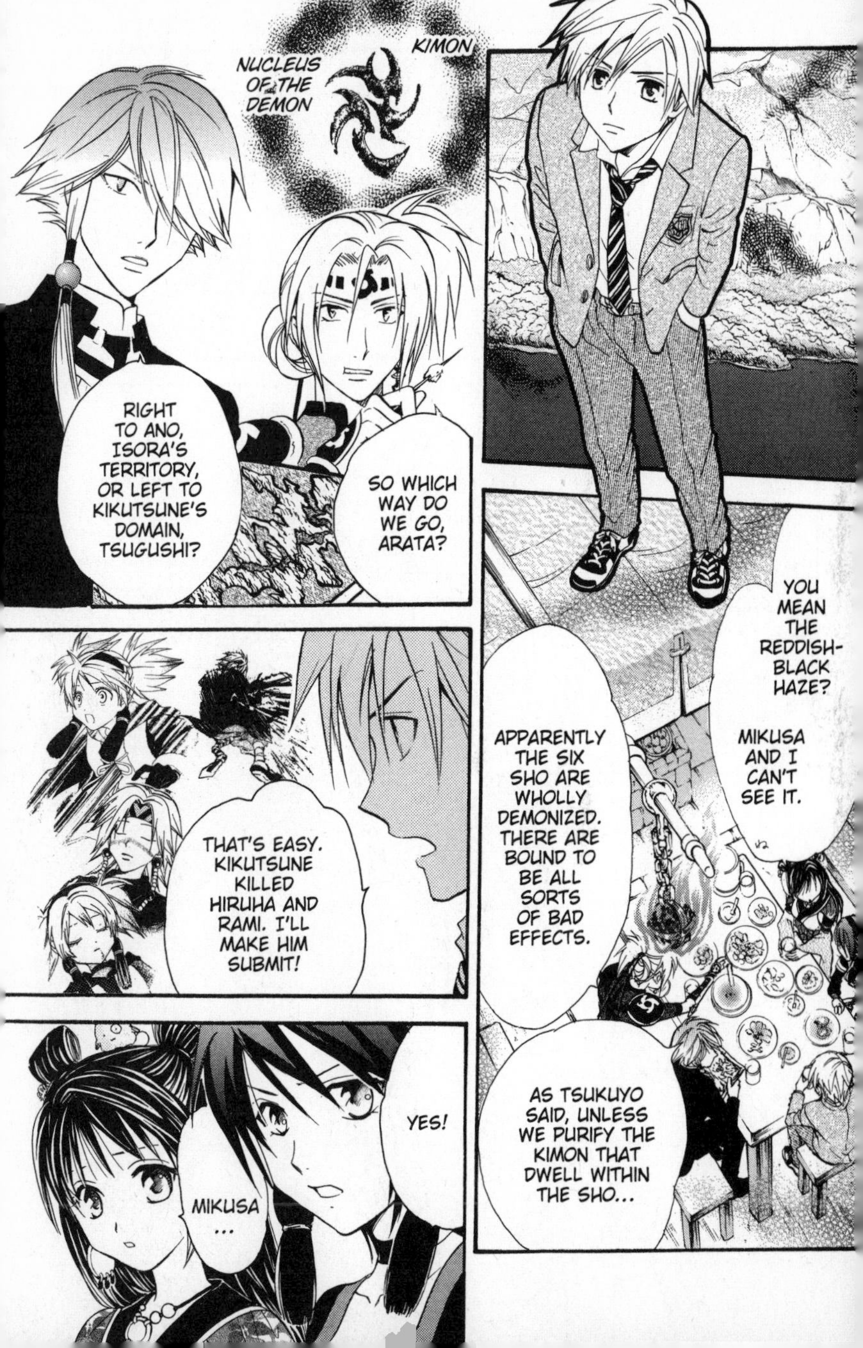
KIMON
NUCLEUS OF THE DEMON
SO WHICH WAY DO WE GO, ARATA?
RIGHT TO ANO, ISORA'S TERRITORY, OR LEFT TO KIKUTSUNE'S DOMAIN, TSUGUSHI?
YOU MEAN THE REDDISH-BLACK HAZE?
MIKUSA AND I CAN'T SEE IT.
APPARENTLY THE SIX SHO ARE WHOLLY DEMONIZED. THERE ARE BOUND TO BE ALL SORTS OF BAD EFFECTS.
AS TSUKUYO SAID, UNLESS WE PURIFY THE KIMON THAT DWELL WITHIN THE SHO...
THAT'S EASY. KIKUTSUNE KILLED HIRUHA AND RAMI. I'LL MAKE HIM SUBMIT!
YES!
MIKUSA...

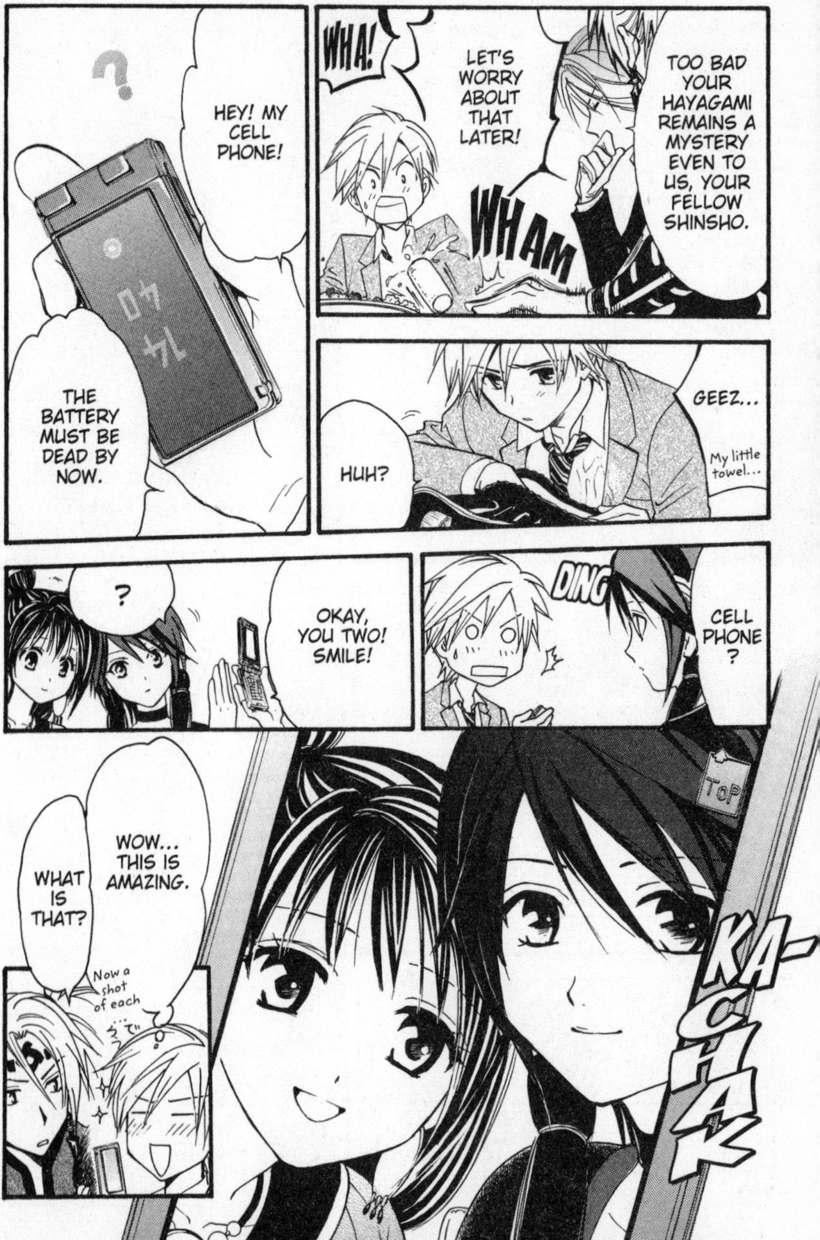
TOO BAD YOUR HAYAGAMI REMAINS A MYSTERY EVEN TO US, YOUR FELLOW SHINSHO.
WHAM
LET'S WORRY ABOUT THAT LATER!
WHA!
GEEZ...
My little towel...
HUH?
HEY! MY CELL PHONE!
THE BATTERY MUST BE DEAD BY NOW.
DING
CELL PHONE?
OKAY, YOU TWO! SMILE!
?
KA-CHAK
WOW... THIS IS AMAZING.
WHAT IS THAT?
Now a shot of each...

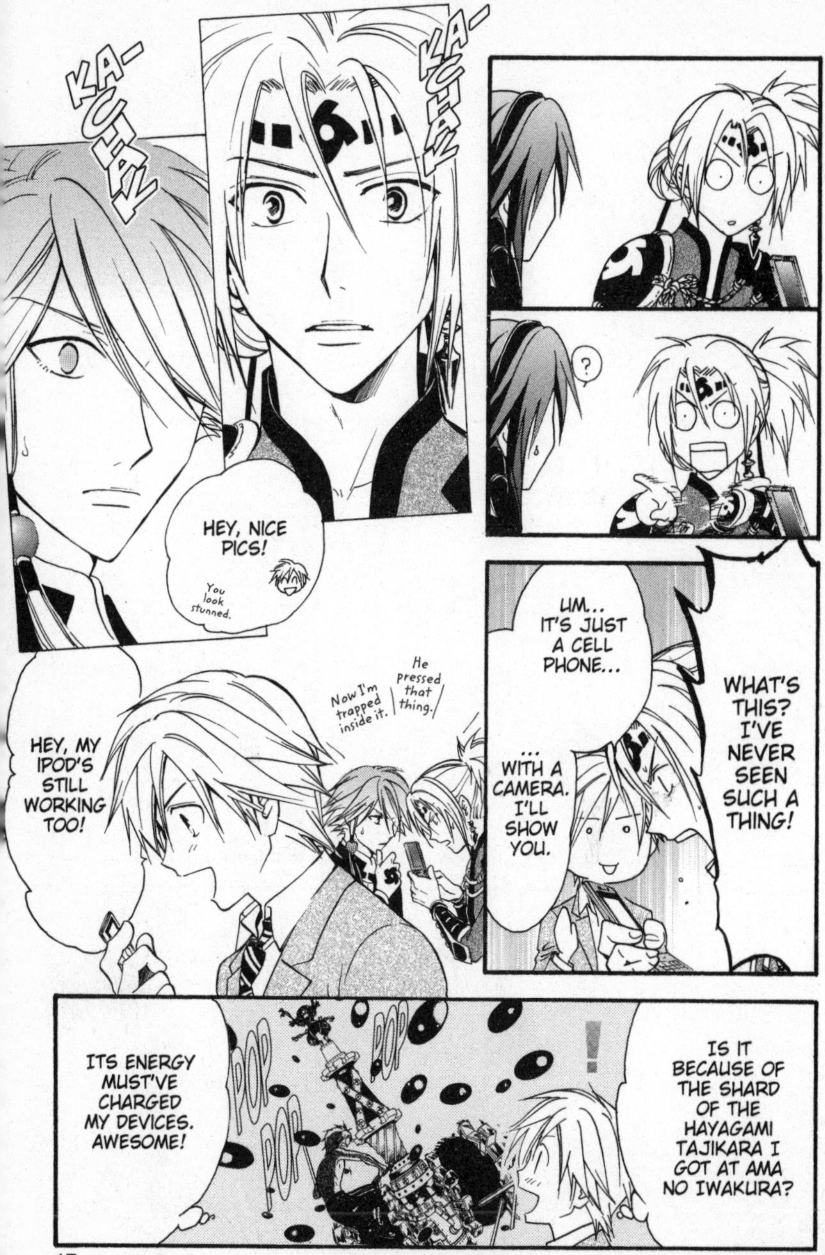
?
KA-CHAY
KA-CHAY
HEY, NICE PICS!
You look stunned.
WHAT'S THIS? I'VE NEVER SEEN SUCH A THING!
UM... IT'S JUST A CELL PHONE...
... WITH A CAMERA. I'LL SHOW YOU.
He pressed that thing.
Now I'm trapped inside it.
HEY, MY IPOD'S STILL WORKING TOO!
!
IS IT BECAUSE OF THE SHARD OF THE HAYAGAMI TAJIKARA I GOT AT AMA NO IWAKURA?
POP
POP
POP
POP
ITS ENERGY MUST'VE CHARGED MY DEVICES. AWESOME!

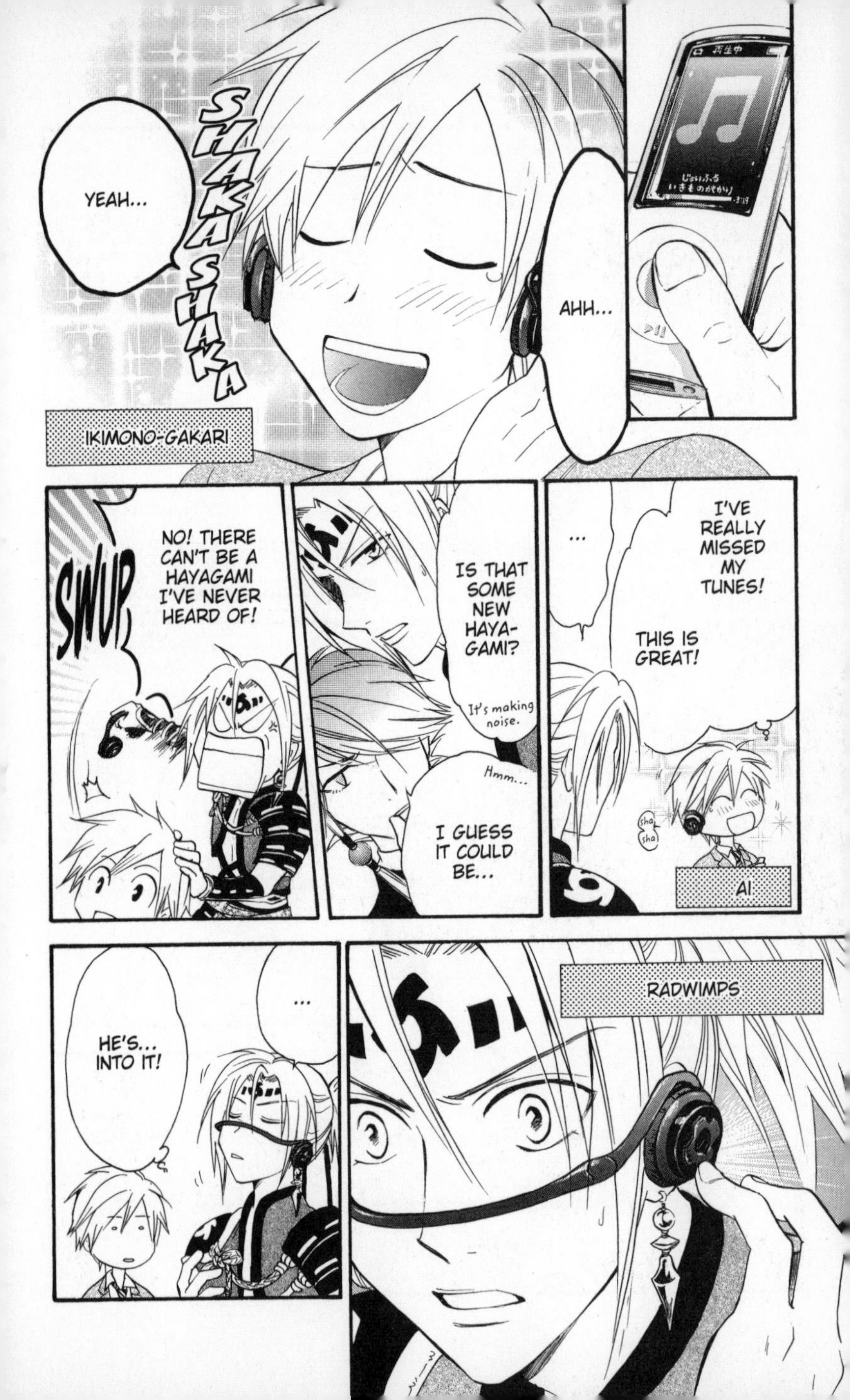
再生中
じょいふる
いきものがかり
AHH...
YEAH...
SHAKA SHAKA
IKIMONO-GAKARI
I'VE REALLY MISSED MY TUNES!
THIS IS GREAT!
...
sha
sha
AI
IS THAT SOME NEW HAYA-GAMI?
It's making noise.
Hmm...
I GUESS IT COULD BE...
NO! THERE CAN'T BE A HAYAGAMI I'VE NEVER HEARD OF!
SWUP
RADWIMPS
...
HE'S... INTO IT!

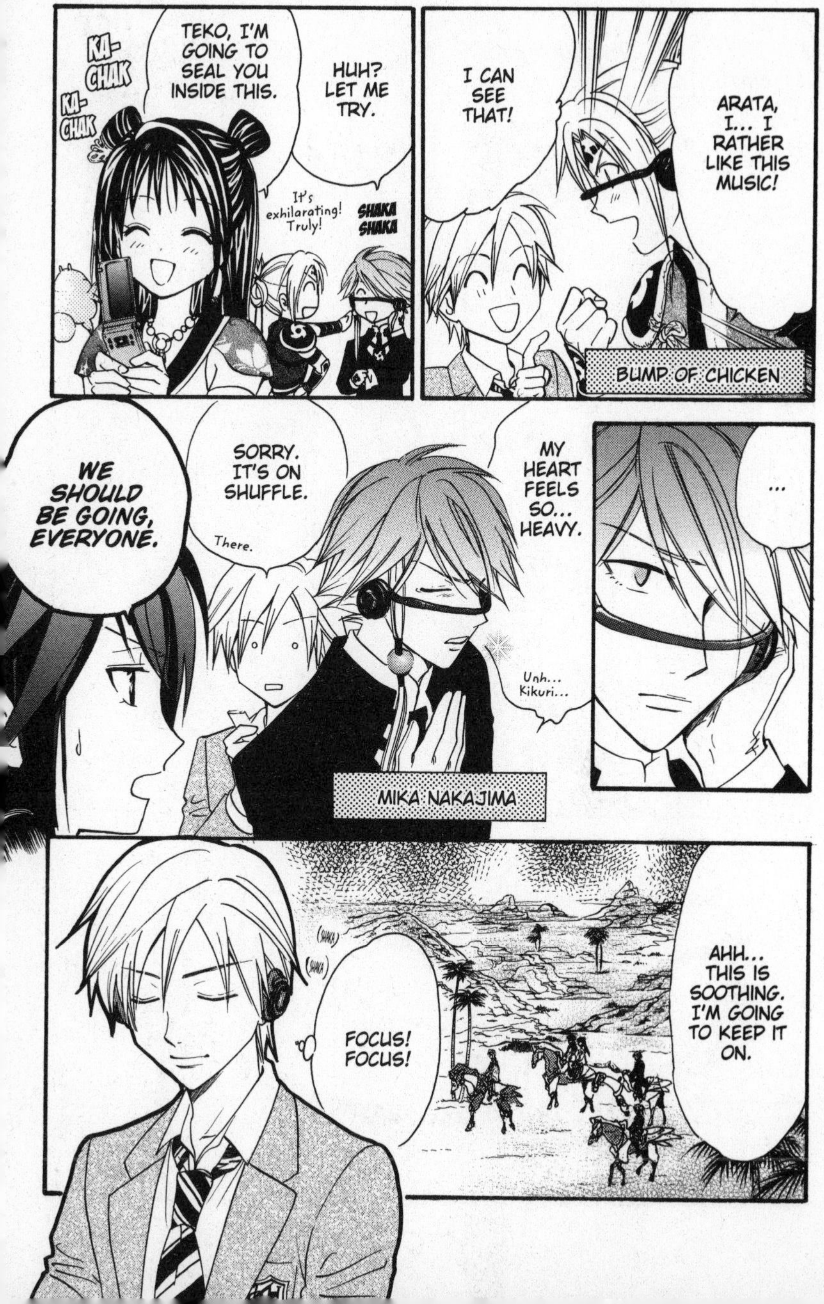
ARATA, I... I RATHER LIKE THIS MUSIC!
I CAN SEE THAT!
BUMP OF CHICKEN
KA-CHAK
KA-CHAK
TEKO, I'M GOING TO SEAL YOU INSIDE THIS.
HUH? LET ME TRY.
SHAKA SHAKA
It's exhilarating! Truly!
...
MY HEART FEELS SO... HEAVY.
Unh... Kikuri...
MIKA NAKAJIMA
SORRY. IT'S ON SHUFFLE.
There.
WE SHOULD BE GOING, EVERYONE.
AHH... THIS IS SOOTHING. I'M GOING TO KEEP IT ON.
(SHAKA)
(SHAKA)
FOCUS! FOCUS!

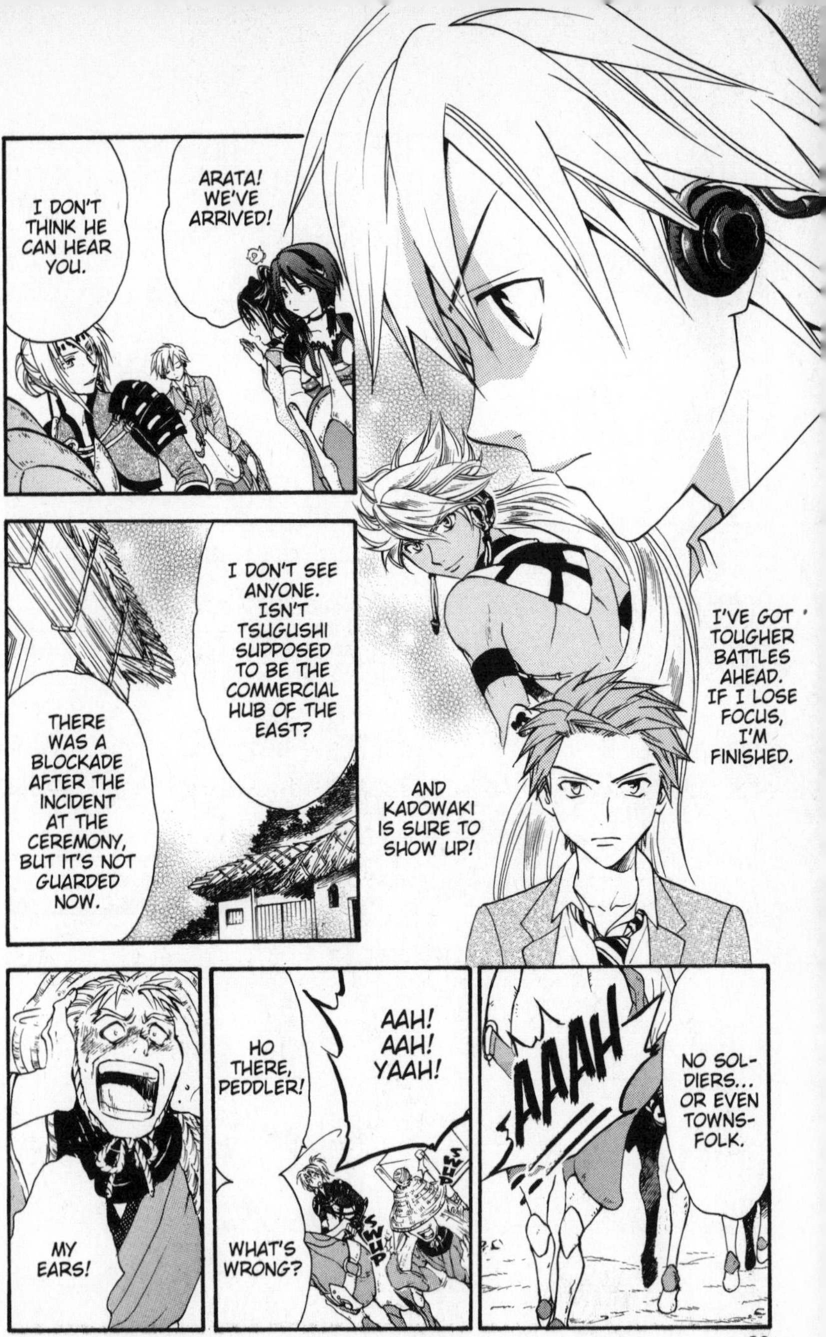
I'VE GOT TOUGHER BATTLES AHEAD. IF I LOSE FOCUS, I'M FINISHED.
AND KADOWAKI IS SURE TO SHOW UP!
ARATA! WE'VE ARRIVED!
I DON'T THINK HE CAN HEAR YOU.
I DON'T SEE ANYONE. ISN'T TSUGUSHI SUPPOSED TO BE THE COMMERCIAL HUB OF THE EAST?
THERE WAS A BLOCKADE AFTER THE INCIDENT AT THE CEREMONY, BUT IT'S NOT GUARDED NOW.
NO SOL-DIERS... OR EVEN TOWNS-FOLK.
AAAH
AAH! AAH! YAAH!
HO THERE, PEDDLER!
SWUP
SWUP
WHAT'S WRONG?
MY EARS!

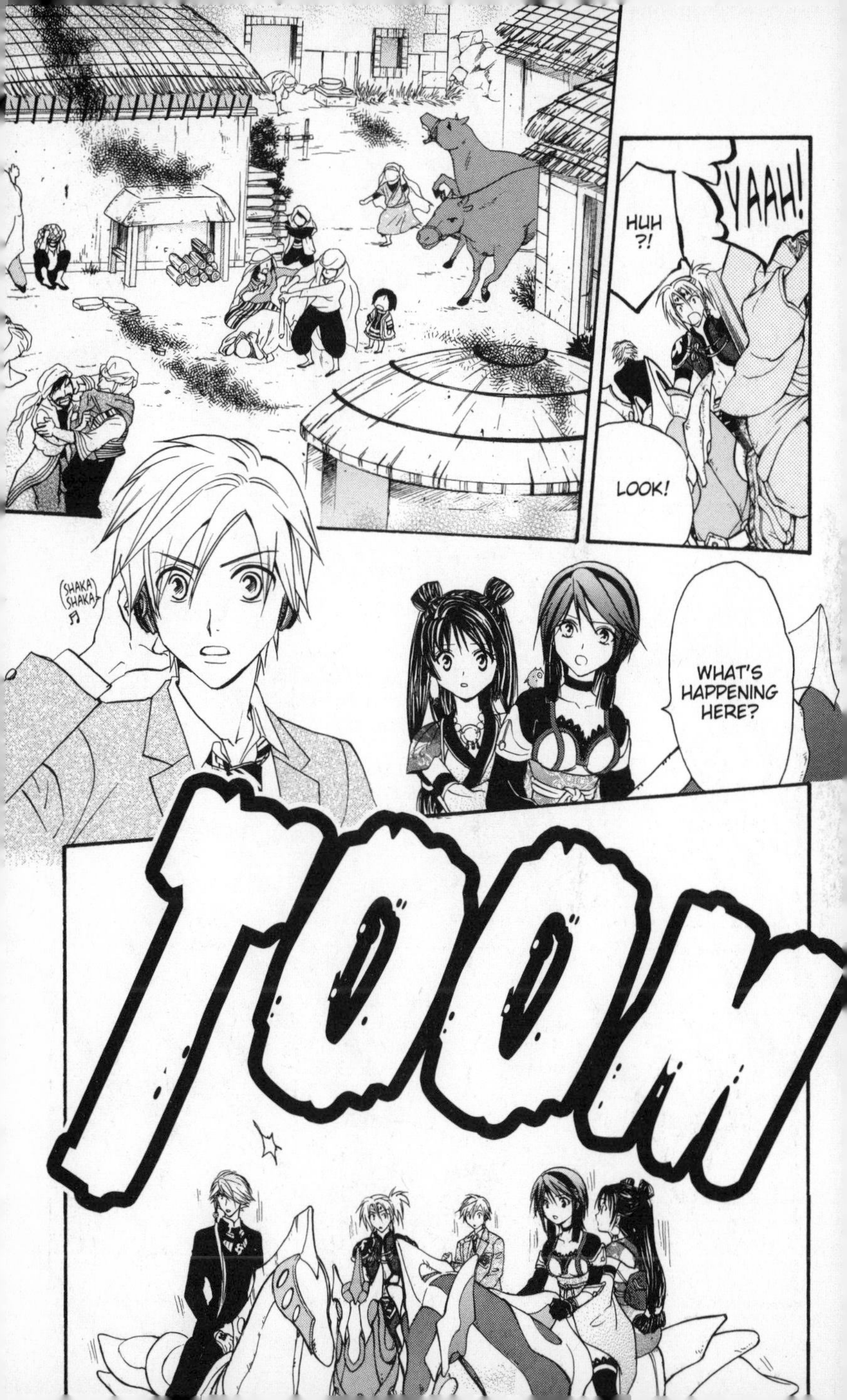
YAAH!
HUH ?!
LOOK!
WHAT'S HAPPENING HERE?
(SHAKA) (SHAKA)
TOOM

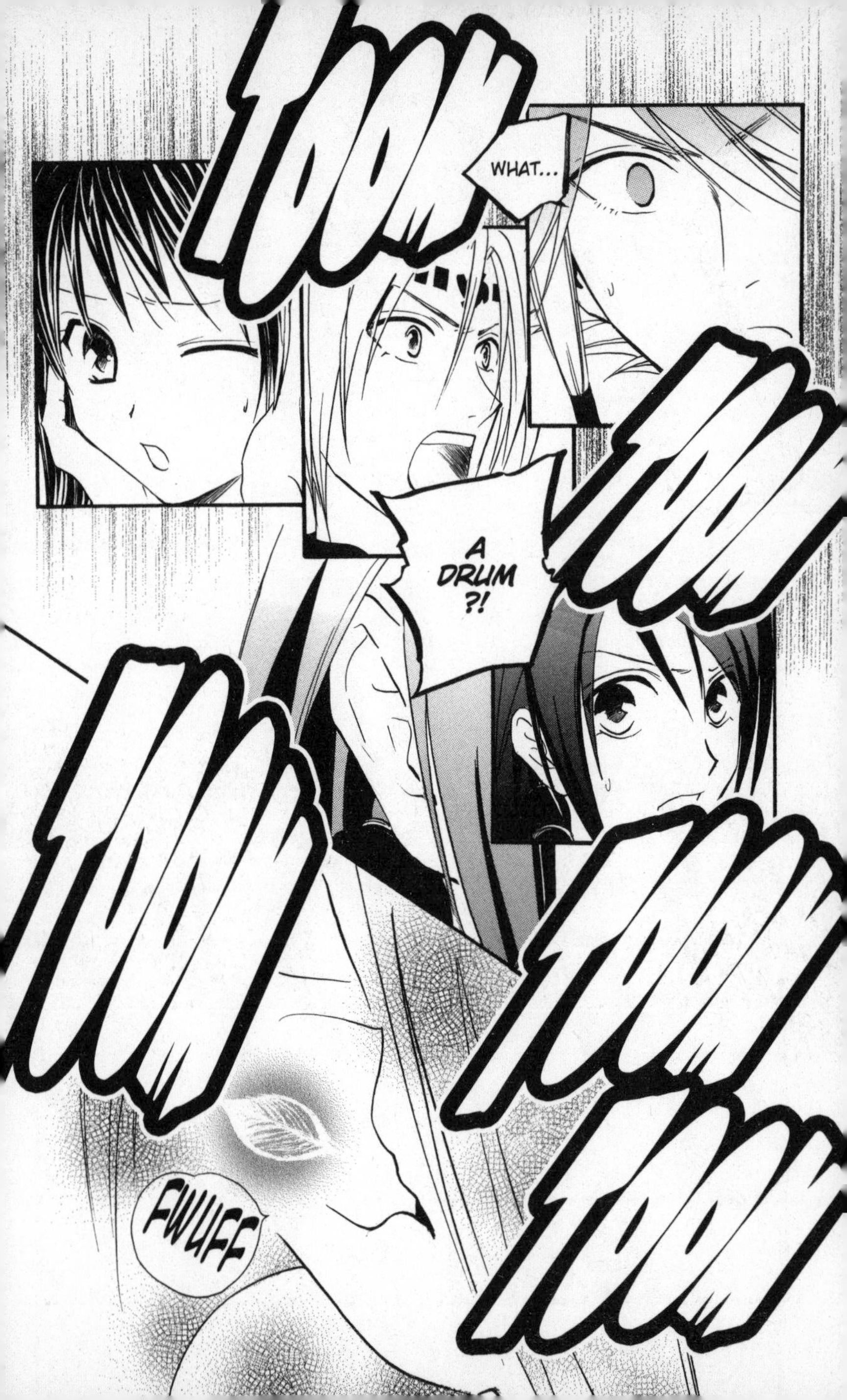
TOON
WHAT...
TOON
A DRUM ?!
TOON
TOON
TOON
FWUFF

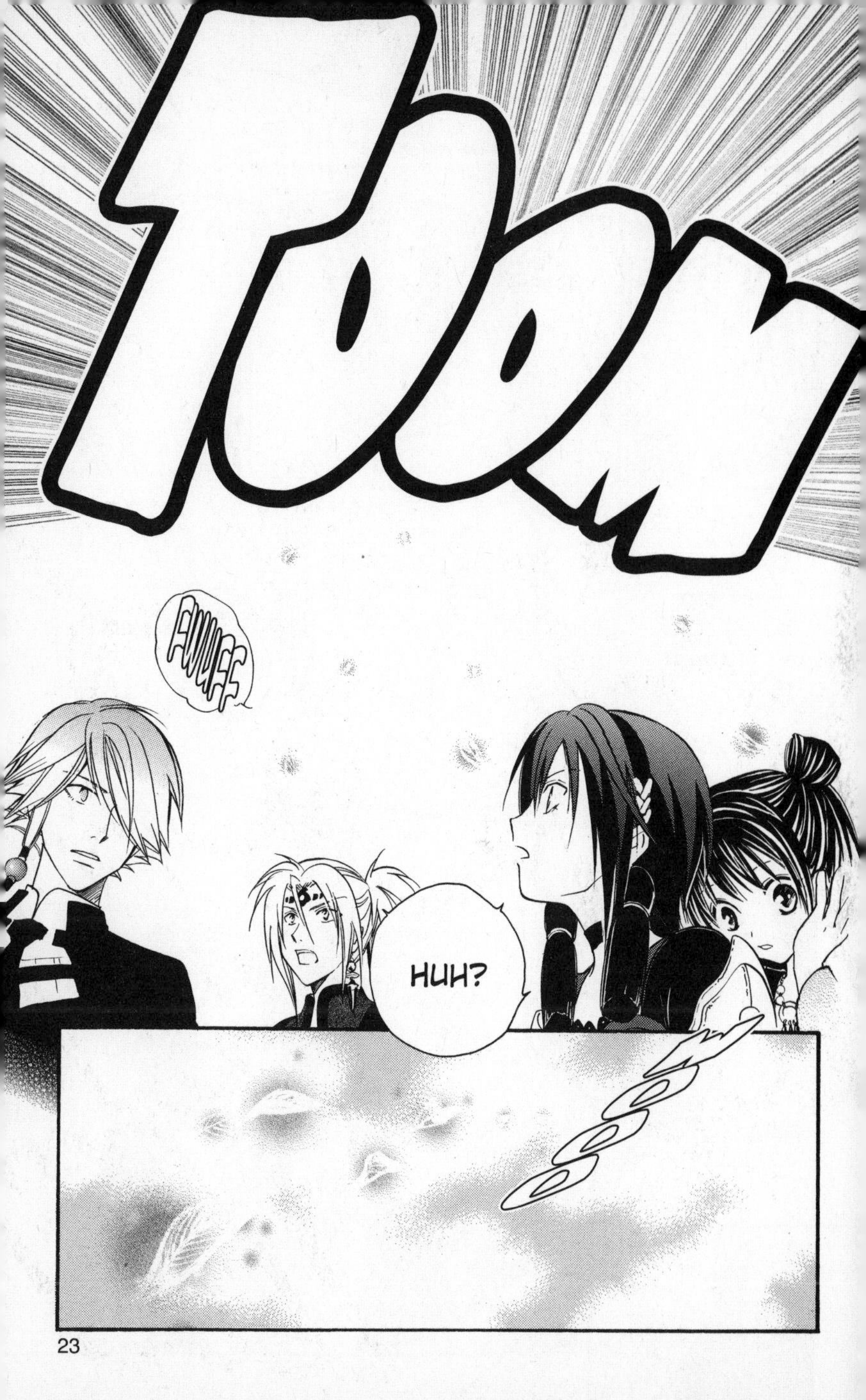
TOOM
HUH?
FWUFF
OOOM

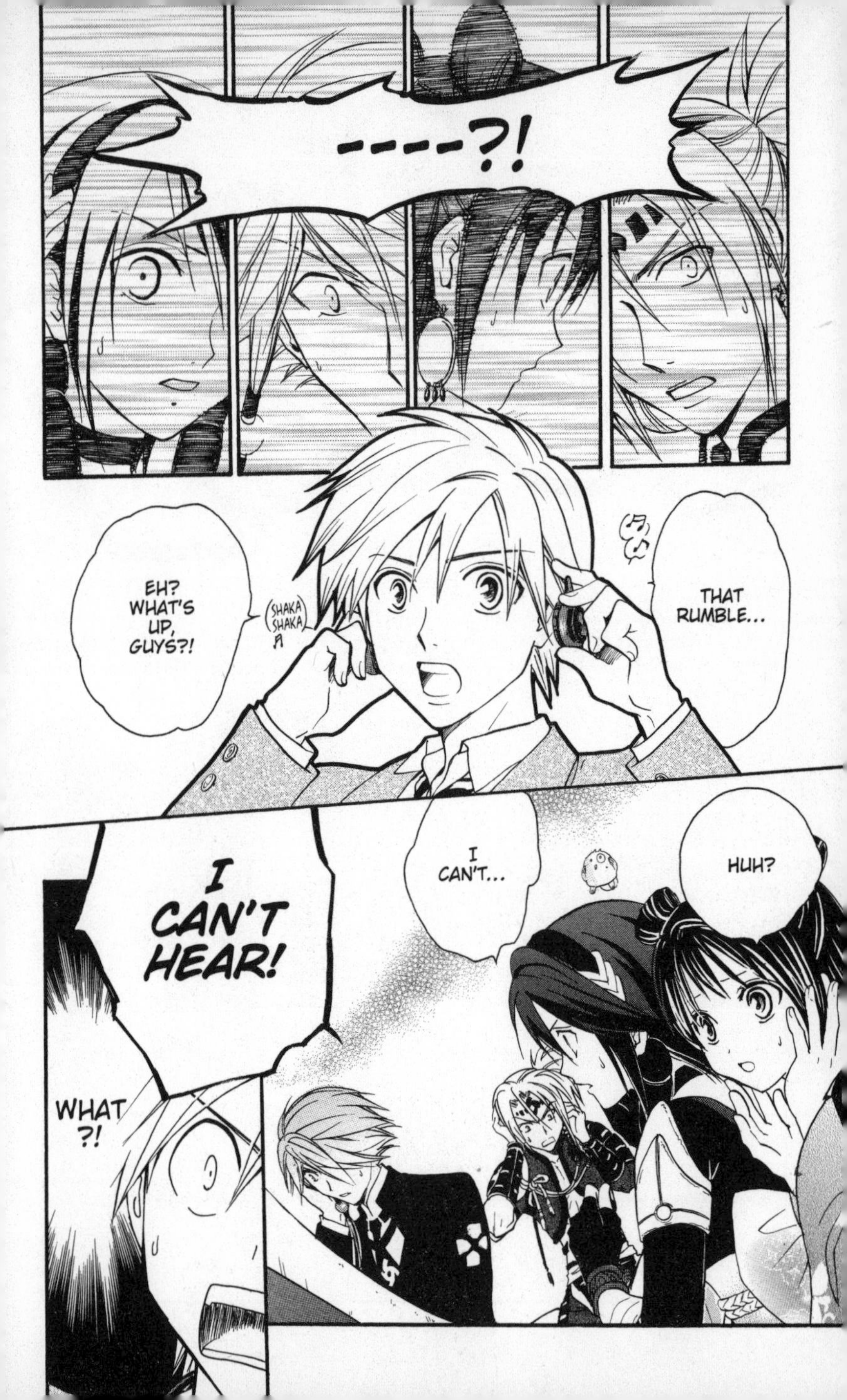
----?!
THAT RUMBLE...
(SHAKA SHAKA)
EH? WHAT'S UP, GUYS?!
HUH?
I CAN'T...
I CAN'T HEAR!
WHAT?!

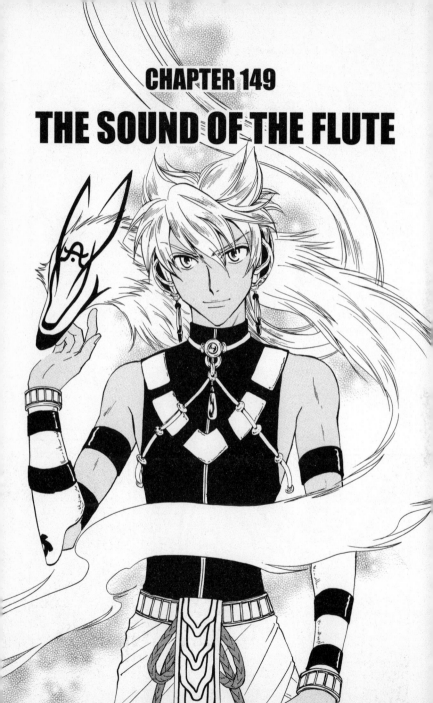

CHAPTER 149
THE SOUND OF THE FLUTE

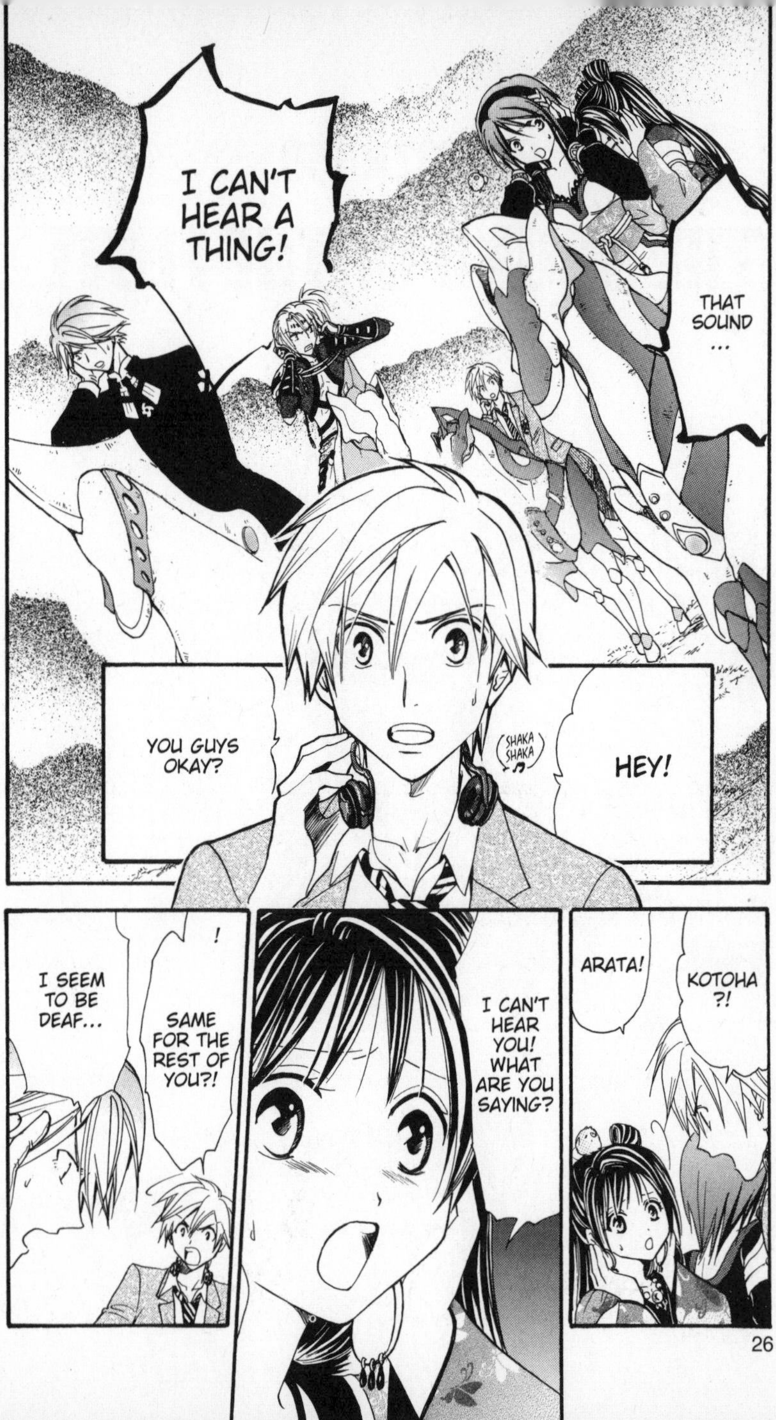
THAT SOUND ...
I CAN'T HEAR A THING!
HEY!
SHAKA SHAKA
YOU GUYS OKAY?
KOTOHA ?!
ARATA!
I CAN'T HEAR YOU! WHAT ARE YOU SAYING?
!
SAME FOR THE REST OF YOU?!
I SEEM TO BE DEAF...

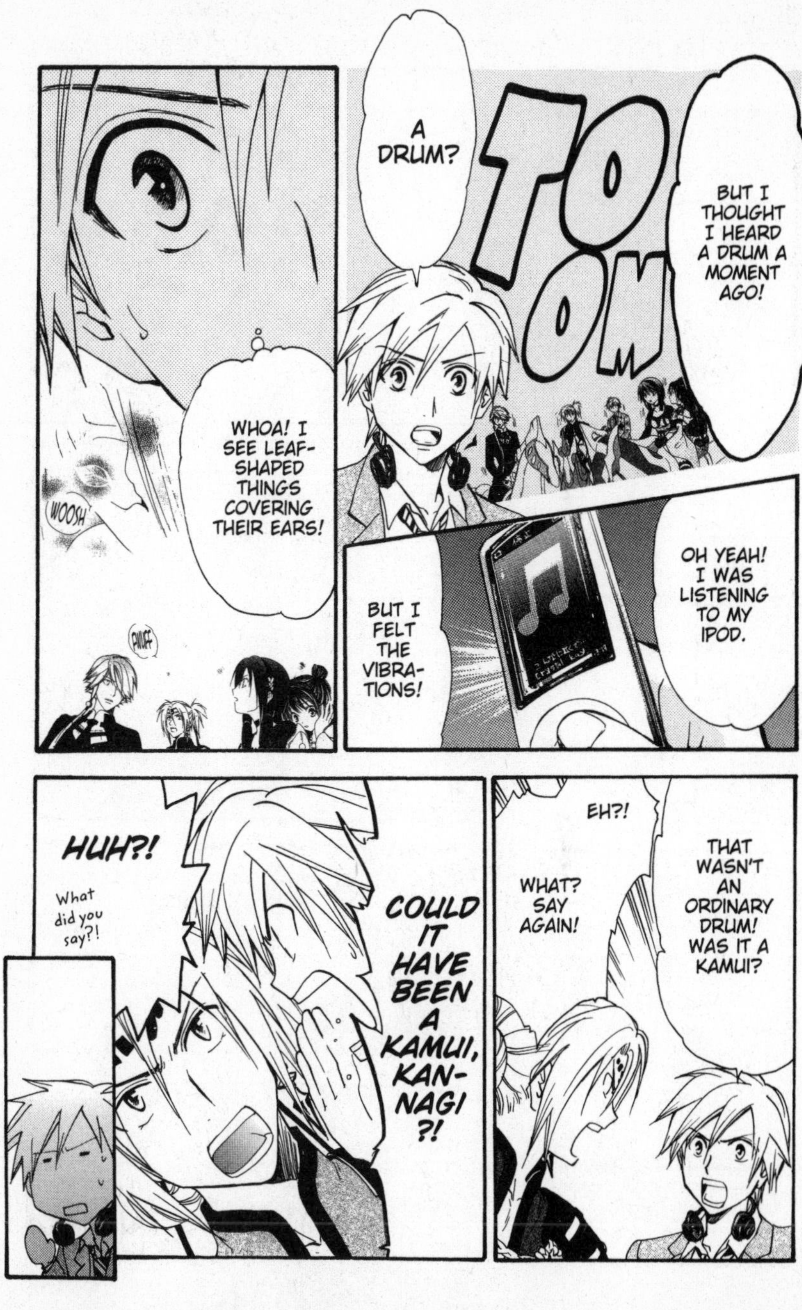
BUT I THOUGHT I HEARD A DRUM A MOMENT AGO!
TOM
A DRUM?
OH YEAH! I WAS LISTENING TO MY IPOD.
BUT I FELT THE VIBRATIONS!
WHOA! I SEE LEAF-SHAPED THINGS COVERING THEIR EARS!
WOOSH
THAT WASN'T AN ORDINARY DRUM! WAS IT A KAMUI?
EH?!
WHAT? SAY AGAIN!
COULD IT HAVE BEEN A KAMUI, KAN-NAGI?!
HUH?!
What did you say?!

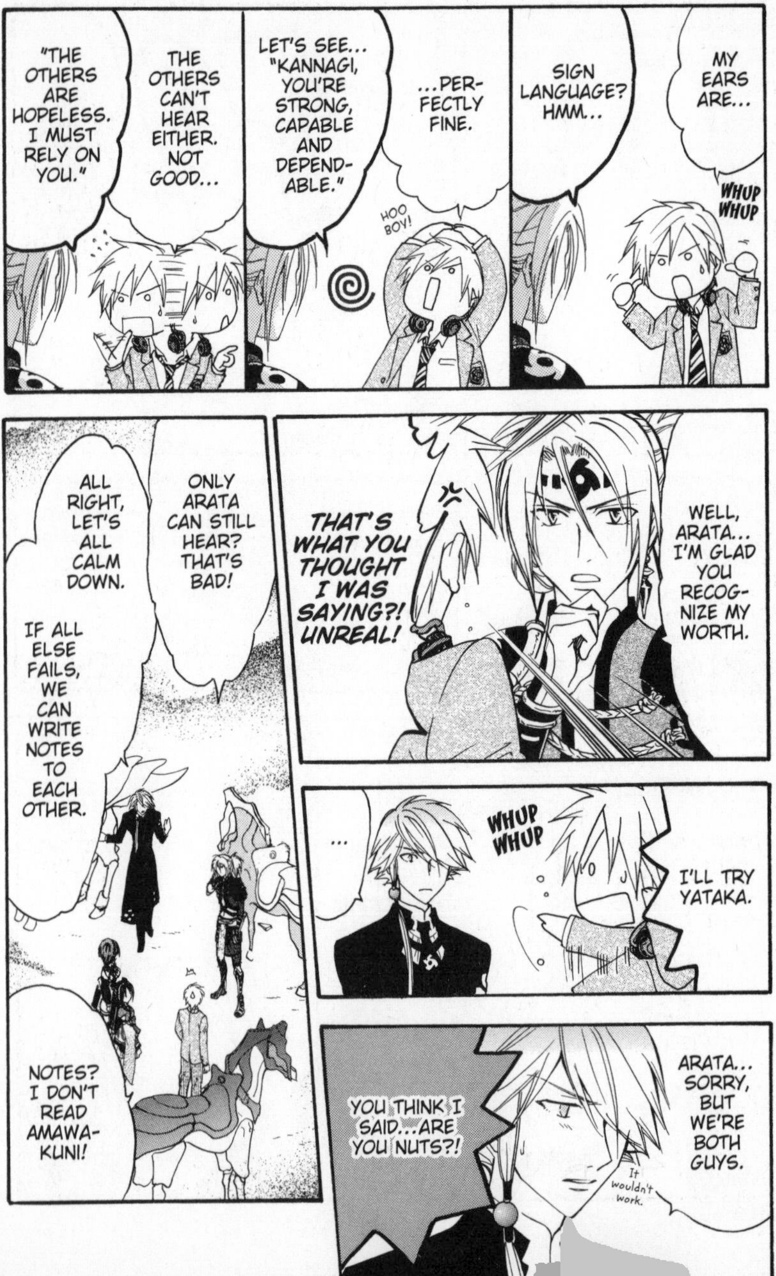
MY EARS ARE...
WHUP WHUP
SIGN LANGUAGE? HMM...
...PERFECTLY FINE.
LET'S SEE... "KANNAGI, YOU'RE STRONG, CAPABLE AND DEPENDABLE."
HOO BOY!
THE OTHERS CAN'T HEAR EITHER. NOT GOOD...
"THE OTHERS ARE HOPELESS. I MUST RELY ON YOU."
WELL, ARATA... I'M GLAD YOU RECOGNIZE MY WORTH.
THAT'S WHAT YOU THOUGHT I WAS SAYING?! UNREAL!
I'LL TRY YATAKA.
WHUP WHUP
...
ARATA... SORRY, BUT WE'RE BOTH GUYS.
It wouldn't work.
YOU THINK I SAID...ARE YOU NUTS?!
ONLY ARATA CAN STILL HEAR? THAT'S BAD!
ALL RIGHT, LET'S ALL CALM DOWN.
IF ALL ELSE FAILS, WE CAN WRITE NOTES TO EACH OTHER.
NOTES? I DON'T READ AMAWAKUNI!

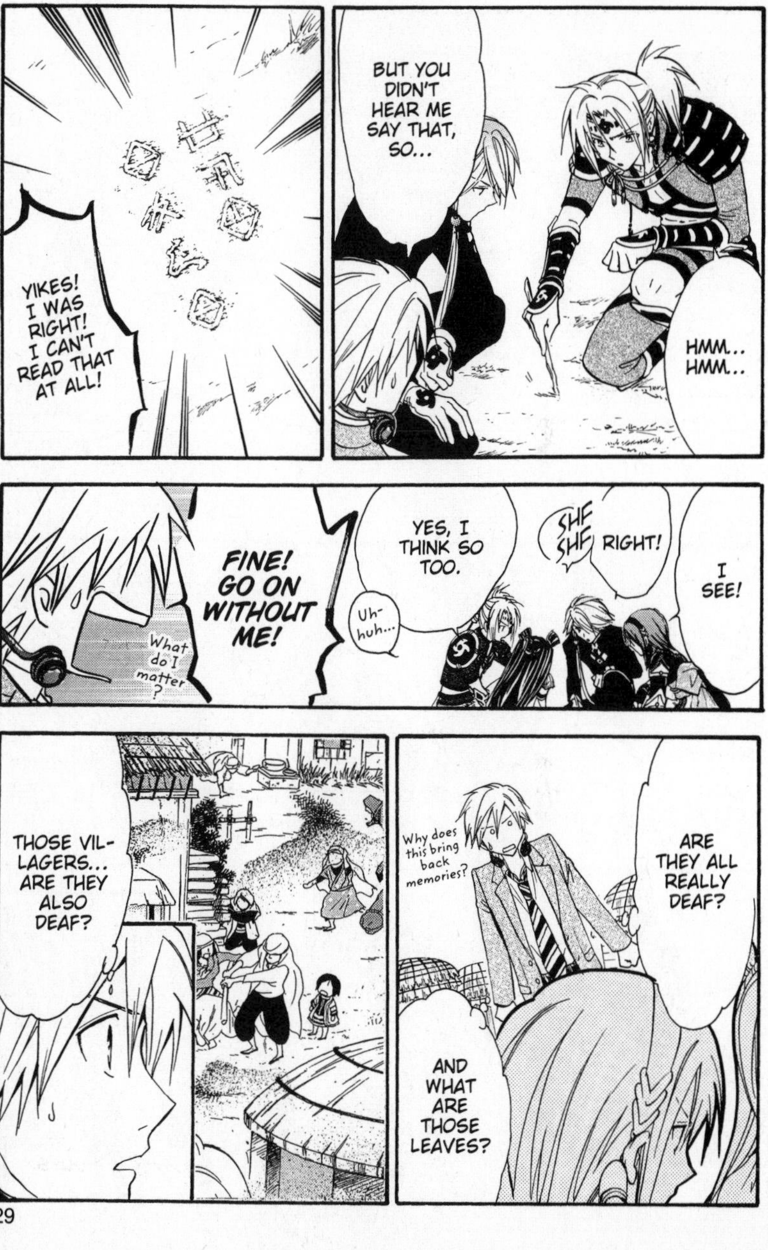
BUT YOU DIDN'T HEAR ME SAY THAT, SO...
HMM... HMM...
YIKES! I WAS RIGHT! I CAN'T READ THAT AT ALL!
I SEE!
SHF SHF
RIGHT!
YES, I THINK SO TOO.
Uh-huh...
FINE! GO ON WITHOUT ME!
What do I matter?
ARE THEY ALL REALLY DEAF?
Why does this bring back memories?
AND WHAT ARE THOSE LEAVES?
THOSE VIL-LAGERS... ARE THEY ALSO DEAF?

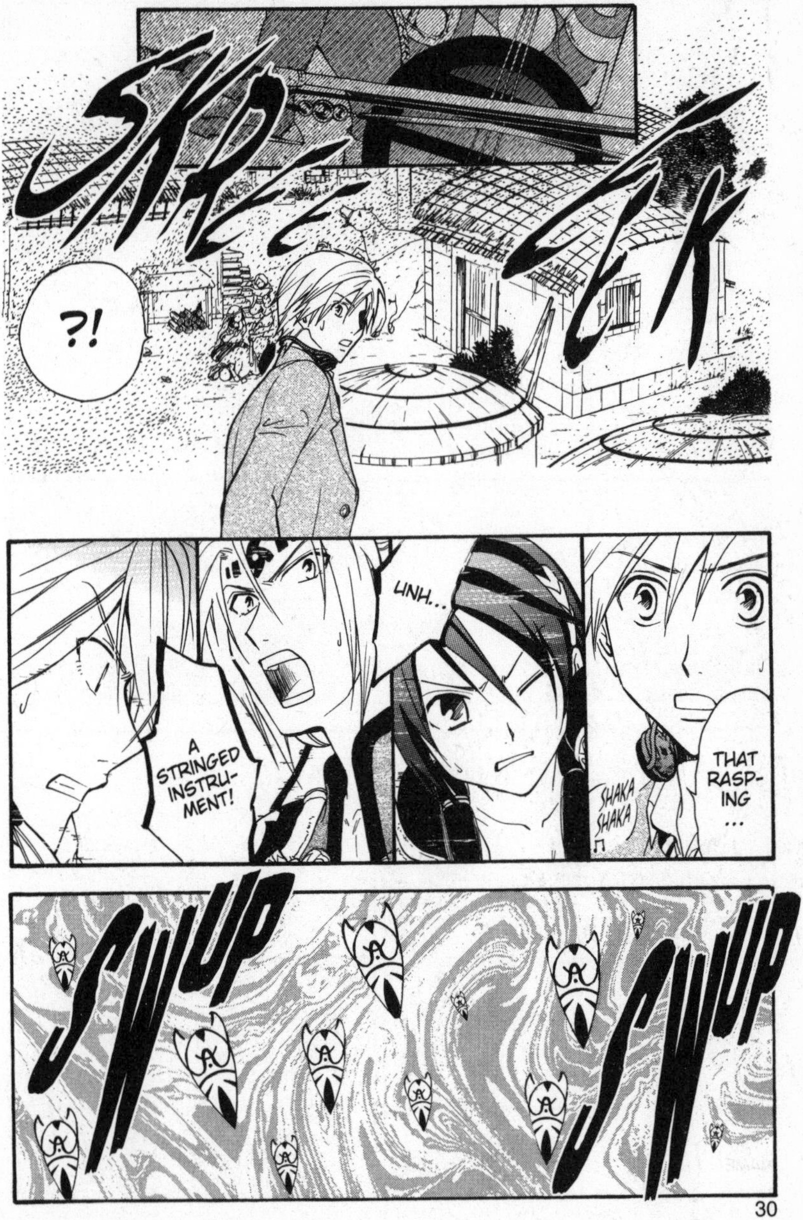
SKREEEEK
?!
THAT RASPING...
SHAKA SHAKA
UNH...
A STRINGED INSTRUMENT!
SHWUP
SHWUP

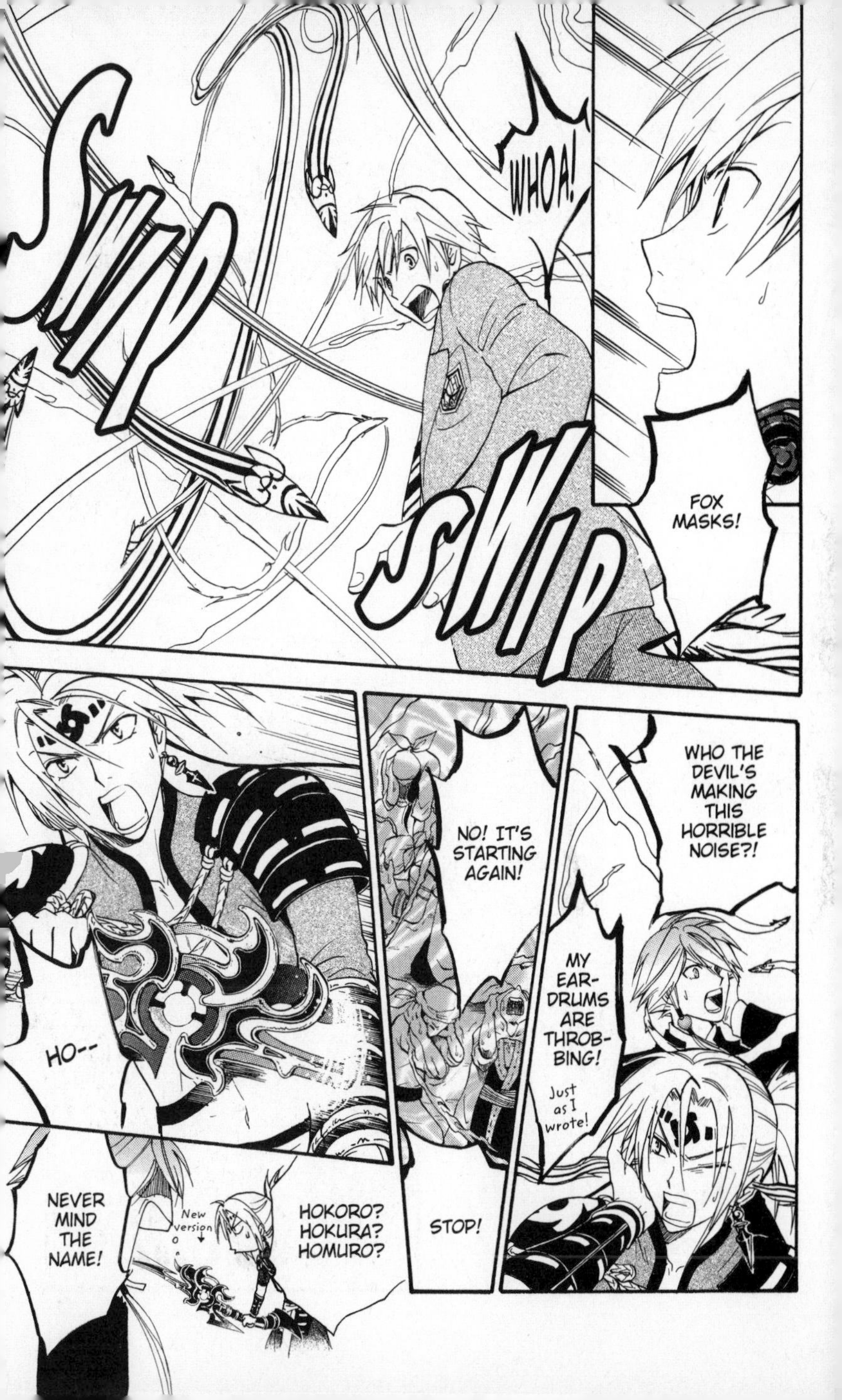
FOX MASKS!
WHOA!
SWIP
SWIP
WHO THE DEVIL'S MAKING THIS HORRIBLE NOISE?!
MY EAR-DRUMS ARE THROB-BING!
Just as I wrote!
NO! IT'S STARTING AGAIN!
STOP!
HO--
HOKORO? HOKURA? HOMURO?
NEVER MIND THE NAME!
New version

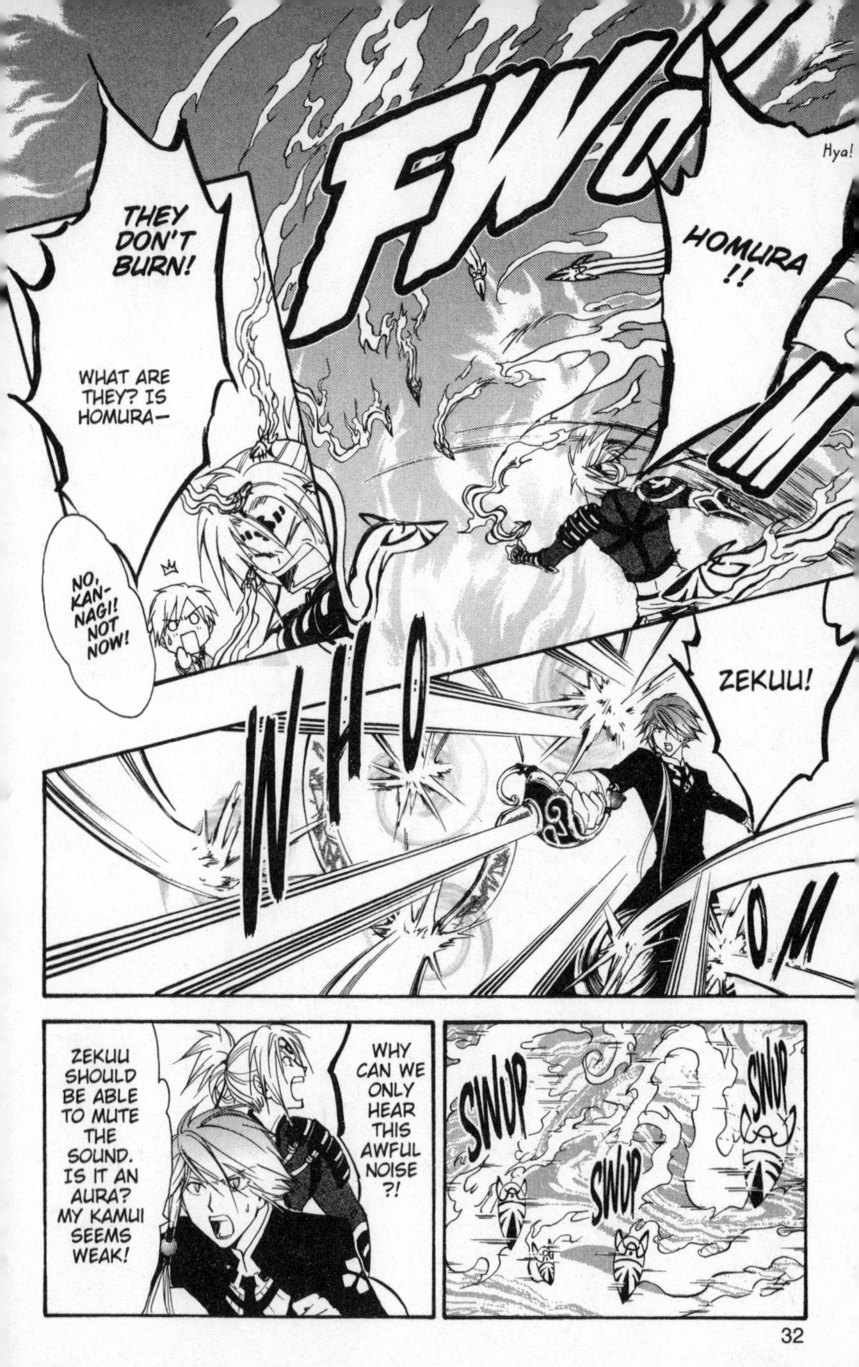
Hya!
HOMURA!!
FWOM
THEY DON'T BURN!
WHAT ARE THEY? IS HOMURA—
NO, KAN-NAGI! NOT NOW!
ZEKUU!
WHOOM
SWUP
SWUP
SWUP
WHY CAN WE ONLY HEAR THIS AWFUL NOISE?!
ZEKUU SHOULD BE ABLE TO MUTE THE SOUND. IS IT AN AURA? MY KAMUI SEEMS WEAK!

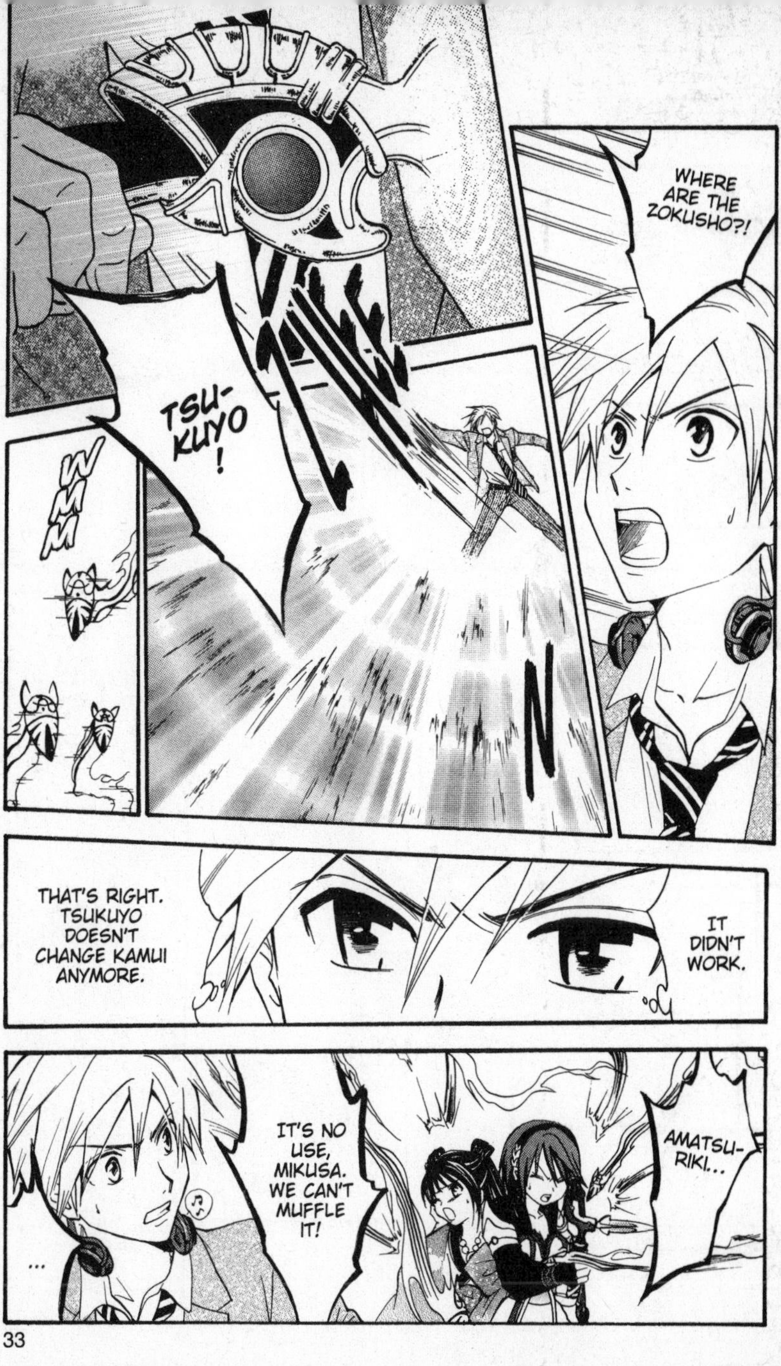
WHERE ARE THE ZOKUSHO?!
TSU-KUYO!
WMMM
N
IT DIDN'T WORK.
THAT'S RIGHT. TSUKUYO DOESN'T CHANGE KAMUI ANYMORE.
AMATSURIKI...
IT'S NO USE, MIKUSA. WE CAN'T MUFFLE IT!
...

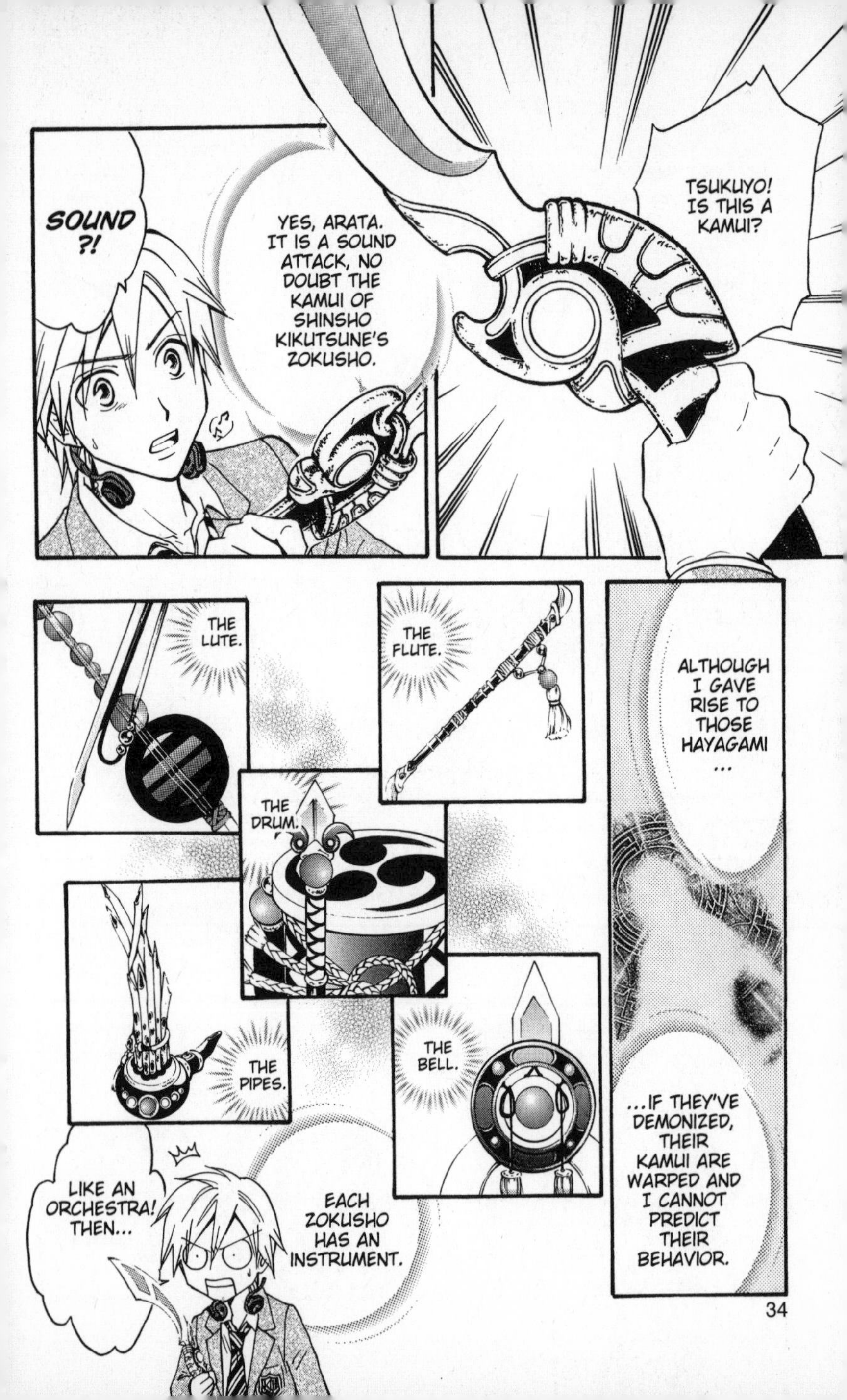
TSUKUYO! IS THIS A KAMUI?
YES, ARATA. IT IS A SOUND ATTACK, NO DOUBT THE KAMUI OF SHINSHO KIKUTSUNE'S ZOKUSHO.
SOUND ?!
ALTHOUGH I GAVE RISE TO THOSE HAYAGAMI...
...IF THEY'VE DEMONIZED, THEIR KAMUI ARE WARPED AND I CANNOT PREDICT THEIR BEHAVIOR.
THE FLUTE.
THE LUTE.
THE DRUM.
THE BELL.
THE PIPES.
EACH ZOKUSHO HAS AN INSTRUMENT.
LIKE AN ORCHESTRA! THEN...

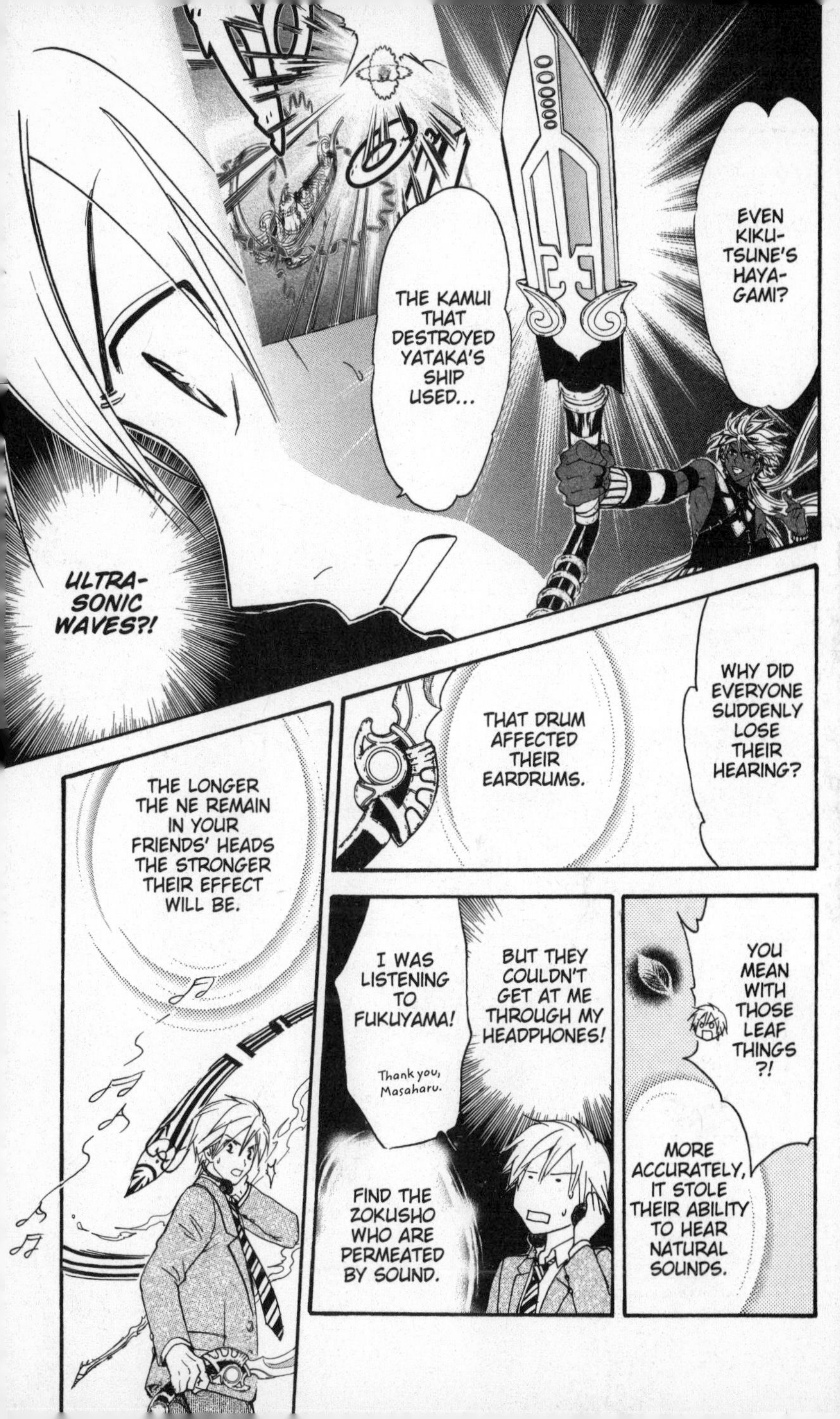
EVEN KIKU-TSUNE'S HAYA-GAMI?
THE KAMUI THAT DESTROYED YATAKA'S SHIP USED...
ULTRA-SONIC WAVES?!
WHY DID EVERYONE SUDDENLY LOSE THEIR HEARING?
THAT DRUM AFFECTED THEIR EARDRUMS.
YOU MEAN WITH THOSE LEAF THINGS?!
MORE ACCURATELY, IT STOLE THEIR ABILITY TO HEAR NATURAL SOUNDS.
BUT THEY COULDN'T GET AT ME THROUGH MY HEADPHONES!
I WAS LISTENING TO FUKUYAMA!
Thank you, Masaharu.
FIND THE ZOKUSHO WHO ARE PERMEATED BY SOUND.
THE LONGER THE NE REMAIN IN YOUR FRIENDS' HEADS THE STRONGER THEIR EFFECT WILL BE.

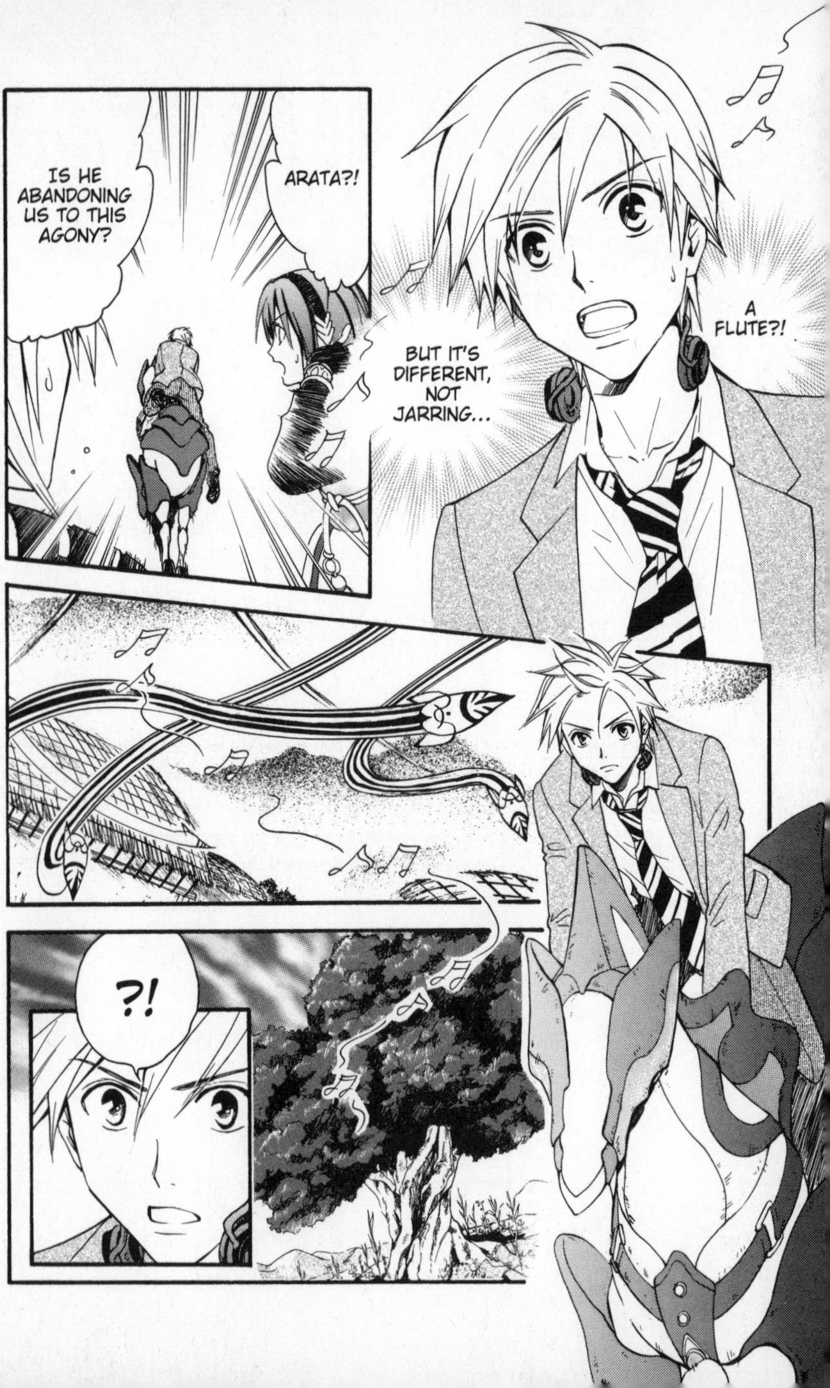
A FLUTE?!
BUT IT'S DIFFERENT, NOT JARRING...
ARATA?!
IS HE ABANDONING US TO THIS AGONY?
?!

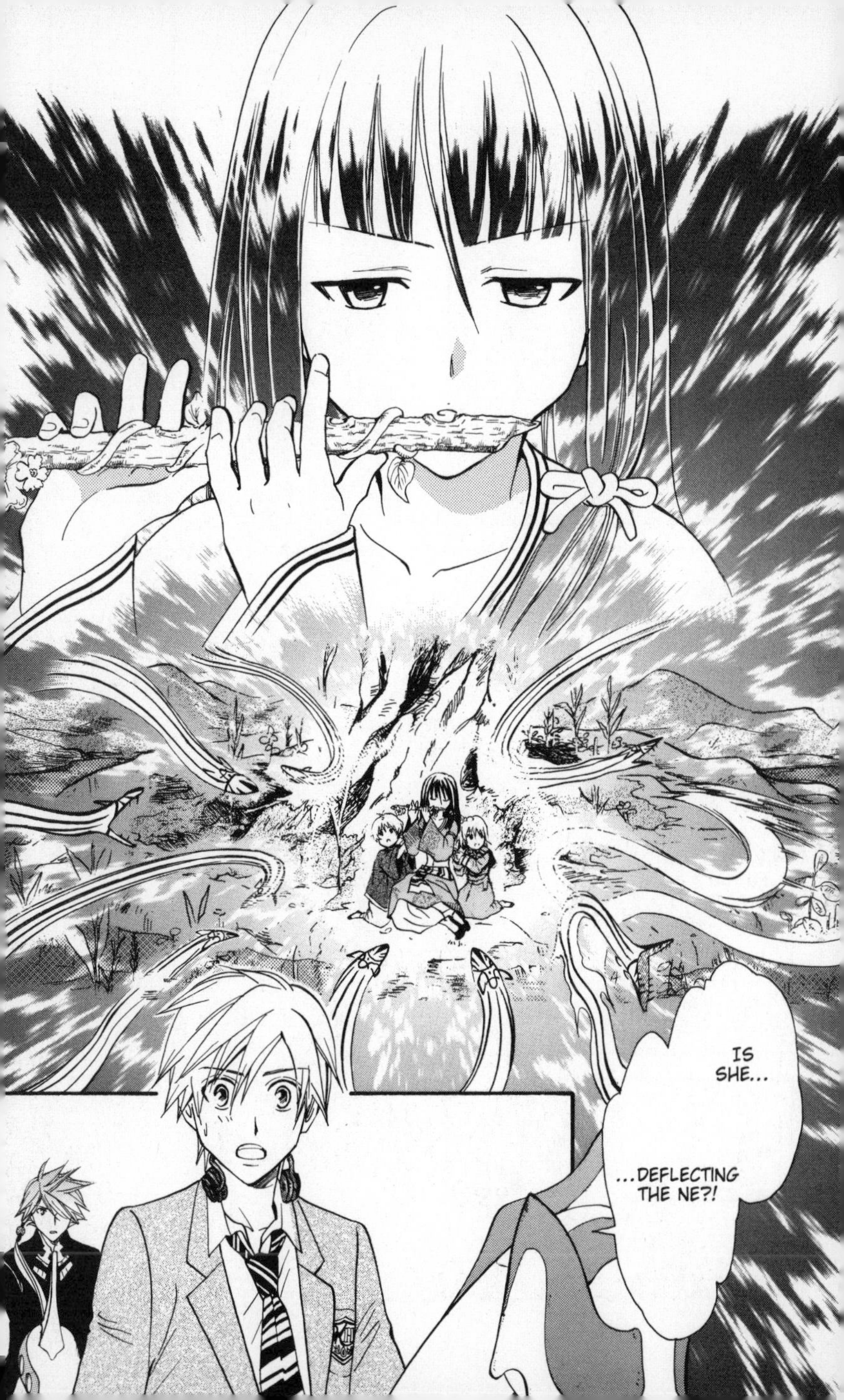
IS SHE...
...DEFLECTING THE NE?!

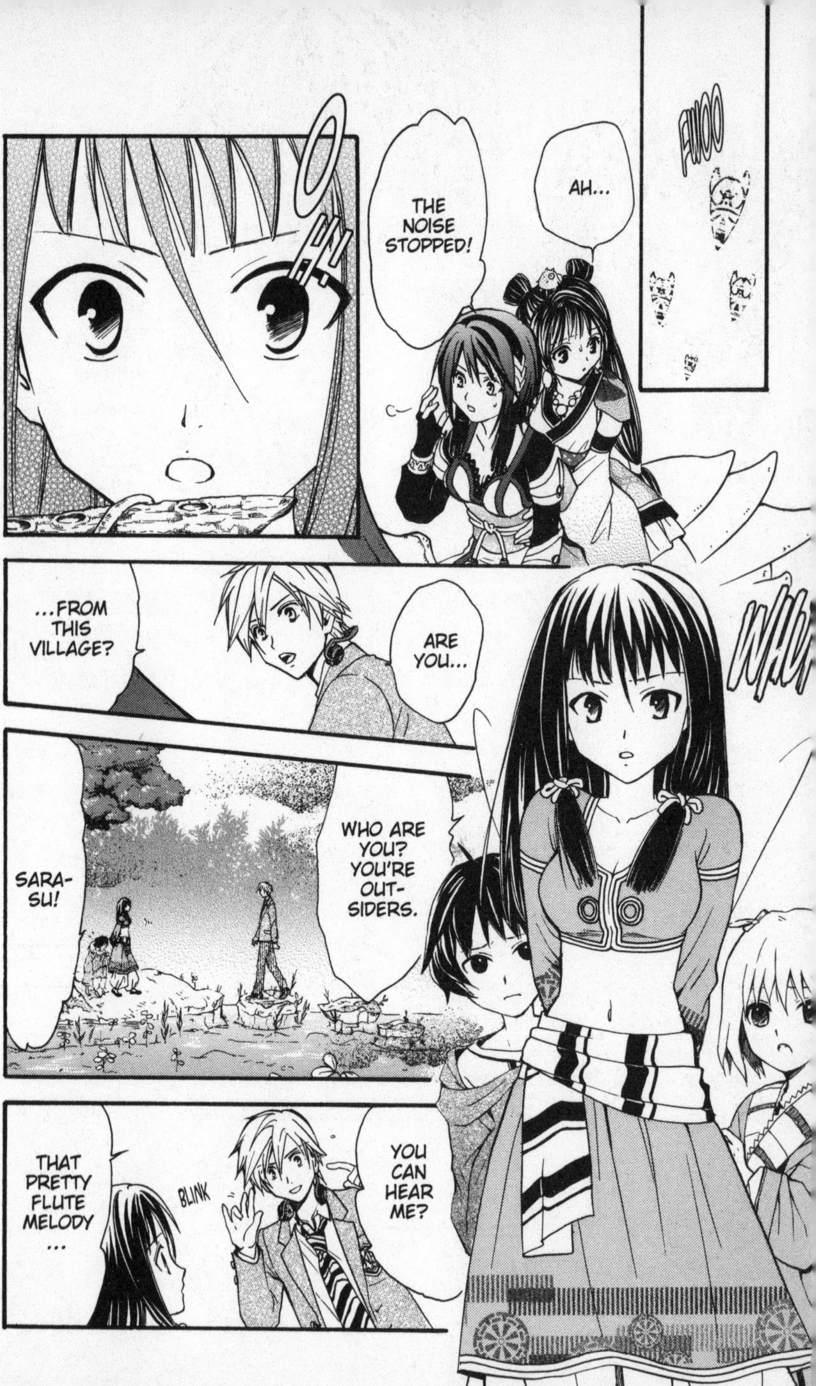

FWOO
AH...
THE NOISE STOPPED!
WHU
ARE YOU...
...FROM THIS VILLAGE?
WHO ARE YOU? YOU'RE OUT-SIDERS.
SARA-SU!
YOU CAN HEAR ME?
BLINK
THAT PRETTY FLUTE MELODY ...

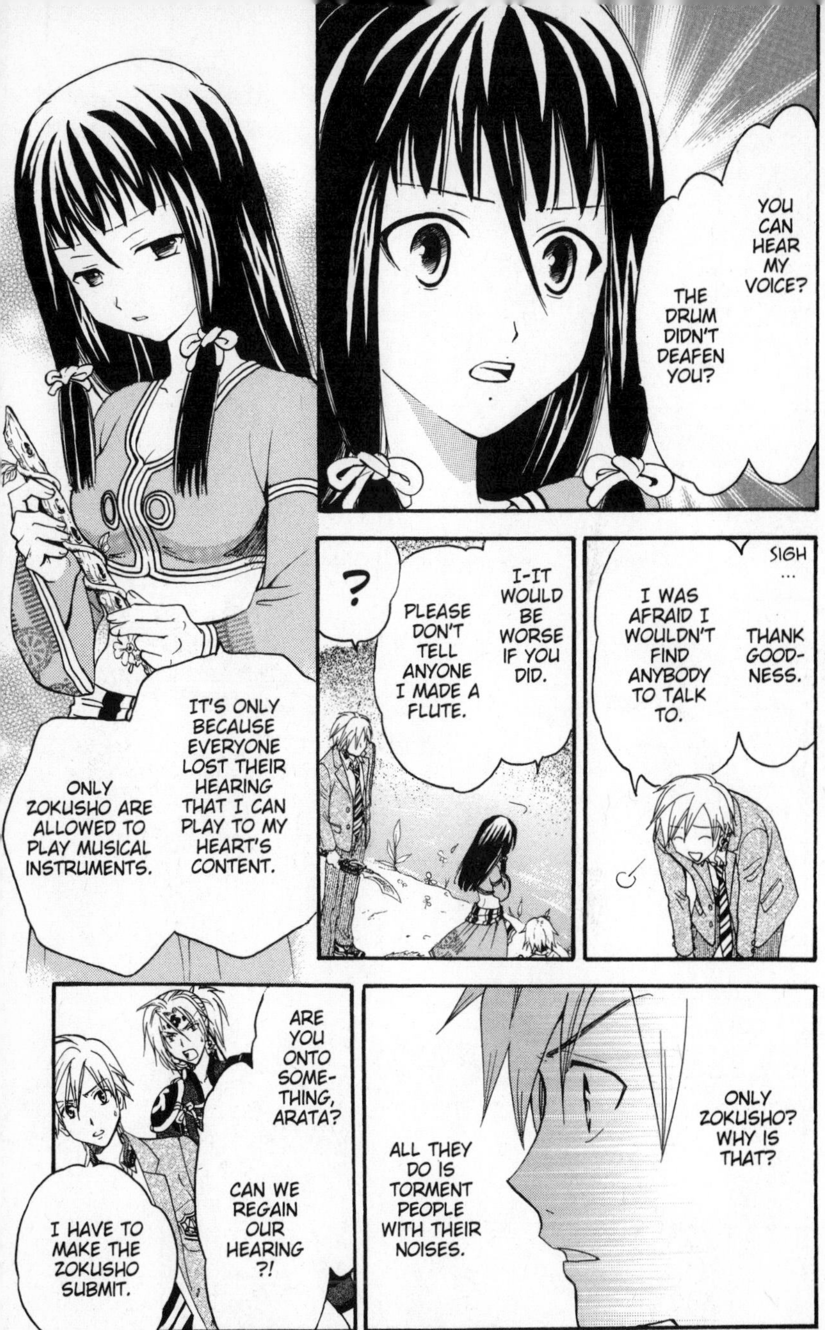
YOU CAN HEAR MY VOICE?
THE DRUM DIDN'T DEAFEN YOU?
SIGH...
THANK GOODNESS.
I WAS AFRAID I WOULDN'T FIND ANYBODY TO TALK TO.
I-IT WOULD BE WORSE IF YOU DID.
PLEASE DON'T TELL ANYONE I MADE A FLUTE.
?
IT'S ONLY BECAUSE EVERYONE LOST THEIR HEARING THAT I CAN PLAY TO MY HEART'S CONTENT.
ONLY ZOKUSHO ARE ALLOWED TO PLAY MUSICAL INSTRUMENTS.
ONLY ZOKUSHO? WHY IS THAT?
ALL THEY DO IS TORMENT PEOPLE WITH THEIR NOISES.
ARE YOU ONTO SOMETHING, ARATA?
CAN WE REGAIN OUR HEARING?!
I HAVE TO MAKE THE ZOKUSHO SUBMIT.

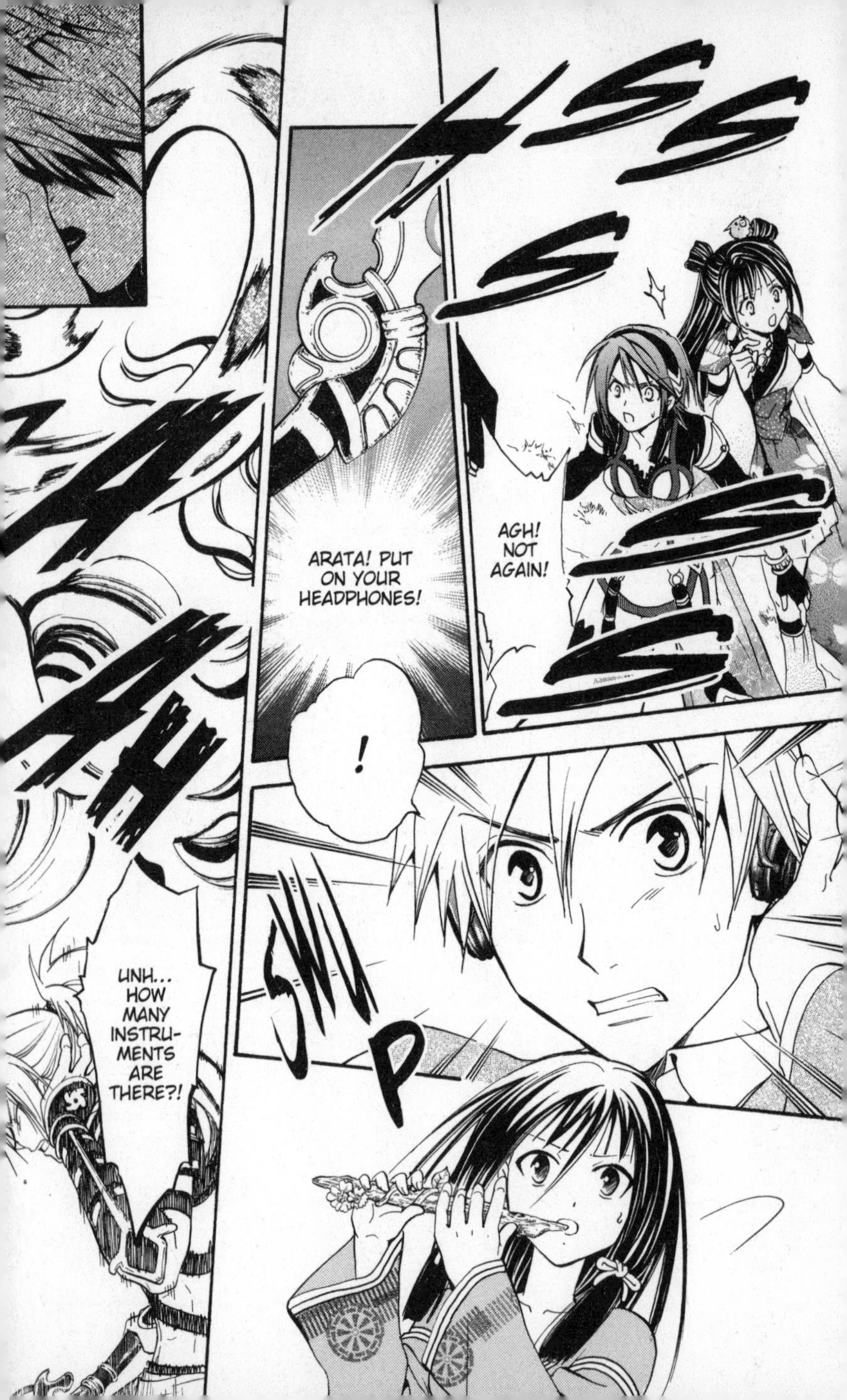
HISSSSS
AGH! NOT AGAIN!
ARATA! PUT ON YOUR HEADPHONES!
!
SNAP
UNH... HOW MANY INSTRUMENTS ARE THERE?!

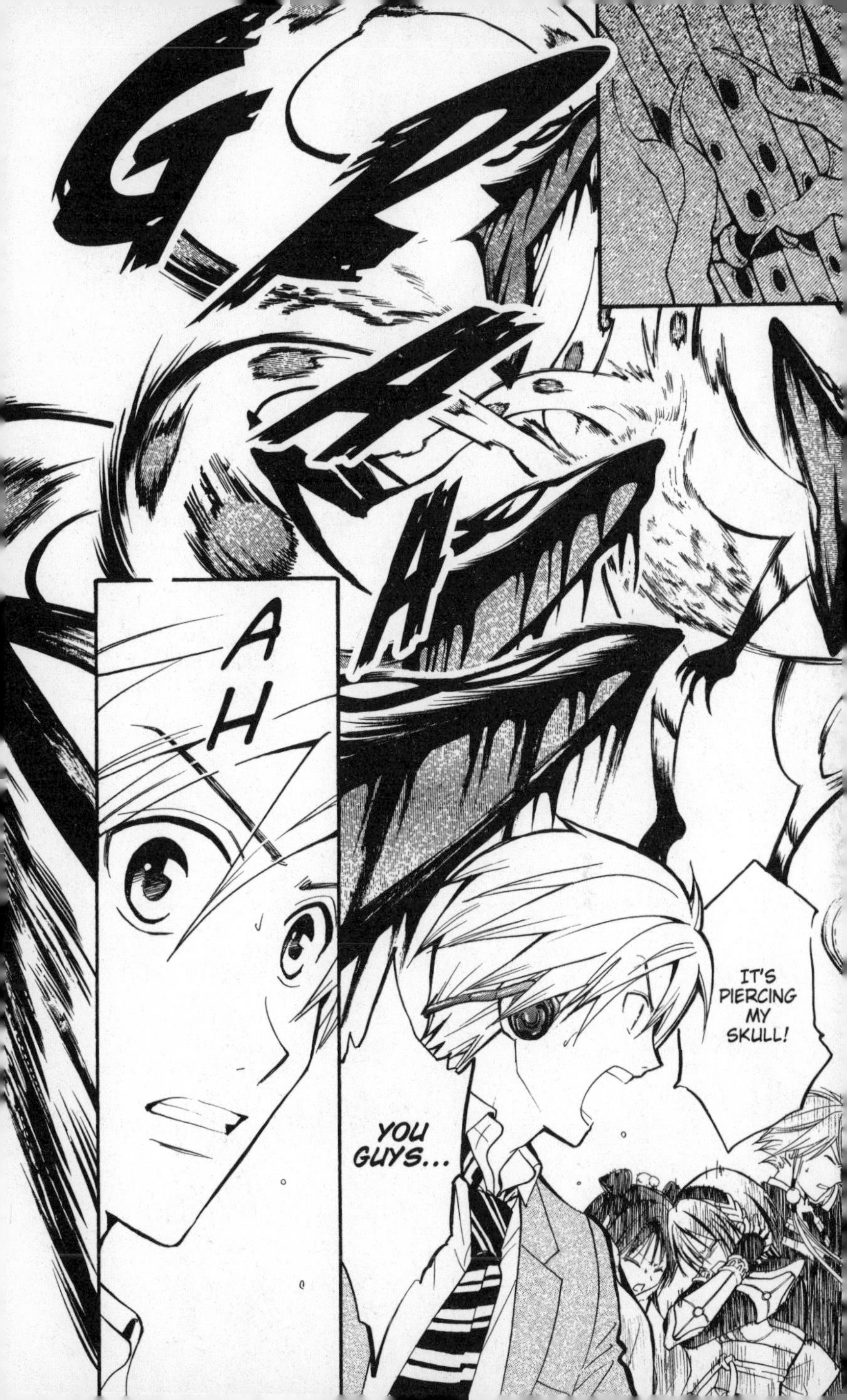
IT'S PIERCING MY SKULL!
YOU GUYS...
AH

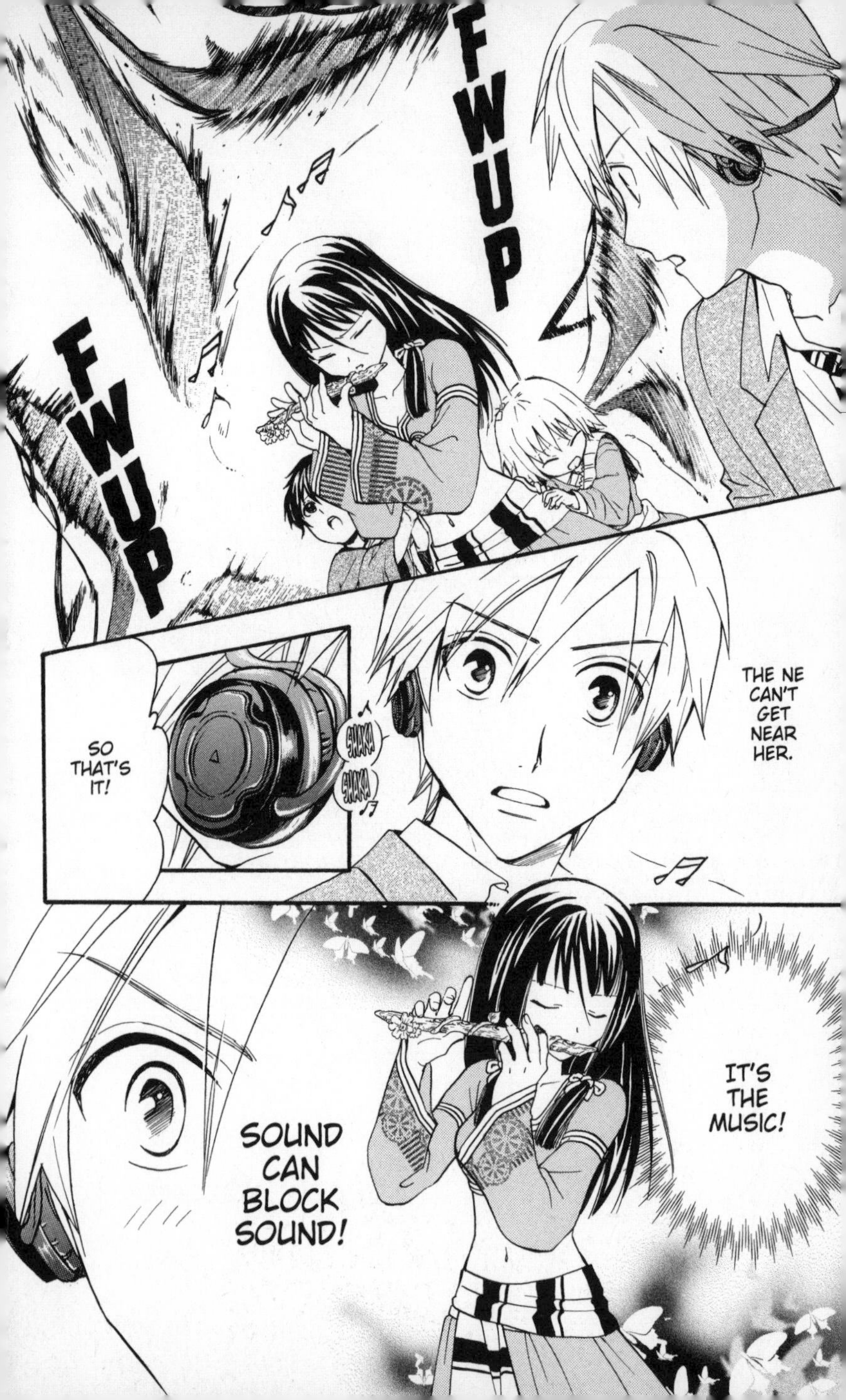
FWUP
FWUP
THE NE CAN'T GET NEAR HER.
SHAKA
SHAKA
SO THAT'S IT!
IT'S THE MUSIC!
SOUND CAN BLOCK SOUND!

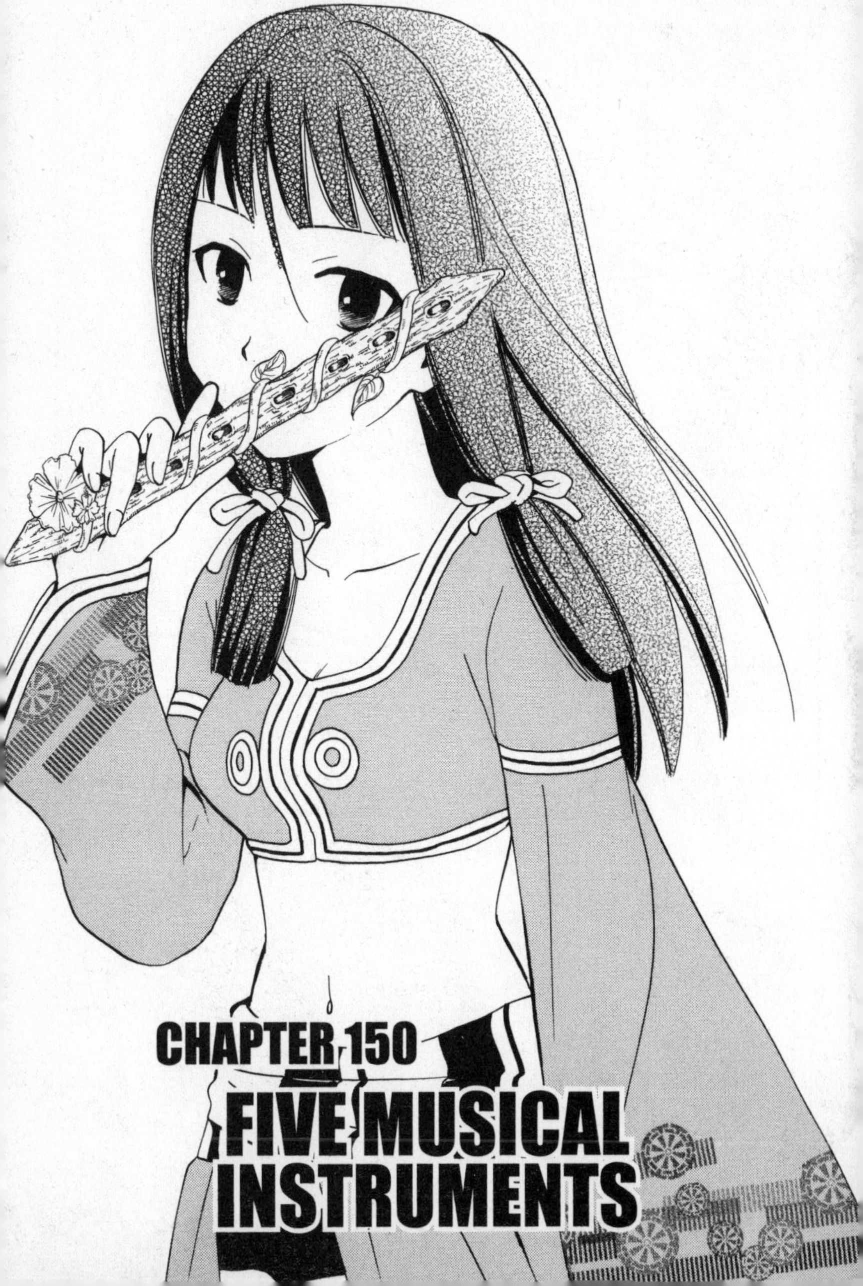
CHAPTER 150
FIVE MUSICAL INSTRUMENTS

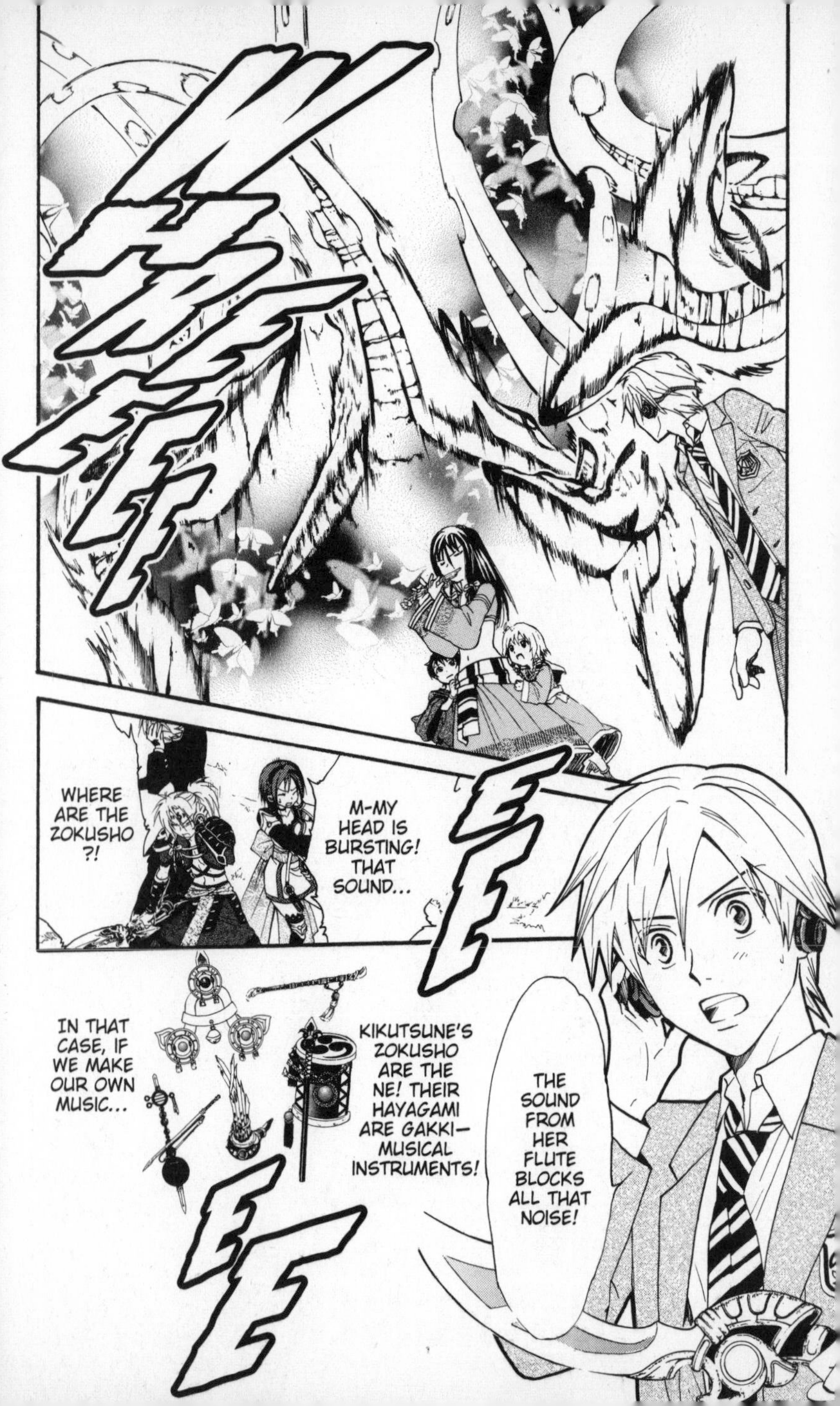
M-MY HEAD IS BURSTING! THAT SOUND...
WHERE ARE THE ZOKUSHO?!
THE SOUND FROM HER FLUTE BLOCKS ALL THAT NOISE!
KIKUTSUNE'S ZOKUSHO ARE THE NE! THEIR HAYAGAMI ARE GAKKI—MUSICAL INSTRUMENTS!
IN THAT CASE, IF WE MAKE OUR OWN MUSIC...

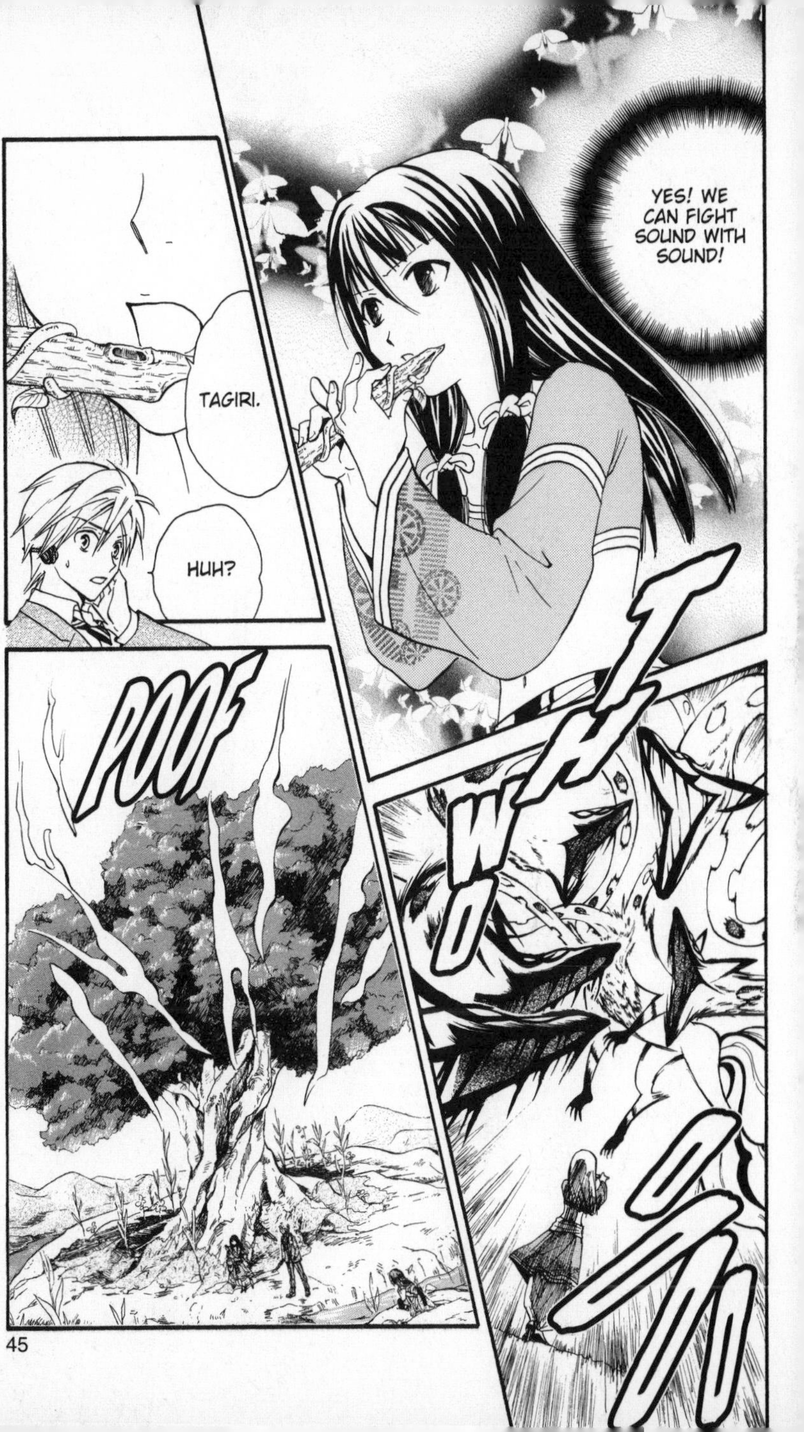
YES! WE CAN FIGHT SOUND WITH SOUND!
TAGIRI.
HUH?
POOF

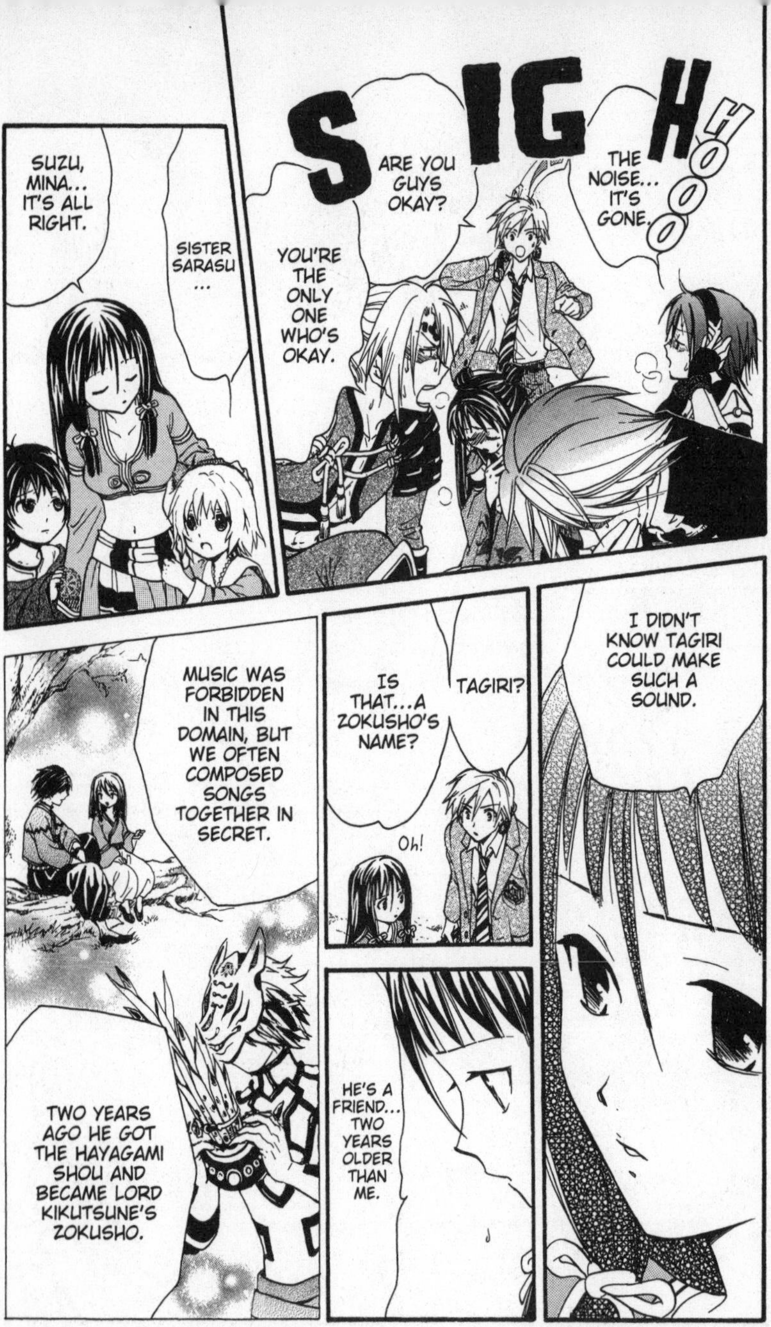
SIGH
HOOOO
THE NOISE... IT'S GONE.
ARE YOU GUYS OKAY?
YOU'RE THE ONLY ONE WHO'S OKAY.
SISTER SARASU...
SUZU, MINA... IT'S ALL RIGHT.
I DIDN'T KNOW TAGIRI COULD MAKE SUCH A SOUND.
TAGIRI?
IS THAT...A ZOKUSHO'S NAME?
Oh!
HE'S A FRIEND... TWO YEARS OLDER THAN ME.
MUSIC WAS FORBIDDEN IN THIS DOMAIN, BUT WE OFTEN COMPOSED SONGS TOGETHER IN SECRET.
TWO YEARS AGO HE GOT THE HAYAGAMI SHOU AND BECAME LORD KIKUTSUNE'S ZOKUSHO.

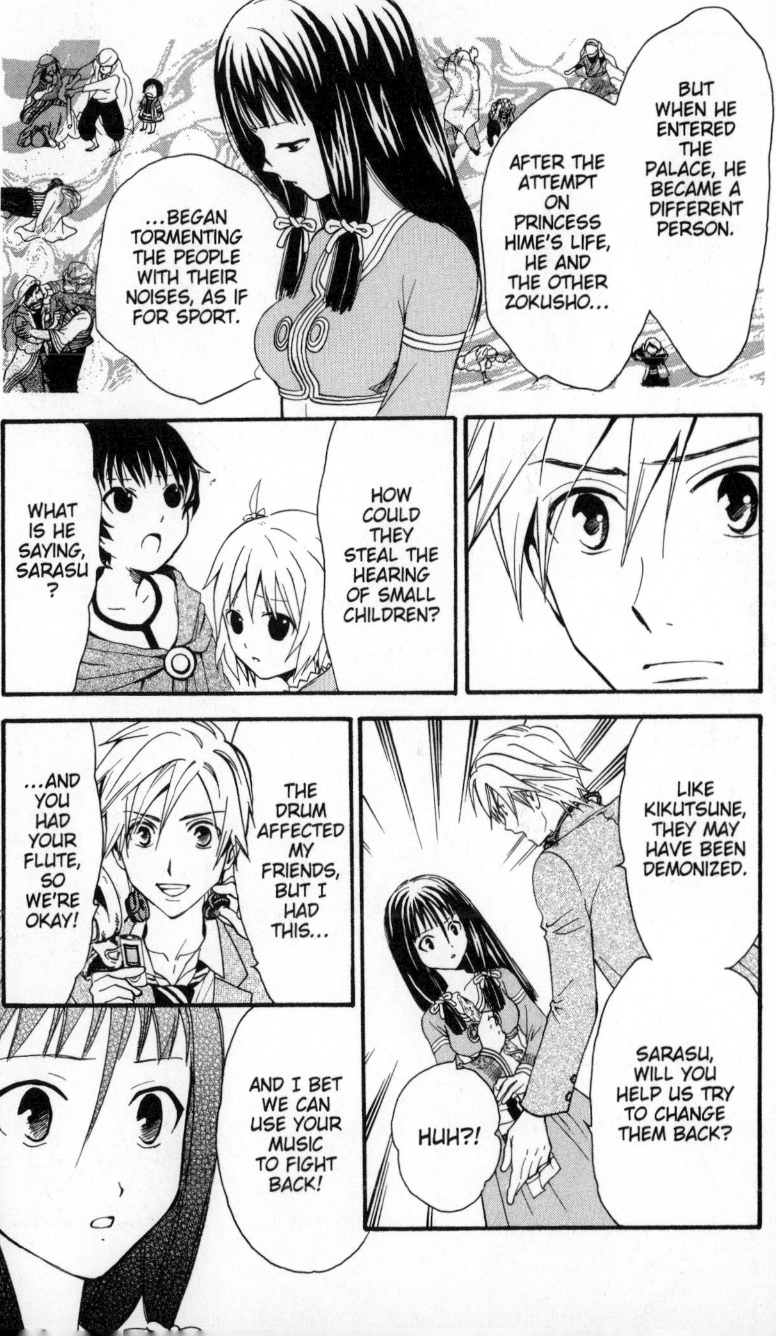
BUT WHEN HE ENTERED THE PALACE, HE BECAME A DIFFERENT PERSON.
AFTER THE ATTEMPT ON PRINCESS HIME'S LIFE, HE AND THE OTHER ZOKUSHO...
...BEGAN TORMENTING THE PEOPLE WITH THEIR NOISES, AS IF FOR SPORT.
HOW COULD THEY STEAL THE HEARING OF SMALL CHILDREN?
WHAT IS HE SAYING, SARASU?
LIKE KIKUTSUNE, THEY MAY HAVE BEEN DEMONIZED.
SARASU, WILL YOU HELP US TRY TO CHANGE THEM BACK?
HUH?!
THE DRUM AFFECTED MY FRIENDS, BUT I HAD THIS...
...AND YOU HAD YOUR FLUTE, SO WE'RE OKAY!
AND I BET WE CAN USE YOUR MUSIC TO FIGHT BACK!

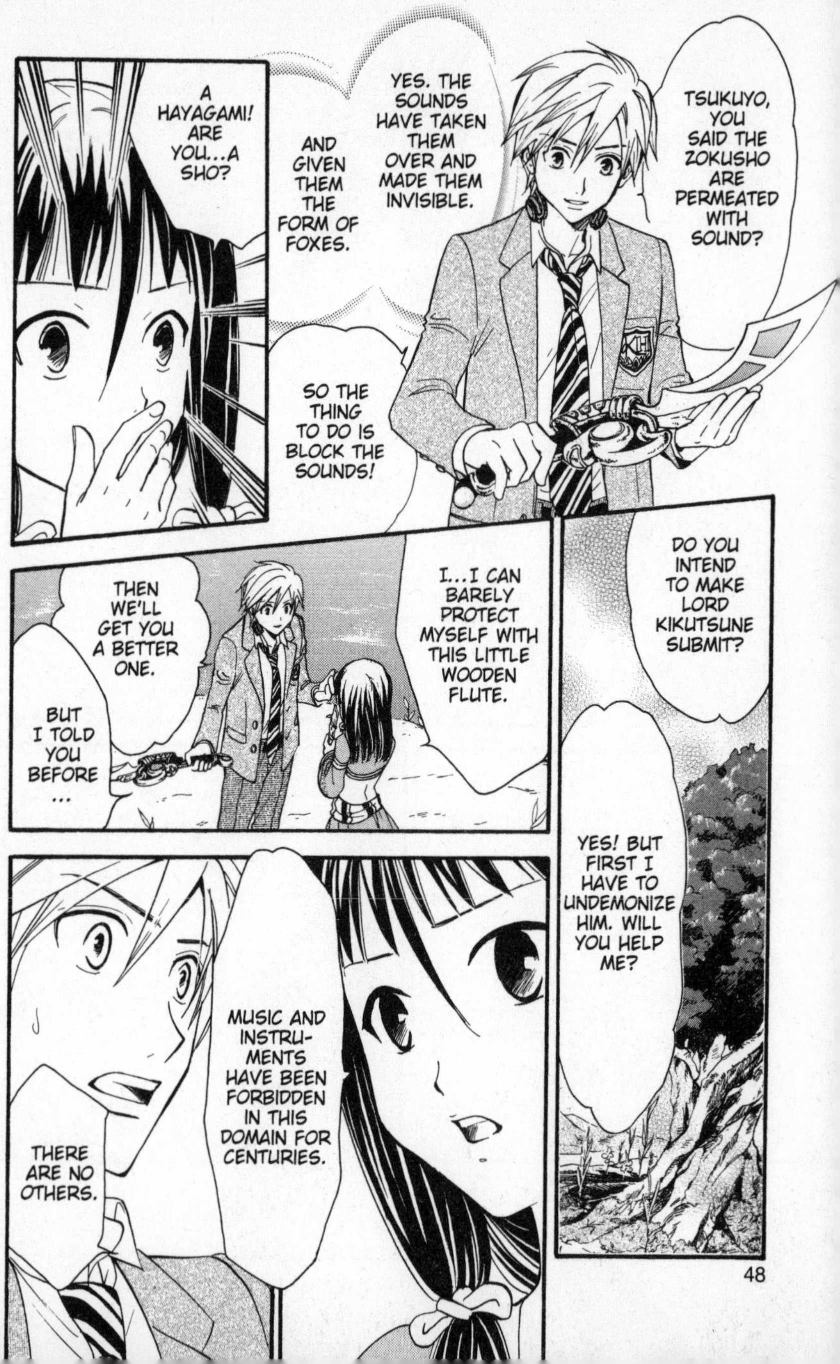
TSUKUYO, YOU SAID THE ZOKUSHO ARE PERMEATED WITH SOUND?
YES. THE SOUNDS HAVE TAKEN THEM OVER AND MADE THEM INVISIBLE.
AND GIVEN THEM THE FORM OF FOXES.
SO THE THING TO DO IS BLOCK THE SOUNDS!
A HAYAGAMI! ARE YOU...A SHO?
DO YOU INTEND TO MAKE LORD KIKUTSUNE SUBMIT?
YES! BUT FIRST I HAVE TO UNDEMONIZE HIM. WILL YOU HELP ME?
I...I CAN BARELY PROTECT MYSELF WITH THIS LITTLE WOODEN FLUTE.
THEN WE'LL GET YOU A BETTER ONE.
BUT I TOLD YOU BEFORE...
MUSIC AND INSTRUMENTS HAVE BEEN FORBIDDEN IN THIS DOMAIN FOR CENTURIES.
THERE ARE NO OTHERS.

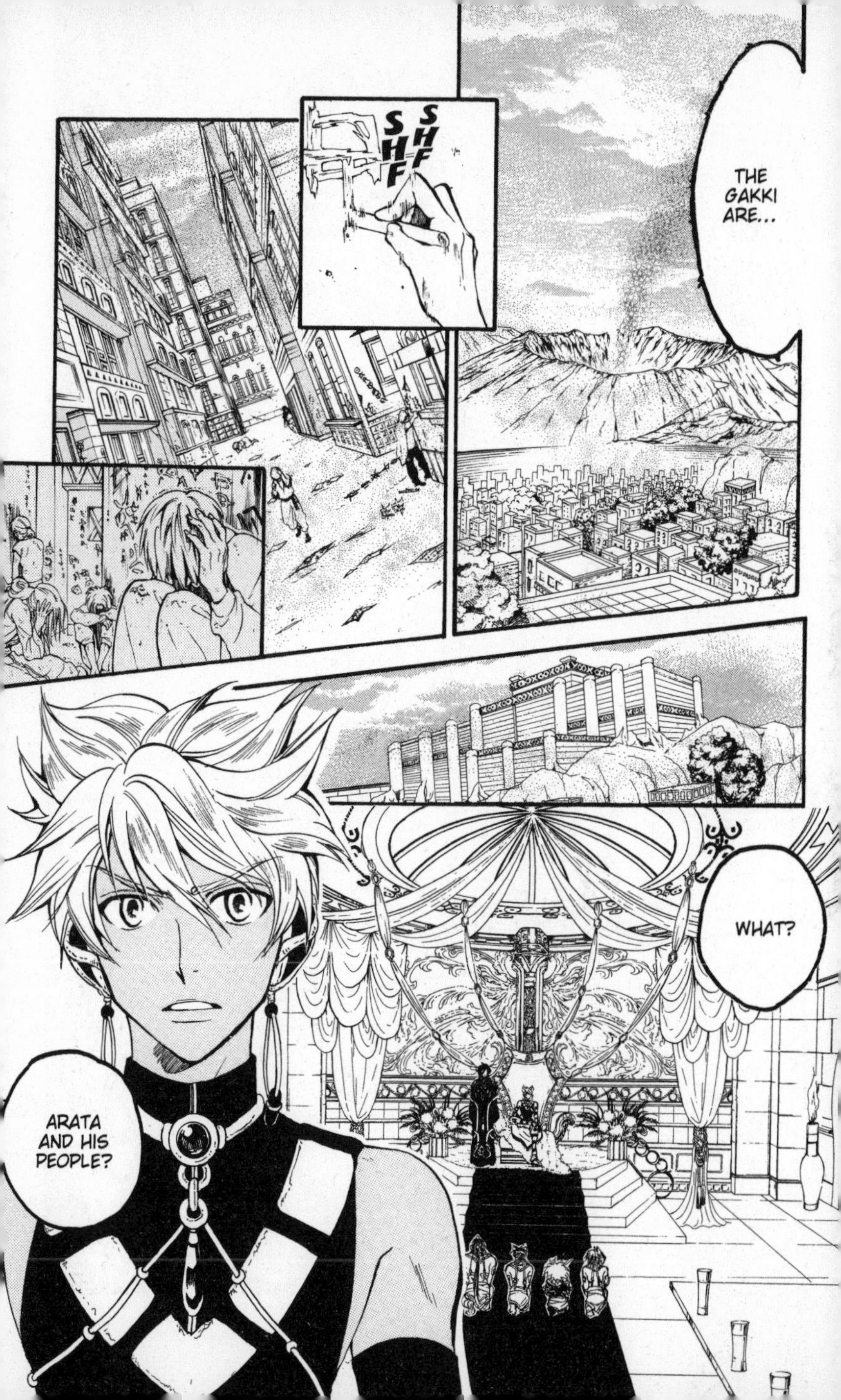
THE GAKKI ARE...
SHF SHF
WHAT?
ARATA AND HIS PEOPLE?

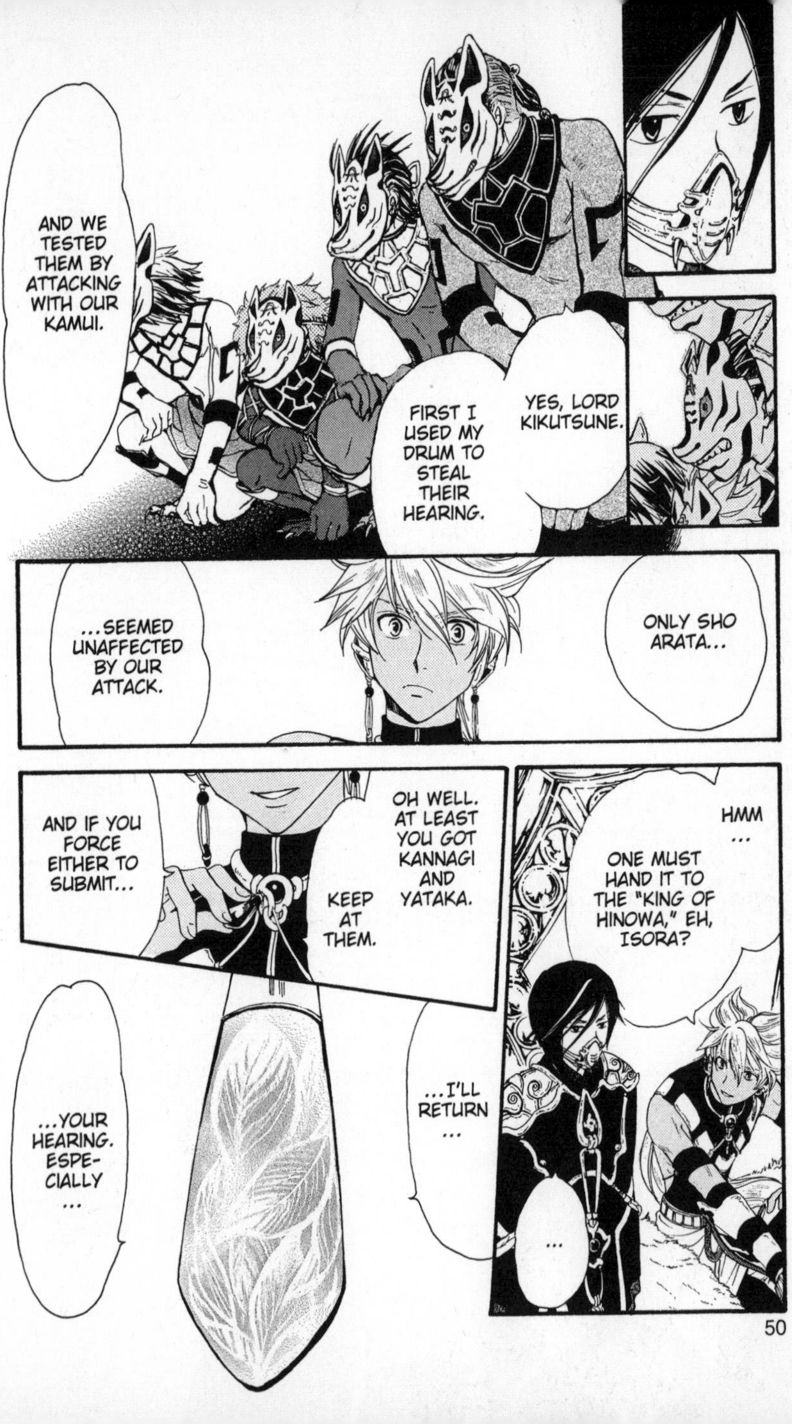
YES, LORD KIKUTSUNE.
FIRST I USED MY DRUM TO STEAL THEIR HEARING.
AND WE TESTED THEM BY ATTACKING WITH OUR KAMUI.
ONLY SHO ARATA...
...SEEMED UNAFFECTED BY OUR ATTACK.
HMM...
ONE MUST HAND IT TO THE "KING OF HINOWA," EH, ISORA?
...
OH WELL. AT LEAST YOU GOT KANNAGI AND YATAKA.
KEEP AT THEM.
AND IF YOU FORCE EITHER TO SUBMIT...
...I'LL RETURN...
...YOUR HEARING. ESPE-CIALLY...

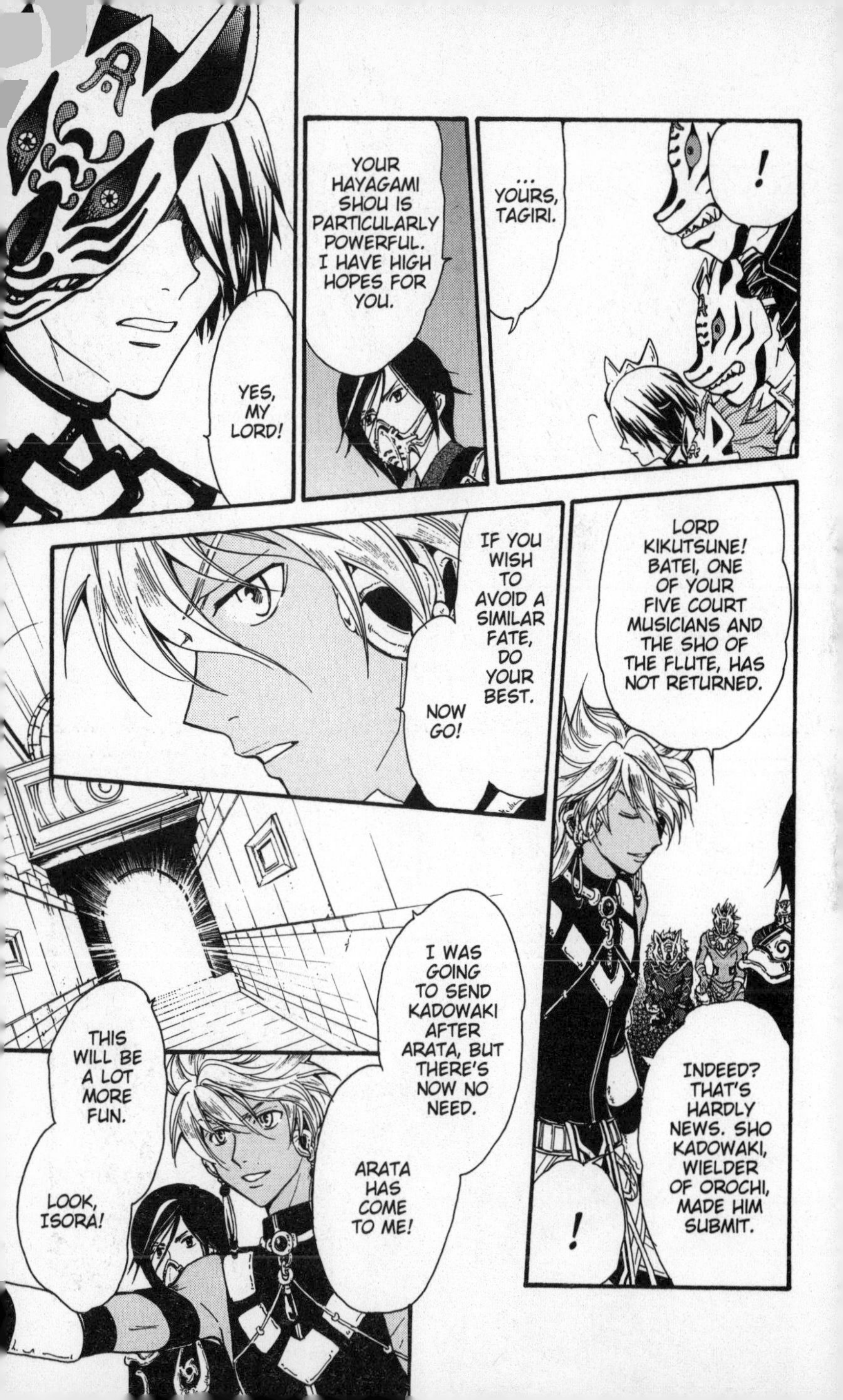
!
... YOURS, TAGIRI.
YOUR HAYAGAMI SHOU IS PARTICULARLY POWERFUL. I HAVE HIGH HOPES FOR YOU.
YES, MY LORD!
LORD KIKUTSUNE! BATEI, ONE OF YOUR FIVE COURT MUSICIANS AND THE SHO OF THE FLUTE, HAS NOT RETURNED.
INDEED? THAT'S HARDLY NEWS. SHO KADOWAKI, WIELDER OF OROCHI, MADE HIM SUBMIT.
!
IF YOU WISH TO AVOID A SIMILAR FATE, DO YOUR BEST.
NOW GO!
I WAS GOING TO SEND KADOWAKI AFTER ARATA, BUT THERE'S NOW NO NEED.
ARATA HAS COME TO ME!
THIS WILL BE A LOT MORE FUN.
LOOK, ISORA!

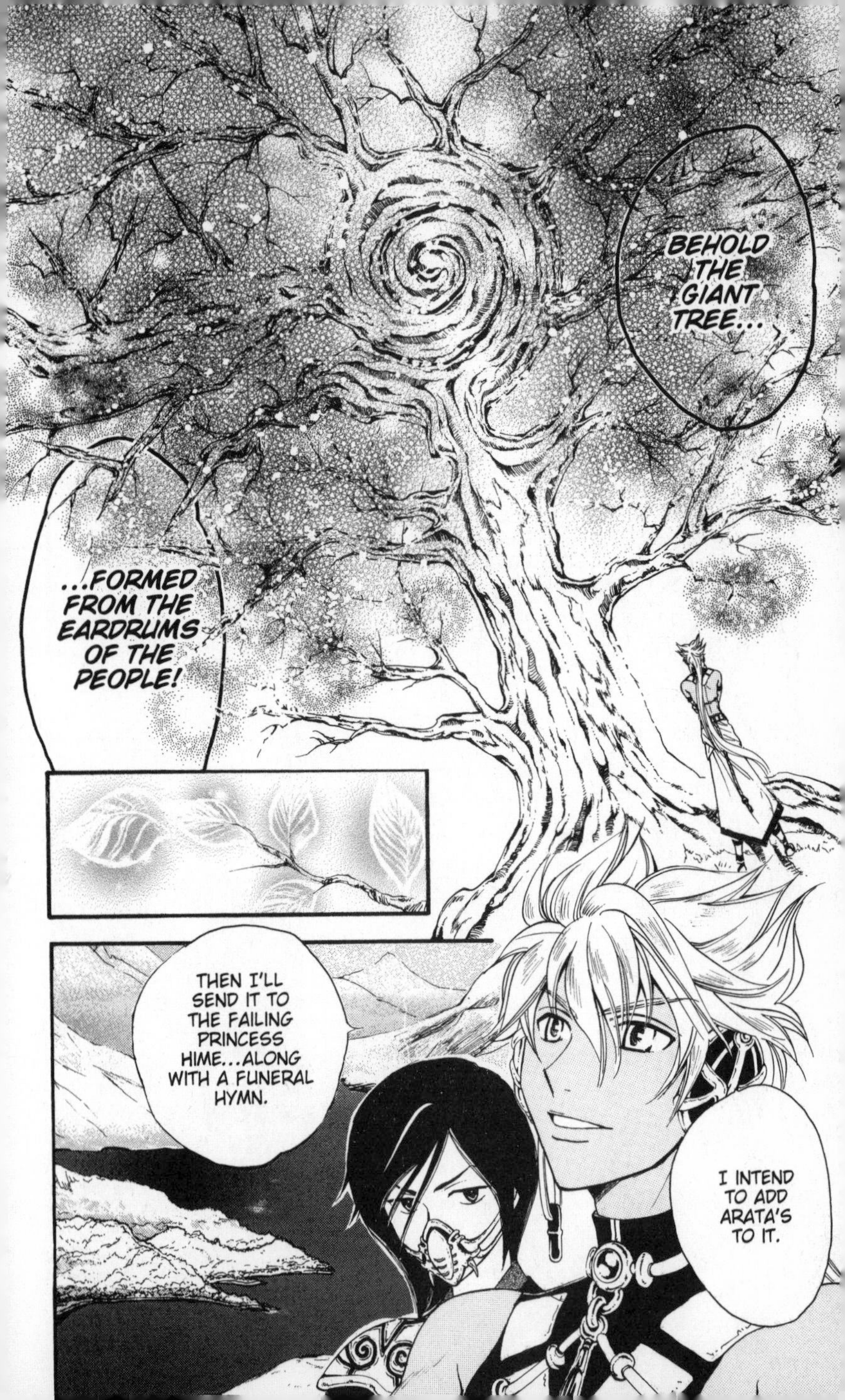
BEHOLD THE GIANT TREE...
...FORMED FROM THE EARDRUMS OF THE PEOPLE!
THEN I'LL SEND IT TO THE FAILING PRINCESS HIME...ALONG WITH A FUNERAL HYMN.
I INTEND TO ADD ARATA'S TO IT.

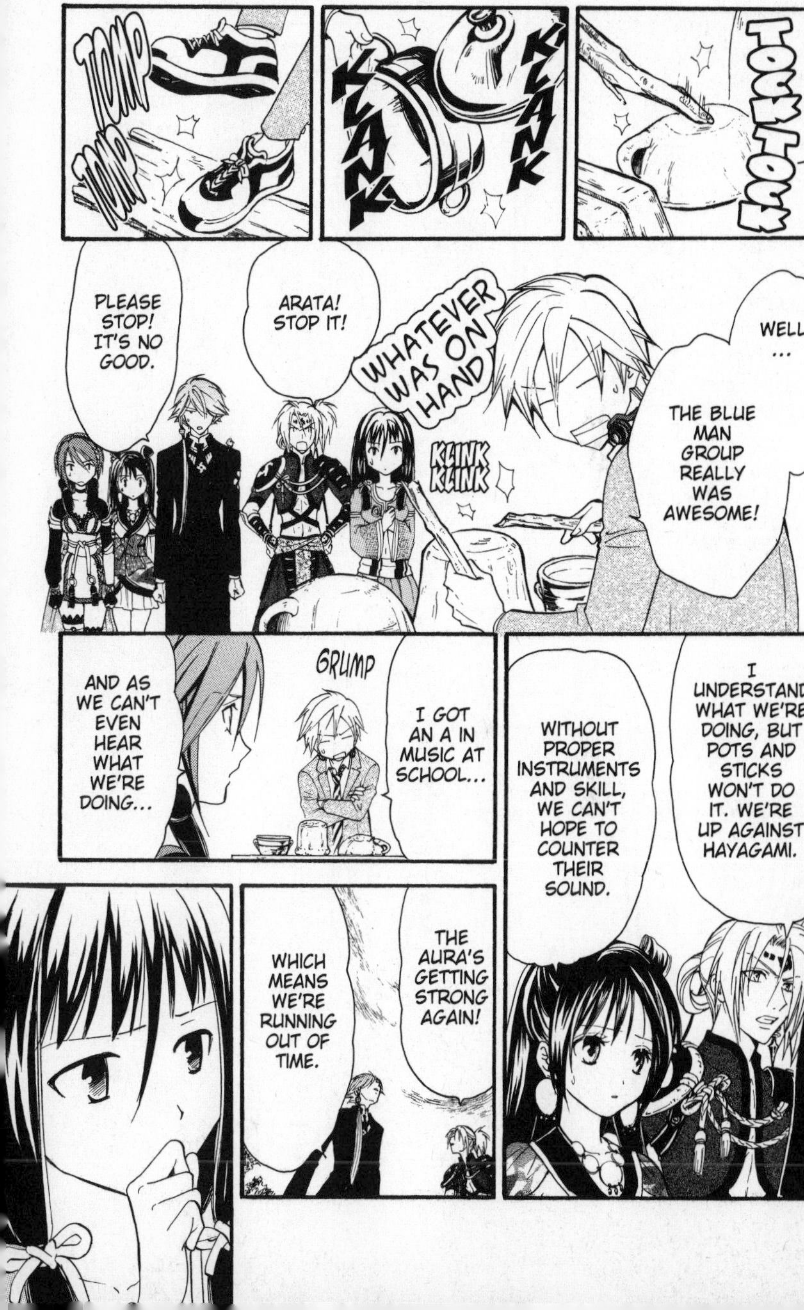
TOCK TOCK
KLANK KLANK
TOMP TOMP
WELL...
THE BLUE MAN GROUP REALLY WAS AWESOME!
WHATEVER WAS ON HAND
KLINK KLINK
ARATA! STOP IT!
PLEASE STOP! IT'S NO GOOD.
I UNDERSTAND WHAT WE'RE DOING, BUT POTS AND STICKS WON'T DO IT. WE'RE UP AGAINST HAYAGAMI.
WITHOUT PROPER INSTRUMENTS AND SKILL, WE CAN'T HOPE TO COUNTER THEIR SOUND.
I GOT AN A IN MUSIC AT SCHOOL...
GRUMP
AND AS WE CAN'T EVEN HEAR WHAT WE'RE DOING...
THE AURA'S GETTING STRONG AGAIN!
WHICH MEANS WE'RE RUNNING OUT OF TIME.

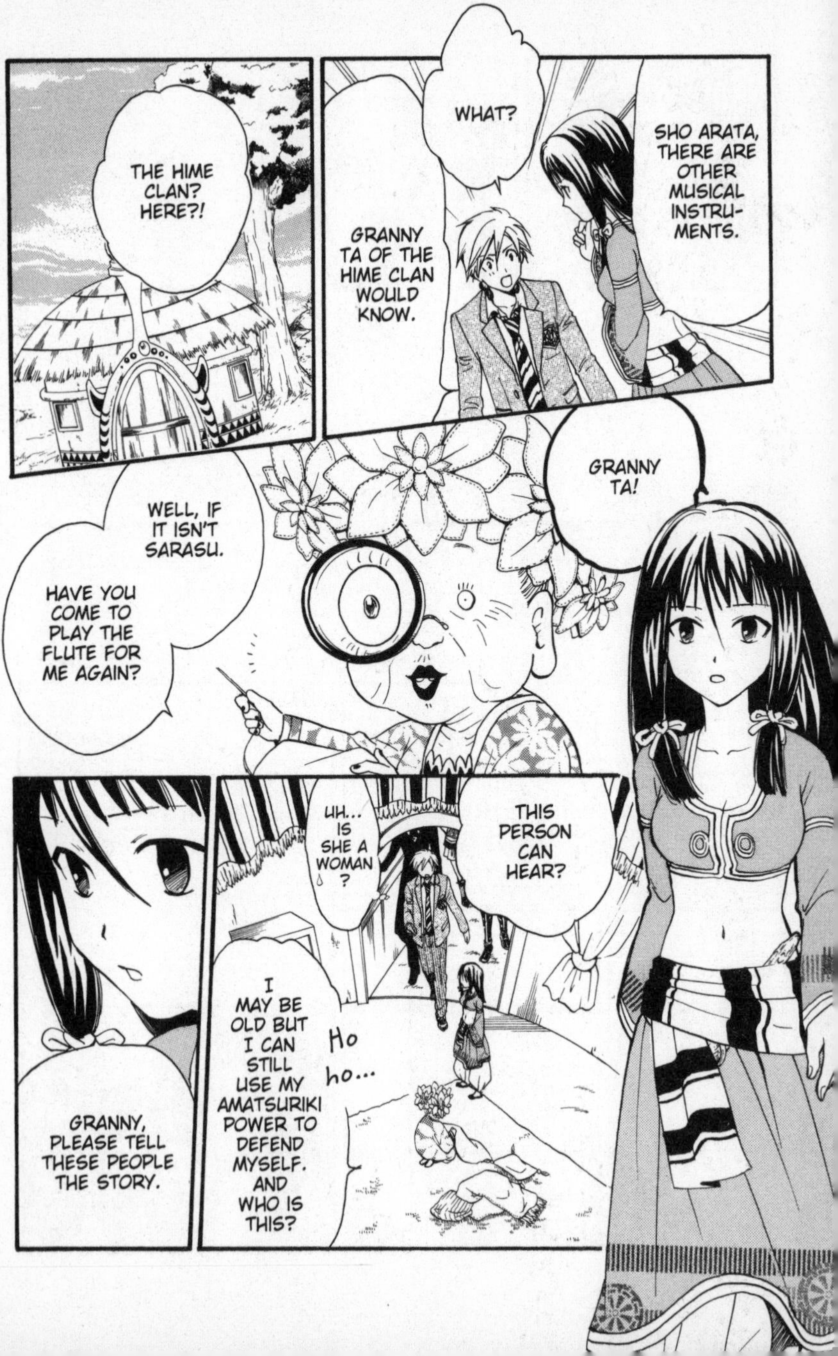
SHO ARATA, THERE ARE OTHER MUSICAL INSTRU-MENTS.
WHAT?
GRANNY TA OF THE HIME CLAN WOULD KNOW.
THE HIME CLAN? HERE?!
GRANNY TA!
WELL, IF IT ISN'T SARASU.
HAVE YOU COME TO PLAY THE FLUTE FOR ME AGAIN?
THIS PERSON CAN HEAR?
UH... IS SHE A WOMAN?
I MAY BE OLD BUT I CAN STILL USE MY AMATSURIKI POWER TO DEFEND MYSELF. AND WHO IS THIS?
Ho ho...
GRANNY, PLEASE TELL THESE PEOPLE THE STORY.

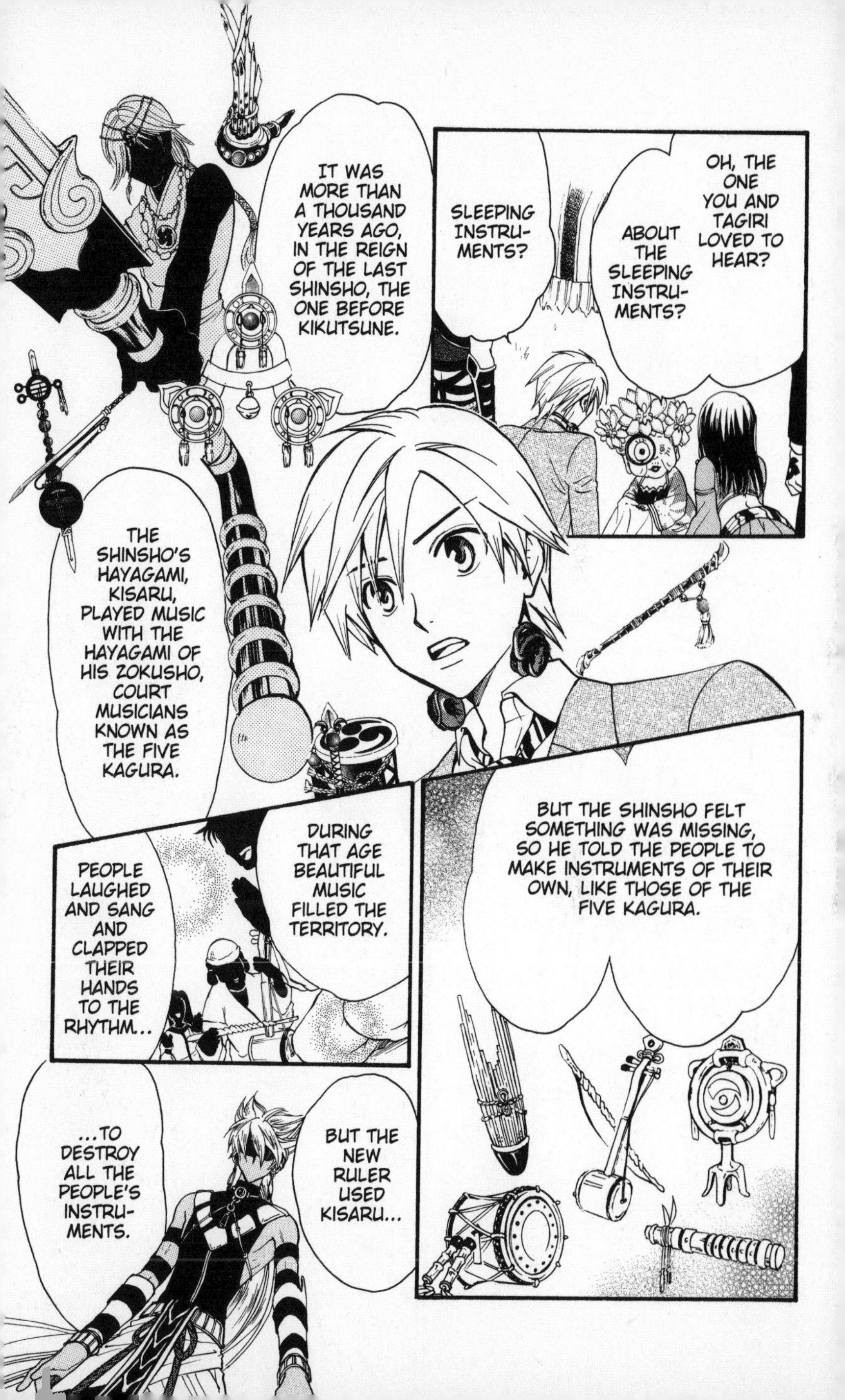
OH, THE ONE YOU AND TAGIRI LOVED TO HEAR?
ABOUT THE SLEEPING INSTRU-MENTS?
SLEEPING INSTRU-MENTS?
IT WAS MORE THAN A THOUSAND YEARS AGO, IN THE REIGN OF THE LAST SHINSHO, THE ONE BEFORE KIKUTSUNE.
THE SHINSHO'S HAYAGAMI, KISARU, PLAYED MUSIC WITH THE HAYAGAMI OF HIS ZOKUSHO, COURT MUSICIANS KNOWN AS THE FIVE KAGURA.
BUT THE SHINSHO FELT SOMETHING WAS MISSING, SO HE TOLD THE PEOPLE TO MAKE INSTRUMENTS OF THEIR OWN, LIKE THOSE OF THE FIVE KAGURA.
DURING THAT AGE BEAUTIFUL MUSIC FILLED THE TERRITORY.
PEOPLE LAUGHED AND SANG AND CLAPPED THEIR HANDS TO THE RHYTHM...
BUT THE NEW RULER USED KISARU...
...TO DESTROY ALL THE PEOPLE'S INSTRU-MENTS.

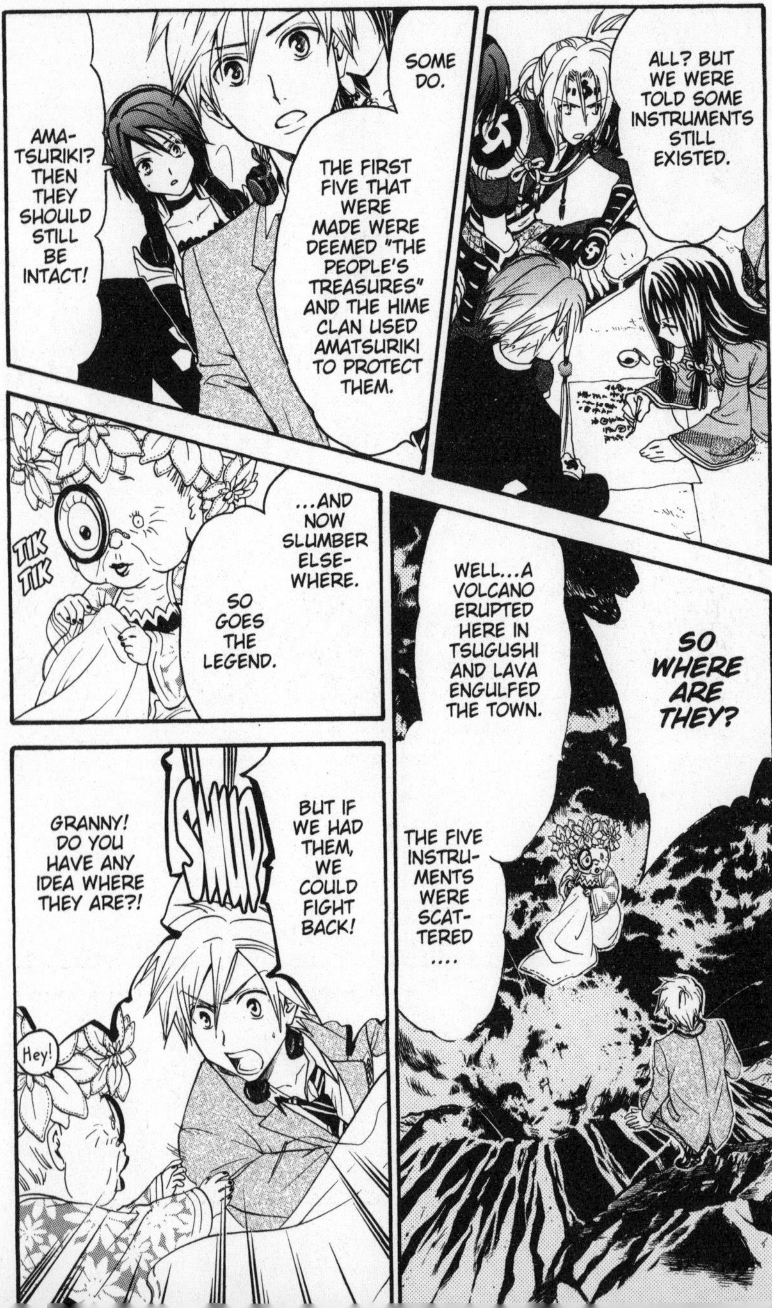
ALL? BUT WE WERE TOLD SOME INSTRUMENTS STILL EXISTED.
SOME DO.
THE FIRST FIVE THAT WERE MADE WERE DEEMED "THE PEOPLE'S TREASURES" AND THE HIME CLAN USED AMATSURIKI TO PROTECT THEM.
AMA-TSURIKI? THEN THEY SHOULD STILL BE INTACT!
SO WHERE ARE THEY?
WELL...A VOLCANO ERUPTED HERE IN TSUGUSHI AND LAVA ENGULFED THE TOWN.
THE FIVE INSTRU-MENTS WERE SCAT-TERED....
...AND NOW SLUMBER ELSE-WHERE.
SO GOES THE LEGEND.
TIK TIK
BUT IF WE HAD THEM, WE COULD FIGHT BACK!
GRANNY! DO YOU HAVE ANY IDEA WHERE THEY ARE?!
Hey!

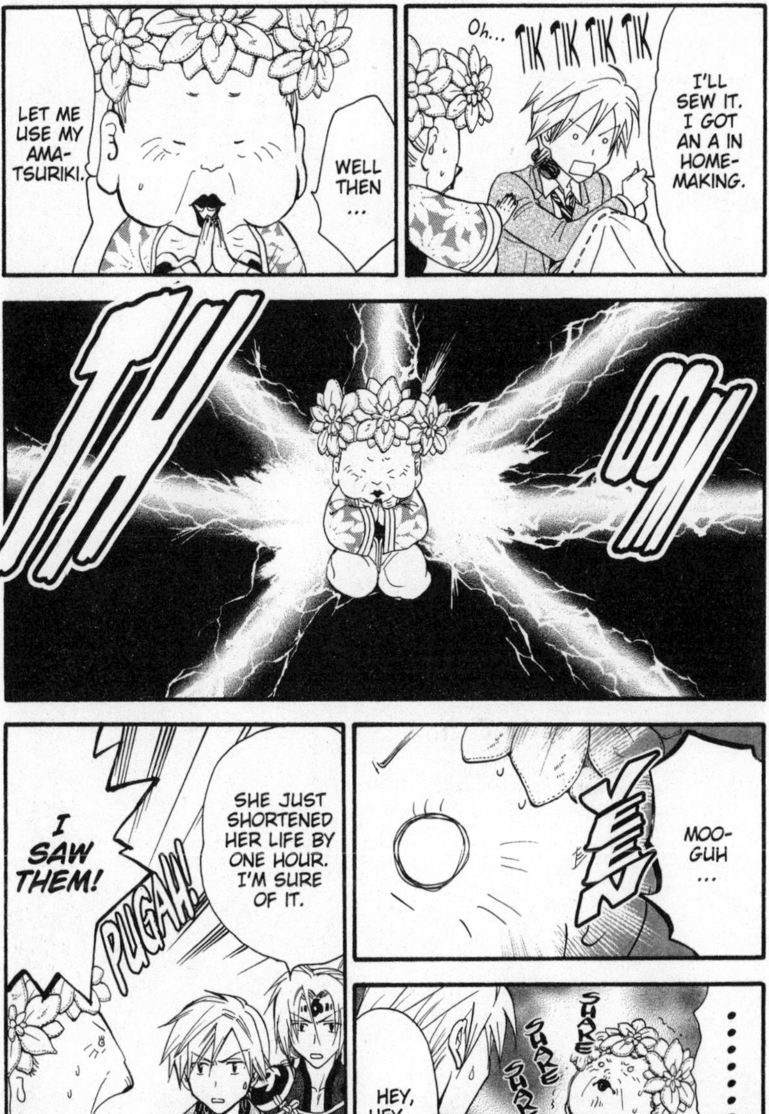
Oh...
TIK TIK TIK TIK
I'LL SEW IT. I GOT AN A IN HOME-MAKING.
WELL THEN ...
LET ME USE MY AMA-TSURIKI.
MOO-GUH ...
SHAKE
SHAKE
SHAKE
......!
HEY, HEY...
SHE JUST SHORTENED HER LIFE BY ONE HOUR. I'M SURE OF IT.
I SAW THEM!
PUGAH!

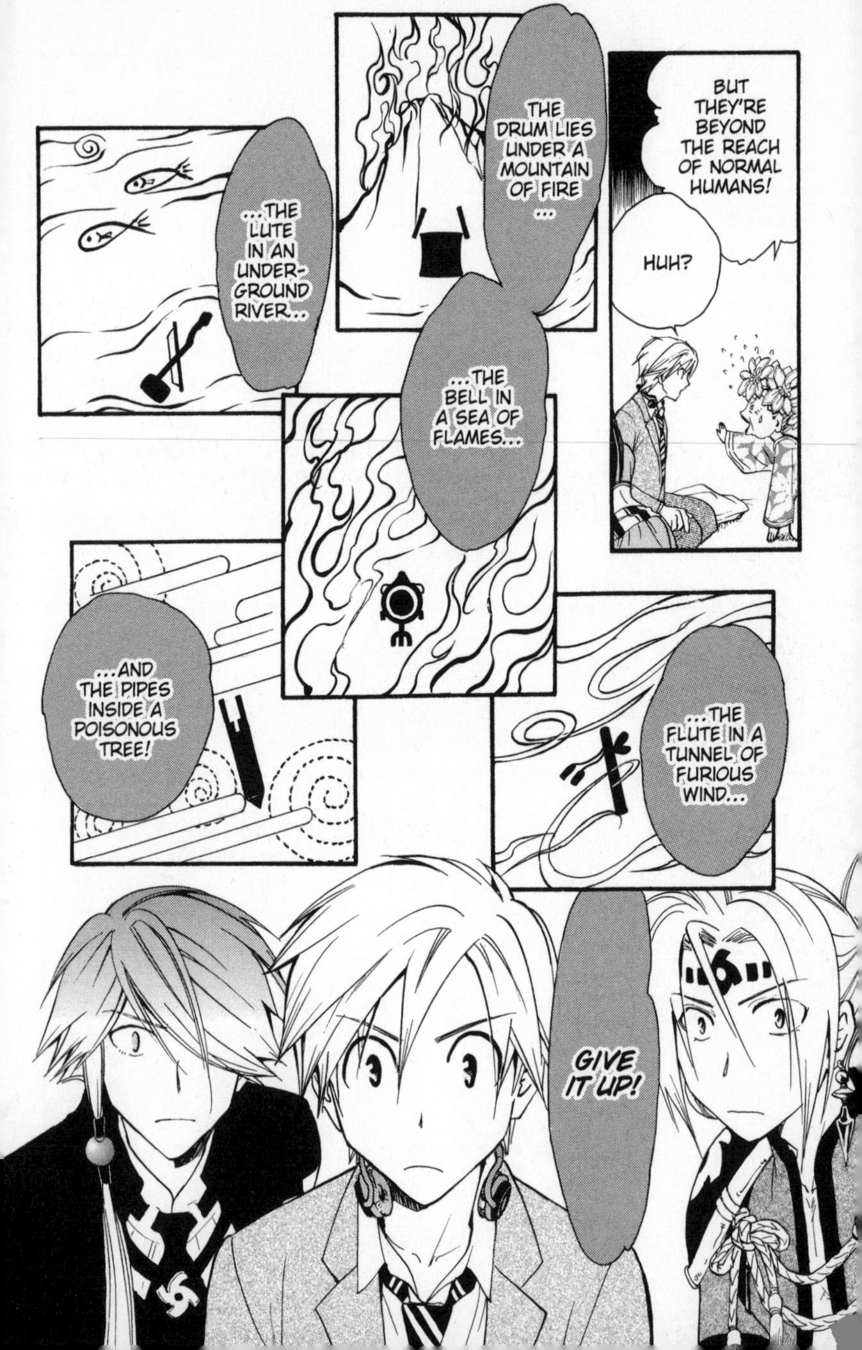
THE DRUM LIES UNDER A MOUNTAIN OF FIRE ...
...THE LUTE IN AN UNDER-GROUND RIVER...
...THE BELL IN A SEA OF FLAMES...
...THE FLUTE IN A TUNNEL OF FURIOUS WIND...
...AND THE PIPES INSIDE A POISONOUS TREE!
BUT THEY'RE BEYOND THE REACH OF NORMAL HUMANS!
HUH?
GIVE IT UP!

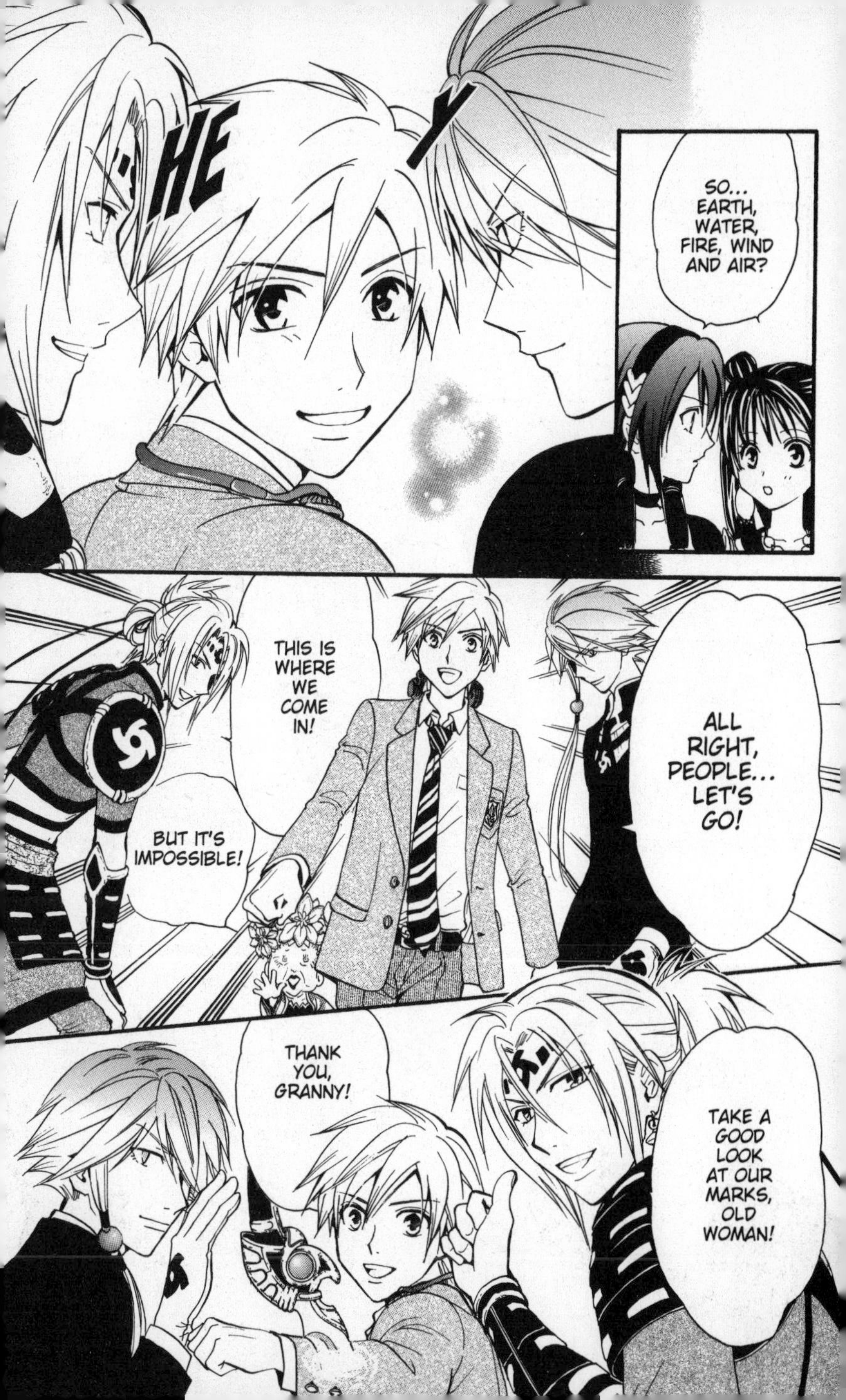
SO... EARTH, WATER, FIRE, WIND AND AIR?
HEY
ALL RIGHT, PEOPLE... LET'S GO!
THIS IS WHERE WE COME IN!
BUT IT'S IMPOSSIBLE!
TAKE A GOOD LOOK AT OUR MARKS, OLD WOMAN!
THANK YOU, GRANNY!

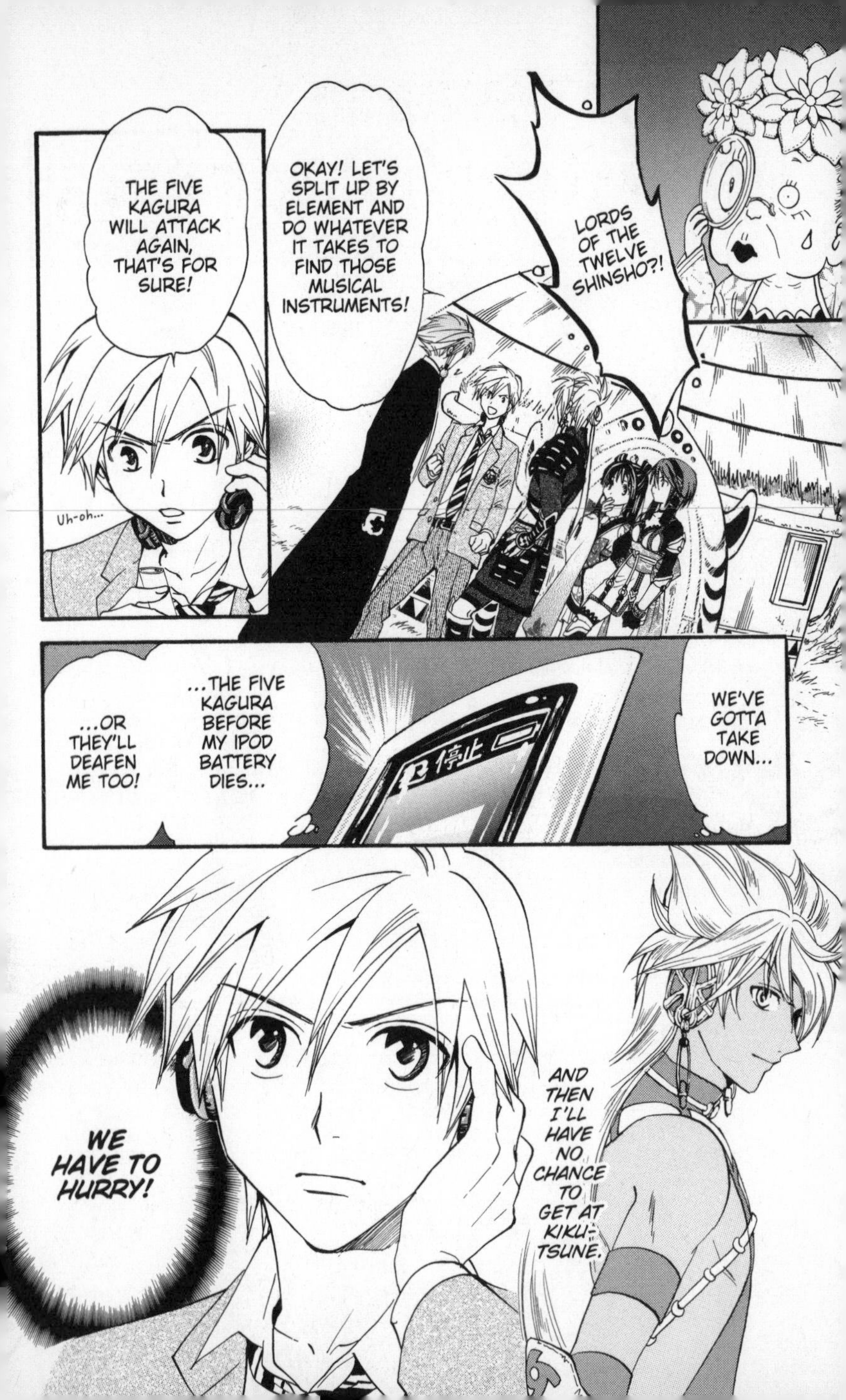
LORDS OF THE TWELVE SHINSHO?!
OKAY! LET'S SPLIT UP BY ELEMENT AND DO WHATEVER IT TAKES TO FIND THOSE MUSICAL INSTRUMENTS!
THE FIVE KAGURA WILL ATTACK AGAIN, THAT'S FOR SURE!
Uh-oh...
WE'VE GOTTA TAKE DOWN...
停止
...THE FIVE KAGURA BEFORE MY IPOD BATTERY DIES...
...OR THEY'LL DEAFEN ME TOO!
AND THEN I'LL HAVE NO CHANCE TO GET AT KIKU-TSUNE.
WE HAVE TO HURRY!

CHAPTER 151
REBELLIOUS ATTRIBUTES

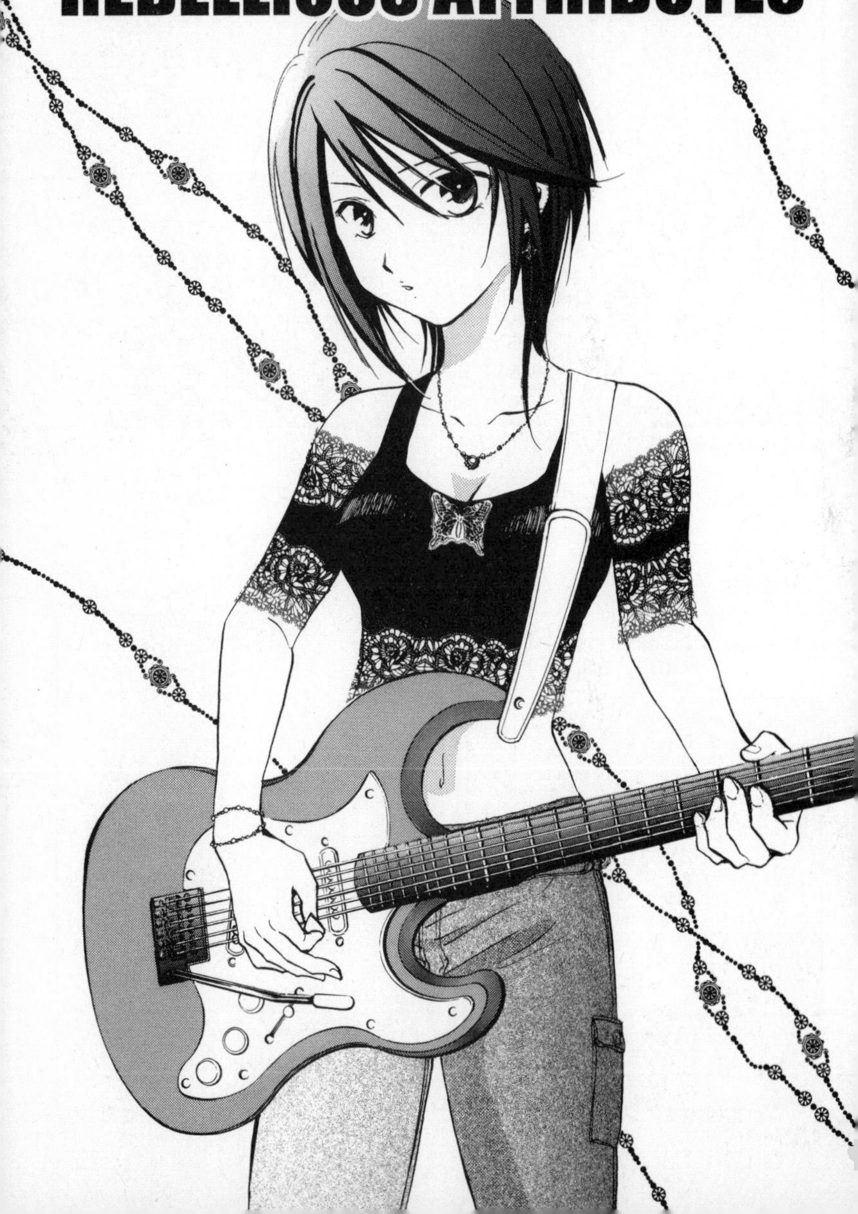

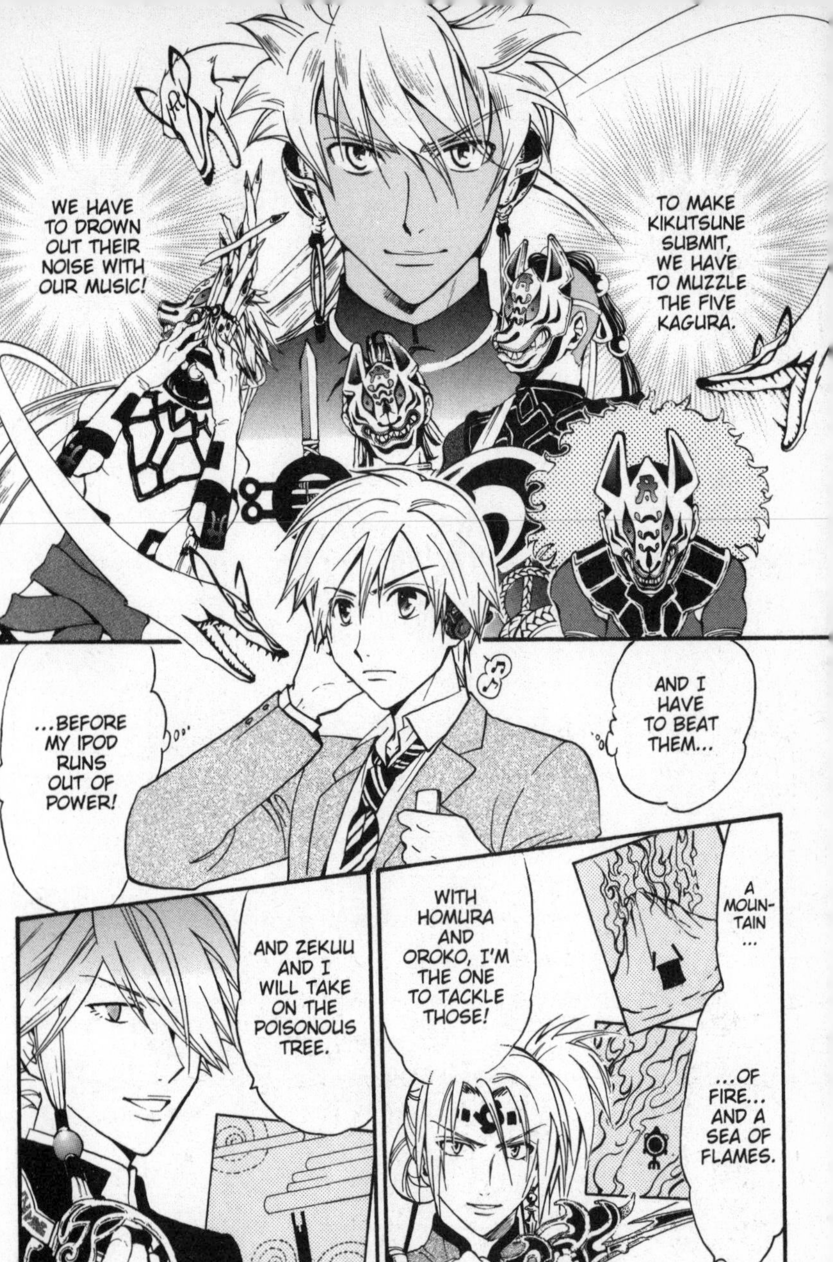
TO MAKE KIKUTSUNE SUBMIT, WE HAVE TO MUZZLE THE FIVE KAGURA.
WE HAVE TO DROWN OUT THEIR NOISE WITH OUR MUSIC!
AND I HAVE TO BEAT THEM...
...BEFORE MY IPOD RUNS OUT OF POWER!
A MOUN-TAIN...
...OF FIRE... AND A SEA OF FLAMES.
WITH HOMURA AND OROKO, I'M THE ONE TO TACKLE THOSE!
AND ZEKUU AND I WILL TAKE ON THE POISONOUS TREE.

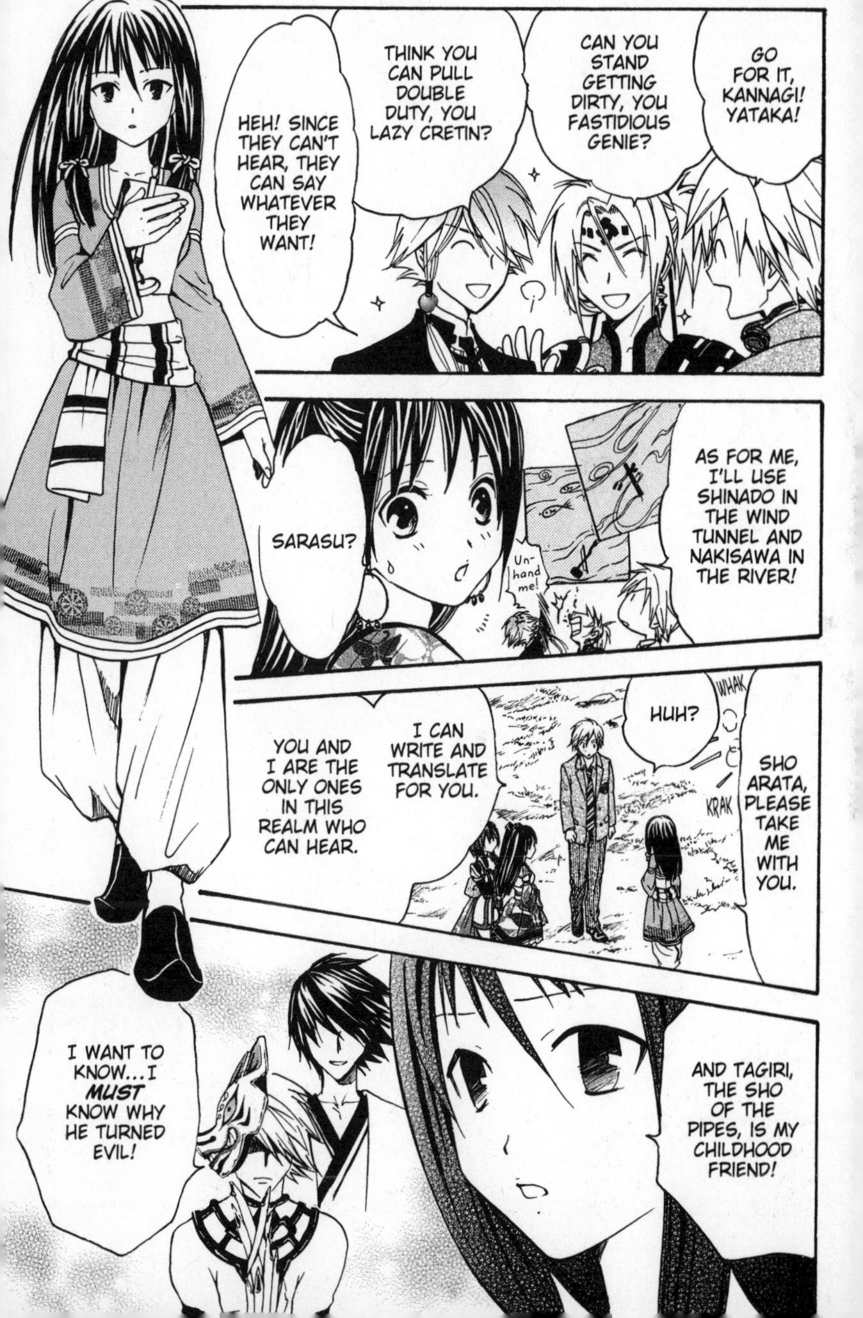
GO FOR IT, KANNAGI! YATAKA!
CAN YOU STAND GETTING DIRTY, YOU FASTIDIOUS GENIE?
THINK YOU CAN PULL DOUBLE DUTY, YOU LAZY CRETIN?
HEH! SINCE THEY CAN'T HEAR, THEY CAN SAY WHATEVER THEY WANT!
AS FOR ME, I'LL USE SHINADO IN THE WIND TUNNEL AND NAKISAWA IN THE RIVER!
Un-hand me!
SARASU?
SHO ARATA, PLEASE TAKE ME WITH YOU.
WHAK
KRAK
HUH?
I CAN WRITE AND TRANSLATE FOR YOU.
YOU AND I ARE THE ONLY ONES IN THIS REALM WHO CAN HEAR.
AND TAGIRI, THE SHO OF THE PIPES, IS MY CHILDHOOD FRIEND!
I WANT TO KNOW...I *MUST* KNOW WHY HE TURNED EVIL!

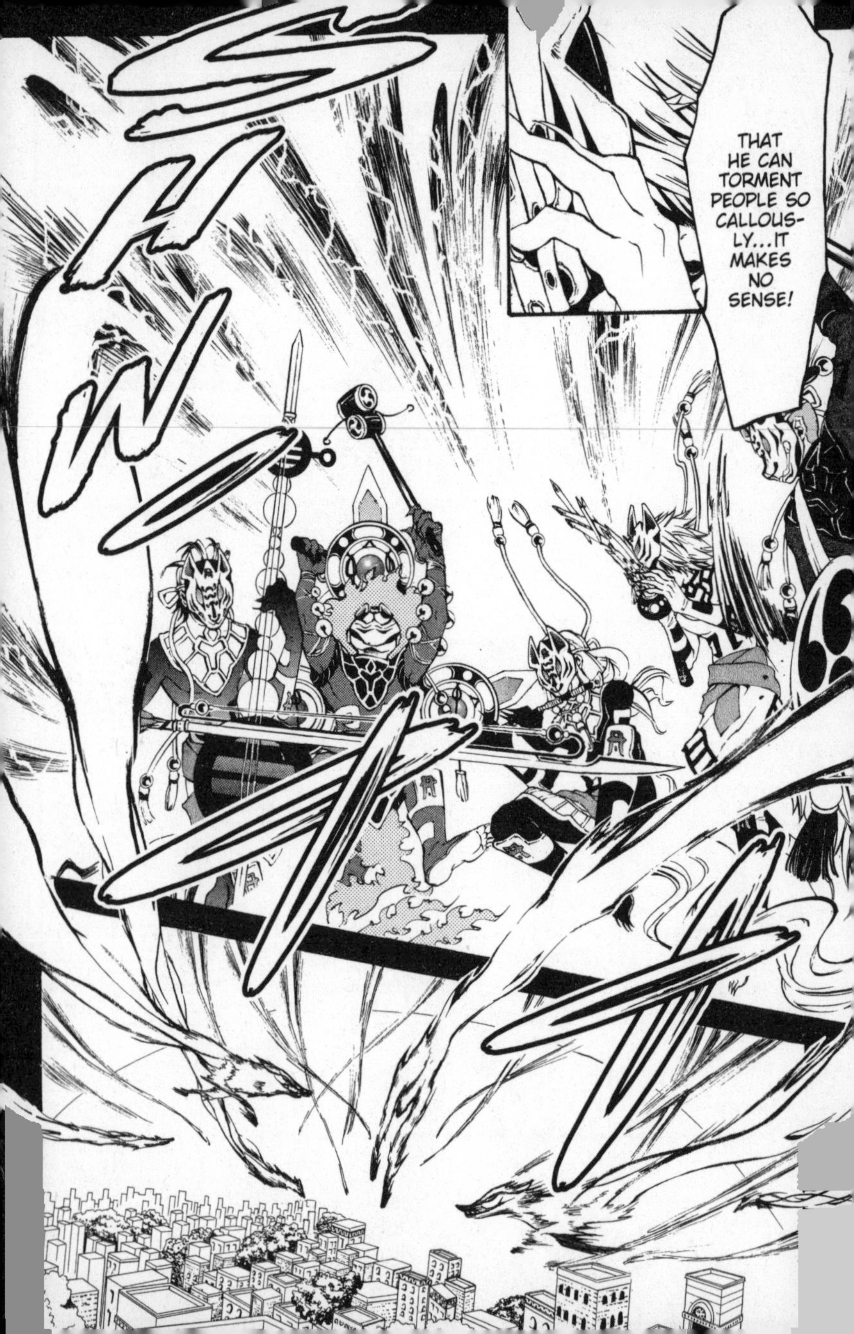
THAT HE CAN TORMENT PEOPLE SO CALLOUS-LY...IT MAKES NO SENSE!

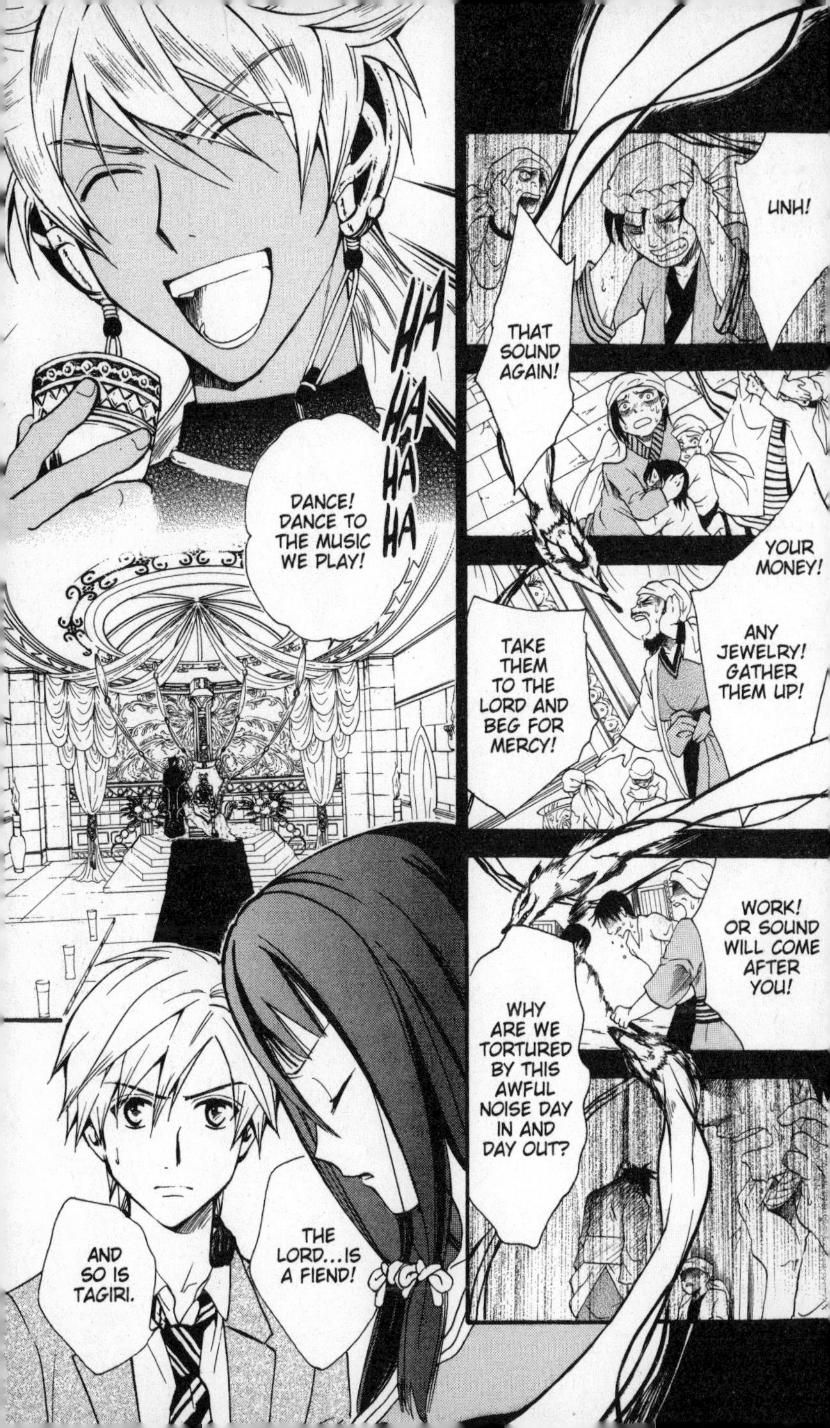
UNH!
THAT SOUND AGAIN!
YOUR MONEY!
ANY JEWELRY! GATHER THEM UP!
TAKE THEM TO THE LORD AND BEG FOR MERCY!
WORK! OR SOUND WILL COME AFTER YOU!
WHY ARE WE TORTURED BY THIS AWFUL NOISE DAY IN AND DAY OUT?
HA HA HA HA HA HA
DANCE! DANCE TO THE MUSIC WE PLAY!
THE LORD...IS A FIEND!
AND SO IS TAGIRI.

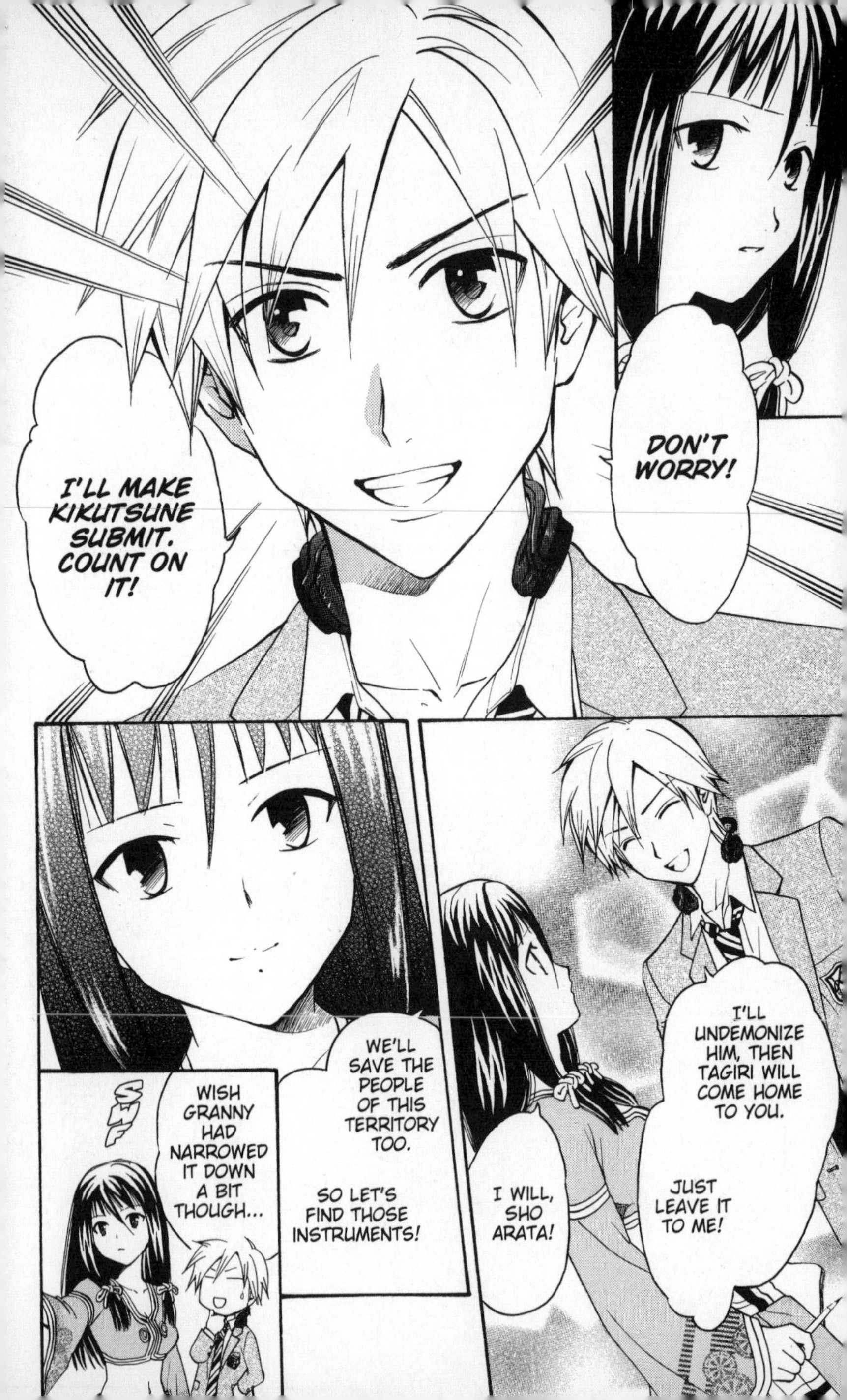
DON'T WORRY!
I'LL MAKE KIKUTSUNE SUBMIT. COUNT ON IT!
I'LL UNDEMONIZE HIM, THEN TAGIRI WILL COME HOME TO YOU.
JUST LEAVE IT TO ME!
I WILL, SHO ARATA!
WE'LL SAVE THE PEOPLE OF THIS TERRITORY TOO.
SO LET'S FIND THOSE INSTRUMENTS!
SWF
WISH GRANNY HAD NARROWED IT DOWN A BIT THOUGH...

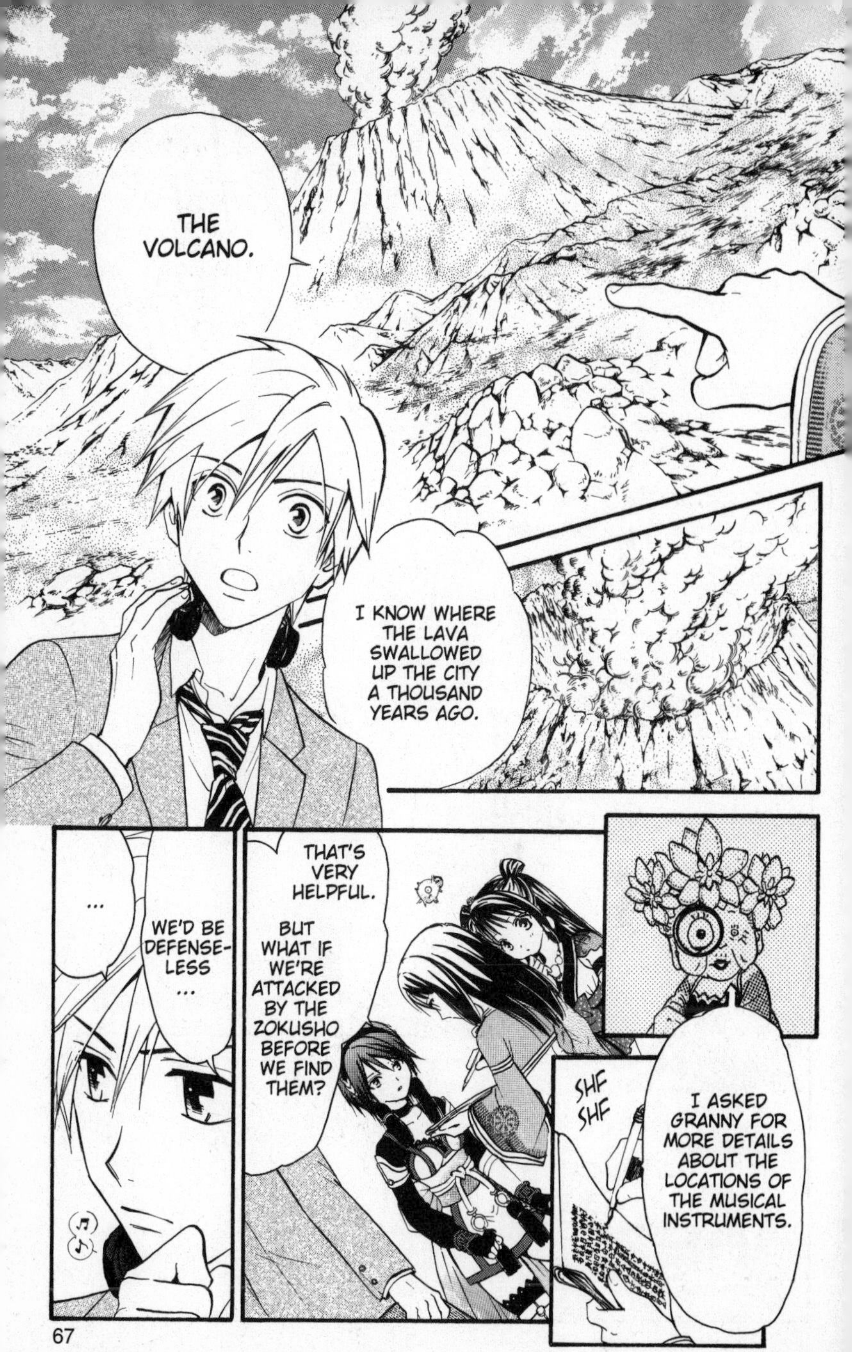
THE VOLCANO.
I KNOW WHERE THE LAVA SWALLOWED UP THE CITY A THOUSAND YEARS AGO.
SHF SHF
I ASKED GRANNY FOR MORE DETAILS ABOUT THE LOCATIONS OF THE MUSICAL INSTRUMENTS.
THAT'S VERY HELPFUL.
BUT WHAT IF WE'RE ATTACKED BY THE ZOKUSHO BEFORE WE FIND THEM?
...
WE'D BE DEFENSE-LESS ...

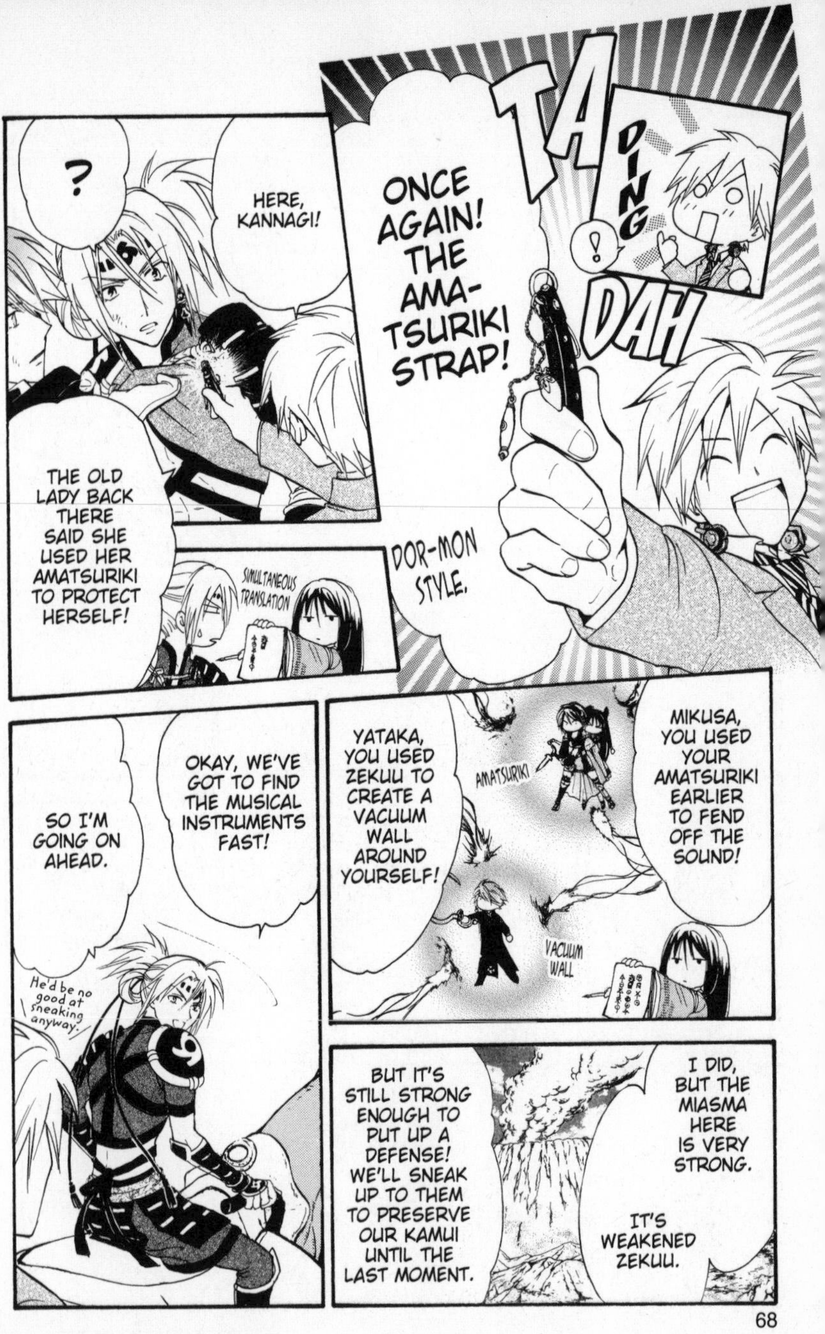
TA
DAH
DING
!
ONCE AGAIN! THE AMA-TSURIKI STRAP!
DOR-MON STYLE.
HERE, KANNAGI!
?
THE OLD LADY BACK THERE SAID SHE USED HER AMATSURIKI TO PROTECT HERSELF!
SIMULTANEOUS TRANSLATION
MIKUSA, YOU USED YOUR AMATSURIKI EARLIER TO FEND OFF THE SOUND!
AMATSURIKI
YATAKA, YOU USED ZEKUU TO CREATE A VACUUM WALL AROUND YOURSELF!
VACUUM WALL
I DID, BUT THE MIASMA HERE IS VERY STRONG.
IT'S WEAKENED ZEKUU.
BUT IT'S STILL STRONG ENOUGH TO PUT UP A DEFENSE! WE'LL SNEAK UP TO THEM TO PRESERVE OUR KAMUI UNTIL THE LAST MOMENT.
OKAY, WE'VE GOT TO FIND THE MUSICAL INSTRUMENTS FAST!
SO I'M GOING ON AHEAD.
He'd be no good at sneaking anyway.

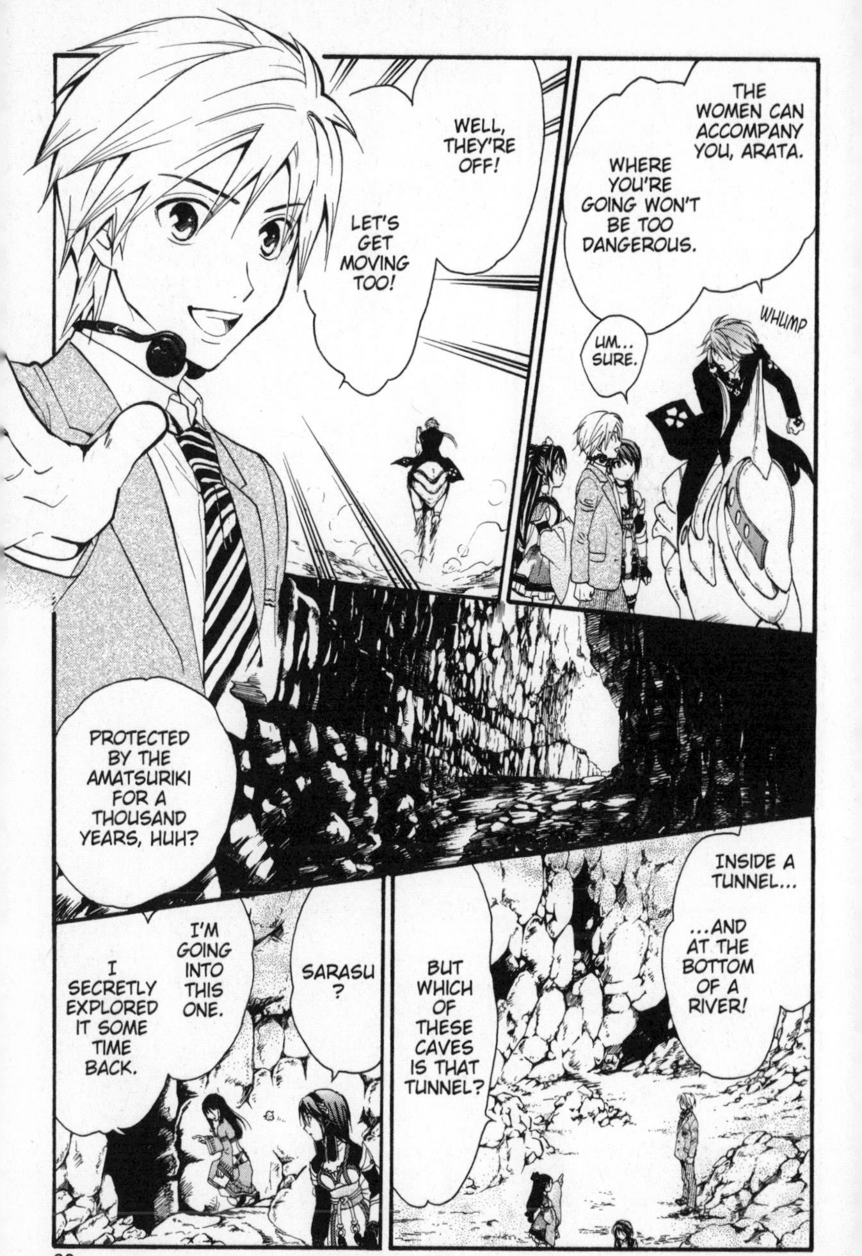
THE WOMEN CAN ACCOMPANY YOU, ARATA.
WHERE YOU'RE GOING WON'T BE TOO DANGEROUS.
WHUMP
UM... SURE.
WELL, THEY'RE OFF!
LET'S GET MOVING TOO!
PROTECTED BY THE AMATSURIKI FOR A THOUSAND YEARS, HUH?
INSIDE A TUNNEL...
...AND AT THE BOTTOM OF A RIVER!
BUT WHICH OF THESE CAVES IS THAT TUNNEL?
SARASU?
I'M GOING INTO THIS ONE.
I SECRETLY EXPLORED IT SOME TIME BACK.

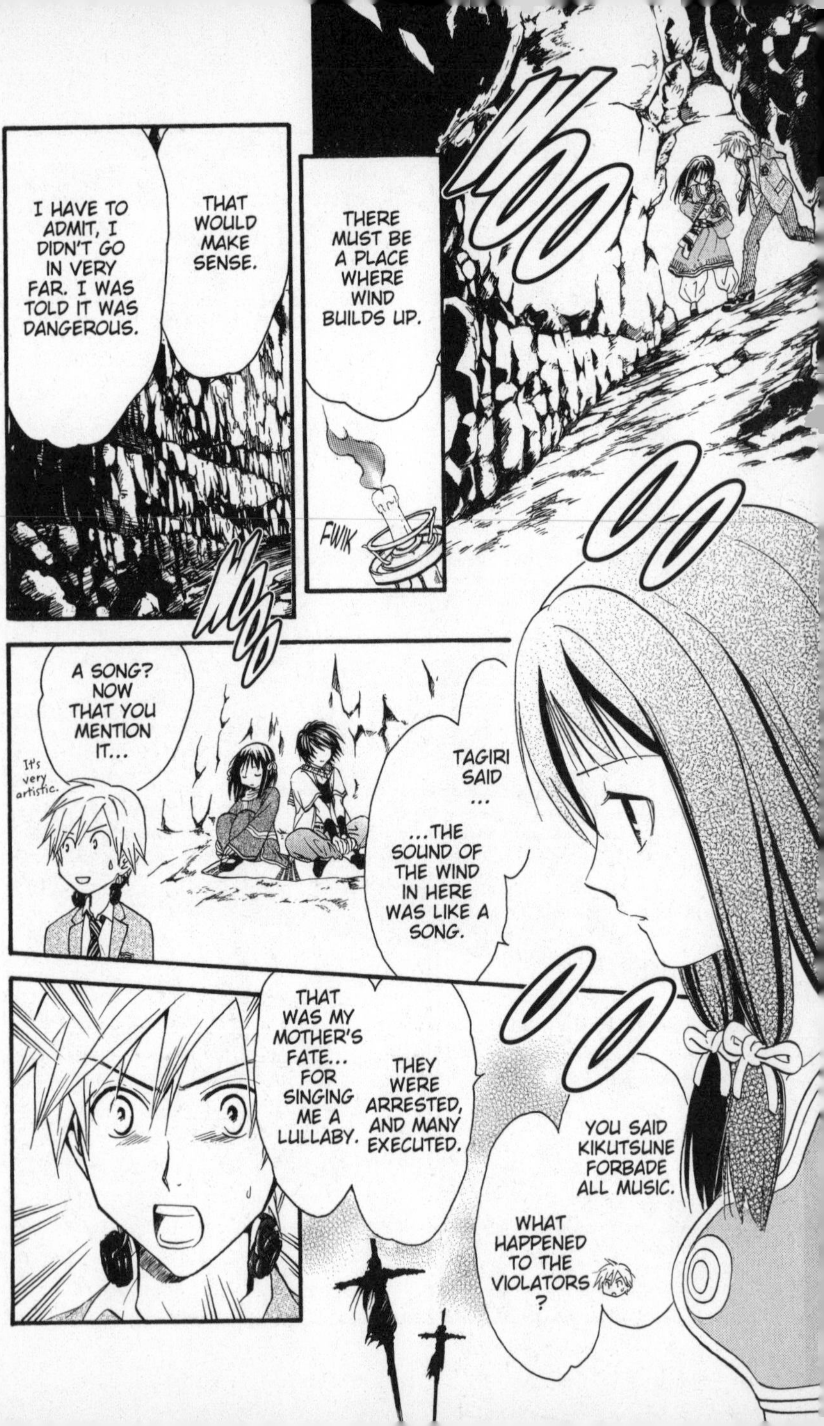
WOOO
THERE MUST BE A PLACE WHERE WIND BUILDS UP.
FWIK
THAT WOULD MAKE SENSE.
I HAVE TO ADMIT, I DIDN'T GO IN VERY FAR. I WAS TOLD IT WAS DANGEROUS.
WOOO
OOO
TAGIRI SAID ...
...THE SOUND OF THE WIND IN HERE WAS LIKE A SONG.
A SONG? NOW THAT YOU MENTION IT...
It's very artistic.
OOO
YOU SAID KIKUTSUNE FORBADE ALL MUSIC.
WHAT HAPPENED TO THE VIOLATORS?
THEY WERE ARRESTED, AND MANY EXECUTED.
THAT WAS MY MOTHER'S FATE... FOR SINGING ME A LULLABY.

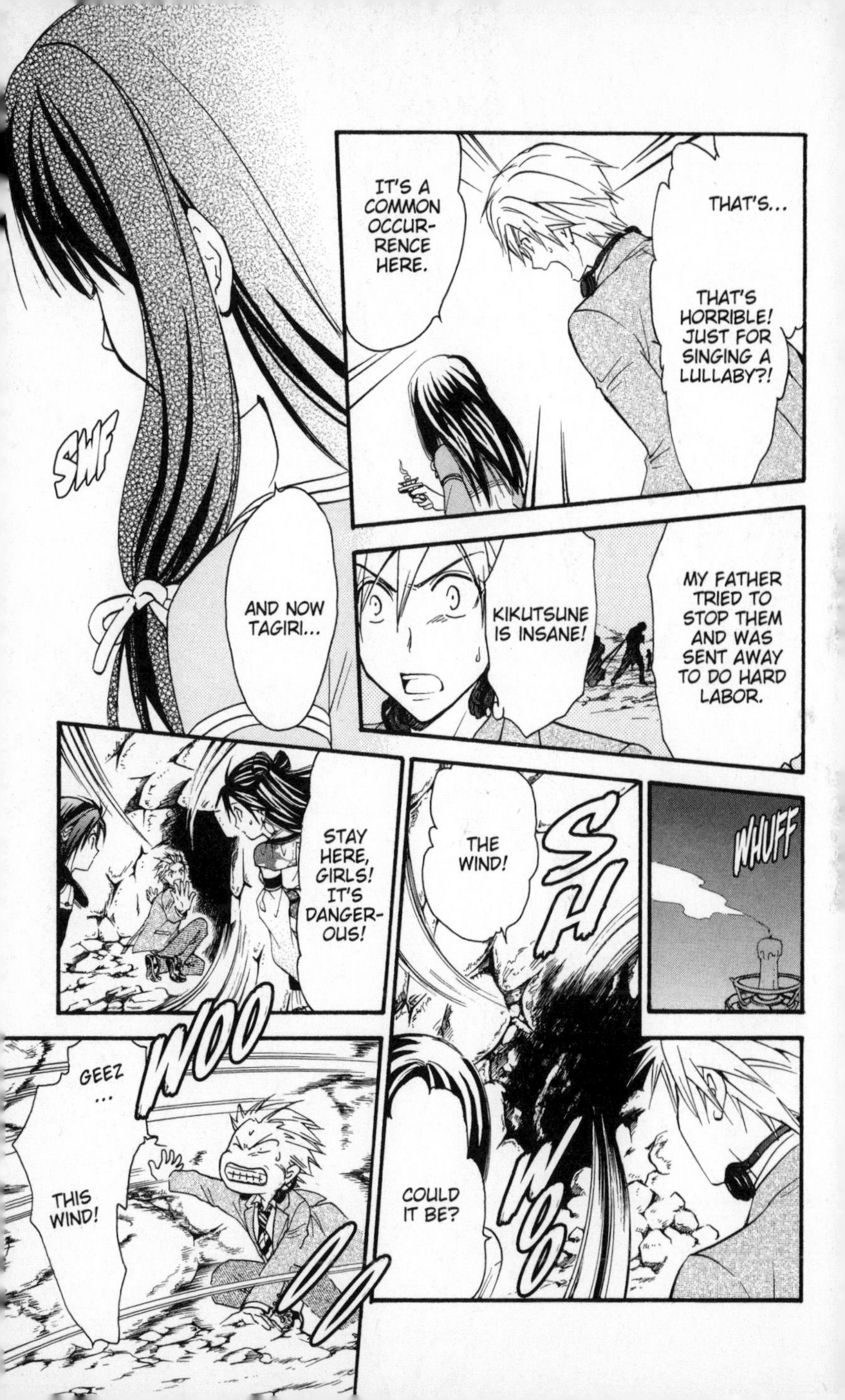
THAT'S...
THAT'S HORRIBLE! JUST FOR SINGING A LULLABY?!
IT'S A COMMON OCCURRENCE HERE.
SWF
MY FATHER TRIED TO STOP THEM AND WAS SENT AWAY TO DO HARD LABOR.
KIKUTSUNE IS INSANE!
AND NOW TAGIRI...
WHUFF
SH
THE WIND!
STAY HERE, GIRLS! IT'S DANGER-OUS!
WOO
COULD IT BE?
WOO
GEEZ ...
THIS WIND!

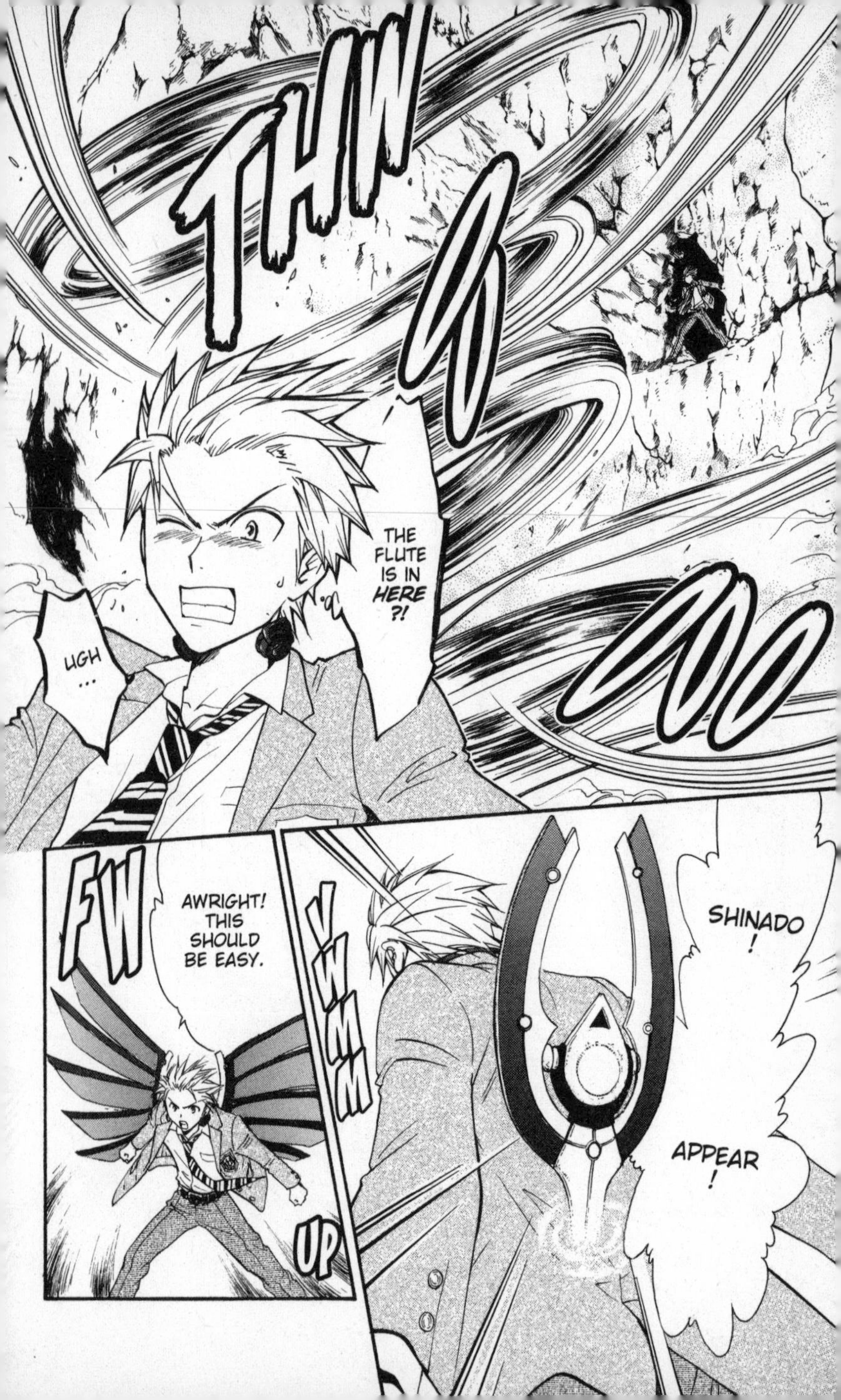

THW
THE FLUTE IS IN HERE ?!
UGH ...
SHINADO !
APPEAR !
VWMM
UP
FW
AWRIGHT! THIS SHOULD BE EASY.

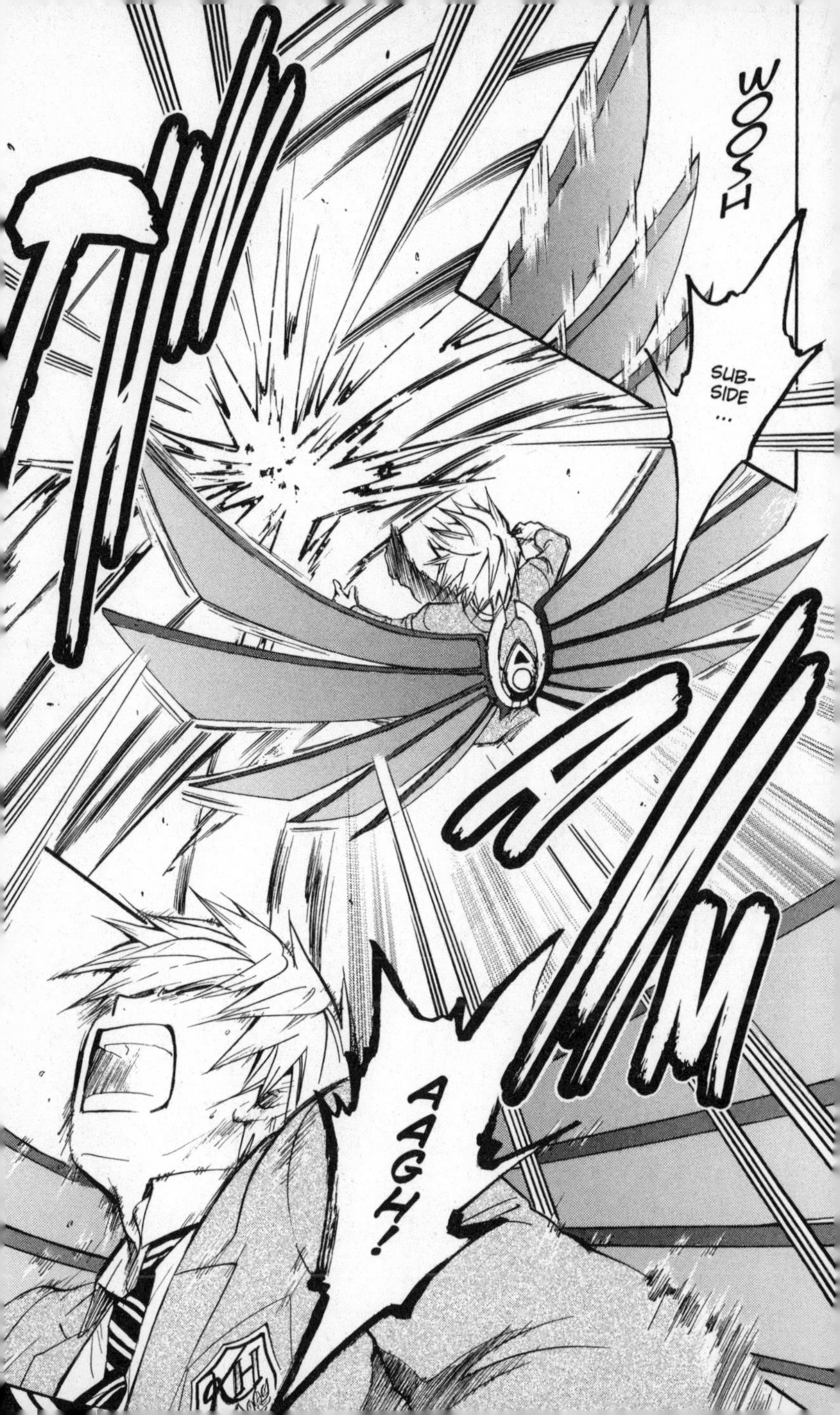
WOOSH
SUB-SIDE ...
AAGH!

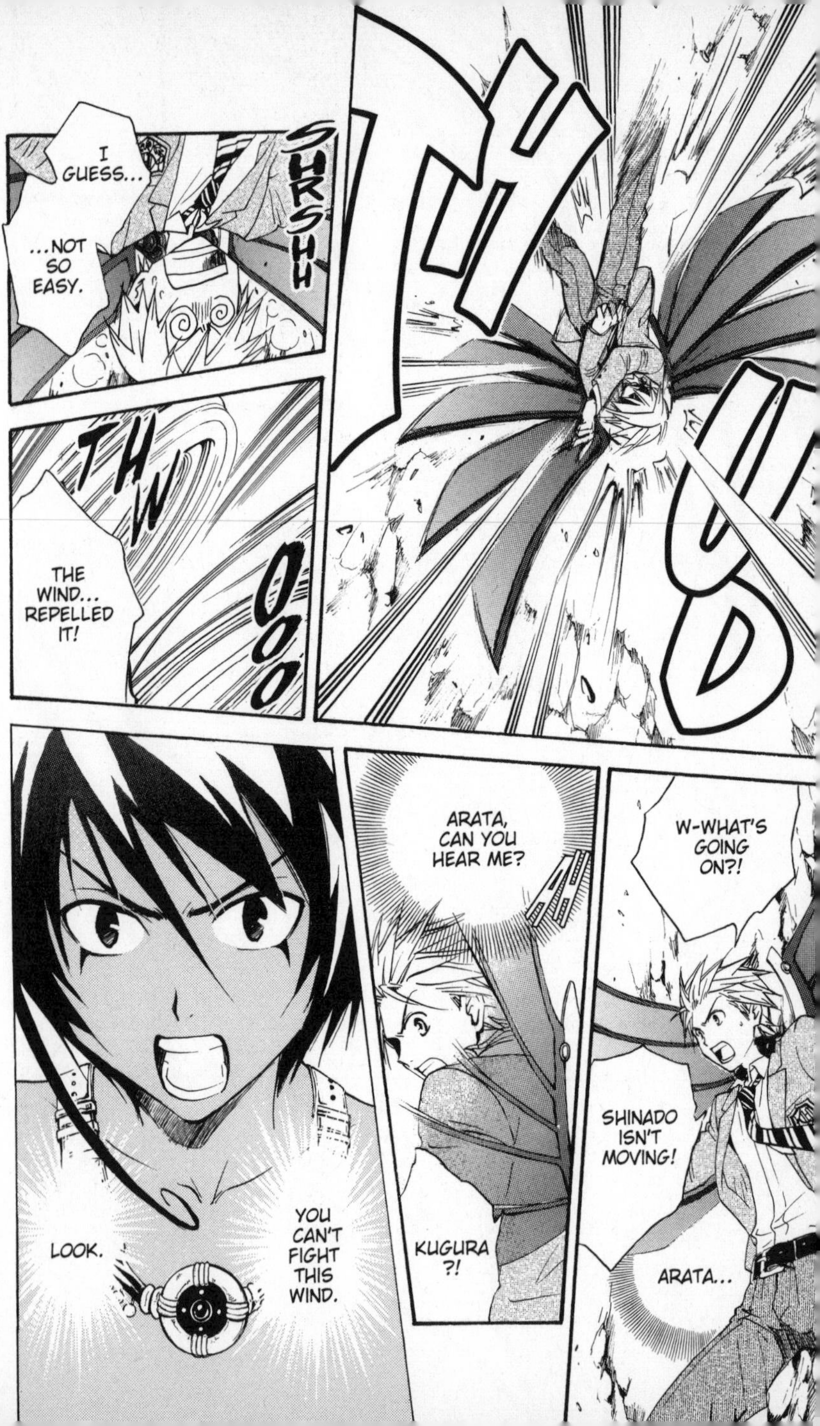
SHRSHH
I GUESS...
...NOT SO EASY.
THWOOO
THE WIND... REPELLED IT!
W-WHAT'S GOING ON?!
SHINADO ISN'T MOVING!
ARATA...
ARATA, CAN YOU HEAR ME?
KUGURA ?!
YOU CAN'T FIGHT THIS WIND.
LOOK.

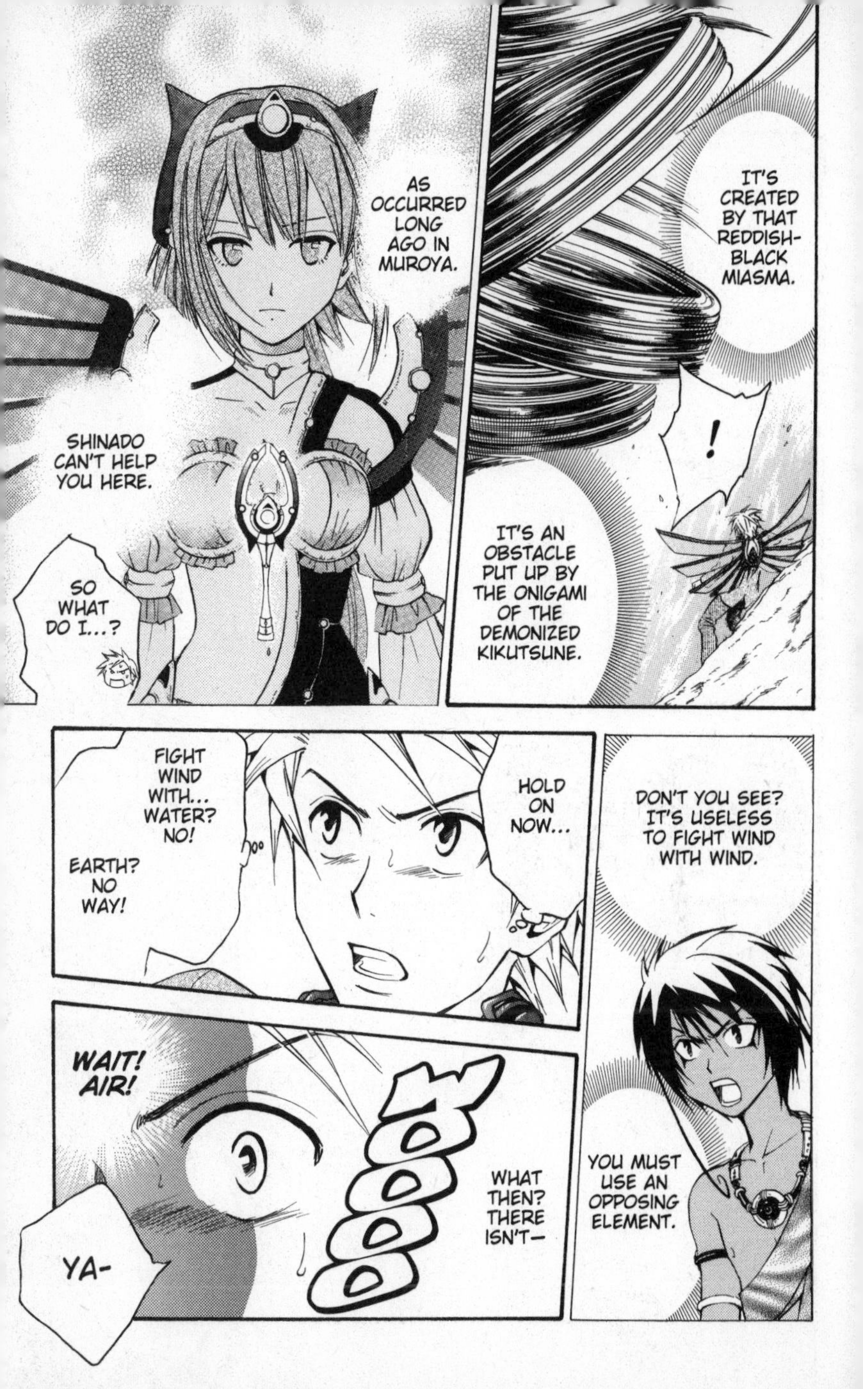
IT'S CREATED BY THAT REDDISH-BLACK MIASMA.
!
IT'S AN OBSTACLE PUT UP BY THE ONIGAMI OF THE DEMONIZED KIKUTSUNE.
AS OCCURRED LONG AGO IN MUROYA.
SHINADO CAN'T HELP YOU HERE.
SO WHAT DO I...?
DON'T YOU SEE? IT'S USELESS TO FIGHT WIND WITH WIND.
YOU MUST USE AN OPPOSING ELEMENT.
HOLD ON NOW...
FIGHT WIND WITH... WATER? NO!
EARTH? NO WAY!
WHAT THEN? THERE ISN'T—
WAIT! AIR!
YA-

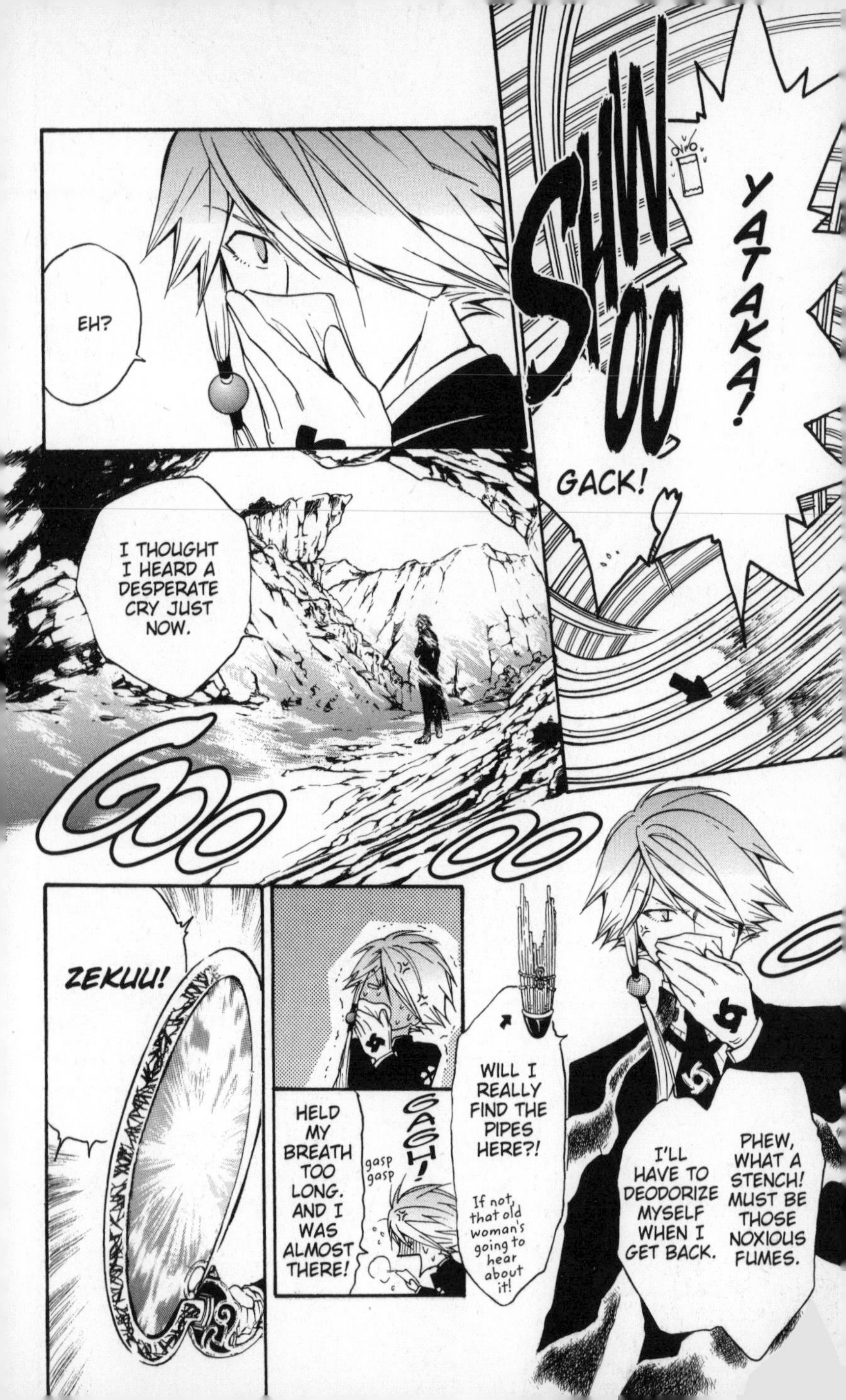
YATAKA!
SHIN
OO
GACK!
EH?
I THOUGHT I HEARD A DESPERATE CRY JUST NOW.
GOOOO
PHEW, WHAT A STENCH! MUST BE THOSE NOXIOUS FUMES.
I'LL HAVE TO DEODORIZE MYSELF WHEN I GET BACK.
WILL I REALLY FIND THE PIPES HERE?!
If not, that old woman's going to hear about it!
GAGH!
gasp gasp
HELD MY BREATH TOO LONG. AND I WAS ALMOST THERE!
ZEKUU!

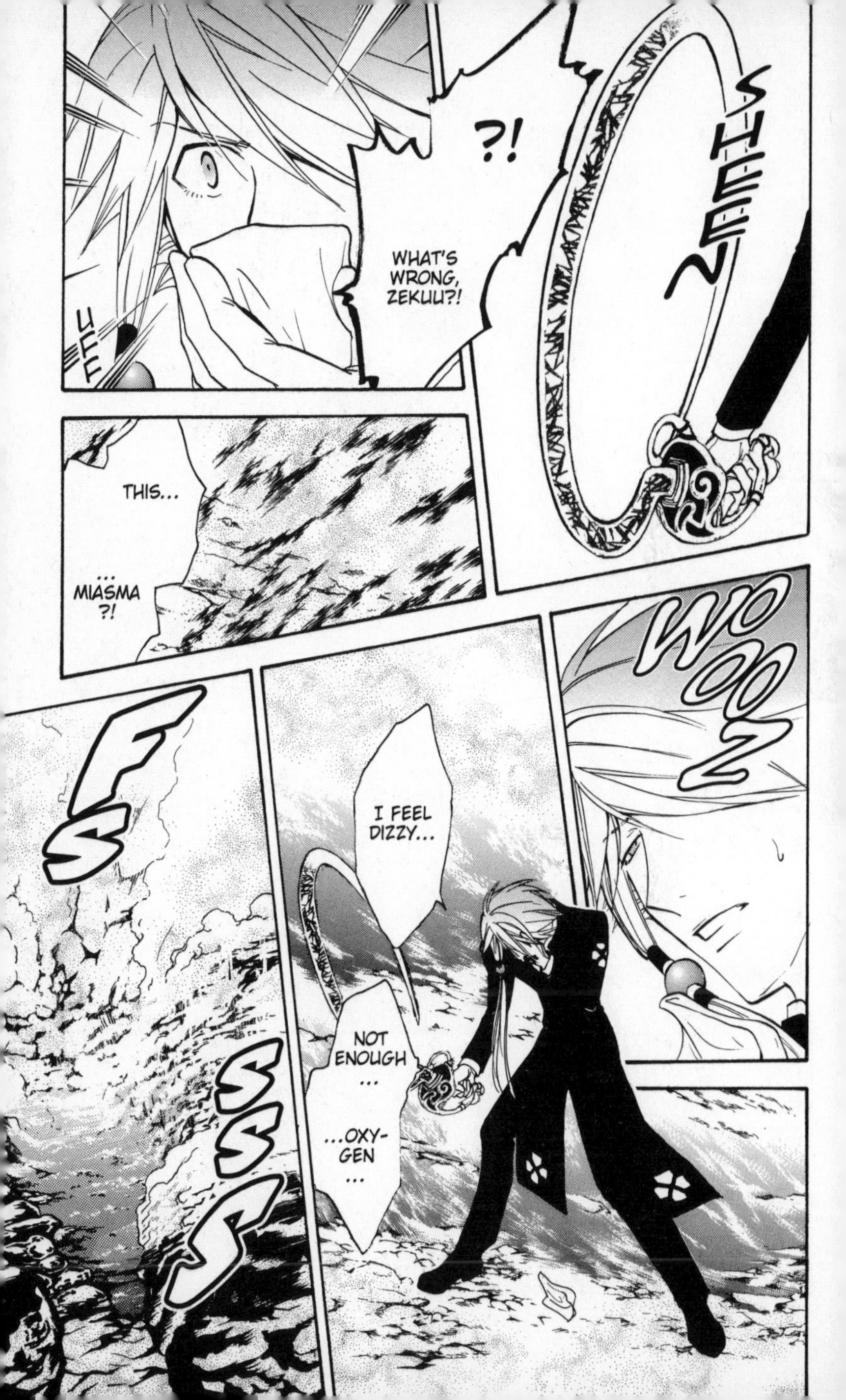
SHEEN
?!
WHAT'S WRONG, ZEKUU?!
UFF
THIS...
...MIASMA?!
WOOZ
I FEEL DIZZY...
NOT ENOUGH...
...OXY-GEN...
FSSSS

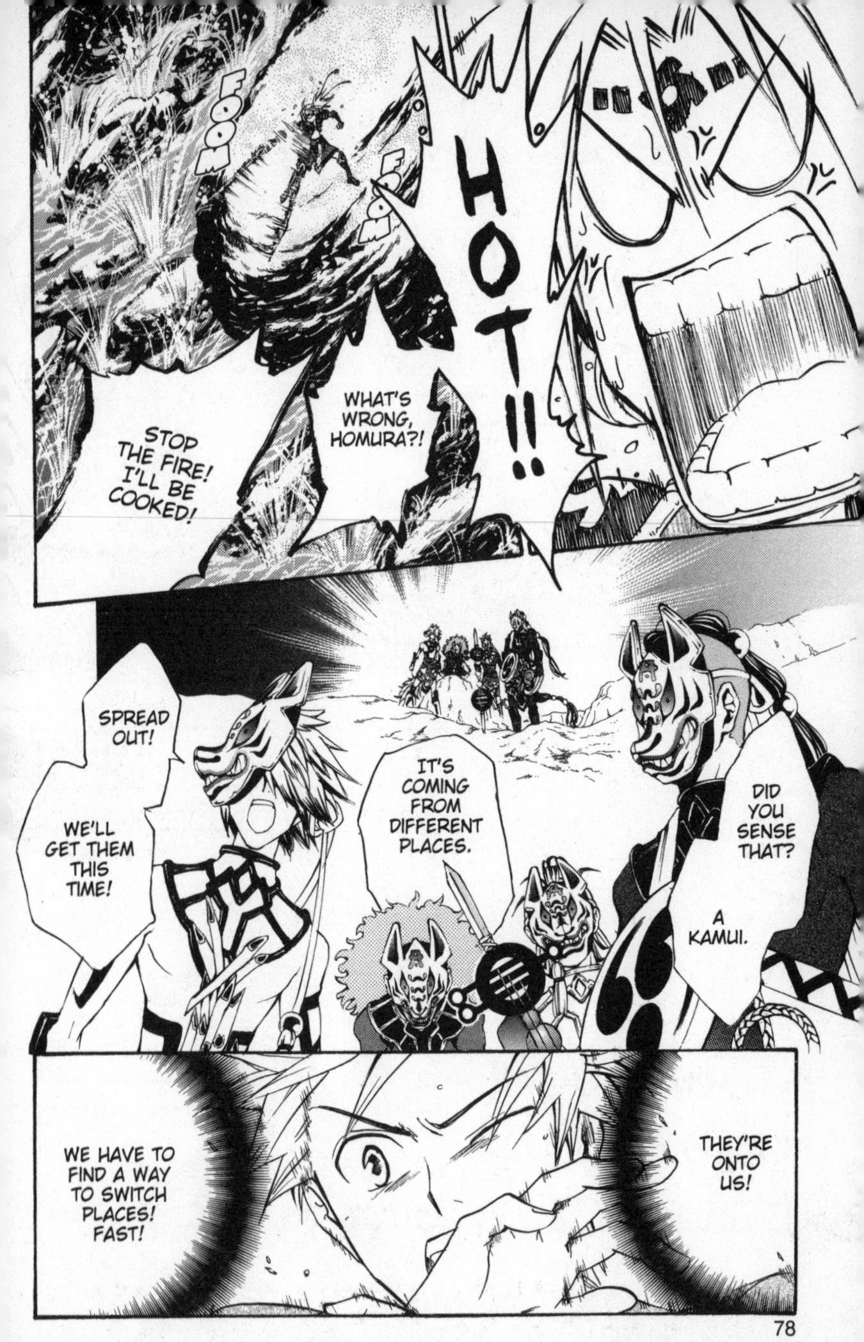
..B..
HOT!!
FOOM
WHAT'S WRONG, HOMURA?!
FOOM
STOP THE FIRE! I'LL BE COOKED!
DID YOU SENSE THAT?
A KAMUI.
IT'S COMING FROM DIFFERENT PLACES.
SPREAD OUT!
WE'LL GET THEM THIS TIME!
THEY'RE ONTO US!
WE HAVE TO FIND A WAY TO SWITCH PLACES! FAST!

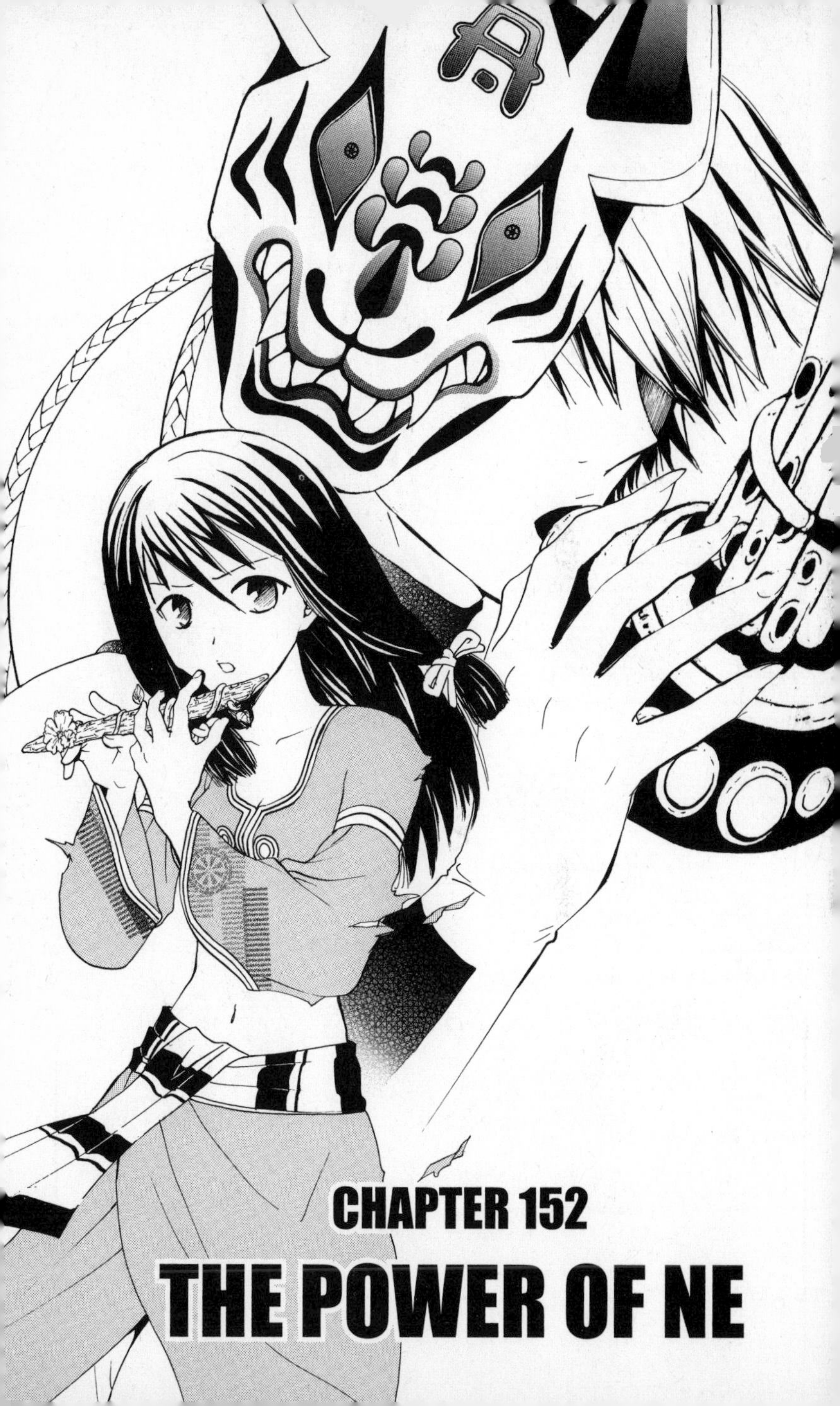
CHAPTER 152
THE POWER OF NE

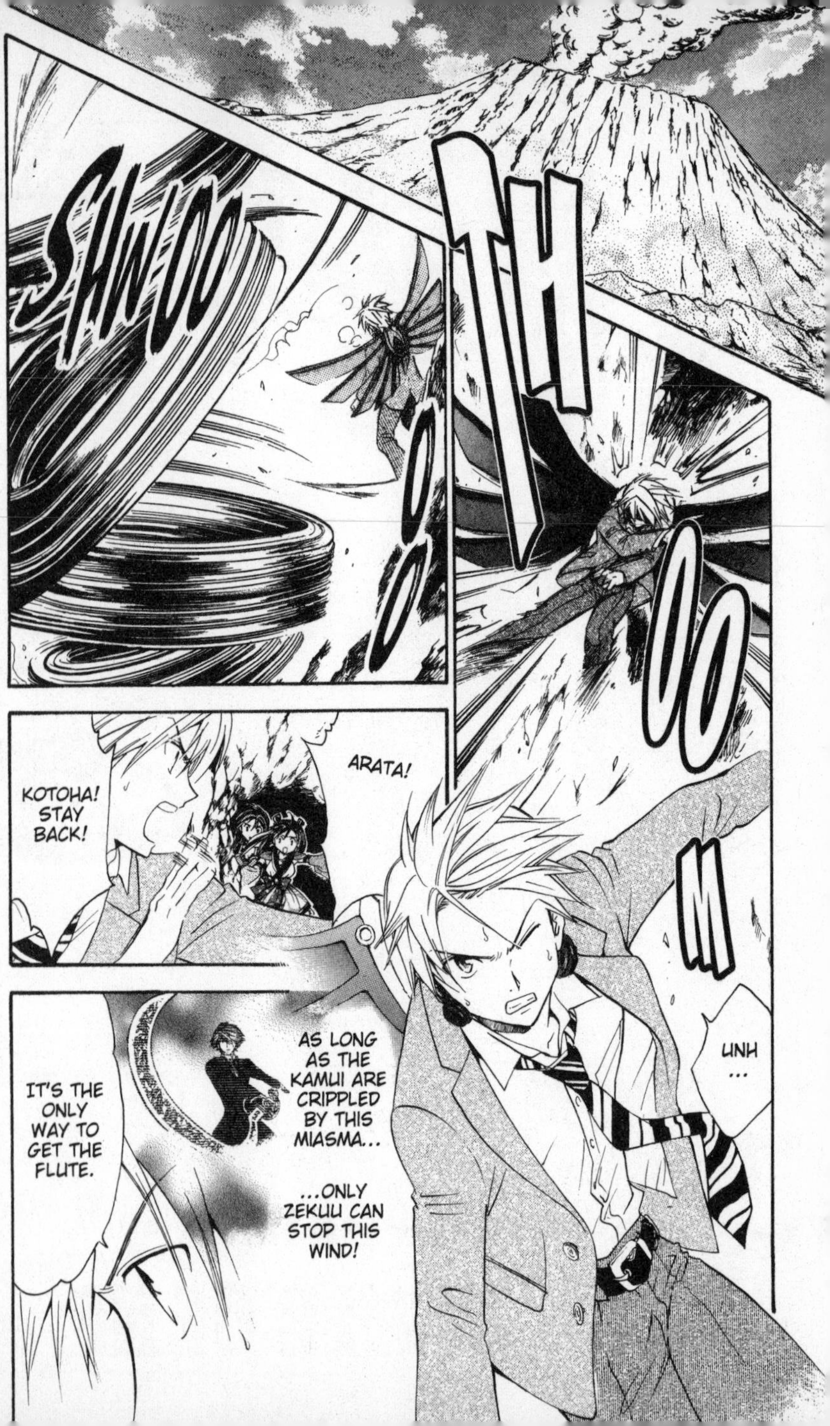
THOOOM
UNH...
SHWOOOO
ARATA!
KOTOHA! STAY BACK!
AS LONG AS THE KAMUI ARE CRIPPLED BY THIS MIASMA...
...ONLY ZEKUU CAN STOP THIS WIND!
IT'S THE ONLY WAY TO GET THE FLUTE.

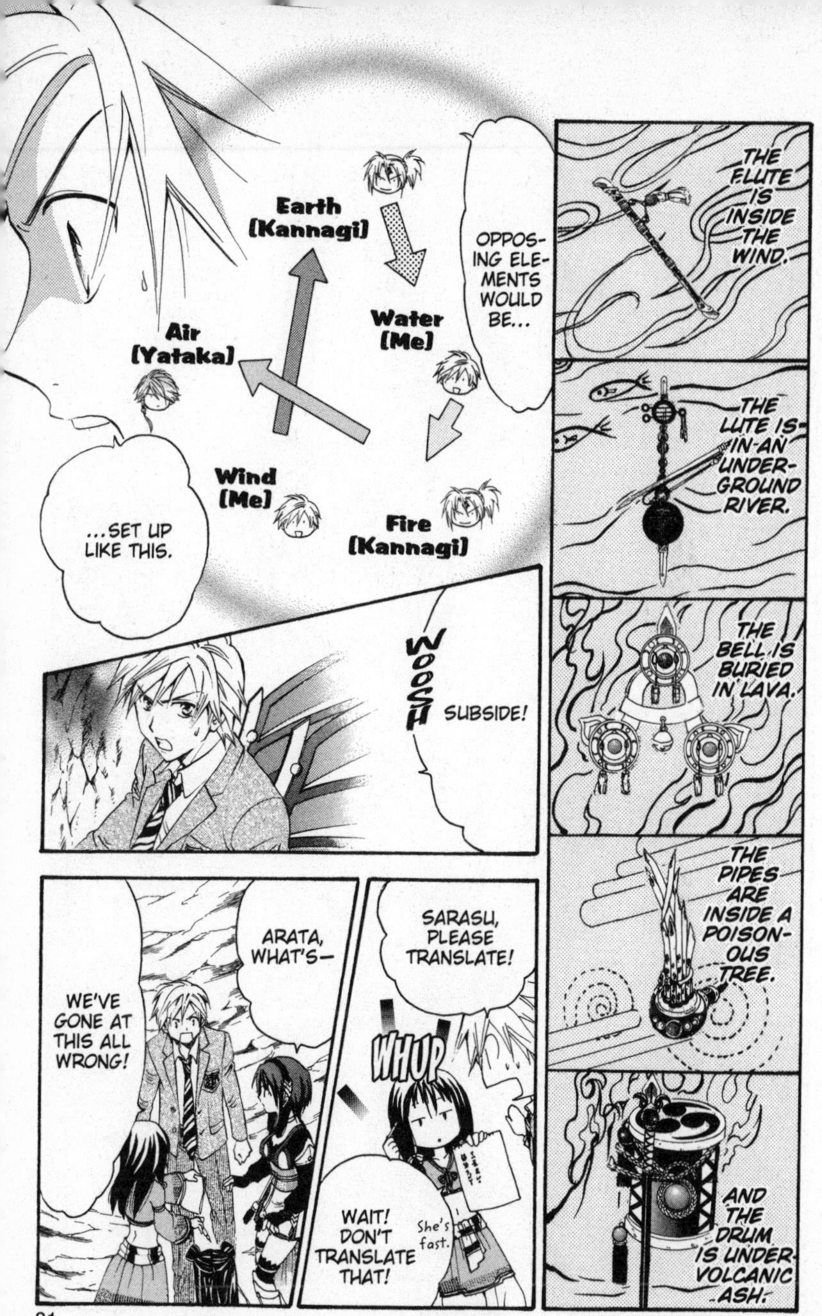
THE FLUTE IS INSIDE THE WIND.
THE LUTE IS IN AN UNDER-GROUND RIVER.
THE BELL IS BURIED IN LAVA.
THE PIPES ARE INSIDE A POISON-OUS TREE.
AND THE DRUM IS UNDER VOLCANIC ASH.
OPPOS-ING ELE-MENTS WOULD BE...
Earth [Kannagi]
Water [Me]
Fire [Kannagi]
Wind [Me]
Air [Yataka]
...SET UP LIKE THIS.
WOOOSH
SUBSIDE!
SARASU, PLEASE TRANSLATE!
WHUP
WAIT! DON'T TRANSLATE THAT!
She's fast.
ARATA, WHAT'S—
WE'VE GONE AT THIS ALL WRONG!

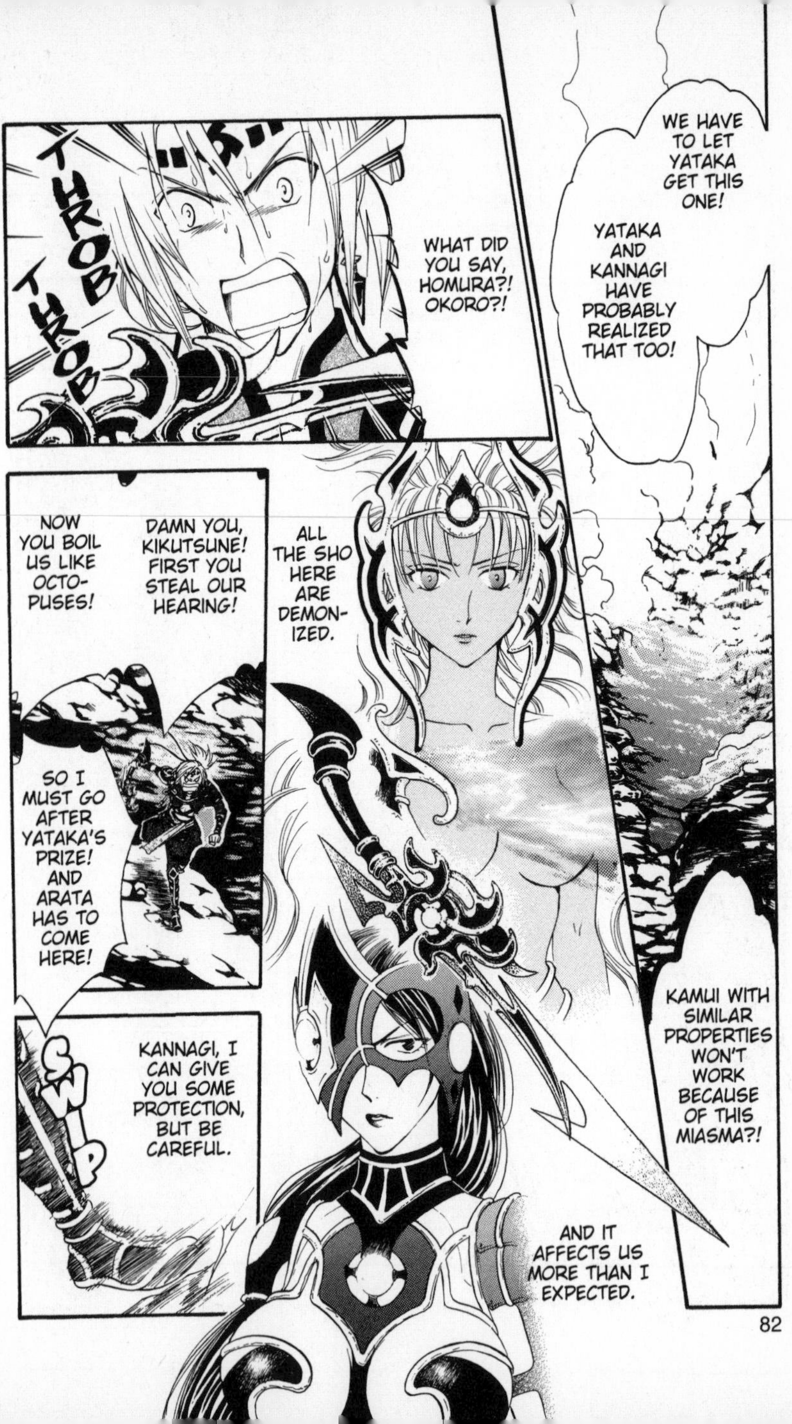
WE HAVE TO LET YATAKA GET THIS ONE!
YATAKA AND KANNAGI HAVE PROBABLY REALIZED THAT TOO!
KAMUI WITH SIMILAR PROPERTIES WON'T WORK BECAUSE OF THIS MIASMA?!
WHAT DID YOU SAY, HOMURA?! OKORO?!
THROB THROB
ALL THE SHO HERE ARE DEMONIZED.
DAMN YOU, KIKUTSUNE! FIRST YOU STEAL OUR HEARING!
NOW YOU BOIL US LIKE OCTO-PUSES!
SO I MUST GO AFTER YATAKA'S PRIZE! AND ARATA HAS TO COME HERE!
AND IT AFFECTS US MORE THAN I EXPECTED.
KANNAGI, I CAN GIVE YOU SOME PROTECTION, BUT BE CAREFUL.
SWIP

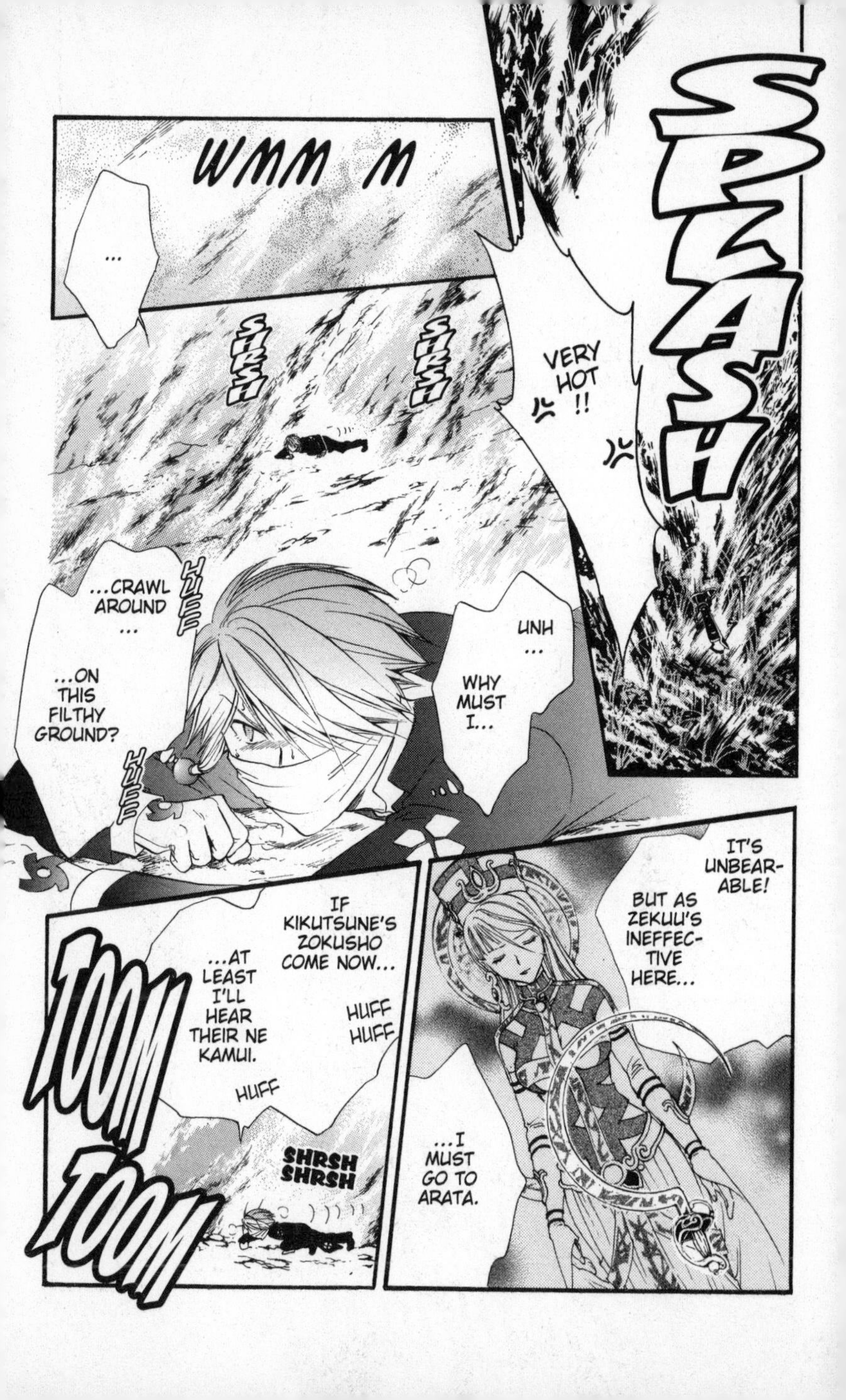
SPLASH
VERY HOT!!
WMMM M
...
SHRSH
SHRSH
UNH...
WHY MUST I...
...CRAWL AROUND...
...ON THIS FILTHY GROUND?
HUFF
HUFF
IT'S UNBEAR-ABLE!
BUT AS ZEKUU'S INEFFEC-TIVE HERE...
...I MUST GO TO ARATA.
IF KIKUTSUNE'S ZOKUSHO COME NOW...
...AT LEAST I'LL HEAR THEIR NE KAMUI.
HUFF HUFF
HUFF
SHRSH SHRSH
TOOM TOOM

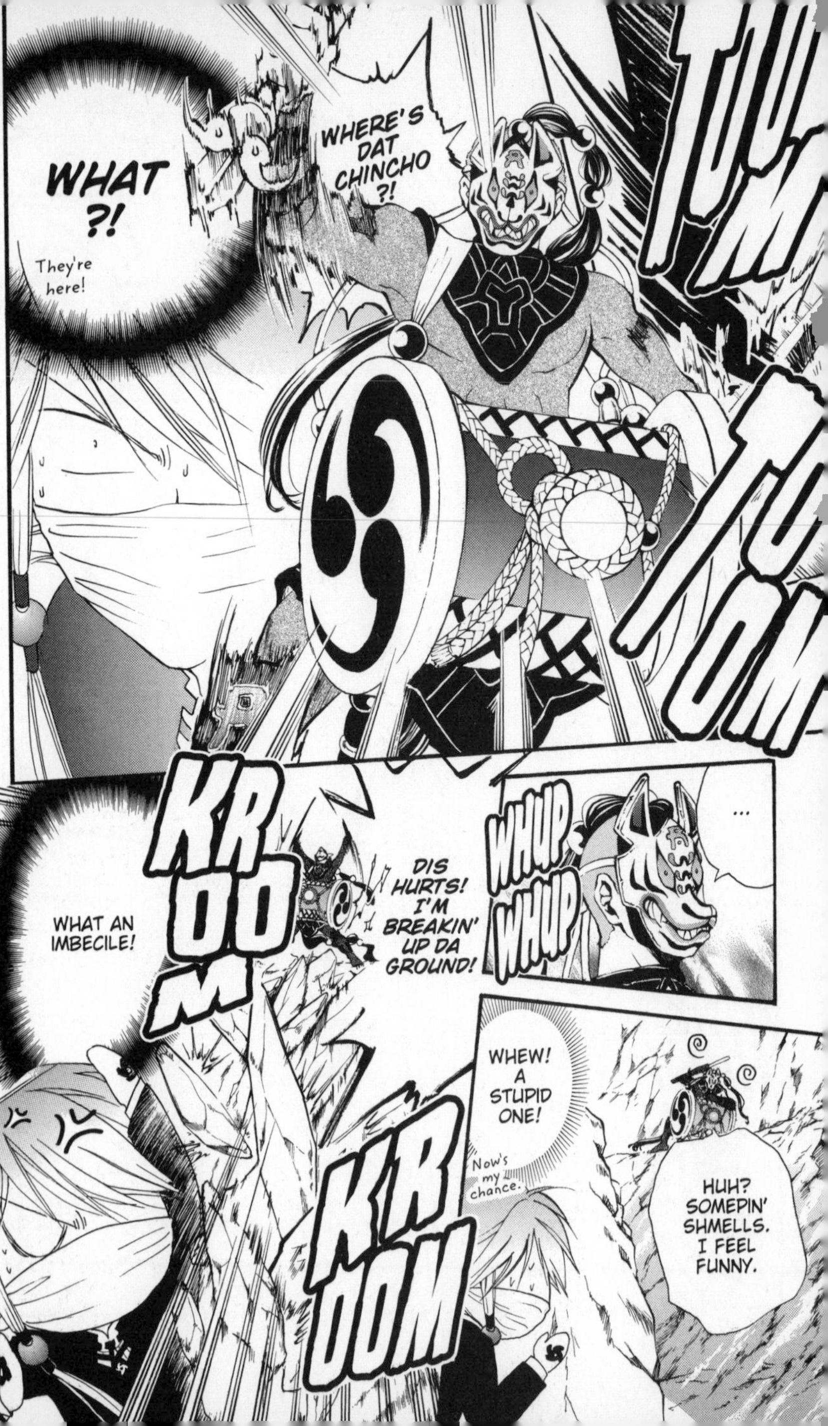
WHERE'S DAT CHINCHO ?!
WHAT ?!
They're here!
...
WHUP WHUP
DIS HURTS! I'M BREAKIN' UP DA GROUND!
KROOM
WHAT AN IMBECILE!
HUH? SOMEPIN' SHMELLS. I FEEL FUNNY.
WHEW! A STUPID ONE!
Now's my chance.
KROOM

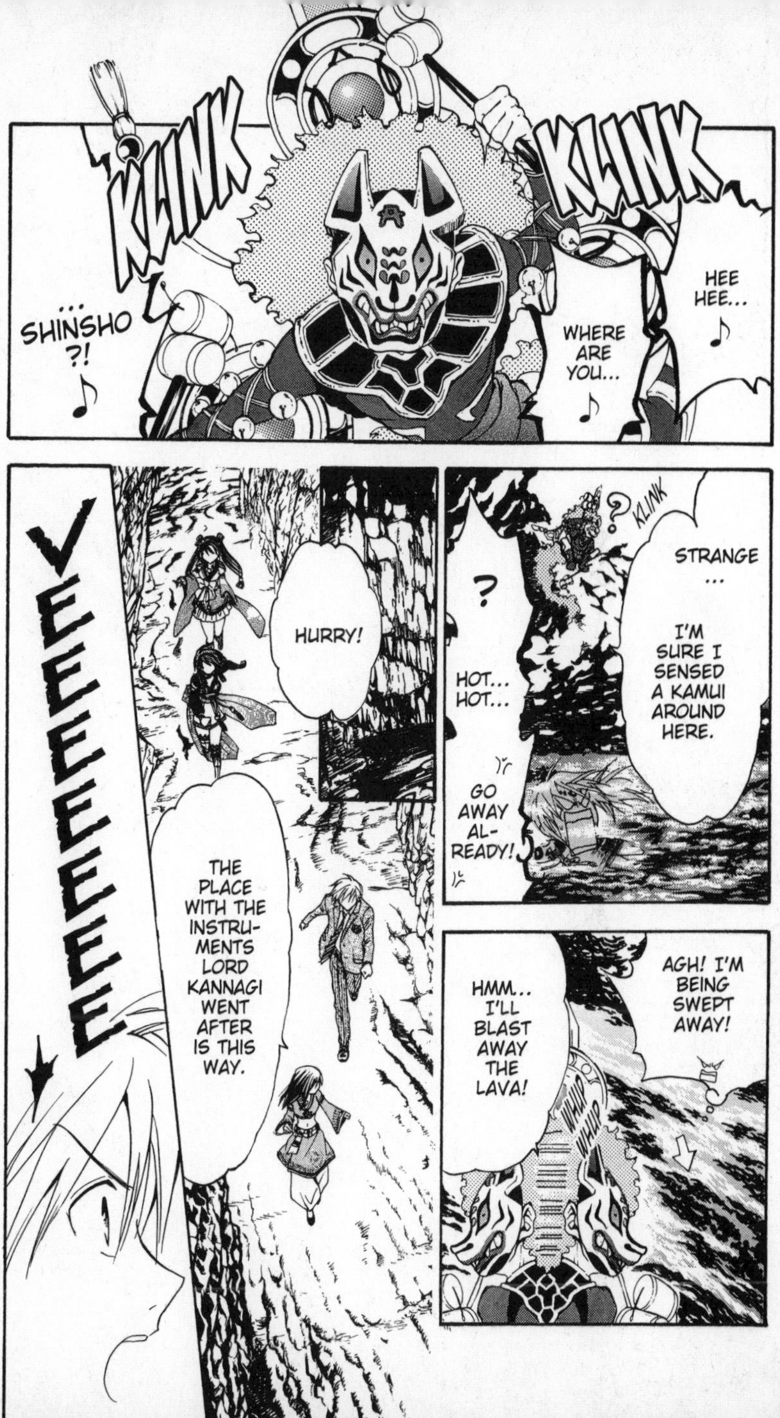
KLINK
HEE HEE... ♪
WHERE ARE YOU... ♪
KLINK
...SHINSHO ?! ♪
KLINK
STRANGE...
I'M SURE I SENSED A KAMUI AROUND HERE.
?
HOT... HOT...
GO AWAY AL-READY!
AGH! I'M BEING SWEPT AWAY!
HMM... I'LL BLAST AWAY THE LAVA!
WHUP
WHUP
HURRY!
THE PLACE WITH THE INSTRU-MENTS LORD KANNAGI WENT AFTER IS THIS WAY.
VEEEEEEEE

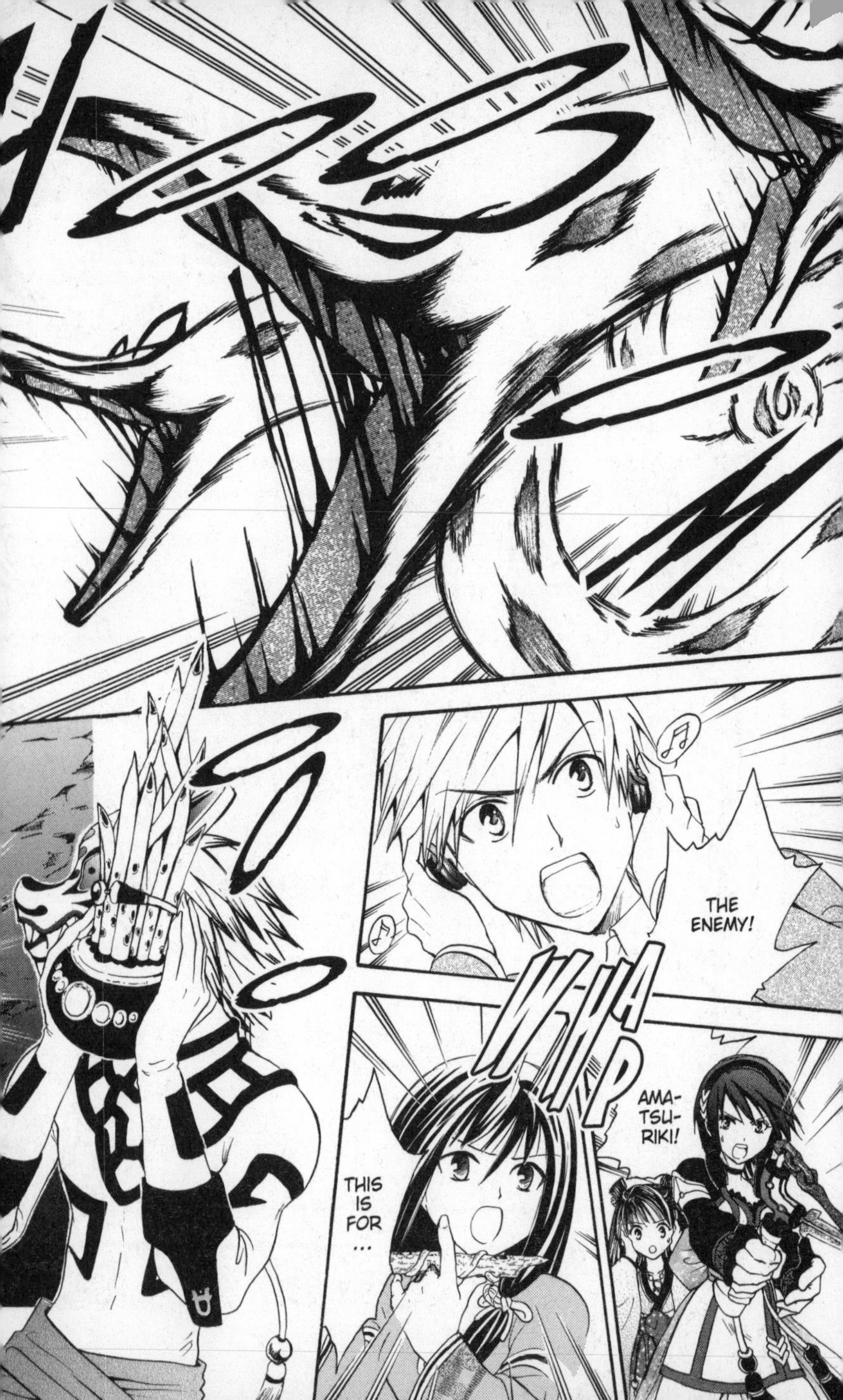
THE ENEMY!
WHAP
AMA-TSU-RIKI!
THIS IS FOR ...

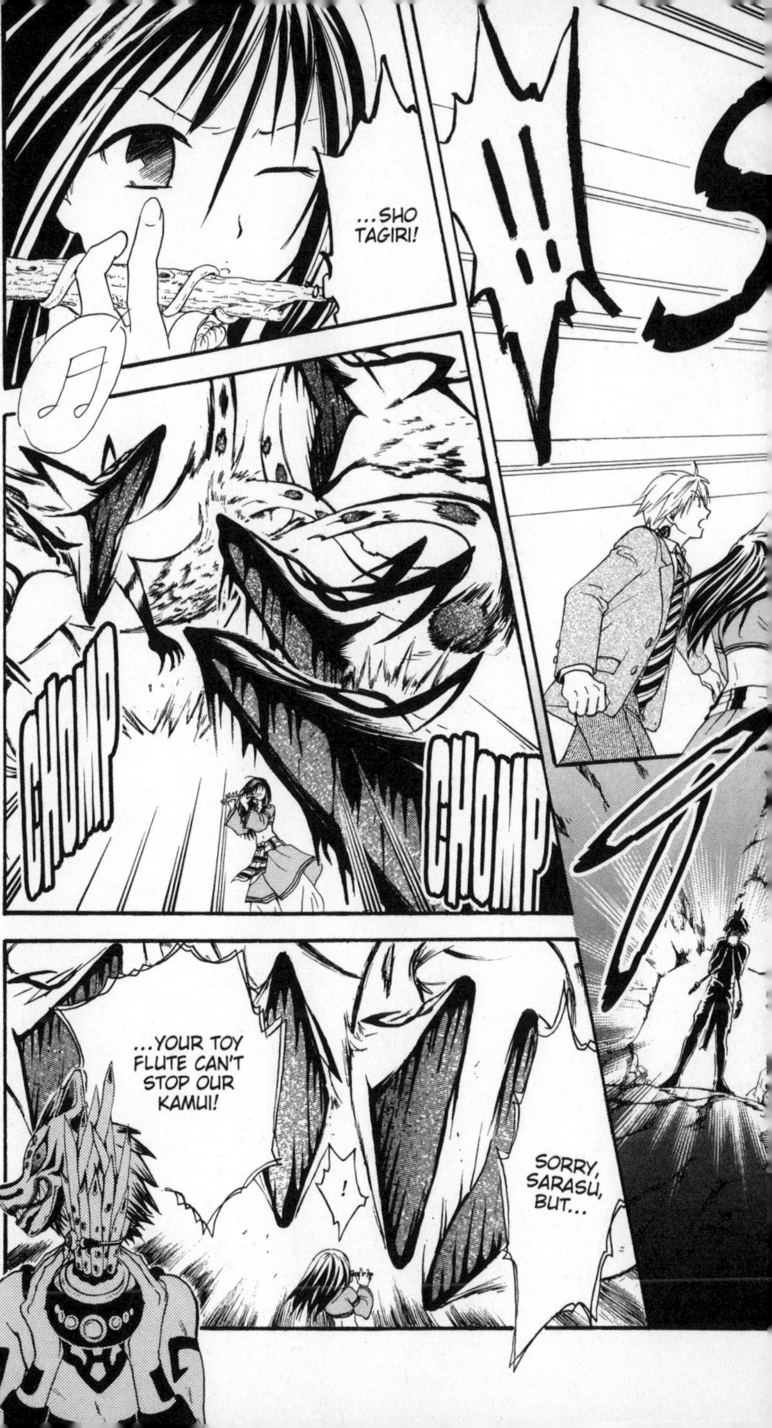
!!
...SHO TAGIRI!
CHOMP
CHOMP
SORRY, SARASU, BUT...
...YOUR TOY FLUTE CAN'T STOP OUR KAMUI!
!

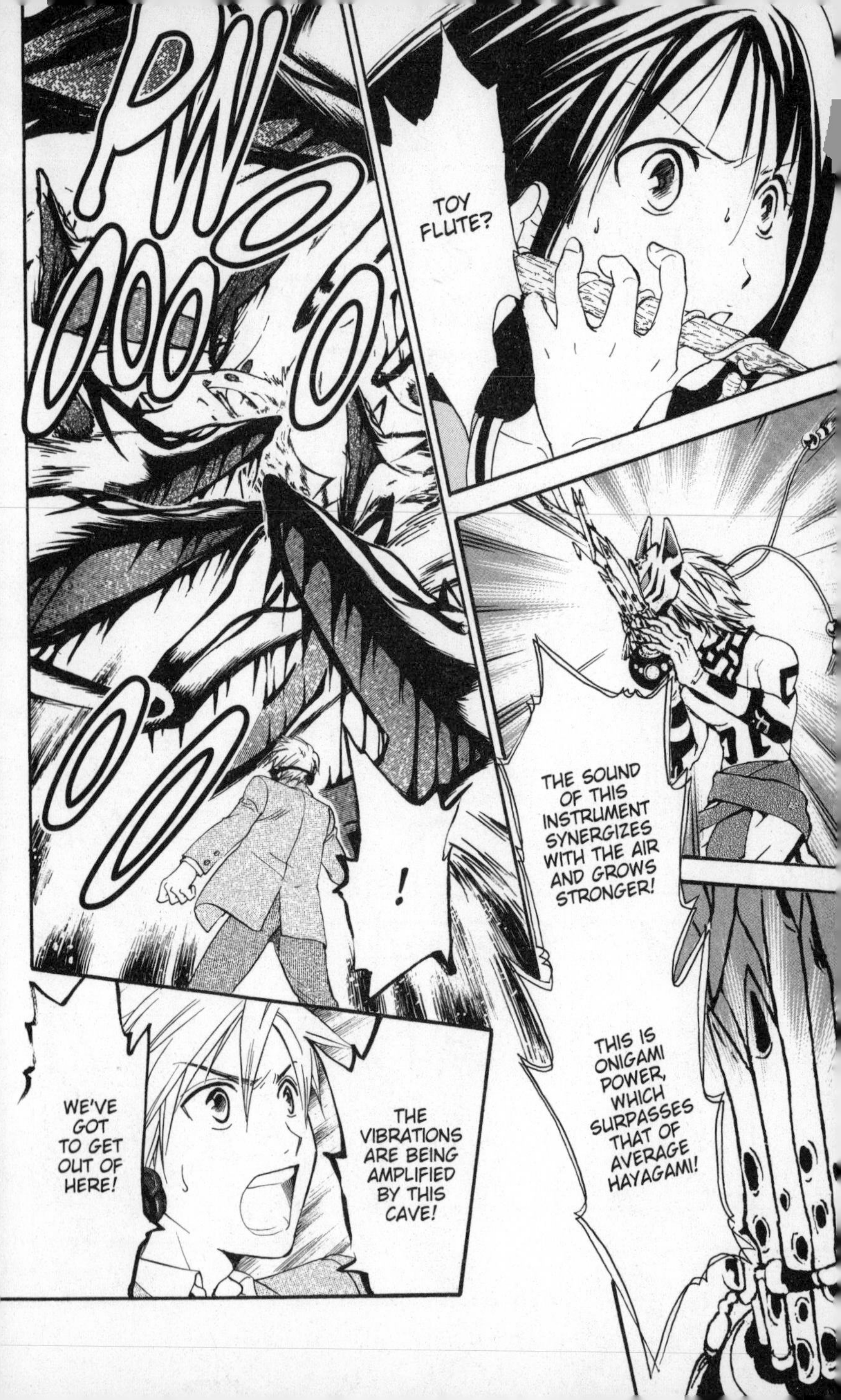

TOY FLUTE?
THE SOUND OF THIS INSTRUMENT SYNERGIZES WITH THE AIR AND GROWS STRONGER!
THIS IS ONIGAMI POWER, WHICH SURPASSES THAT OF AVERAGE HAYAGAMI!
PWOOOOOOOO
!
THE VIBRATIONS ARE BEING AMPLIFIED BY THIS CAVE!
WE'VE GOT TO GET OUT OF HERE!

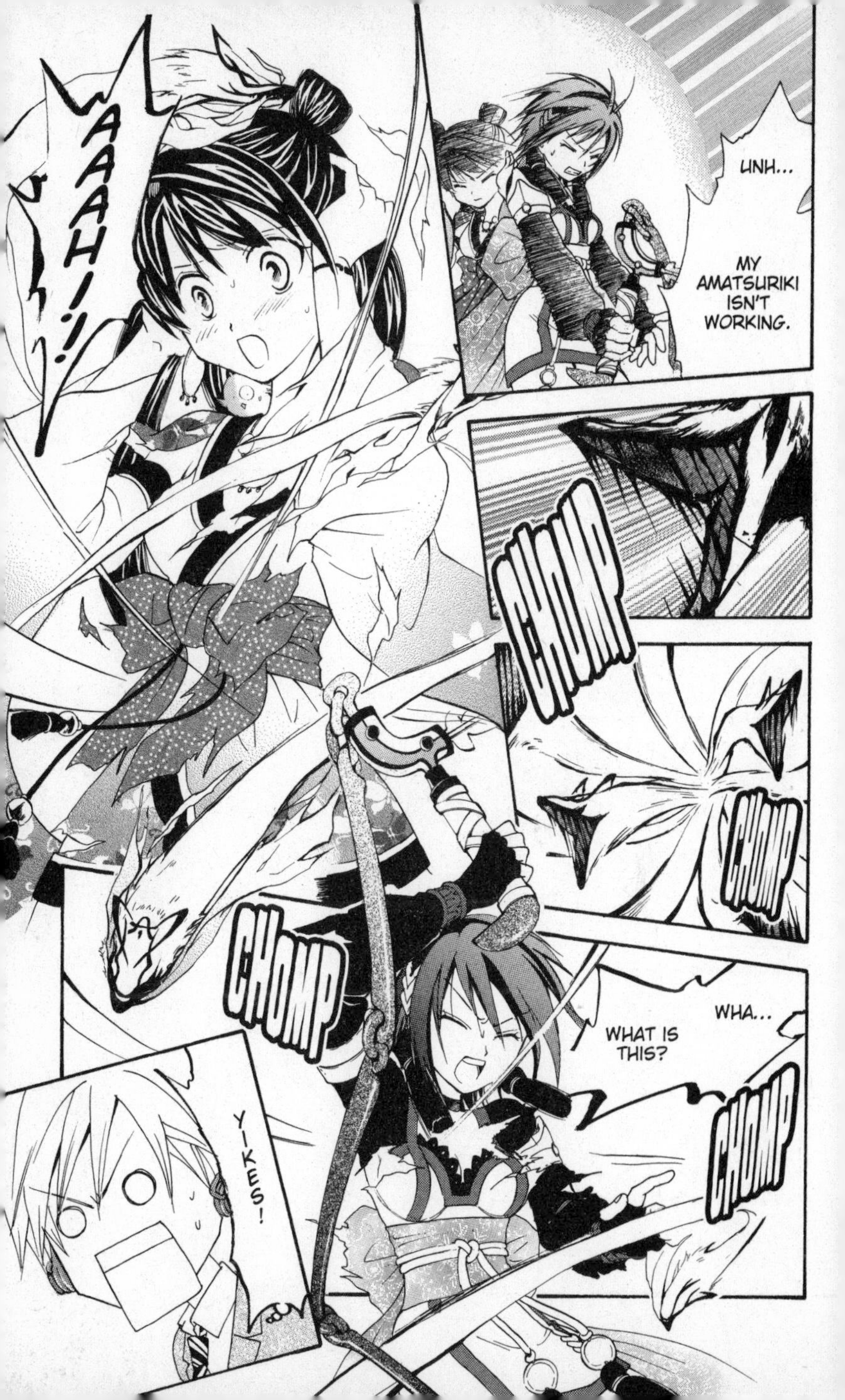
UNH...
MY AMATSURIKI ISN'T WORKING.
WAAAAH!!!
CHOMP
CHOMP
CHOMP
WHA...
WHAT IS THIS?
CHOMP
YIKES!

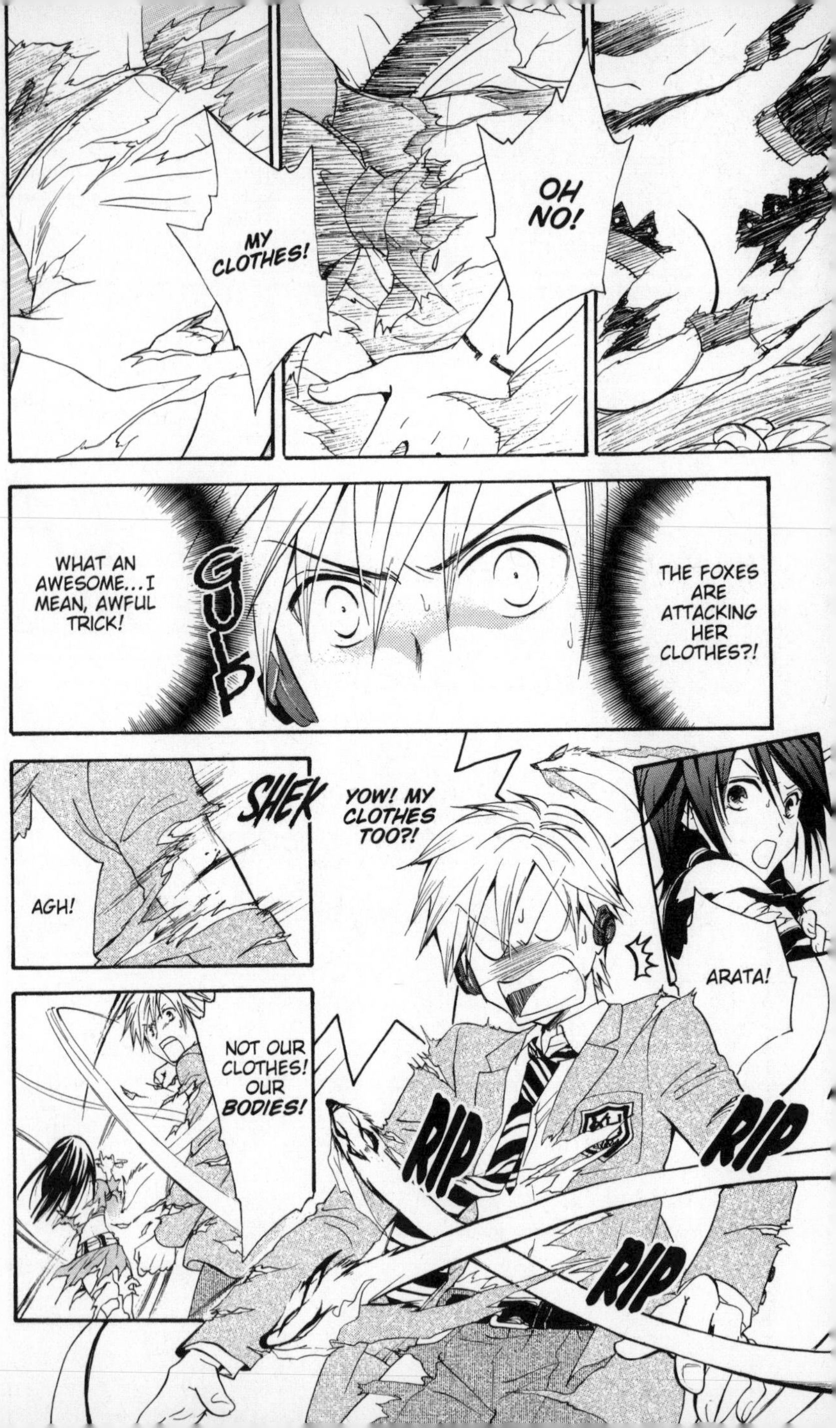
OH NO!
MY CLOTHES!
THE FOXES ARE ATTACKING HER CLOTHES?!
GULP
WHAT AN AWESOME...I MEAN, AWFUL TRICK!
YOW! MY CLOTHES TOO?!
ARATA!
RIP
RIP
RIP
SHEK
AGH!
NOT OUR CLOTHES! OUR BODIES!

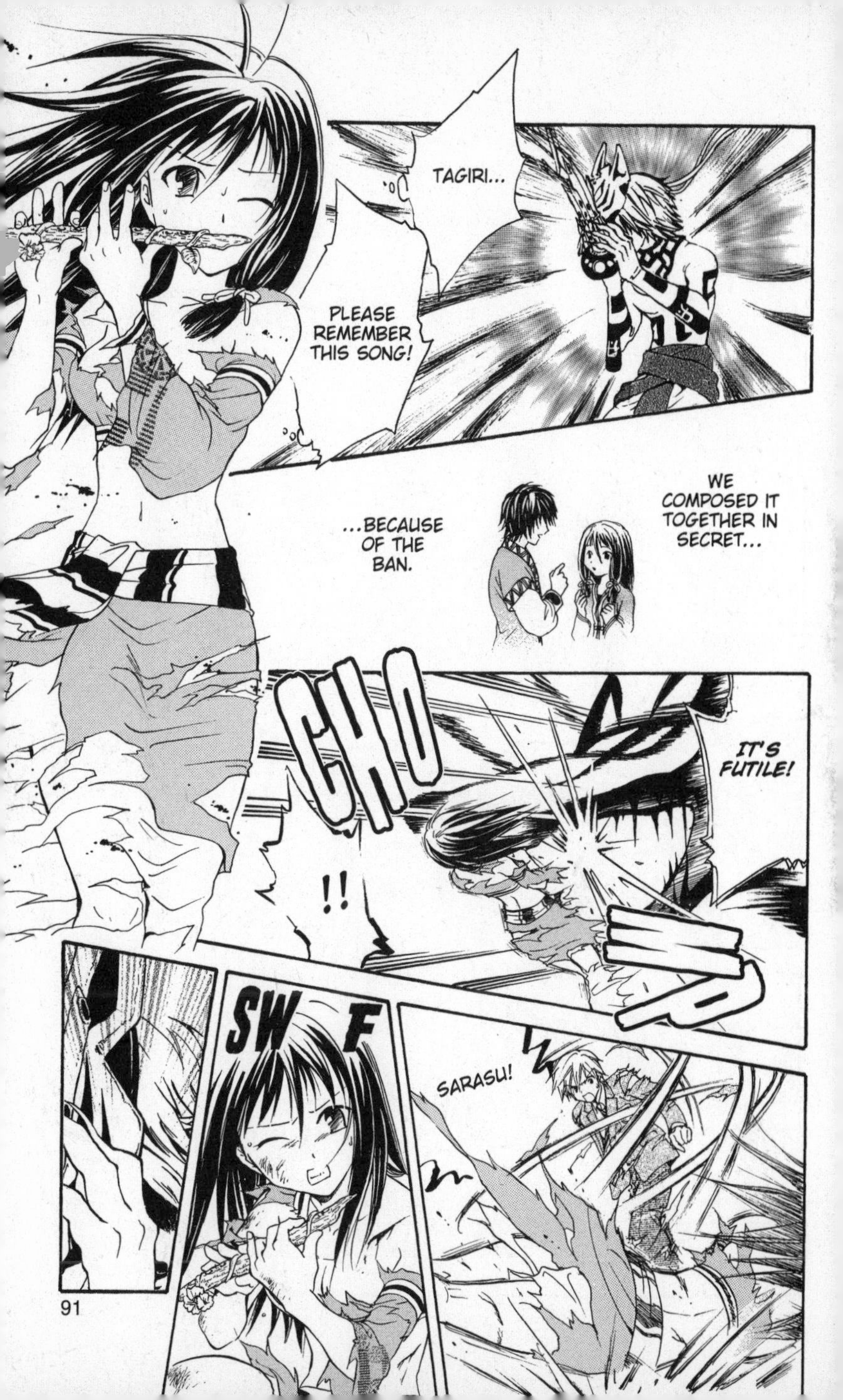
TAGIRI...
PLEASE REMEMBER THIS SONG!
WE COMPOSED IT TOGETHER IN SECRET...
...BECAUSE OF THE BAN.
IT'S FUTILE!
CHO
!!
SARASU!
SW F

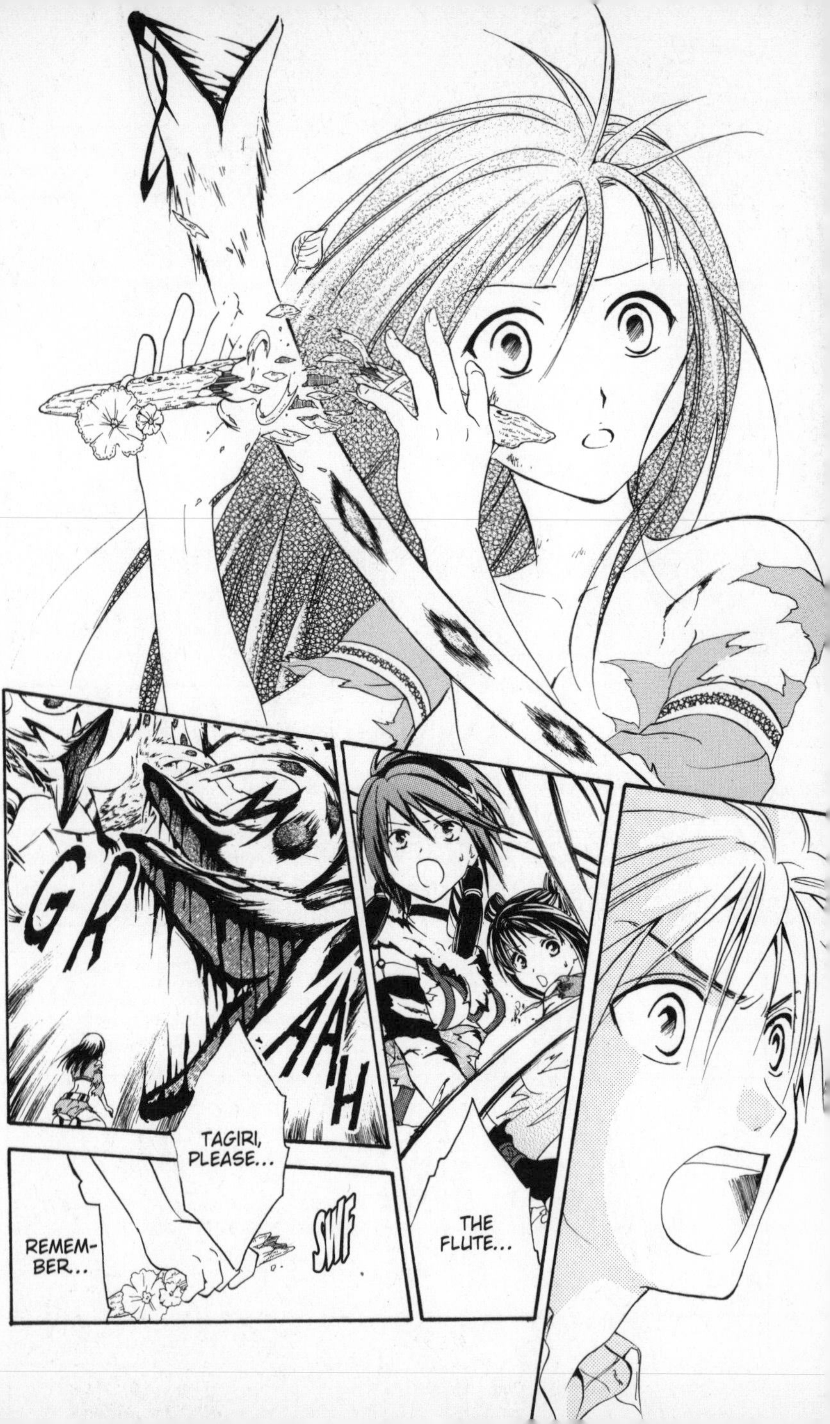
THE FLUTE...
GRAAAH
TAGIRI, PLEASE...
REMEMBER...
SWF

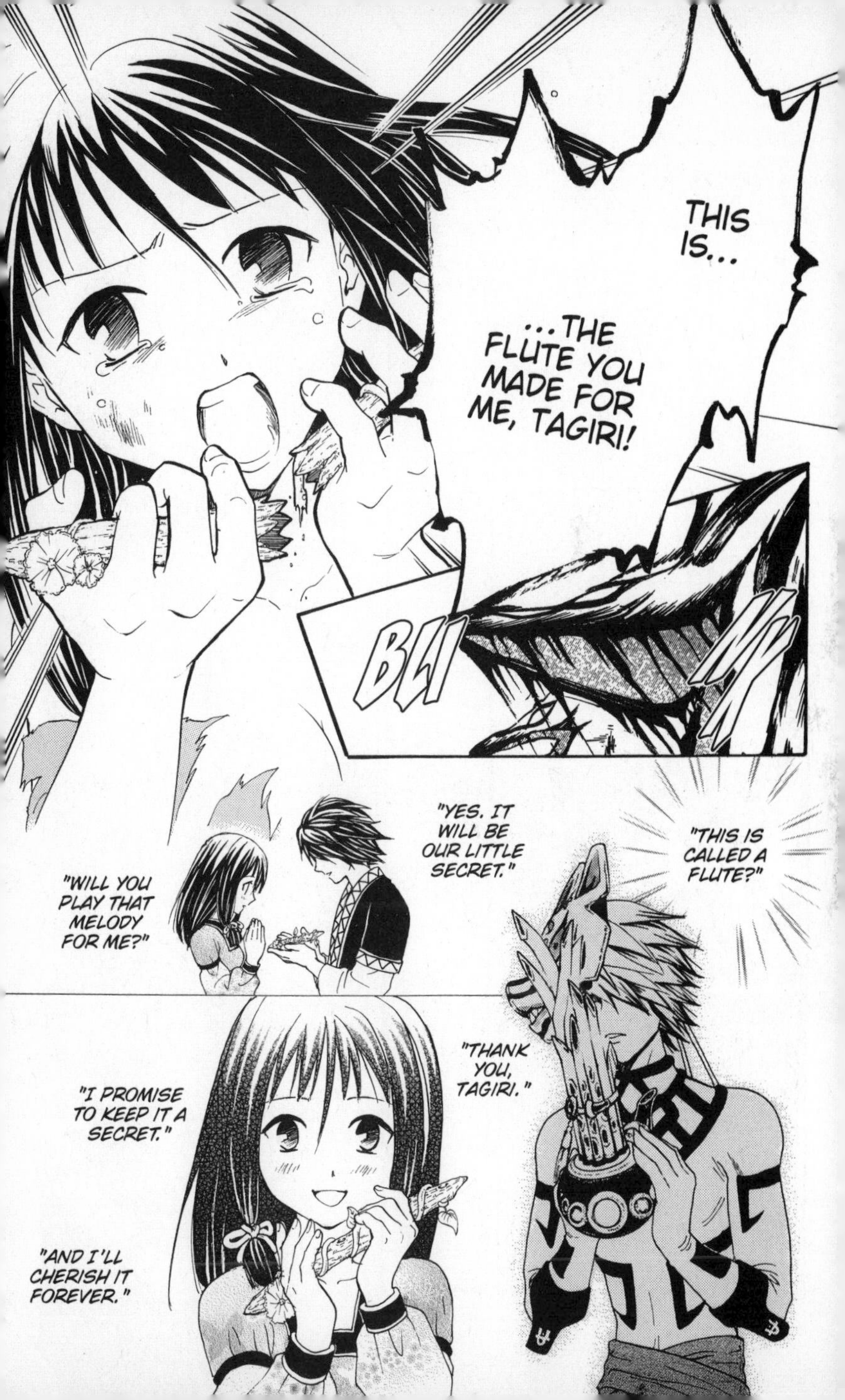
THIS IS...
...THE FLUTE YOU MADE FOR ME, TAGIRI!
BLI
"THIS IS CALLED A FLUTE?"
"YES. IT WILL BE OUR LITTLE SECRET."
"WILL YOU PLAY THAT MELODY FOR ME?"
"THANK YOU, TAGIRI."
"I PROMISE TO KEEP IT A SECRET."
"AND I'LL CHERISH IT FOREVER."

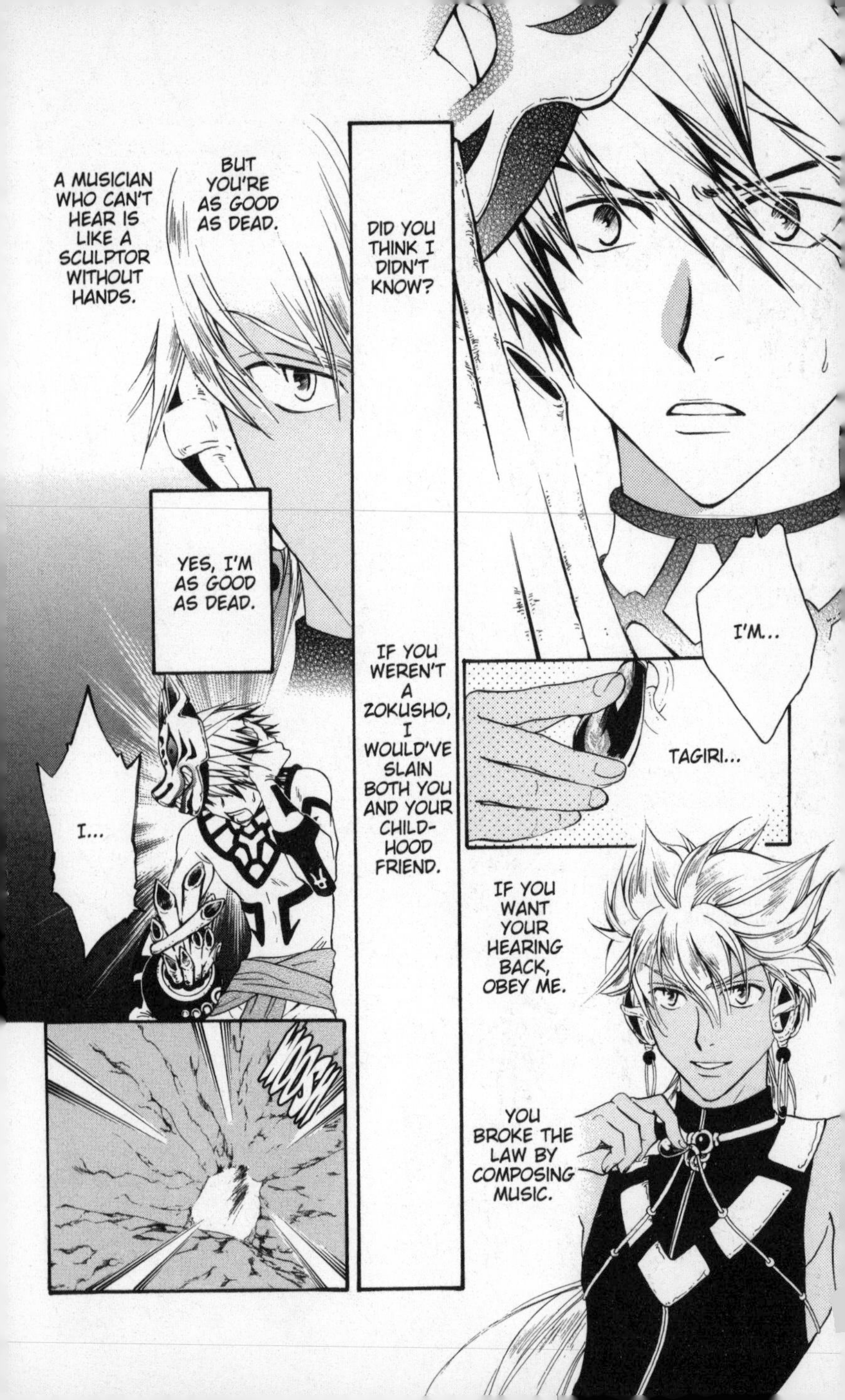

I'M...
TAGIRI...
YOU BROKE THE LAW BY COMPOSING MUSIC.
DID YOU THINK I DIDN'T KNOW?
IF YOU WEREN'T A ZOKUSHO, I WOULD'VE SLAIN BOTH YOU AND YOUR CHILDHOOD FRIEND.
IF YOU WANT YOUR HEARING BACK, OBEY ME.
BUT YOU'RE AS GOOD AS DEAD.
A MUSICIAN WHO CAN'T HEAR IS LIKE A SCULPTOR WITHOUT HANDS.
YES, I'M AS GOOD AS DEAD.
I...
WOOSH

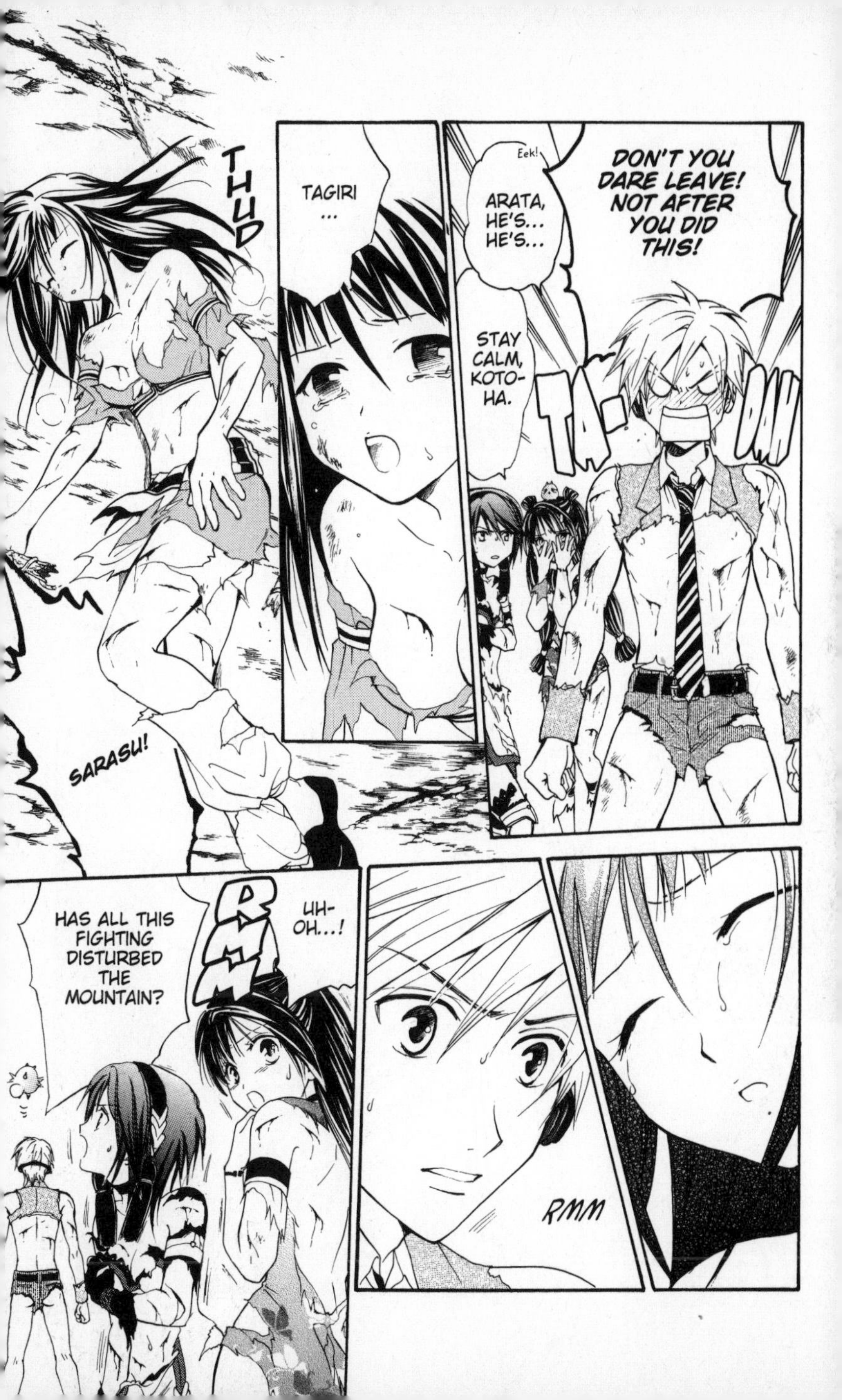
DON'T YOU DARE LEAVE! NOT AFTER YOU DID THIS!
Eek!
ARATA, HE'S... HE'S...
STAY CALM, KOTOHA.
TA-
TAGIRI ...
THUD
SARASU!
RMM
UH-OH...!
RMM
HAS ALL THIS FIGHTING DISTURBED THE MOUNTAIN?

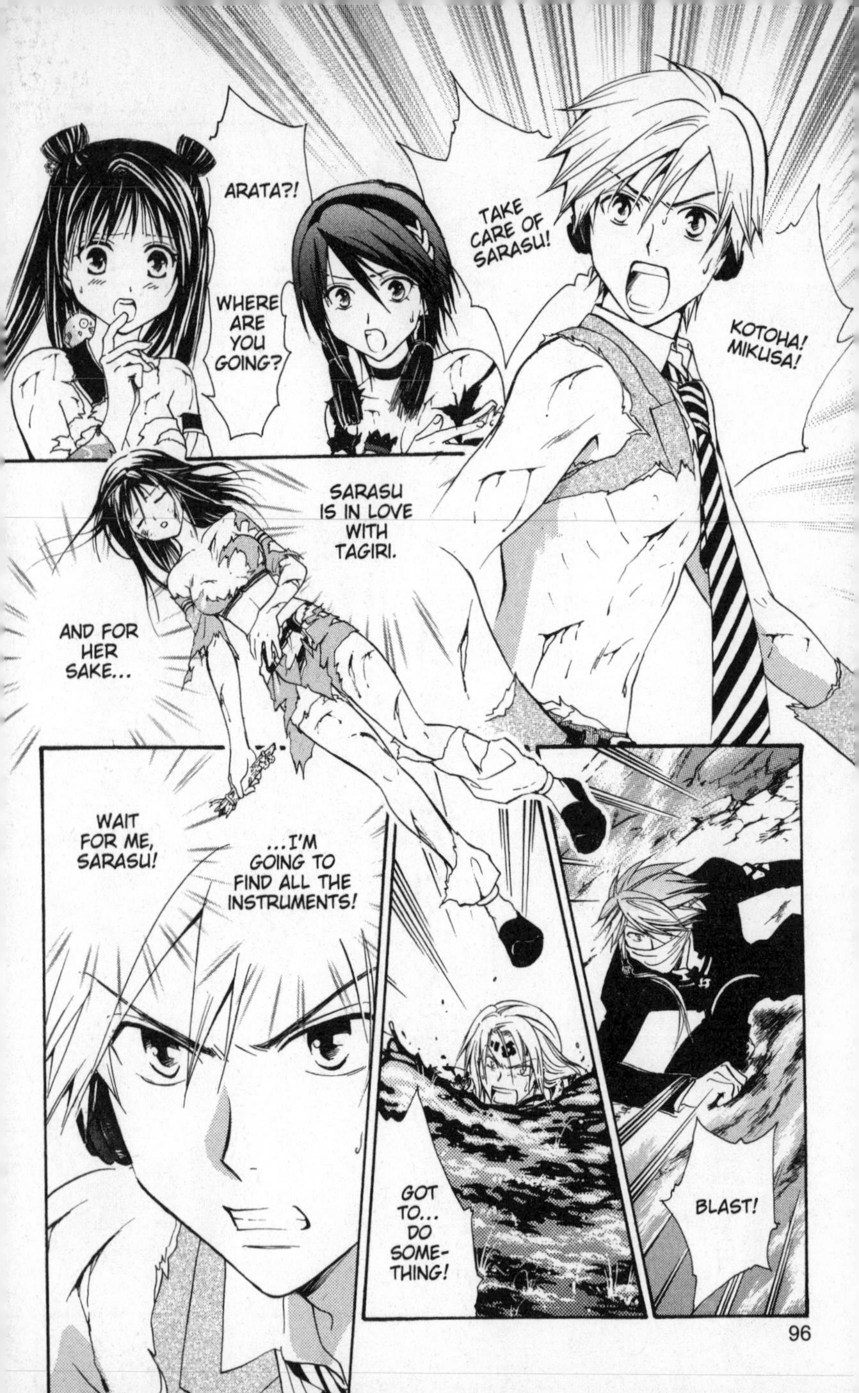
KOTOHA! MIKUSA!
TAKE CARE OF SARASU!
ARATA?!
WHERE ARE YOU GOING?
SARASU IS IN LOVE WITH TAGIRI.
AND FOR HER SAKE...
BLAST!
GOT TO... DO SOME-THING!
...I'M GOING TO FIND ALL THE INSTRUMENTS!
WAIT FOR ME, SARASU!

CHAPTER 153
SEND BACK THE SOUND

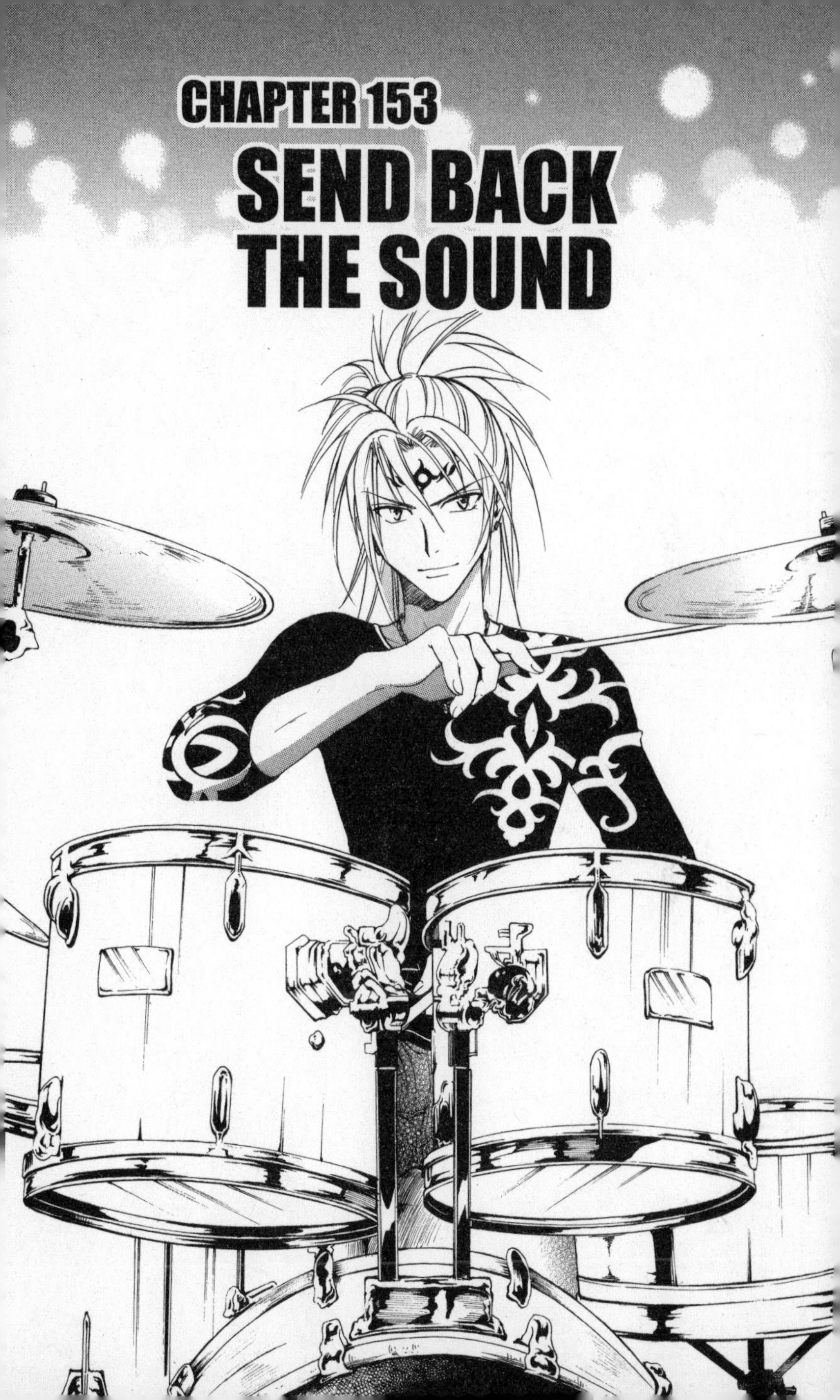

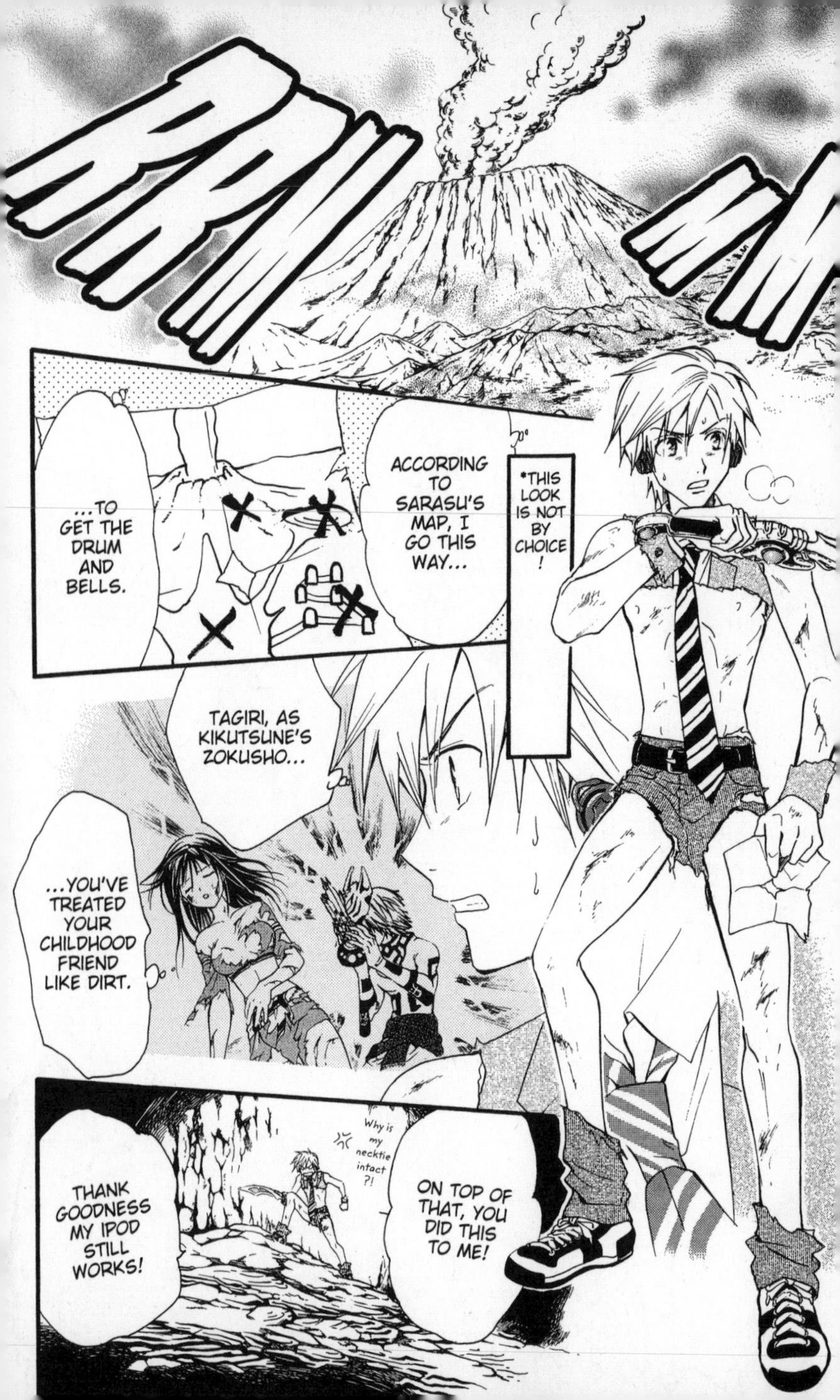
*THIS LOOK IS NOT BY CHOICE!
ACCORDING TO SARASU'S MAP, I GO THIS WAY...
...TO GET THE DRUM AND BELLS.
TAGIRI, AS KIKUTSUNE'S ZOKUSHO...
...YOU'VE TREATED YOUR CHILDHOOD FRIEND LIKE DIRT.
ON TOP OF THAT, YOU DID THIS TO ME!
Why is my necktie intact?!
THANK GOODNESS MY IPOD STILL WORKS!

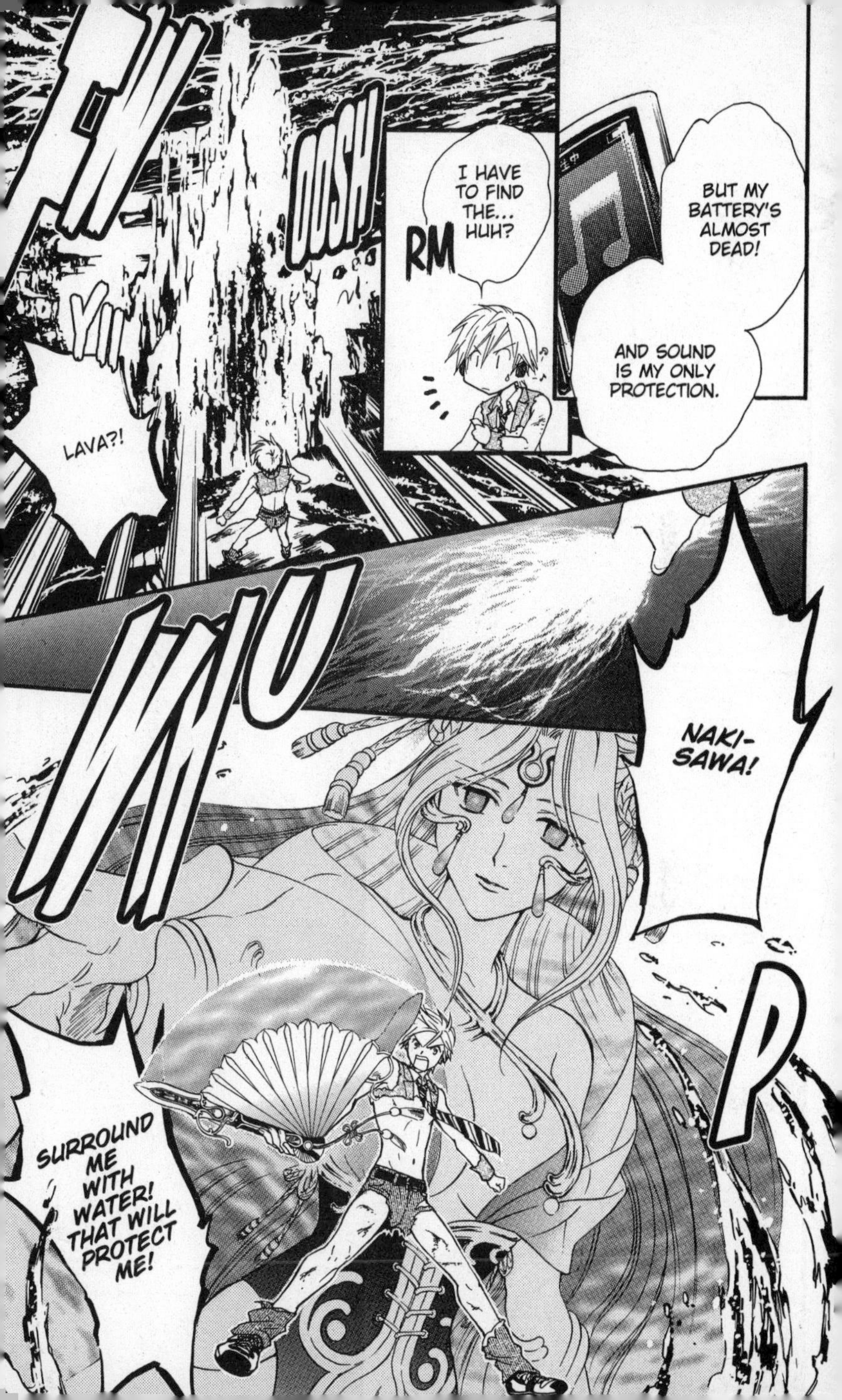
BUT MY BATTERY'S ALMOST DEAD!
AND SOUND IS MY ONLY PROTECTION.
I HAVE TO FIND THE... HUH?
RM
OOSH
LAVA?!
NAKI-SAWA!
P
SURROUND ME WITH WATER! THAT WILL PROTECT ME!

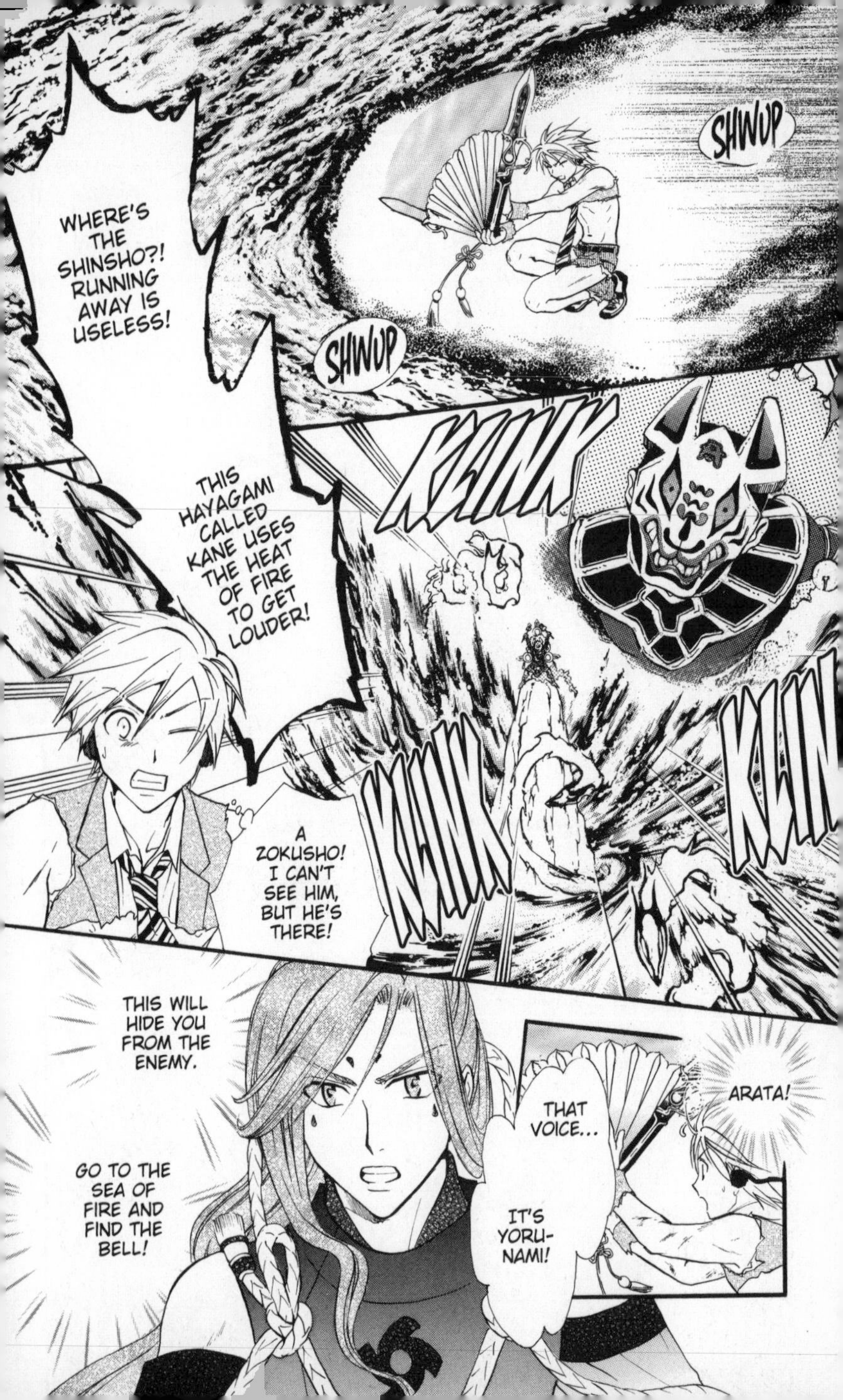
SHWUP
WHERE'S THE SHINSHO?! RUNNING AWAY IS USELESS!
SHWUP
KLINK
KLIN
THIS HAYAGAMI CALLED KANE USES THE HEAT OF FIRE TO GET LOUDER!
KLINK
A ZOKUSHO! I CAN'T SEE HIM, BUT HE'S THERE!
ARATA!
THAT VOICE...
IT'S YORU-NAMI!
THIS WILL HIDE YOU FROM THE ENEMY.
GO TO THE SEA OF FIRE AND FIND THE BELL!

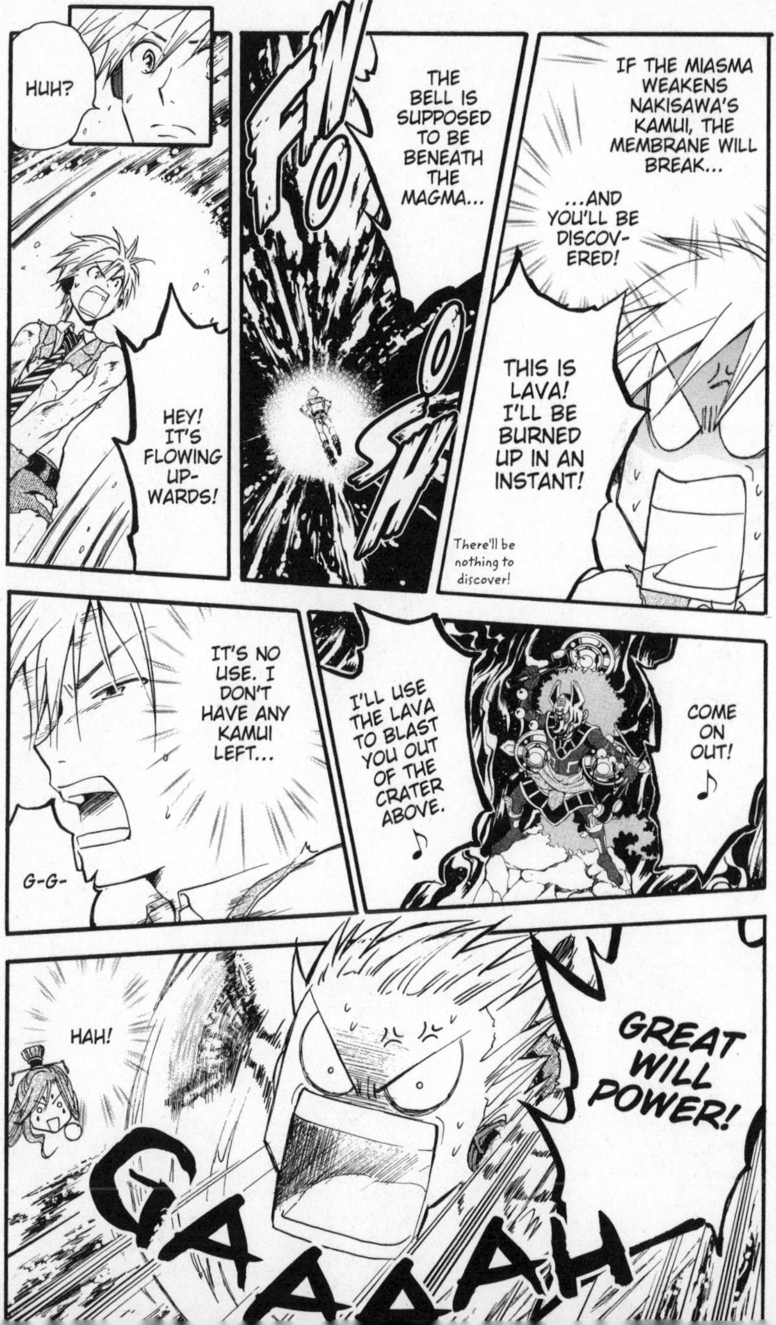
IF THE MIASMA WEAKENS NAKISAWA'S KAMUI, THE MEMBRANE WILL BREAK...
...AND YOU'LL BE DISCOVERED!
THIS IS LAVA! I'LL BE BURNED UP IN AN INSTANT!
There'll be nothing to discover!
FOOSH
THE BELL IS SUPPOSED TO BE BENEATH THE MAGMA...
HUH?
HEY! IT'S FLOWING UPWARDS!
COME ON OUT! ♪
I'LL USE THE LAVA TO BLAST YOU OUT OF THE CRATER ABOVE. ♪
IT'S NO USE. I DON'T HAVE ANY KAMUI LEFT...
G-G-
GREAT WILL POWER!
HAH!
GAAAH

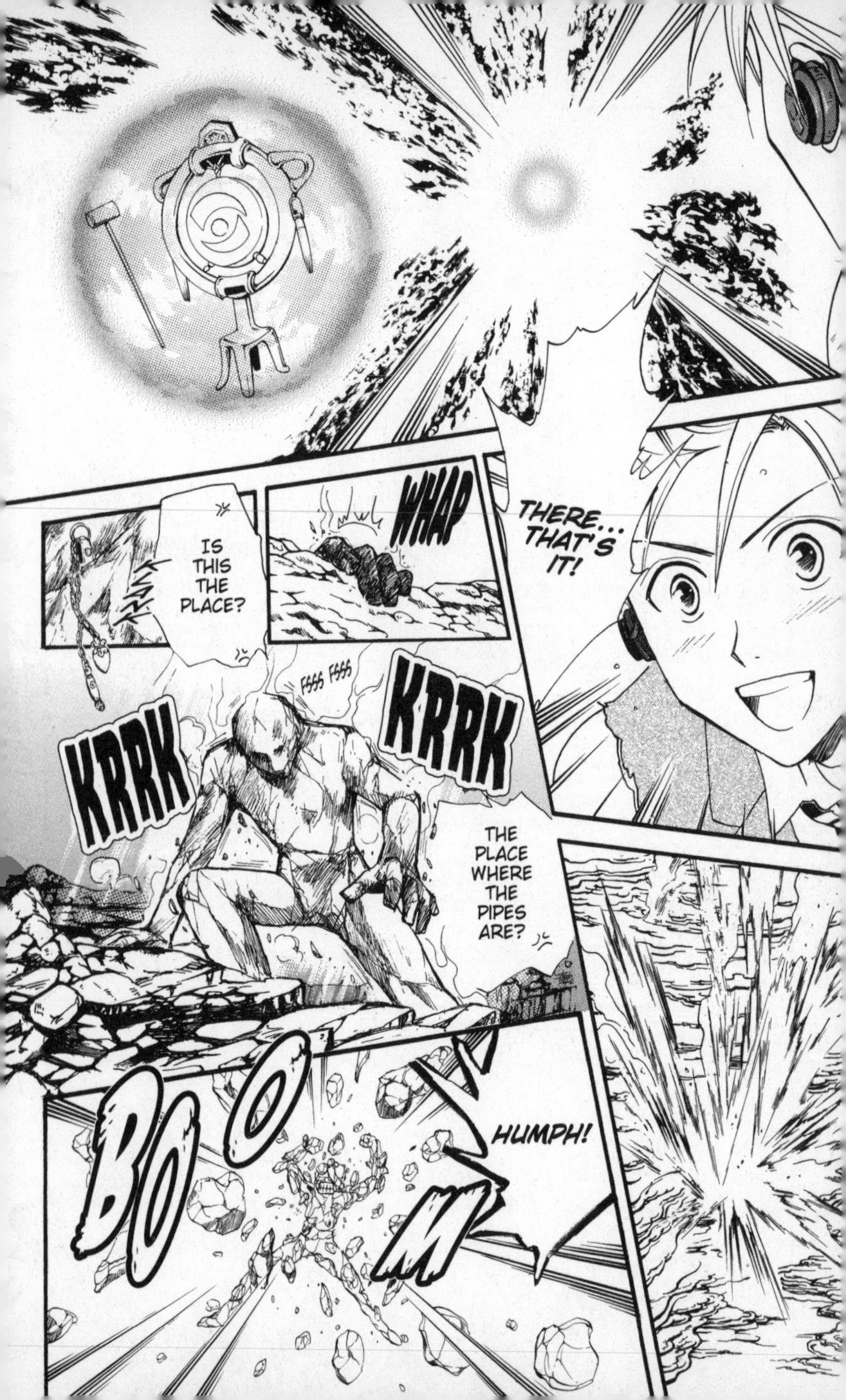
THERE... THAT'S IT!
WHAP
IS THIS THE PLACE?
KRRK
FSSS FSSS
KRRK
THE PLACE WHERE THE PIPES ARE?
HUMPH!
BOOOM

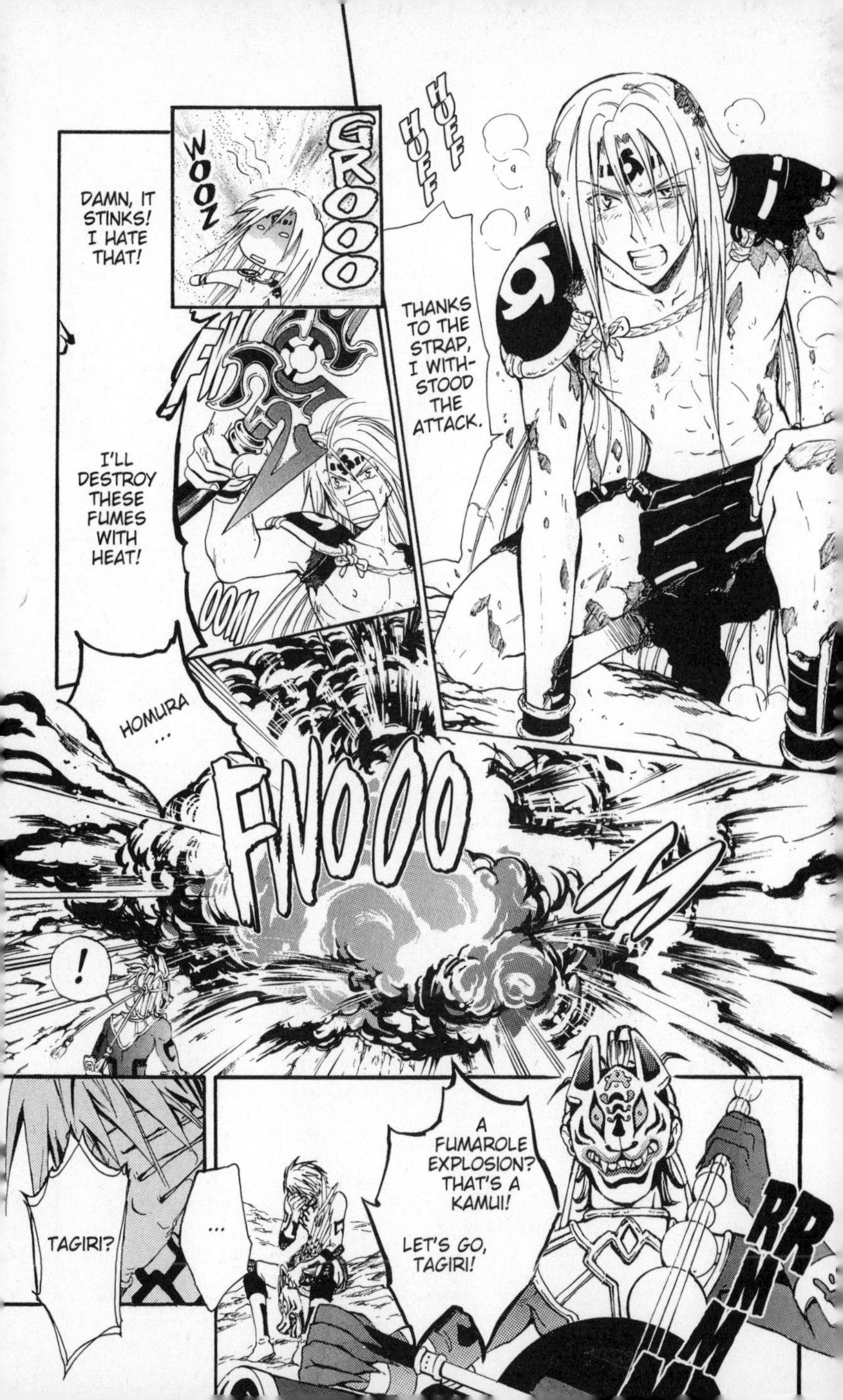
HUFF HUFF
THANKS TO THE STRAP, I WITHSTOOD THE ATTACK.
GROOO
WOOZ
DAMN, IT STINKS! I HATE THAT!
I'LL DESTROY THESE FUMES WITH HEAT!
OOM
HOMURA ...
FWOOOM
!
A FUMAROLE EXPLOSION? THAT'S A KAMUI!
LET'S GO, TAGIRI!
RRMMM
...
TAGIRI?

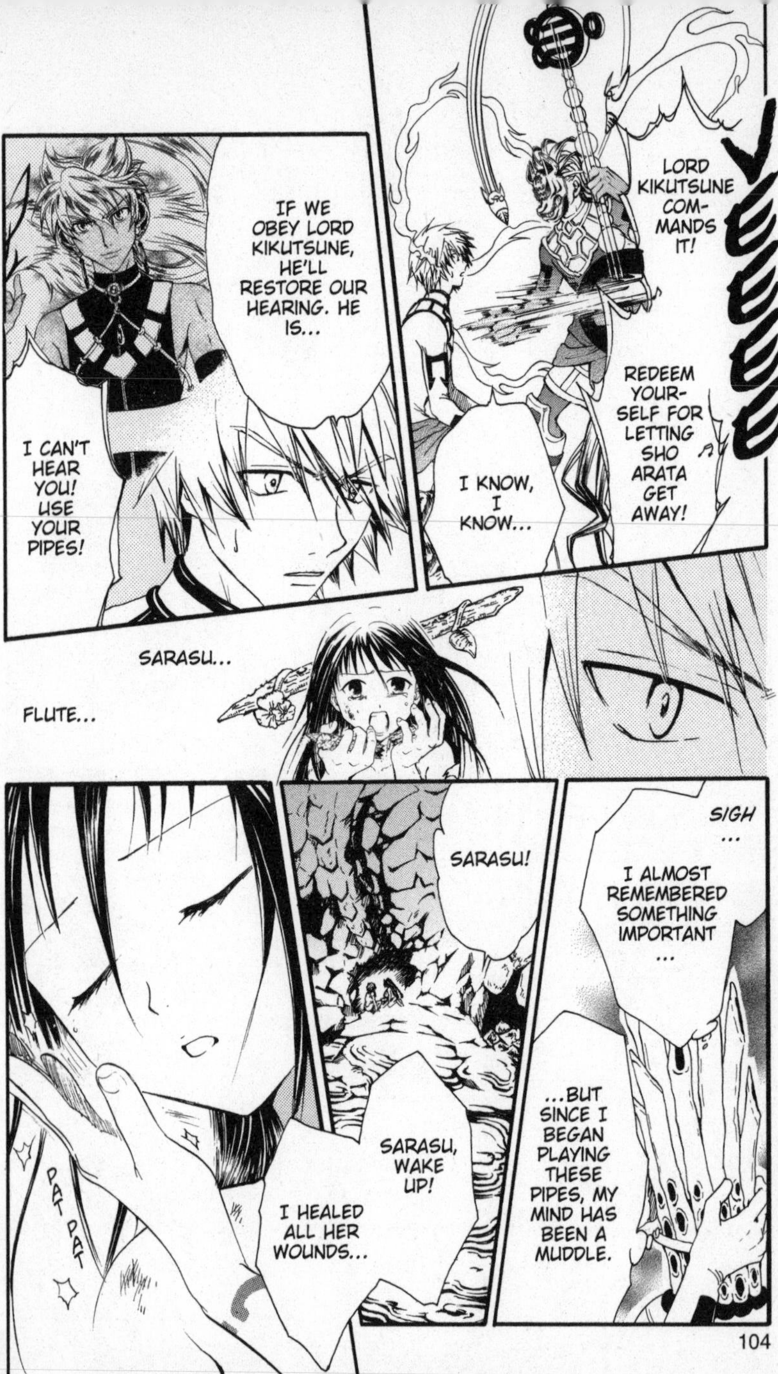
YEEEE
LORD KIKUTSUNE COM-MANDS IT!
REDEEM YOUR-SELF FOR LETTING SHO ARATA GET AWAY!
I KNOW, I KNOW...
IF WE OBEY LORD KIKUTSUNE, HE'LL RESTORE OUR HEARING. HE IS...
I CAN'T HEAR YOU! USE YOUR PIPES!
SARASU...
FLUTE...
SIGH...
I ALMOST REMEMBERED SOMETHING IMPORTANT...
...BUT SINCE I BEGAN PLAYING THESE PIPES, MY MIND HAS BEEN A MUDDLE.
SARASU!
SARASU, WAKE UP!
I HEALED ALL HER WOUNDS...
PAT PAT

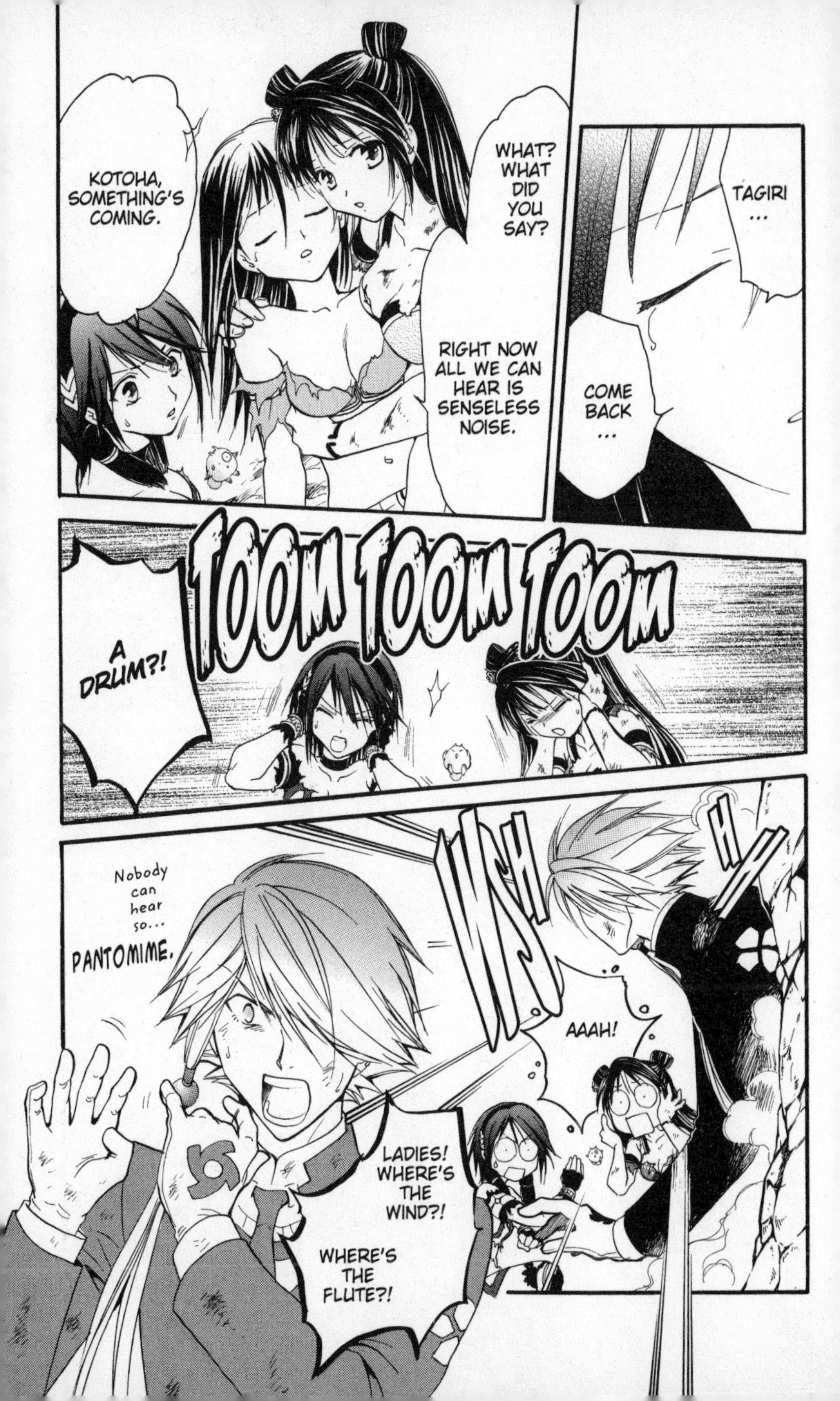
TAGIRI ...
COME BACK ...
KOTOHA, SOMETHING'S COMING.
WHAT? WHAT DID YOU SAY?
RIGHT NOW ALL WE CAN HEAR IS SENSELESS NOISE.
TOOM TOOM TOOM
A DRUM?!
WSH
Nobody can hear so...
PANTOMIME.
AAAH!
LADIES! WHERE'S THE WIND?!
WHERE'S THE FLUTE?!

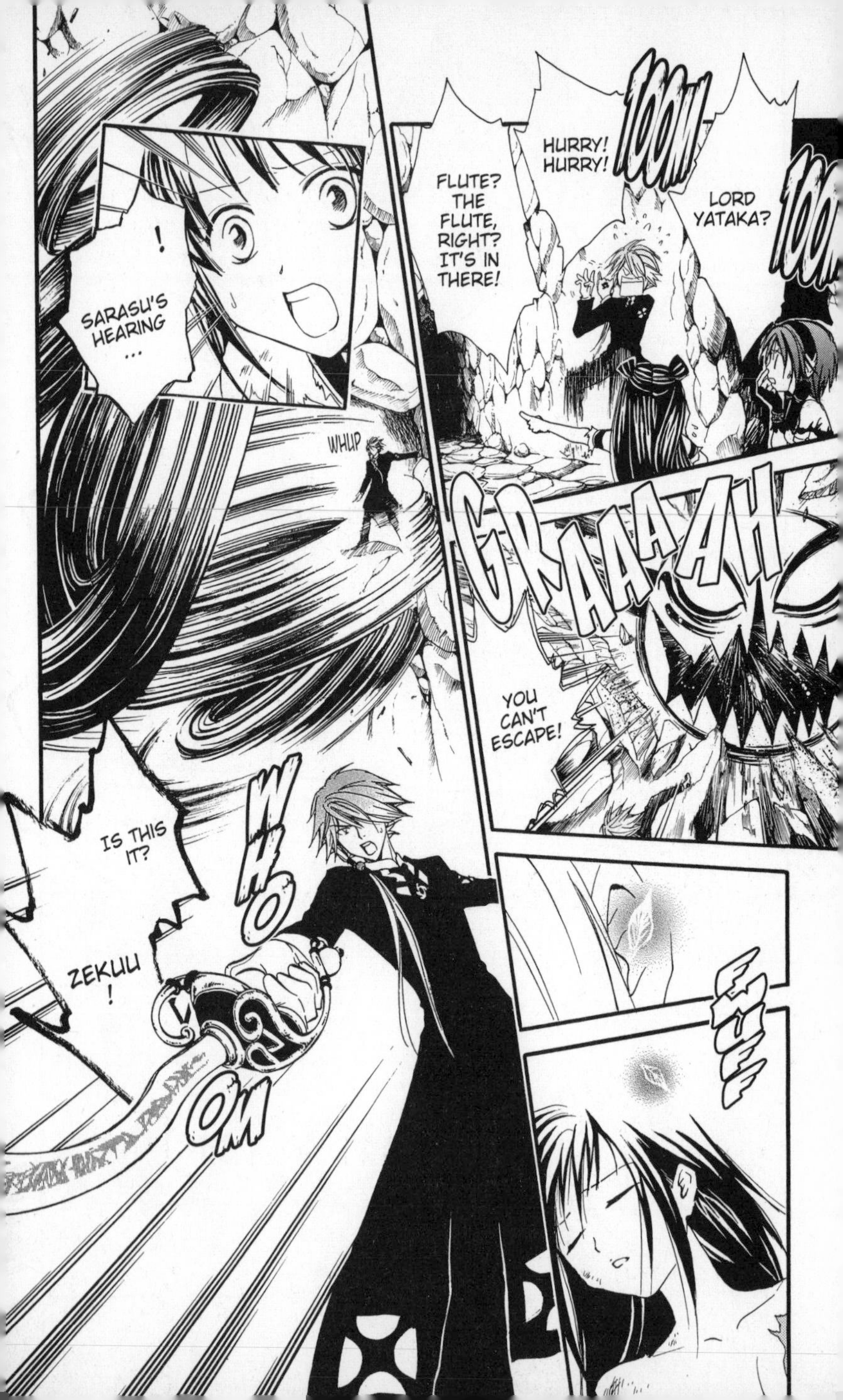
TOOM
LORD YATAKA?
TOOM
HURRY! HURRY!
FLUTE? THE FLUTE, RIGHT? IT'S IN THERE!
GRAAAAH
YOU CAN'T ESCAPE!
!
SARASU'S HEARING ...
WHUP
IS THIS IT?
ZEKUU!
WHOOM

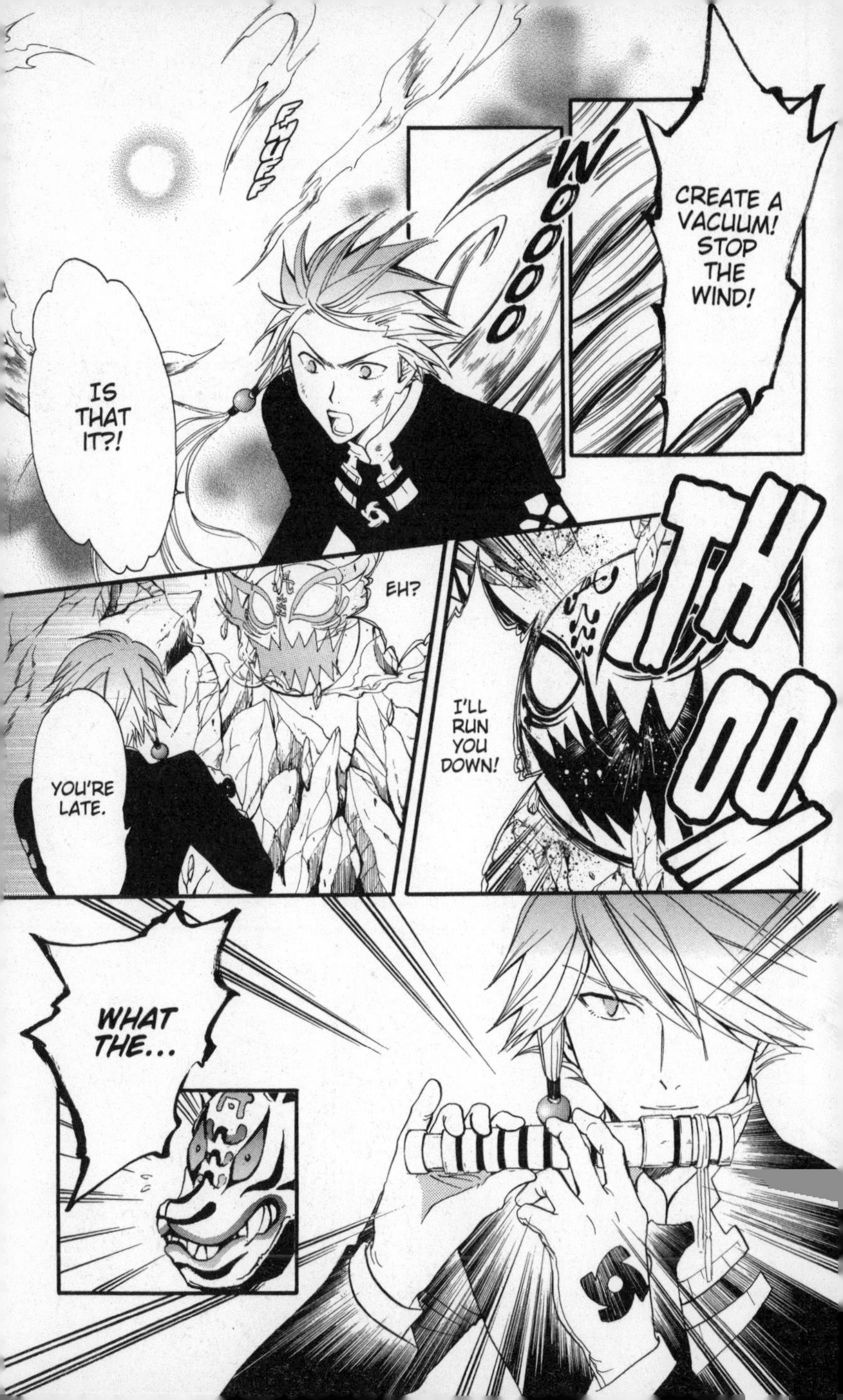
CREATE A VACUUM! STOP THE WIND!
WOOOOOO
FWUFF
IS THAT IT?!
THOOO
I'LL RUN YOU DOWN!
EH?
YOU'RE LATE.
WHAT THE...

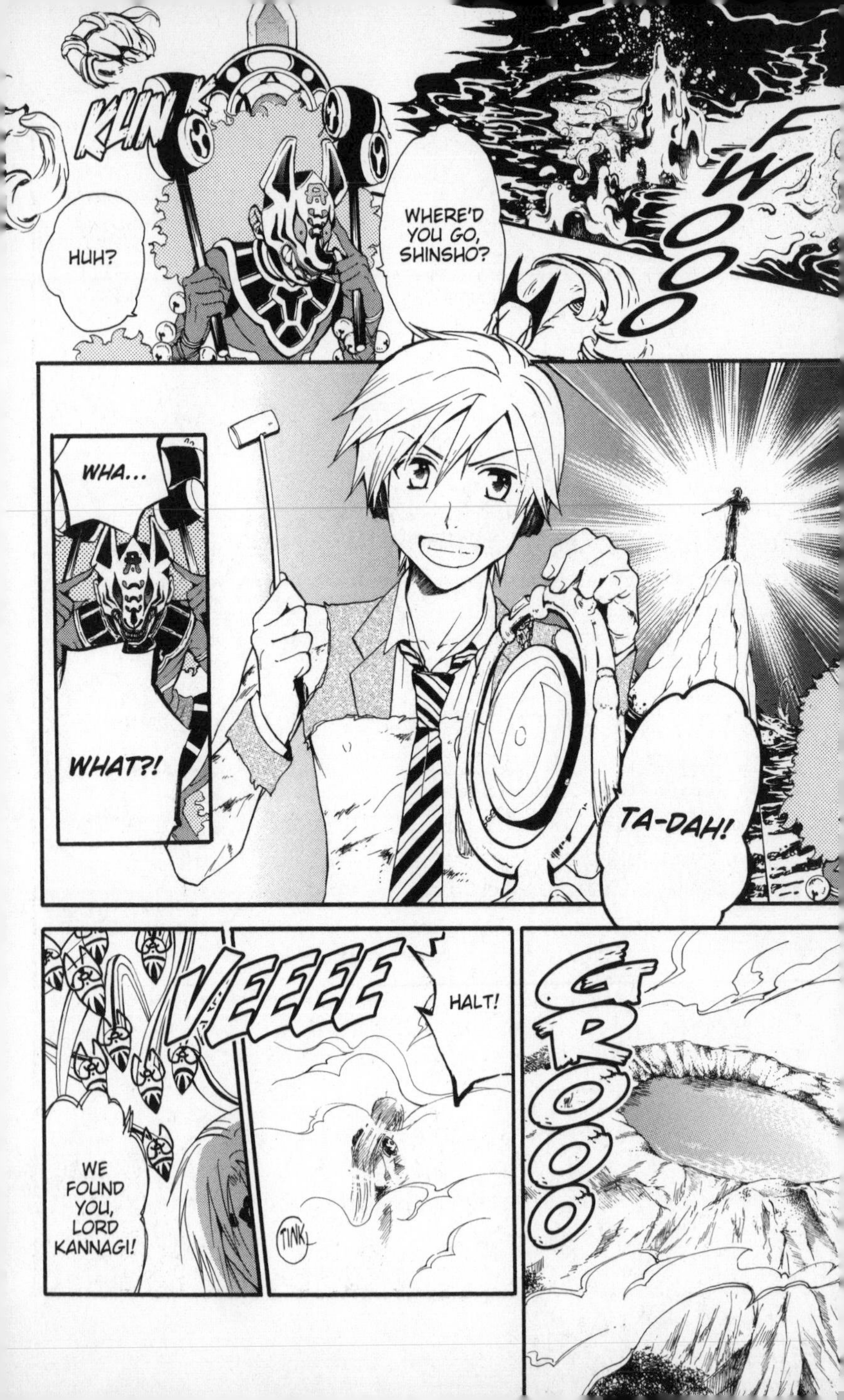
FWOOOO
WHERE'D YOU GO, SHINSHO?
KLINK
HUH?
TA-DAH!
WHA...
WHAT?!
GROOOO
HALT!
TINK
VEEEE
WE FOUND YOU, LORD KANNAGI!

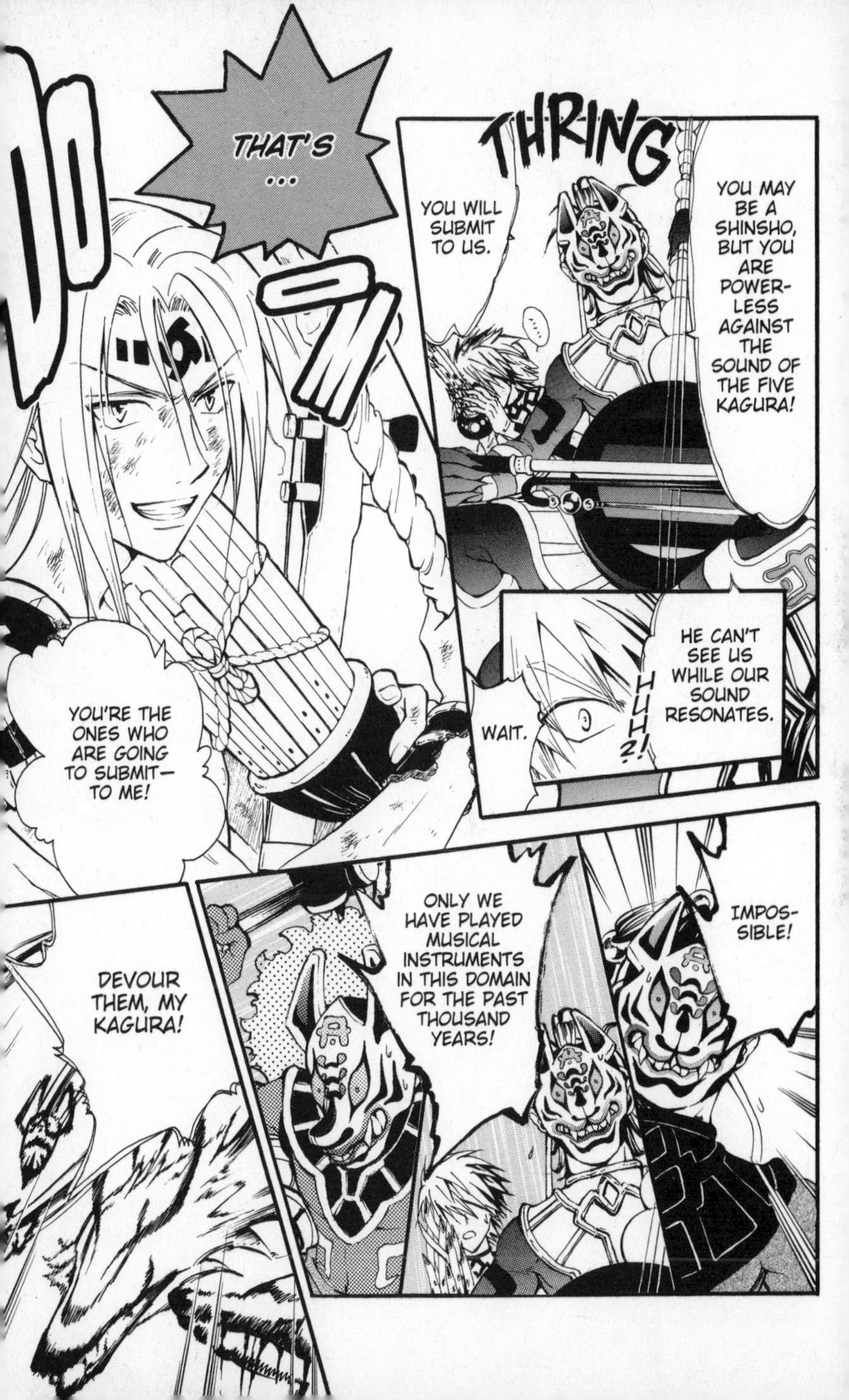
THRING
YOU MAY BE A SHINSHO, BUT YOU ARE POWERLESS AGAINST THE SOUND OF THE FIVE KAGURA!
YOU WILL SUBMIT TO US.
...
HE CAN'T SEE US WHILE OUR SOUND RESONATES.
HUH?!
WAIT.
DO
THAT'S ...
YOU'RE THE ONES WHO ARE GOING TO SUBMIT— TO ME!
IMPOSSIBLE!
ONLY WE HAVE PLAYED MUSICAL INSTRUMENTS IN THIS DOMAIN FOR THE PAST THOUSAND YEARS!
DEVOUR THEM, MY KAGURA!

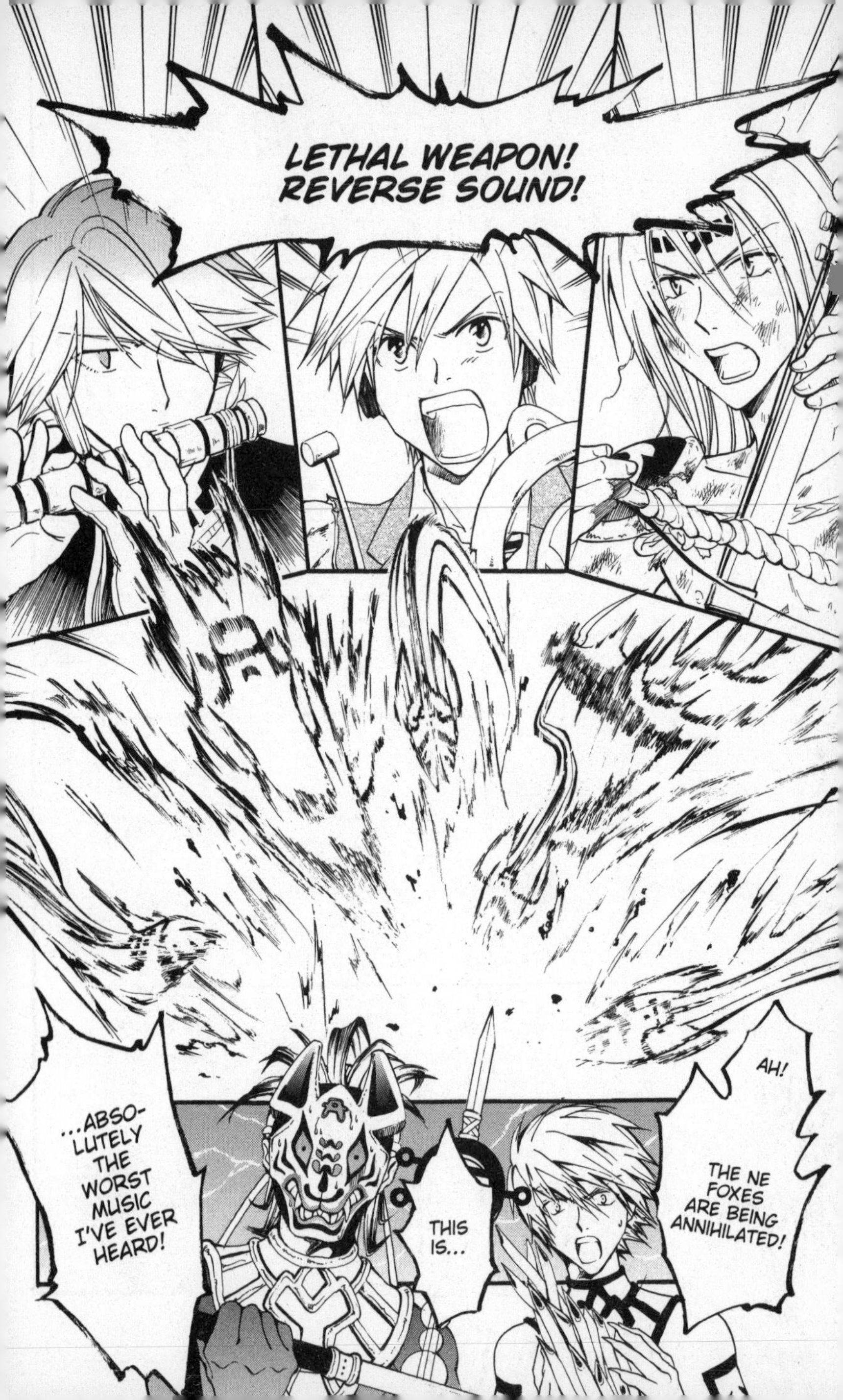
LETHAL WEAPON! REVERSE SOUND!
AH!
THE NE FOXES ARE BEING ANNIHILATED!
THIS IS...
...ABSOLUTELY THE WORST MUSIC I'VE EVER HEARD!

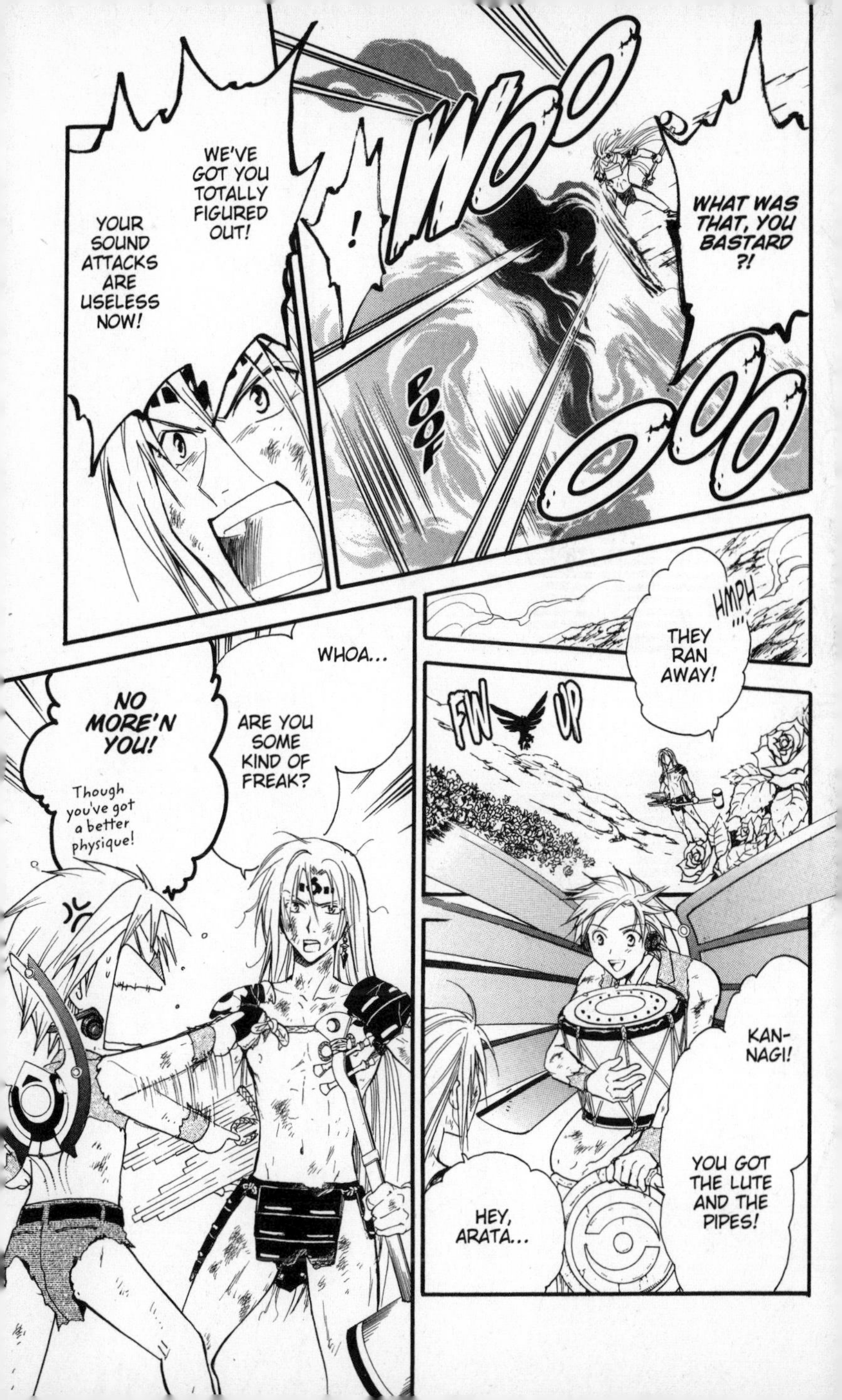
WHAT WAS THAT, YOU BASTARD?!
WOOO
OOOO
!
POOF
WE'VE GOT YOU TOTALLY FIGURED OUT!
YOUR SOUND ATTACKS ARE USELESS NOW!
HMPH...
THEY RAN AWAY!
FWUP
KAN-NAGI!
YOU GOT THE LUTE AND THE PIPES!
HEY, ARATA...
WHOA...
ARE YOU SOME KIND OF FREAK?
NO MORE'N YOU!
Though you've got a better physique!

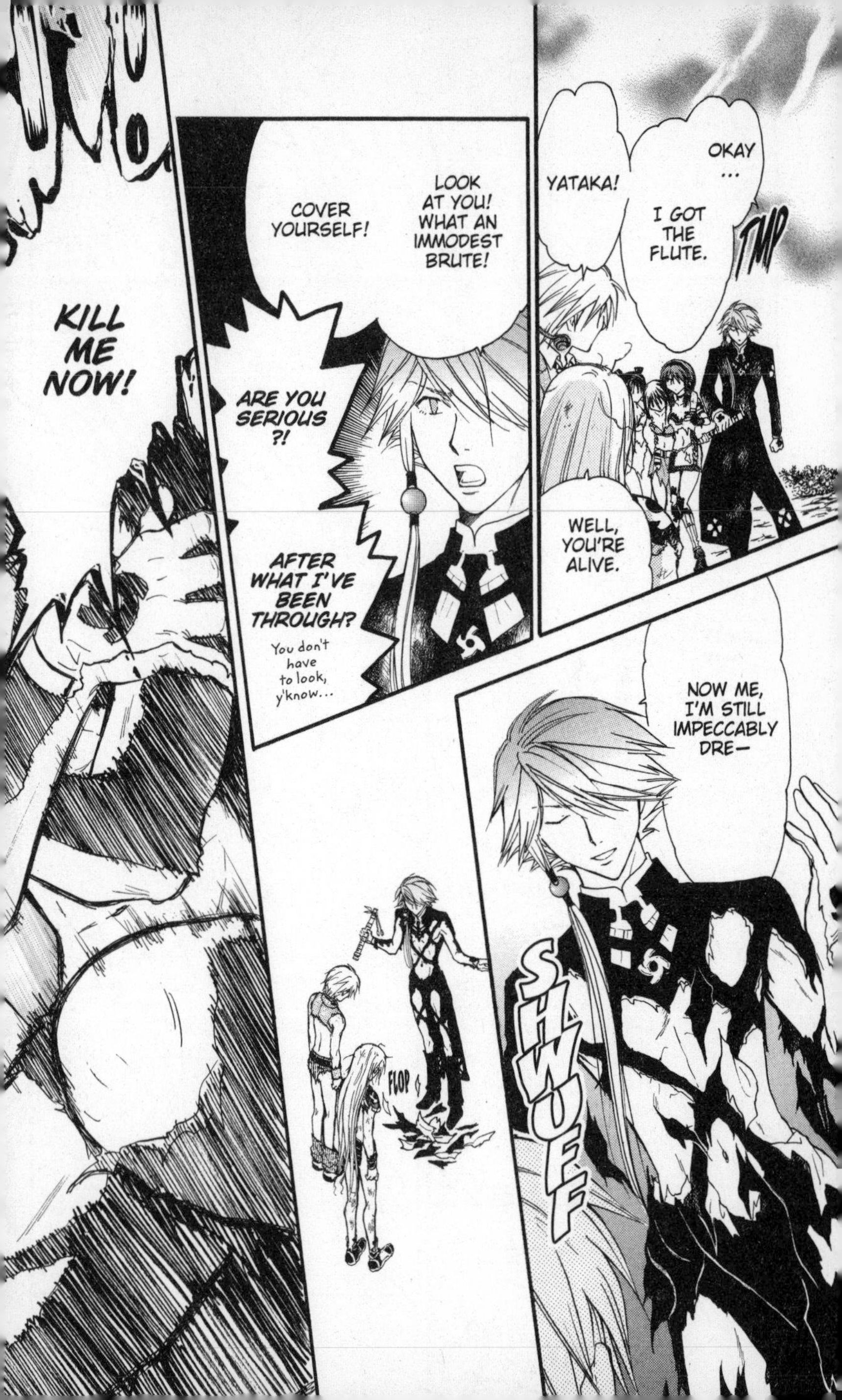
OKAY... I GOT THE FLUTE.
YATAKA!
TMP
WELL, YOU'RE ALIVE.
LOOK AT YOU! WHAT AN IMMODEST BRUTE!
COVER YOURSELF!
ARE YOU SERIOUS?!
AFTER WHAT I'VE BEEN THROUGH?
You don't have to look, y'know...
NOW ME, I'M STILL IMPECCABLY DRE—
SHWUFF
FLOP
KILL ME NOW!

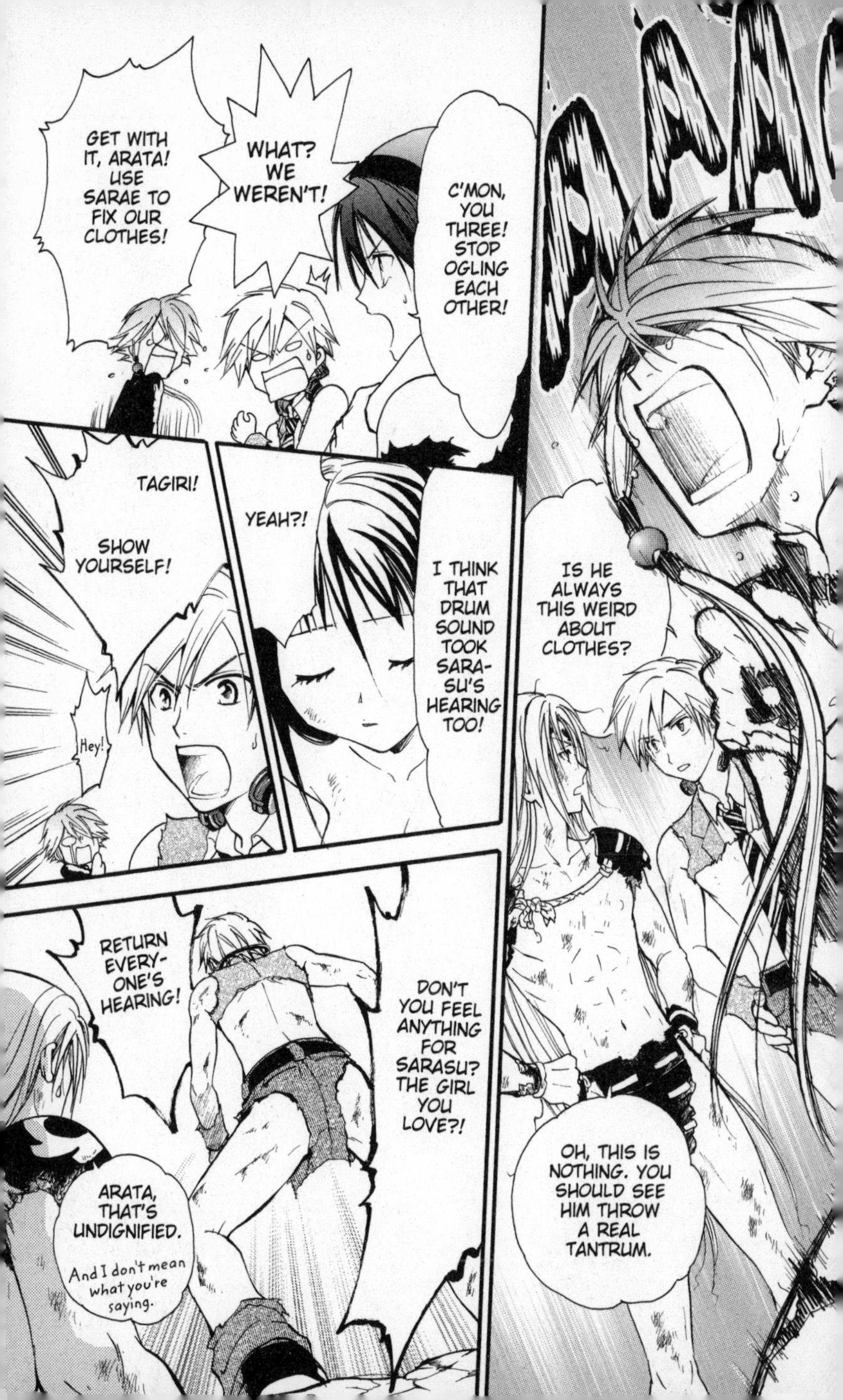
AAA
IS HE ALWAYS THIS WEIRD ABOUT CLOTHES?
OH, THIS IS NOTHING. YOU SHOULD SEE HIM THROW A REAL TANTRUM.
C'MON, YOU THREE! STOP OGLING EACH OTHER!
WHAT? WE WEREN'T!
GET WITH IT, ARATA! USE SARAE TO FIX OUR CLOTHES!
I THINK THAT DRUM SOUND TOOK SARA-SU'S HEARING TOO!
YEAH?!
TAGIRI!
SHOW YOURSELF!
Hey!
DON'T YOU FEEL ANYTHING FOR SARASU? THE GIRL YOU LOVE?!
RETURN EVERY-ONE'S HEARING!
ARATA, THAT'S UNDIGNIFIED.
And I don't mean what you're saying.

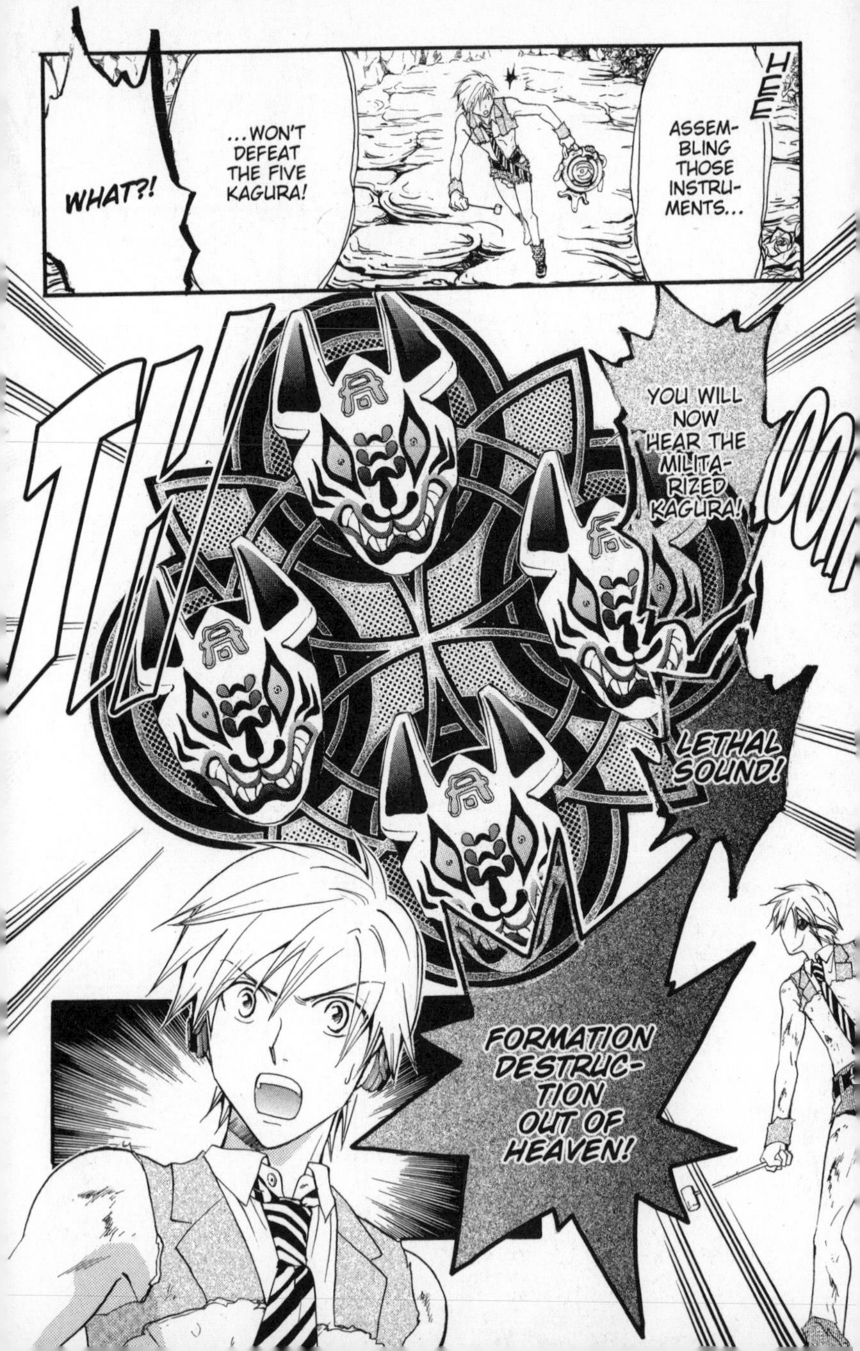
HEE
ASSEM-
BLING
THOSE
INSTRU-
MENTS...
...WON'T
DEFEAT
THE FIVE
KAGURA!
WHAT?!
YOU WILL
NOW
HEAR THE
MILITA-
RIZED
KAGURA!
LETHAL
SOUND!
FORMATION
DESTRUC-
TION
OUT OF
HEAVEN!

CHAPTER 154: ON THE SIGNAL

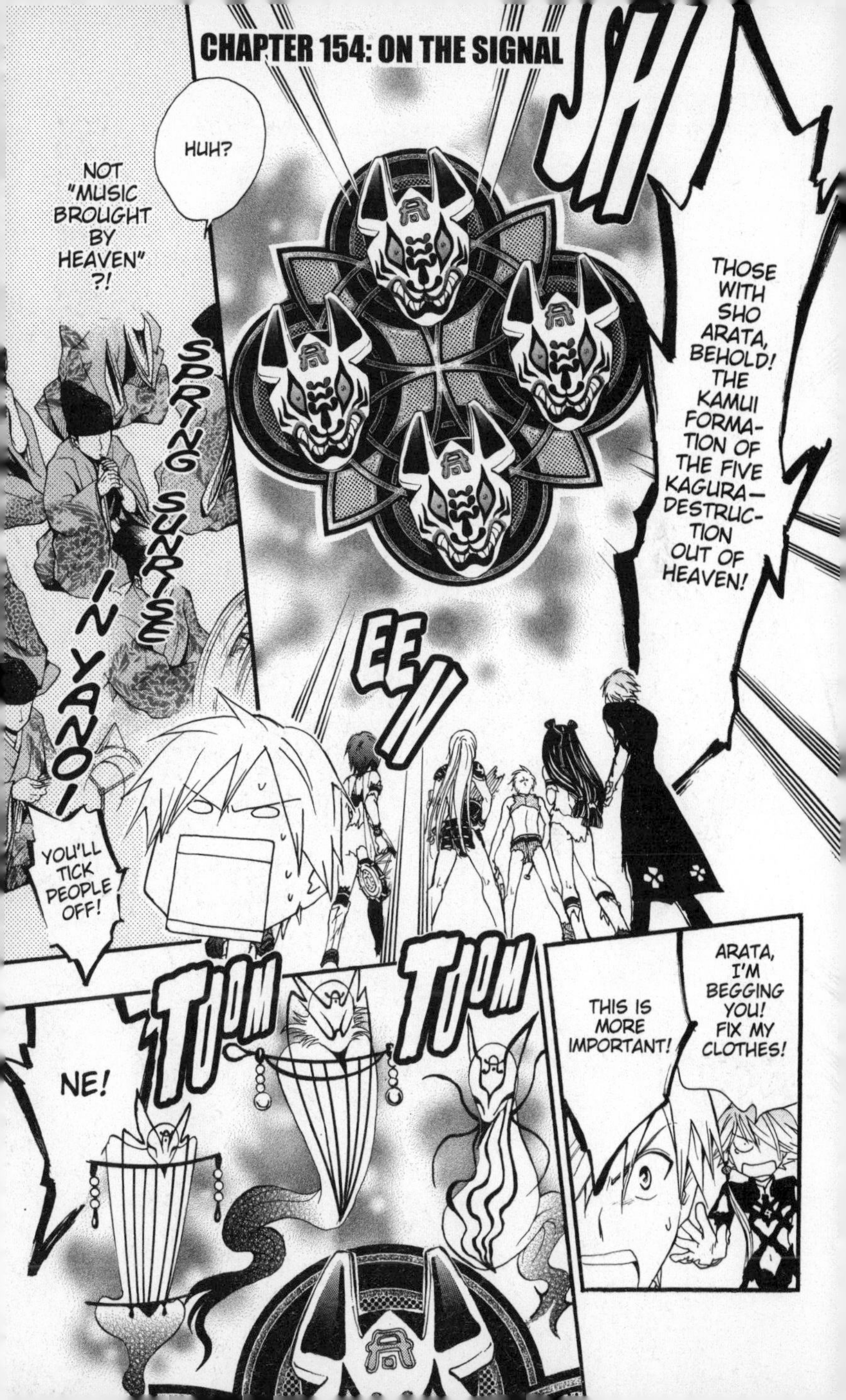
SHI
THOSE WITH SHO ARATA, BEHOLD! THE KAMUI FORMATION OF THE FIVE KAGURA-DESTRUCTION OUT OF HEAVEN!
EE N
HUH?
NOT "MUSIC BROUGHT BY HEAVEN" ?!
SPRING SUNRISE IN YANOI!
YOU'LL TICK PEOPLE OFF!
ARATA, I'M BEGGING YOU! FIX MY CLOTHES!
THIS IS MORE IMPORTANT!
TUOM
TUOM
NE!

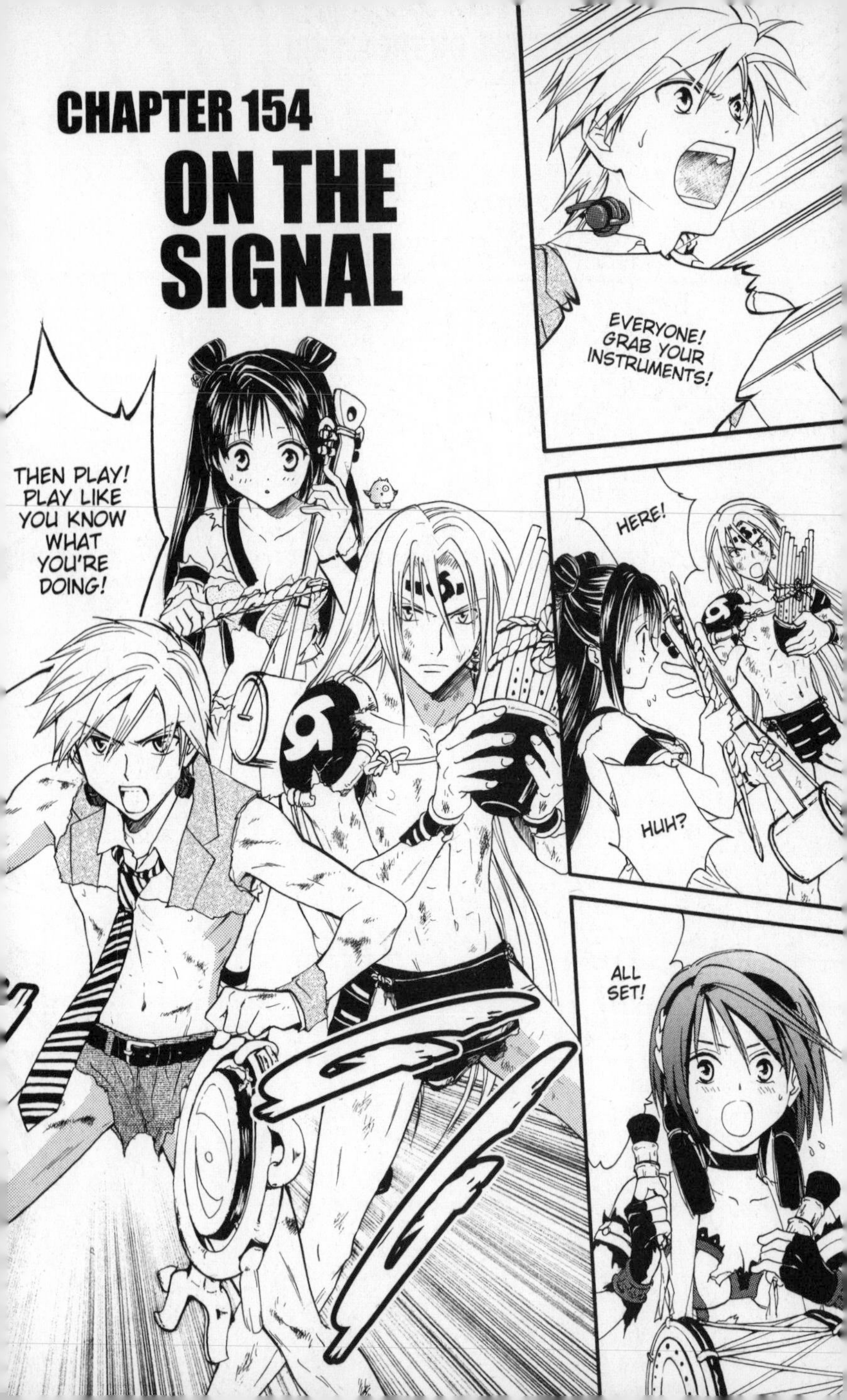
CHAPTER 154
ON THE SIGNAL
EVERYONE! GRAB YOUR INSTRUMENTS!
HERE!
HUH?
ALL SET!
THEN PLAY! PLAY LIKE YOU KNOW WHAT YOU'RE DOING!

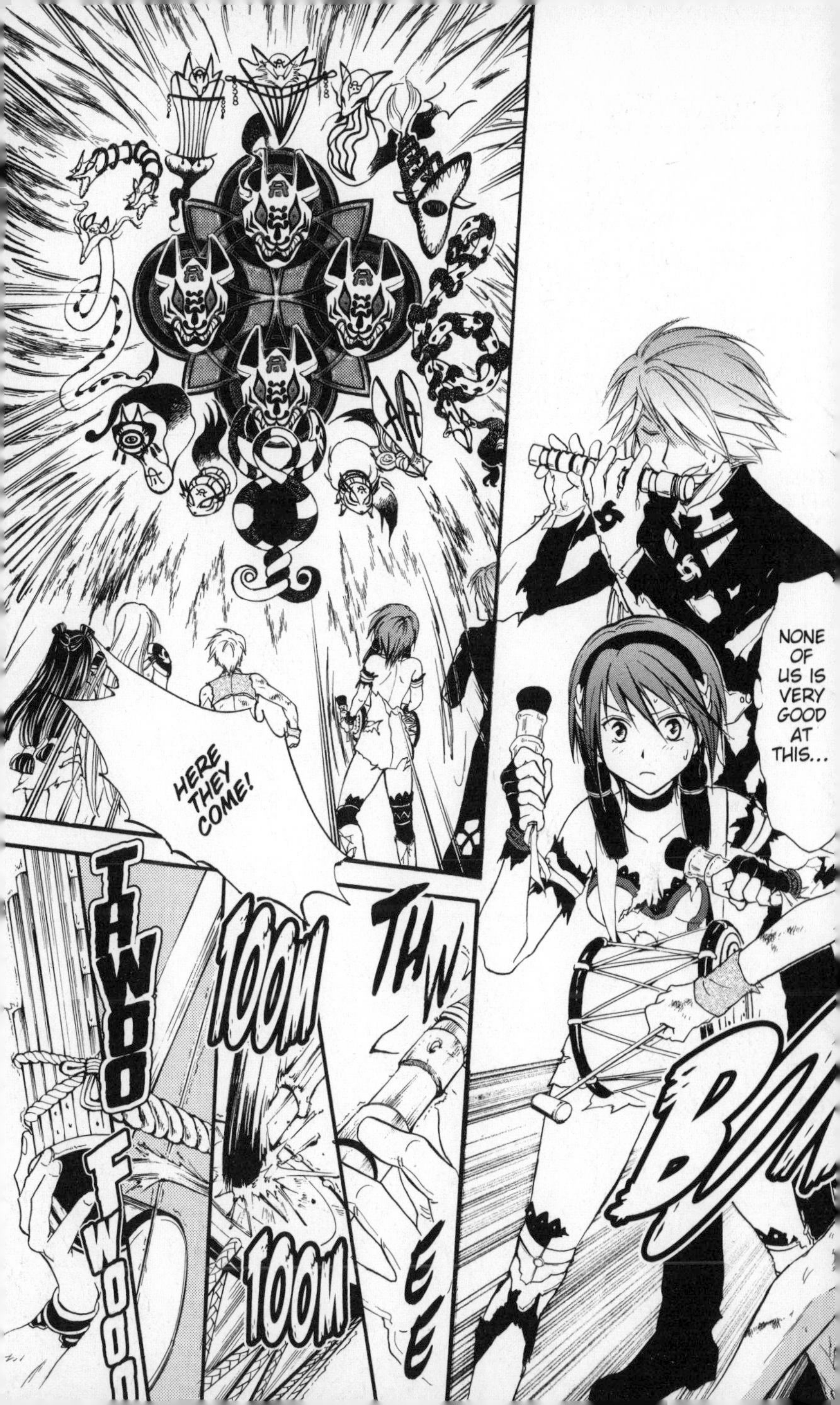
NONE OF US IS VERY GOOD AT THIS...
HERE THEY COME!
BA
THWEEE
TOOM
TOOM
THWOO
FWOOO

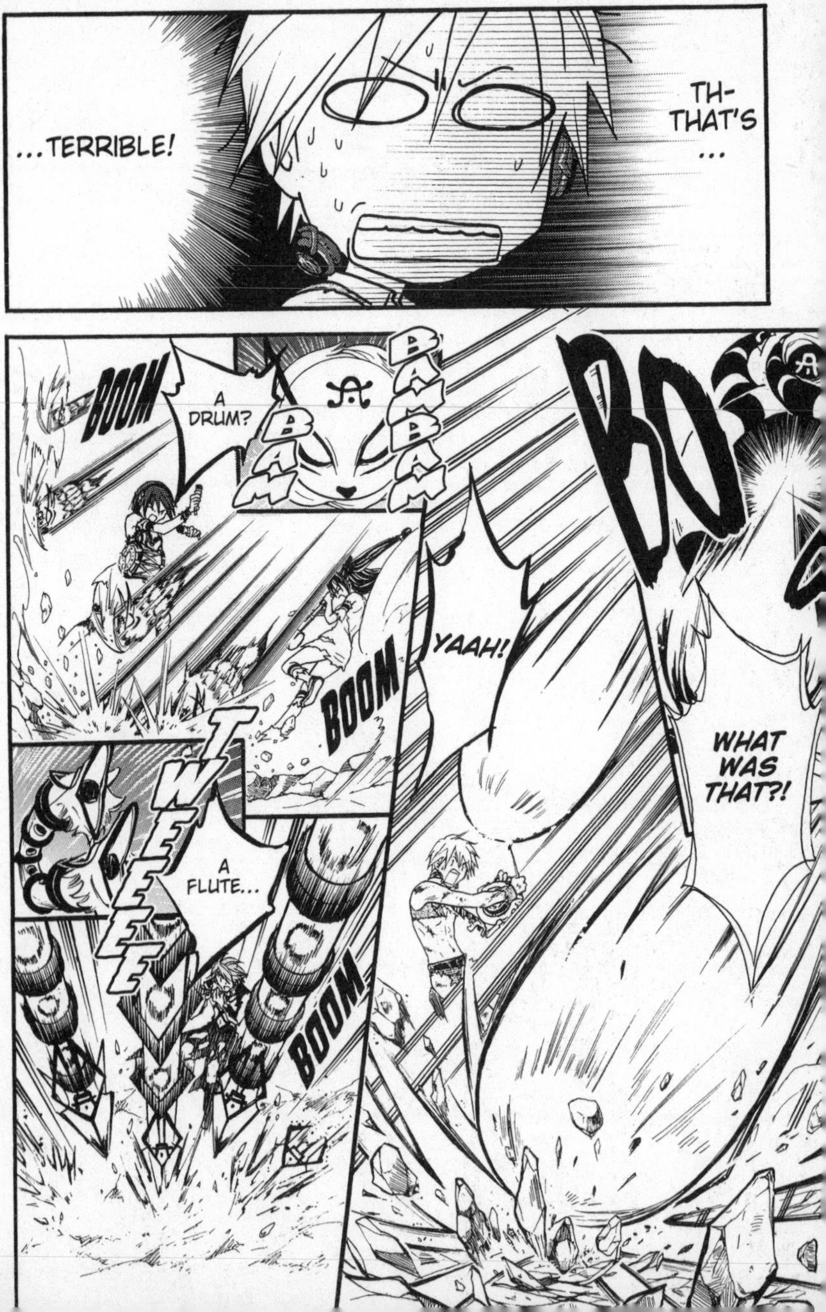
TH- THAT'S ...
...TERRIBLE!
BO
YAAH!
WHAT WAS THAT?!
BAM BAM
BAM BAM
A DRUM?
BOOM
BOOM
TWEEEEEE
A FLUTE...
BOOM

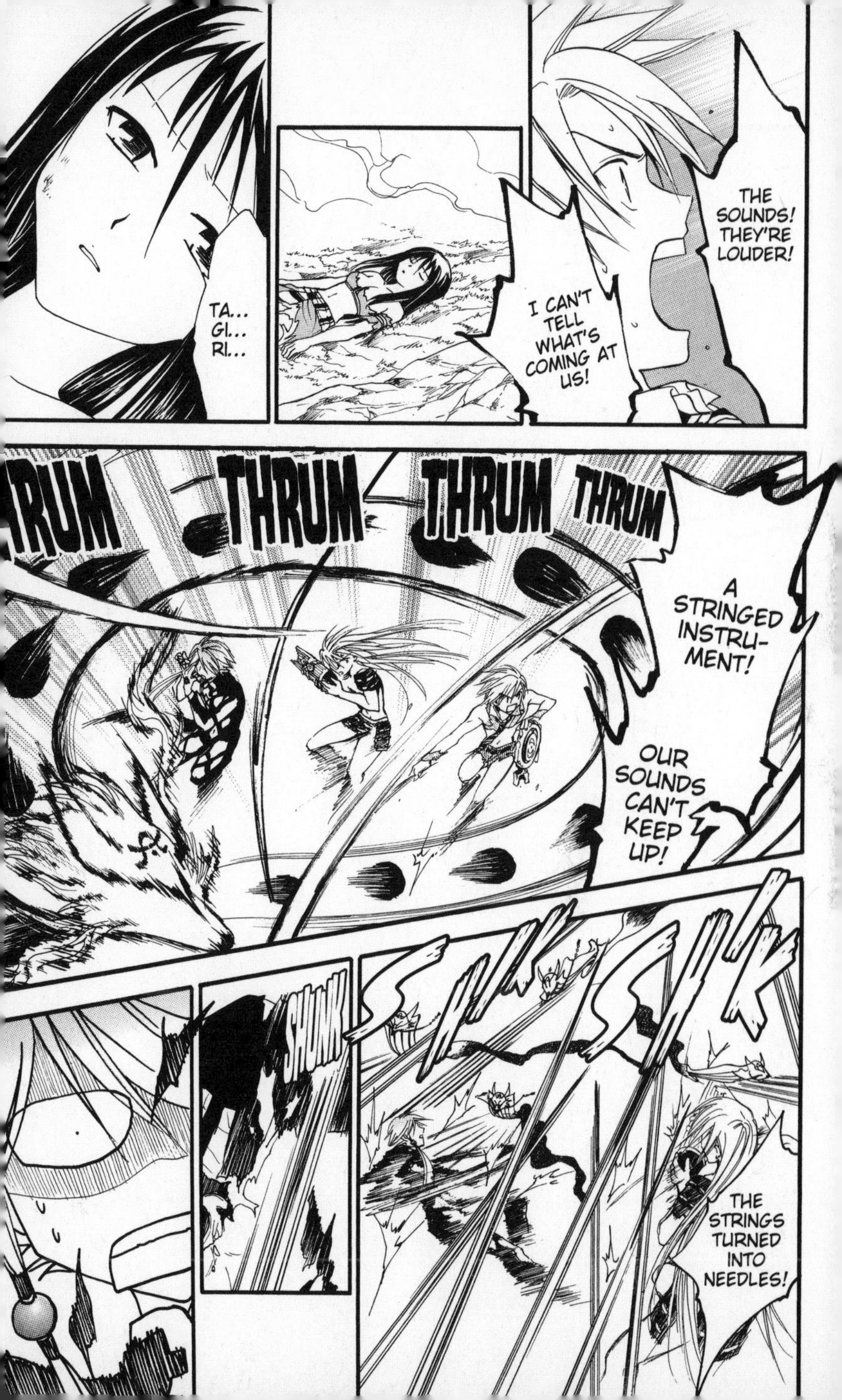
THE SOUNDS! THEY'RE LOUDER!
I CAN'T TELL WHAT'S COMING AT US!
TA... GI... RI...
A STRINGED INSTRU-MENT!
OUR SOUNDS CAN'T KEEP UP!
THRUM THRUM THRUM THRUM
SHK SHK
THE STRINGS TURNED INTO NEEDLES!
SHUNK

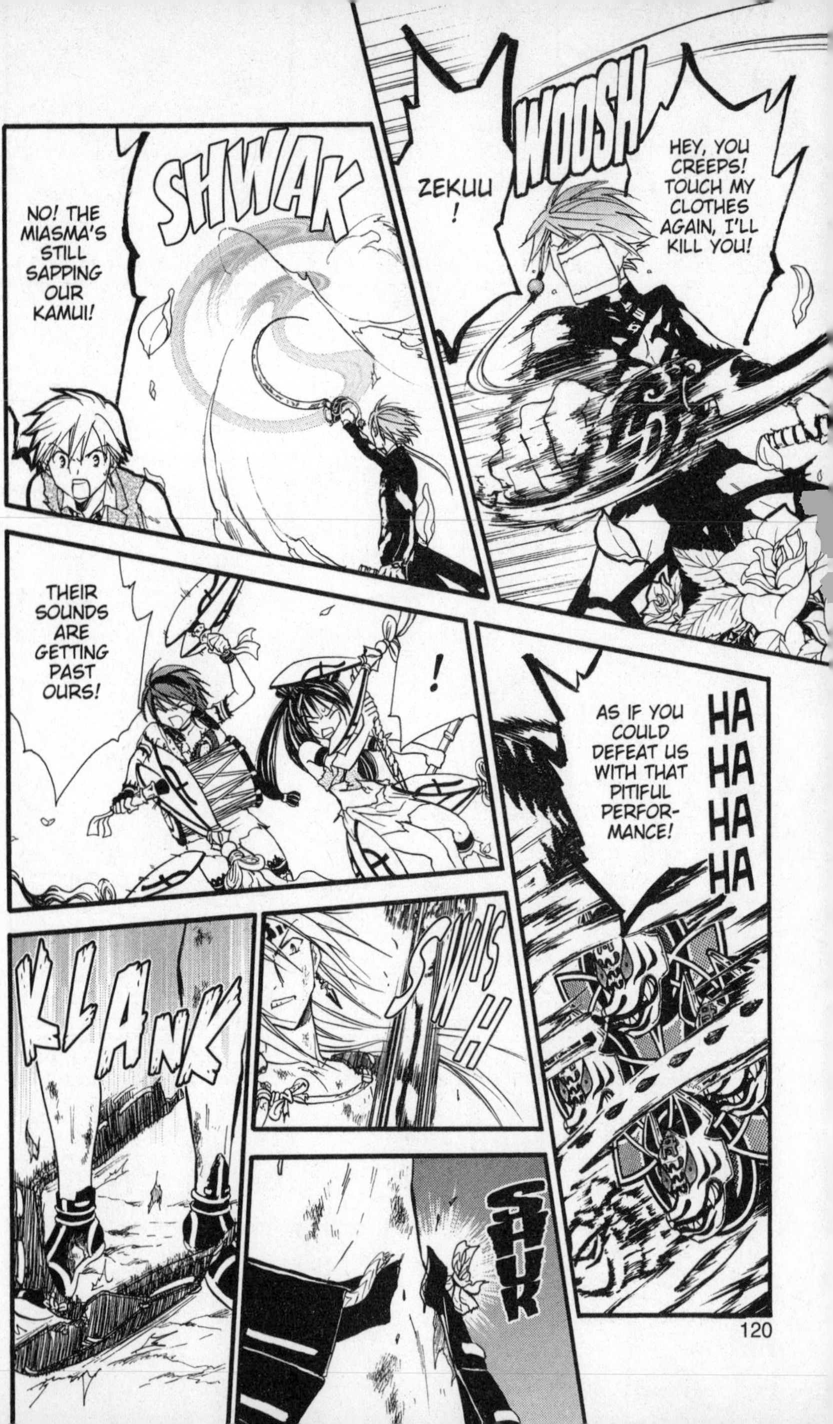
WOOSH
HEY, YOU CREEPS! TOUCH MY CLOTHES AGAIN, I'LL KILL YOU!
ZEKUU!
SHWAK
NO! THE MIASMA'S STILL SAPPING OUR KAMUI!
HA HA HA HA HA
AS IF YOU COULD DEFEAT US WITH THAT PITIFUL PERFORMANCE!
!
THEIR SOUNDS ARE GETTING PAST OURS!
SWISH
SHUK
KLANK

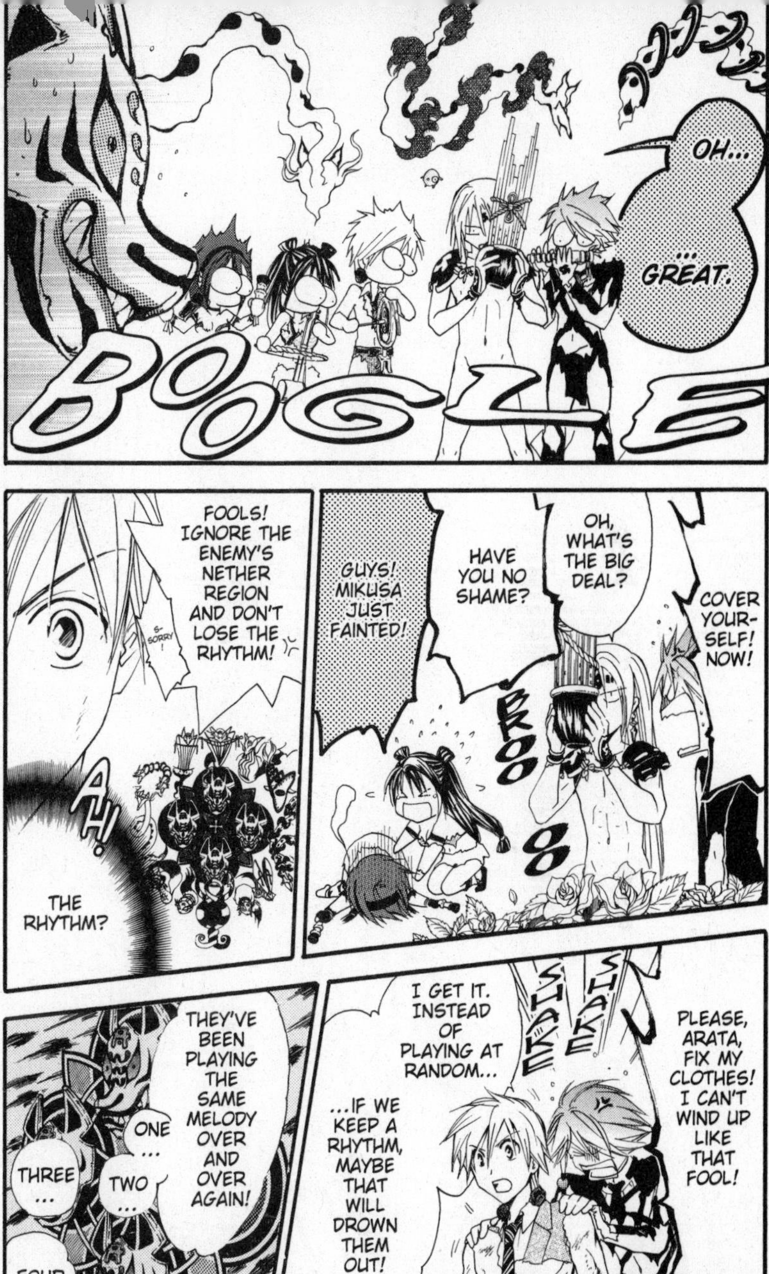
OH...
...GREAT.
BOOGLE
COVER YOURSELF! NOW!
OH, WHAT'S THE BIG DEAL?
HAVE YOU NO SHAME?
GUYS! MIKUSA JUST FAINTED!
BROOO
FOOLS! IGNORE THE ENEMY'S NETHER REGION AND DON'T LOSE THE RHYTHM!
S-SORRY!
AH!
THE RHYTHM?
PLEASE, ARATA, FIX MY CLOTHES! I CAN'T WIND UP LIKE THAT FOOL!
SHAKE
SHAKE
I GET IT. INSTEAD OF PLAYING AT RANDOM...
...IF WE KEEP A RHYTHM, MAYBE THAT WILL DROWN THEM OUT!
THEY'VE BEEN PLAYING THE SAME MELODY OVER AND OVER AGAIN!
ONE...
TWO...
THREE...
FOUR...

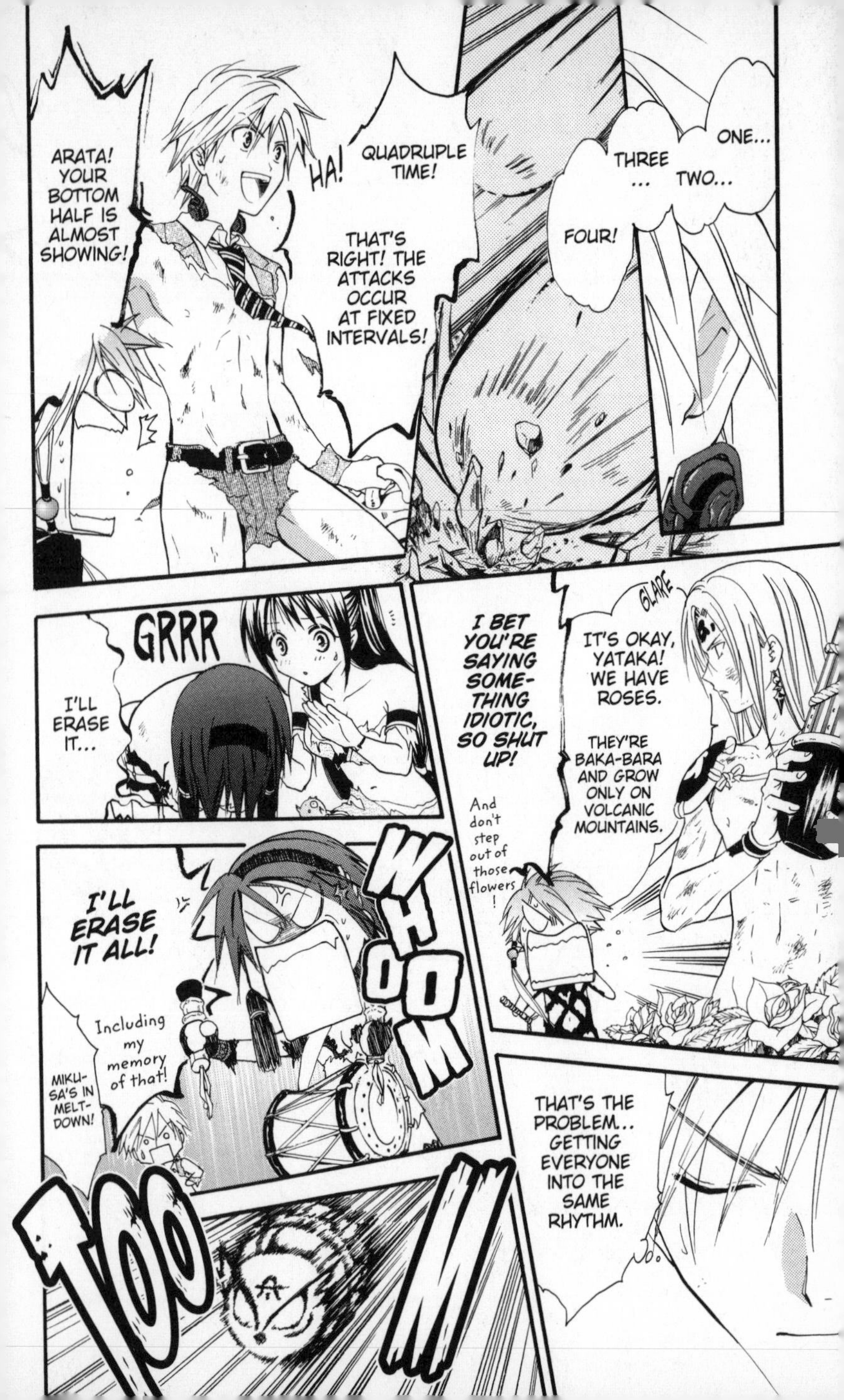
ONE... TWO... THREE... FOUR!
QUADRUPLE TIME!
HA!
THAT'S RIGHT! THE ATTACKS OCCUR AT FIXED INTERVALS!
ARATA! YOUR BOTTOM HALF IS ALMOST SHOWING!
GLARE
IT'S OKAY, YATAKA! WE HAVE ROSES.
THEY'RE BAKA-BARA AND GROW ONLY ON VOLCANIC MOUNTAINS.
I BET YOU'RE SAYING SOME-THING IDIOTIC, SO SHUT UP!
And don't step out of those flowers!
GRRR
I'LL ERASE IT...
WHOOM
I'LL ERASE IT ALL!
Including my memory of that!
MIKU-SA'S IN MELT-DOWN!
TOOM
THAT'S THE PROBLEM... GETTING EVERYONE INTO THE SAME RHYTHM.

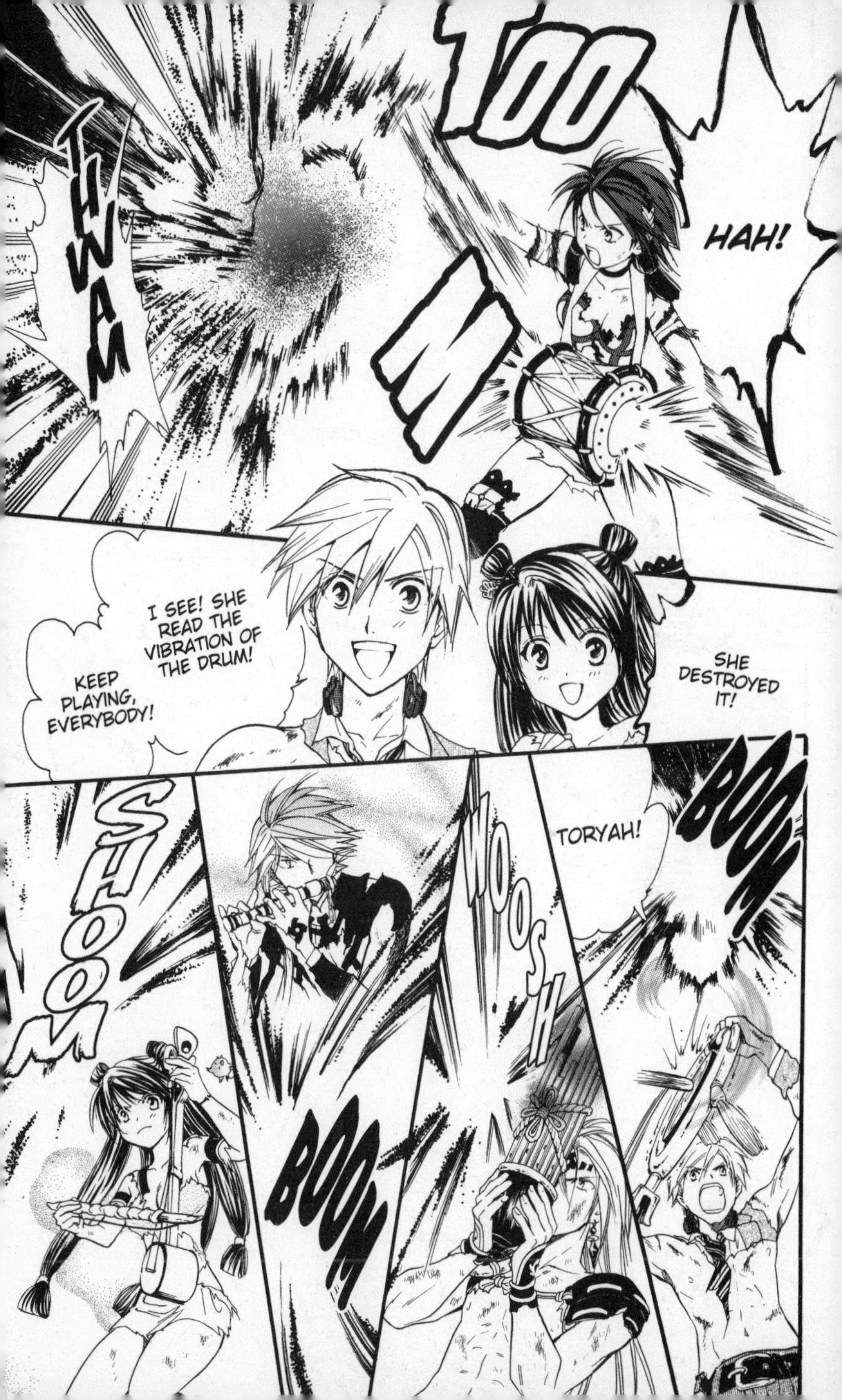
TOOM
HAH!
THWAM
SHE DESTROYED IT!
I SEE! SHE READ THE VIBRATION OF THE DRUM!
KEEP PLAYING, EVERYBODY!
BOOM
TORYAH!
WOOSH
BOOM
SHOOM

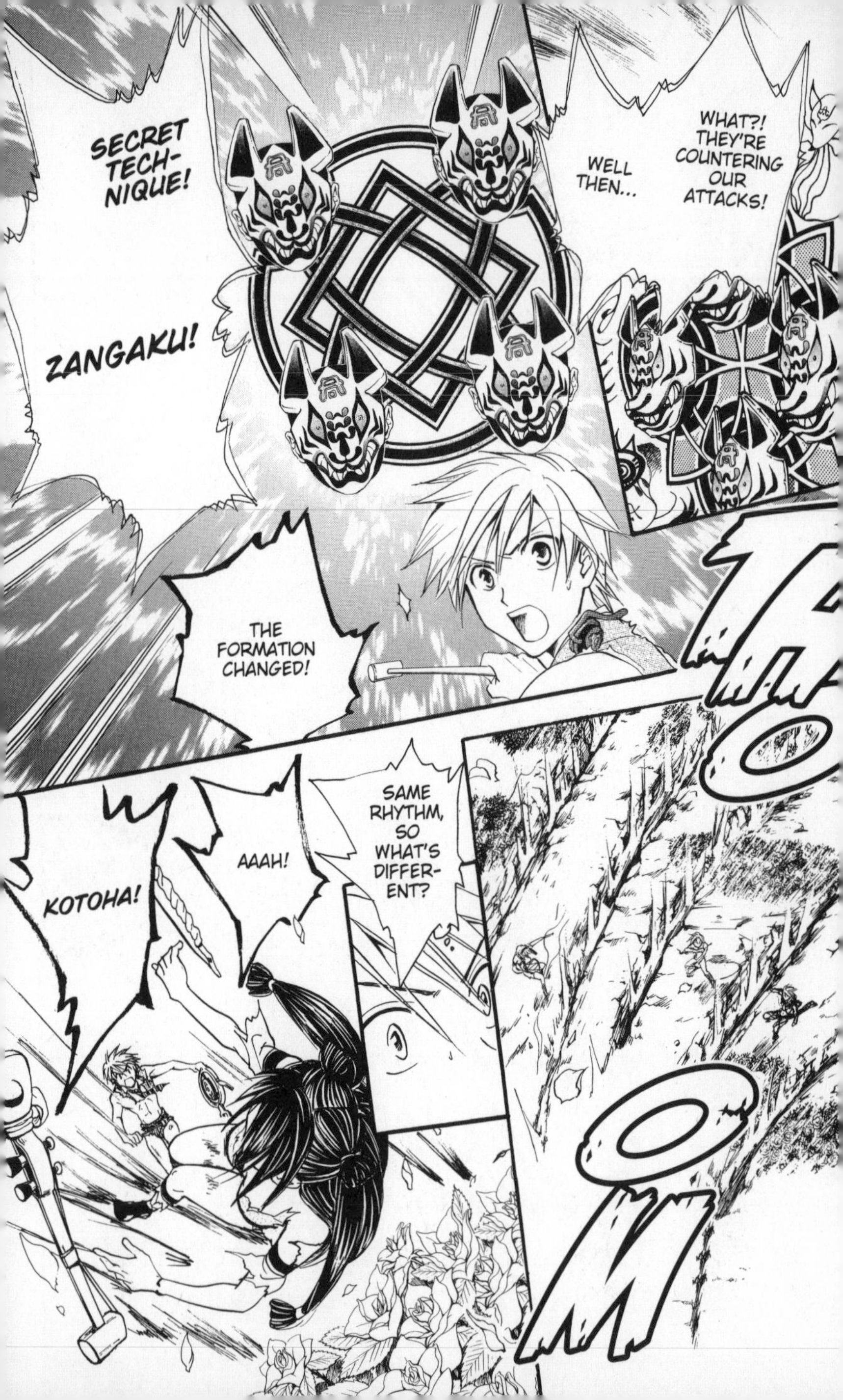
WHAT?! THEY'RE COUNTERING OUR ATTACKS!
WELL THEN...
SECRET TECHNIQUE!
ZANGAKU!
THE FORMATION CHANGED!
SAME RHYTHM, SO WHAT'S DIFFERENT?
AAAH!
KOTOHA!

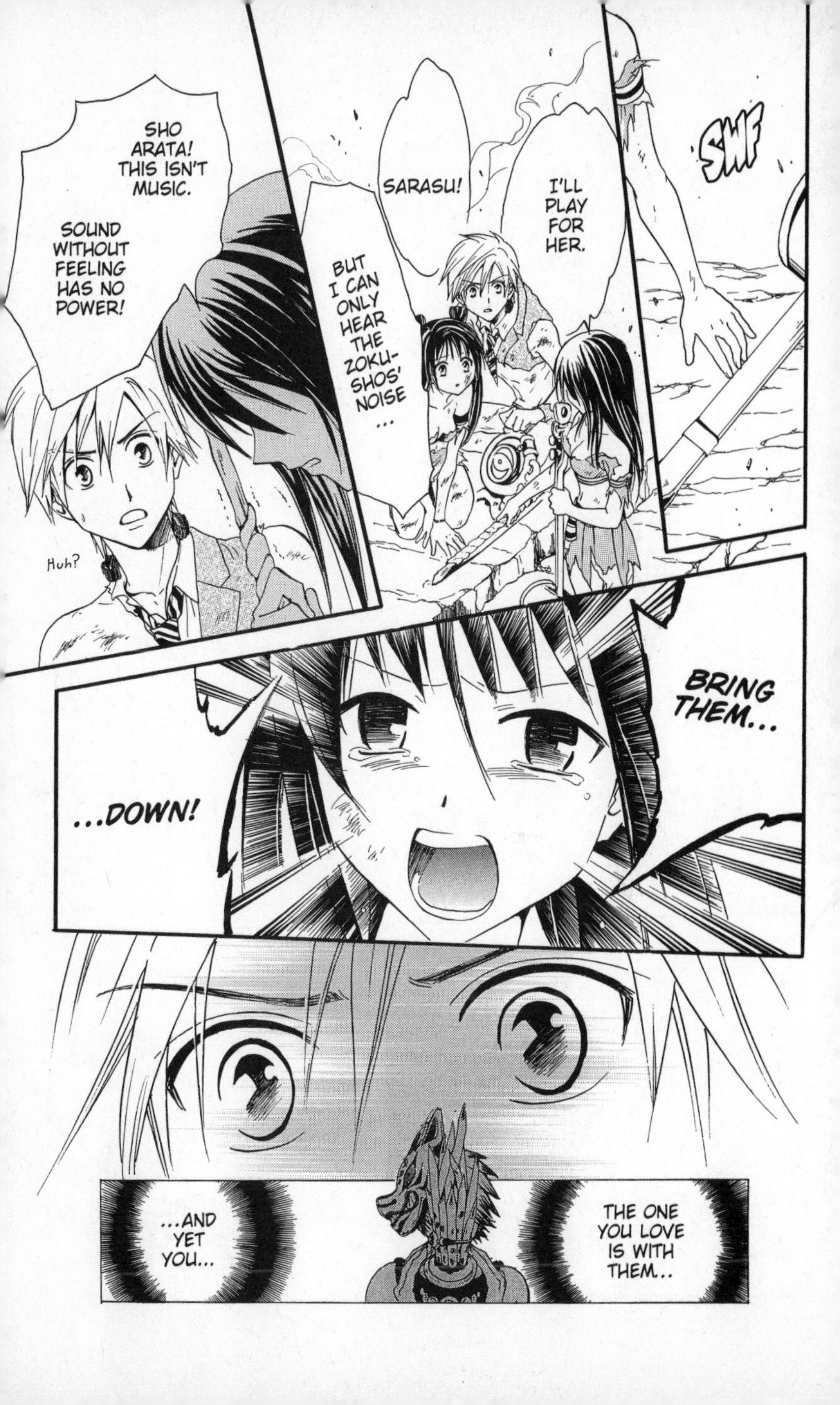
SWF
I'LL PLAY FOR HER.
SARASU!
BUT I CAN ONLY HEAR THE ZOKU-SHOS' NOISE...
SHO ARATA! THIS ISN'T MUSIC.
SOUND WITHOUT FEELING HAS NO POWER!
Huh?
BRING THEM...
...DOWN!
THE ONE YOU LOVE IS WITH THEM..
...AND YET YOU...

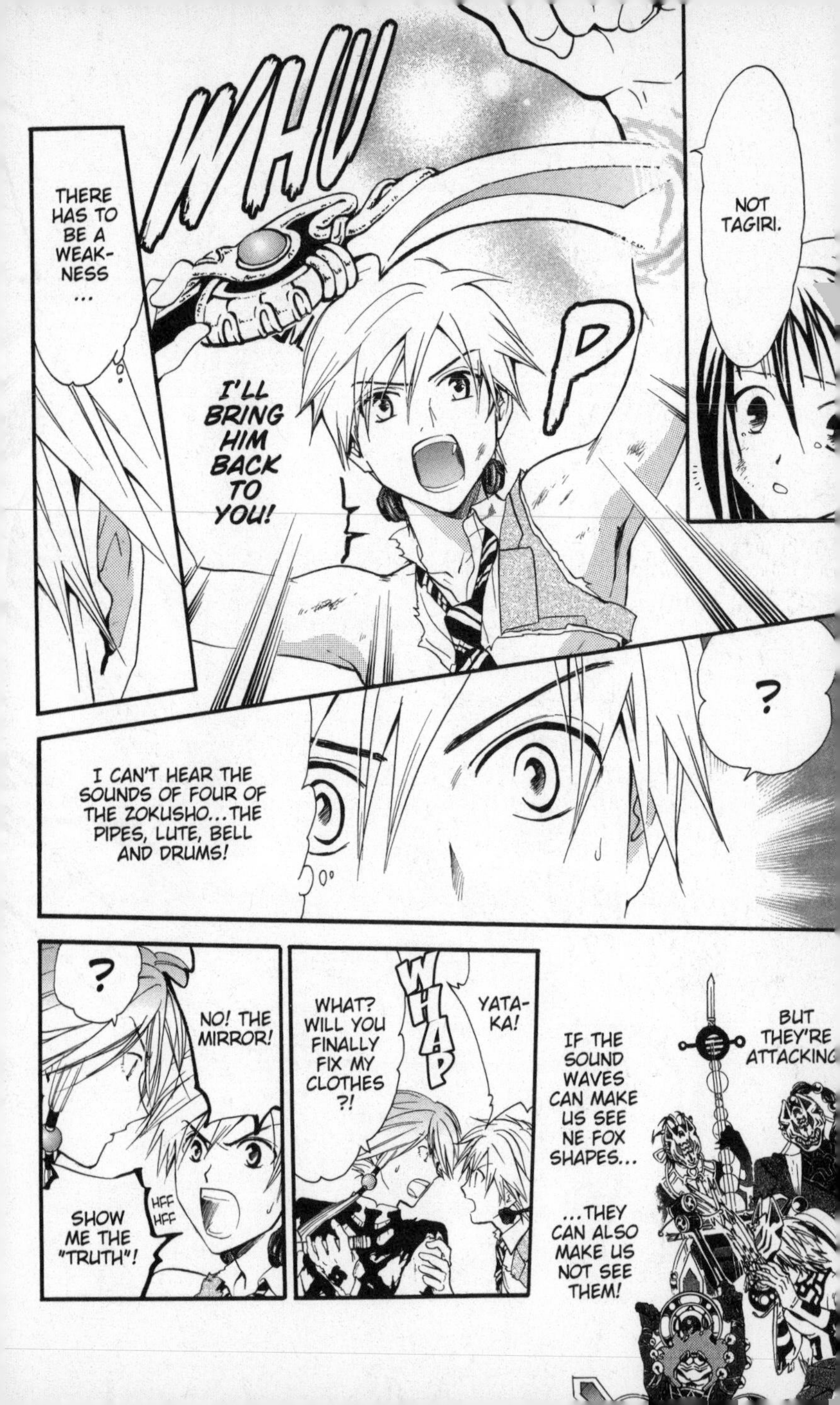
NOT TAGIRI.
WHU
P
I'LL BRING HIM BACK TO YOU!
THERE HAS TO BE A WEAKNESS...
?
I CAN'T HEAR THE SOUNDS OF FOUR OF THE ZOKUSHO...THE PIPES, LUTE, BELL AND DRUMS!
BUT THEY'RE ATTACKING
IF THE SOUND WAVES CAN MAKE US SEE NE FOX SHAPES...
...THEY CAN ALSO MAKE US NOT SEE THEM!
YATA-KA!
WHAP
WHAT? WILL YOU FINALLY FIX MY CLOTHES?!
?
NO! THE MIRROR!
HFF HFF
SHOW ME THE "TRUTH"!

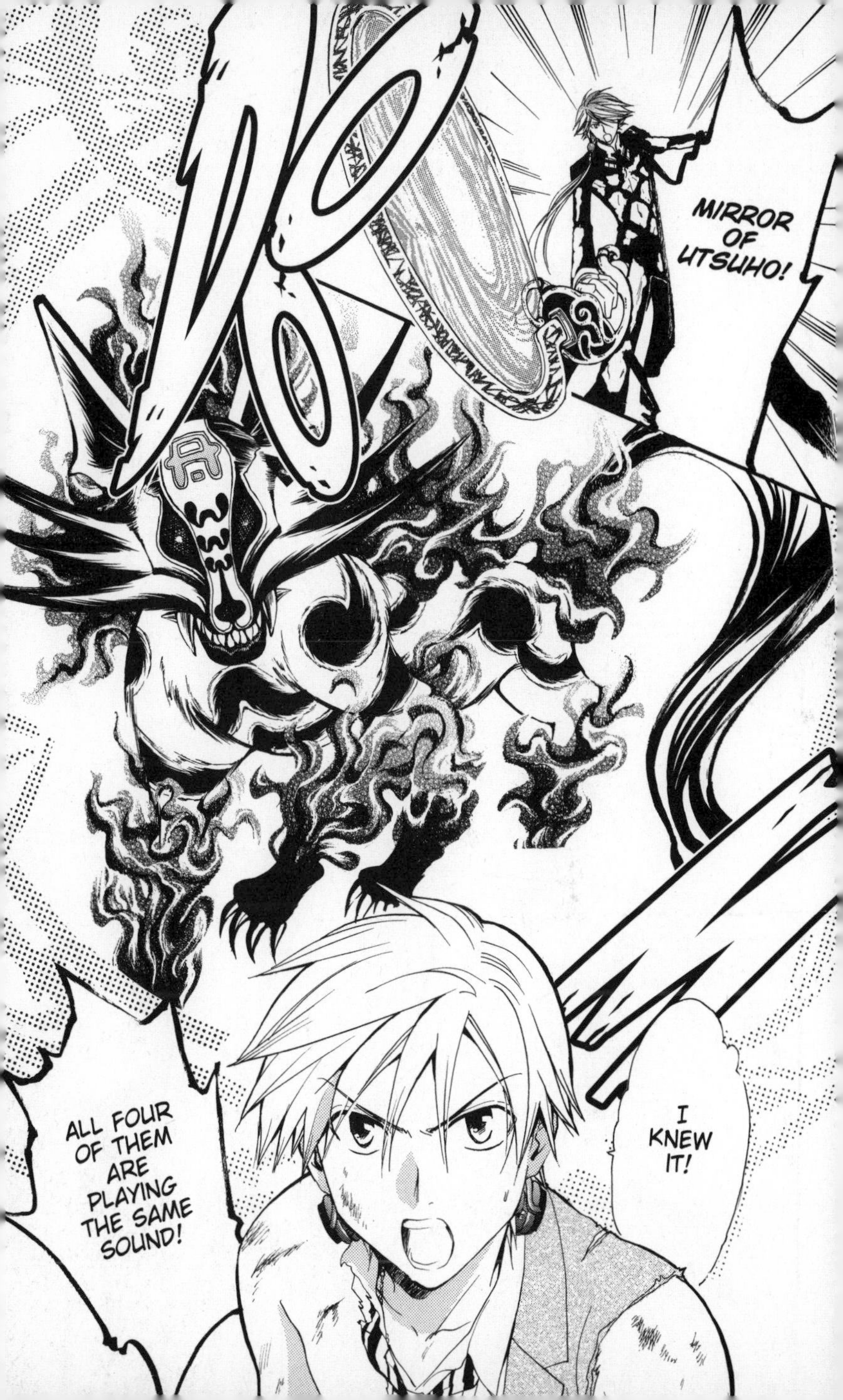
MIRROR OF UTSUHO!
I KNEW IT!
ALL FOUR OF THEM ARE PLAYING THE SAME SOUND!

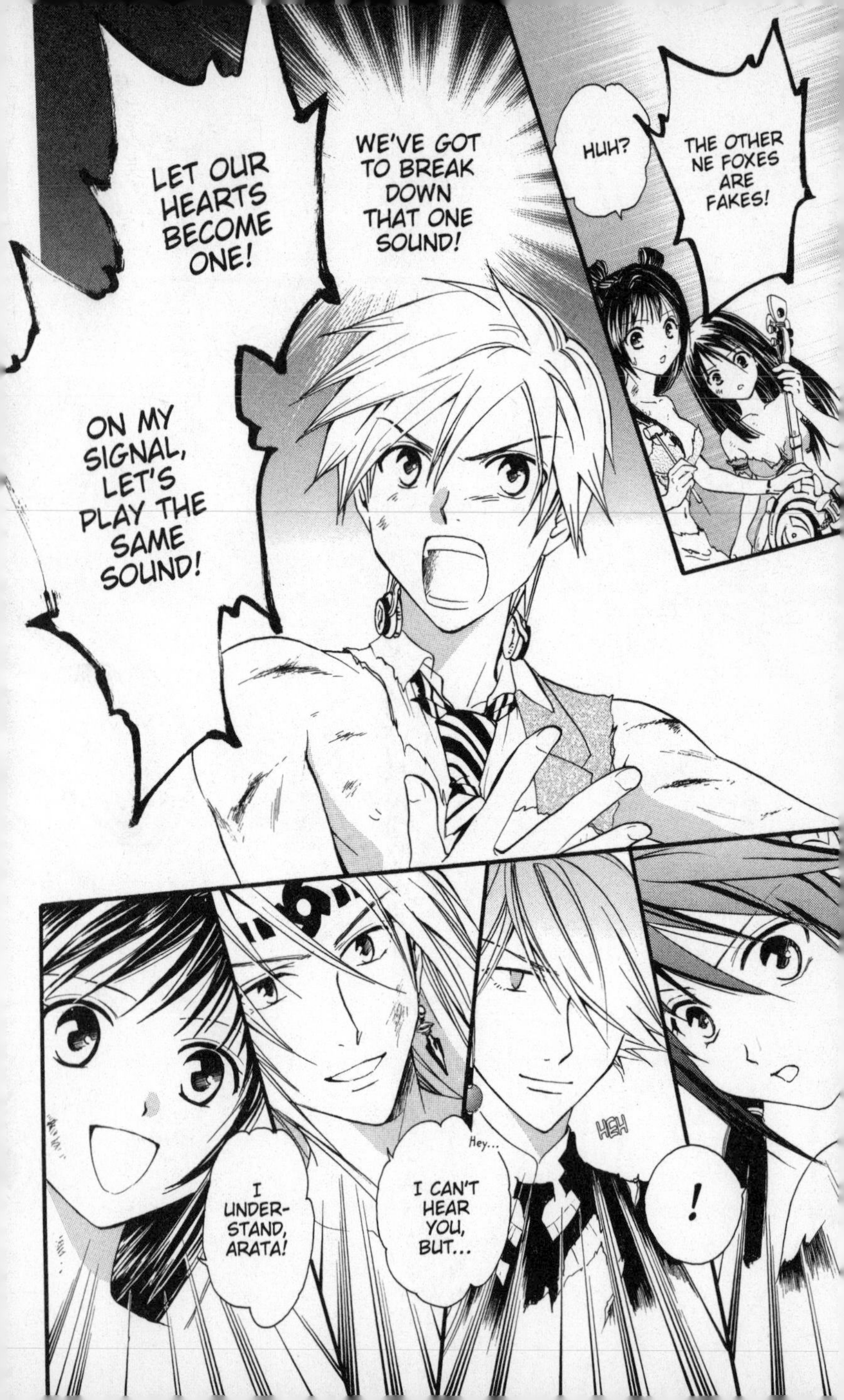
THE OTHER NE FOXES ARE FAKES!
HUH?
WE'VE GOT TO BREAK DOWN THAT ONE SOUND!
LET OUR HEARTS BECOME ONE!
ON MY SIGNAL, LET'S PLAY THE SAME SOUND!
!
HEH
Hey...
I CAN'T HEAR YOU, BUT...
I UNDER-STAND, ARATA!

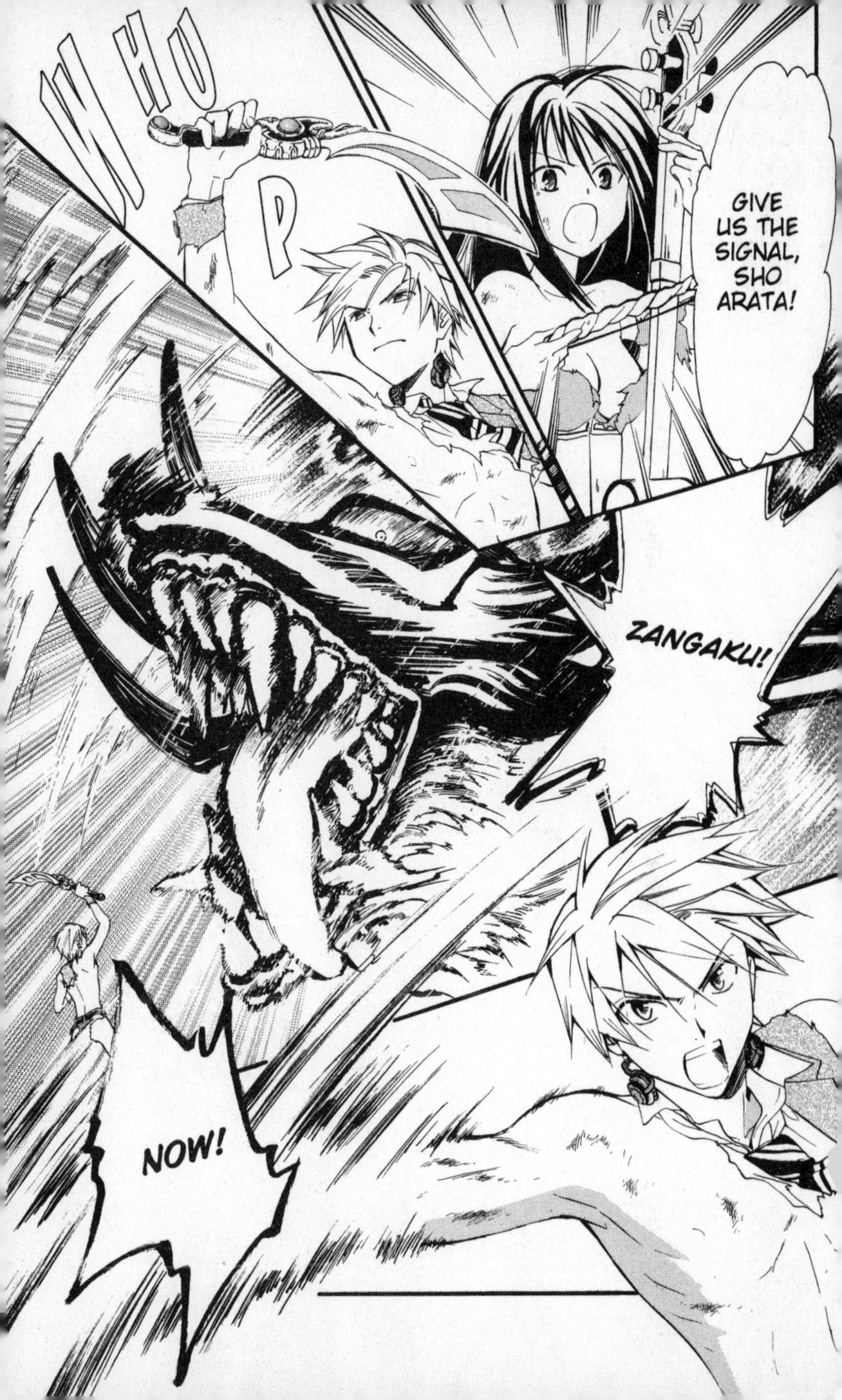
GIVE US THE SIGNAL, SHO ARATA!
WHUP
ZANGAKU!
NOW!

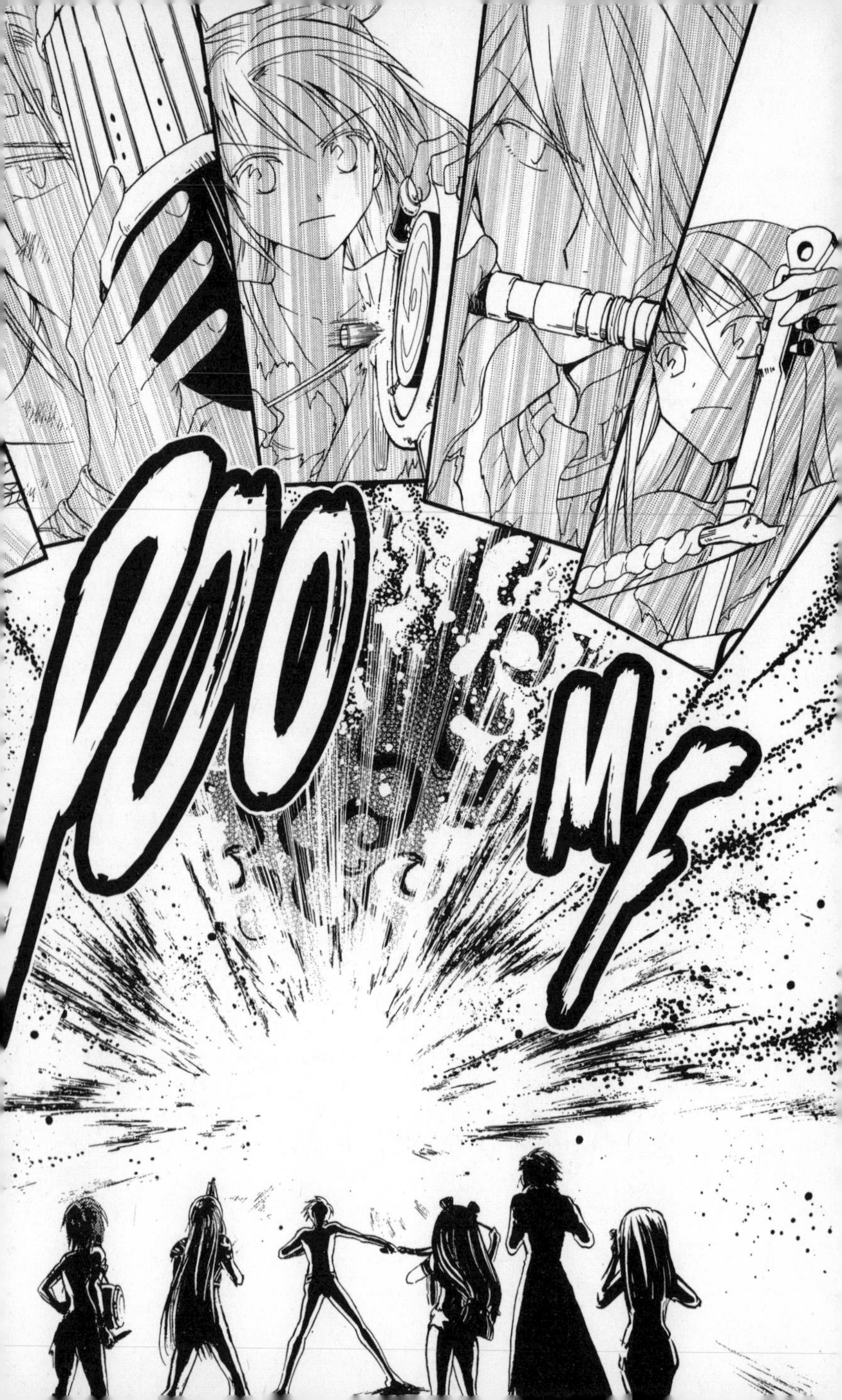

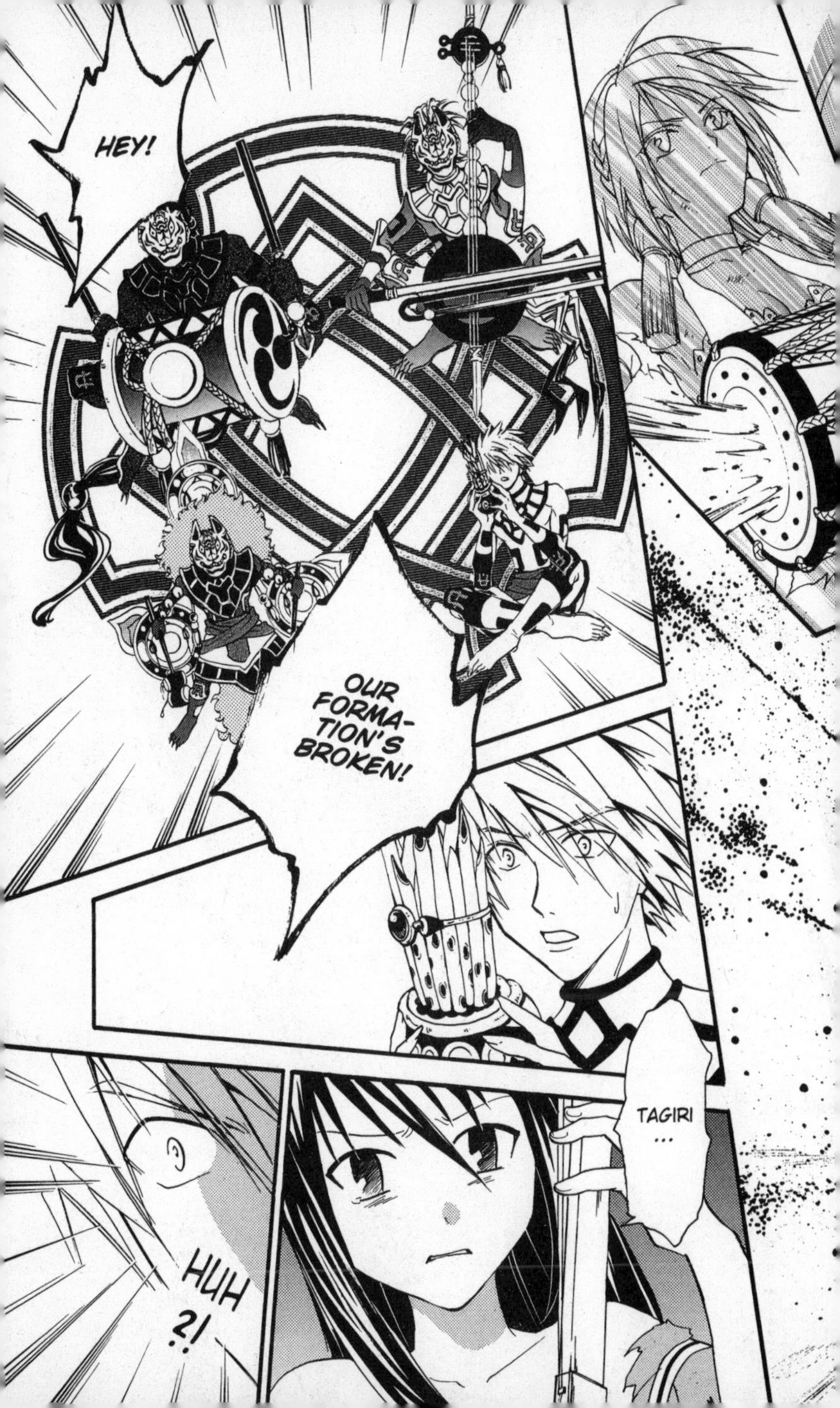
HEY!
OUR FORMATION'S BROKEN!
TAGIRI ...
HUH ?!

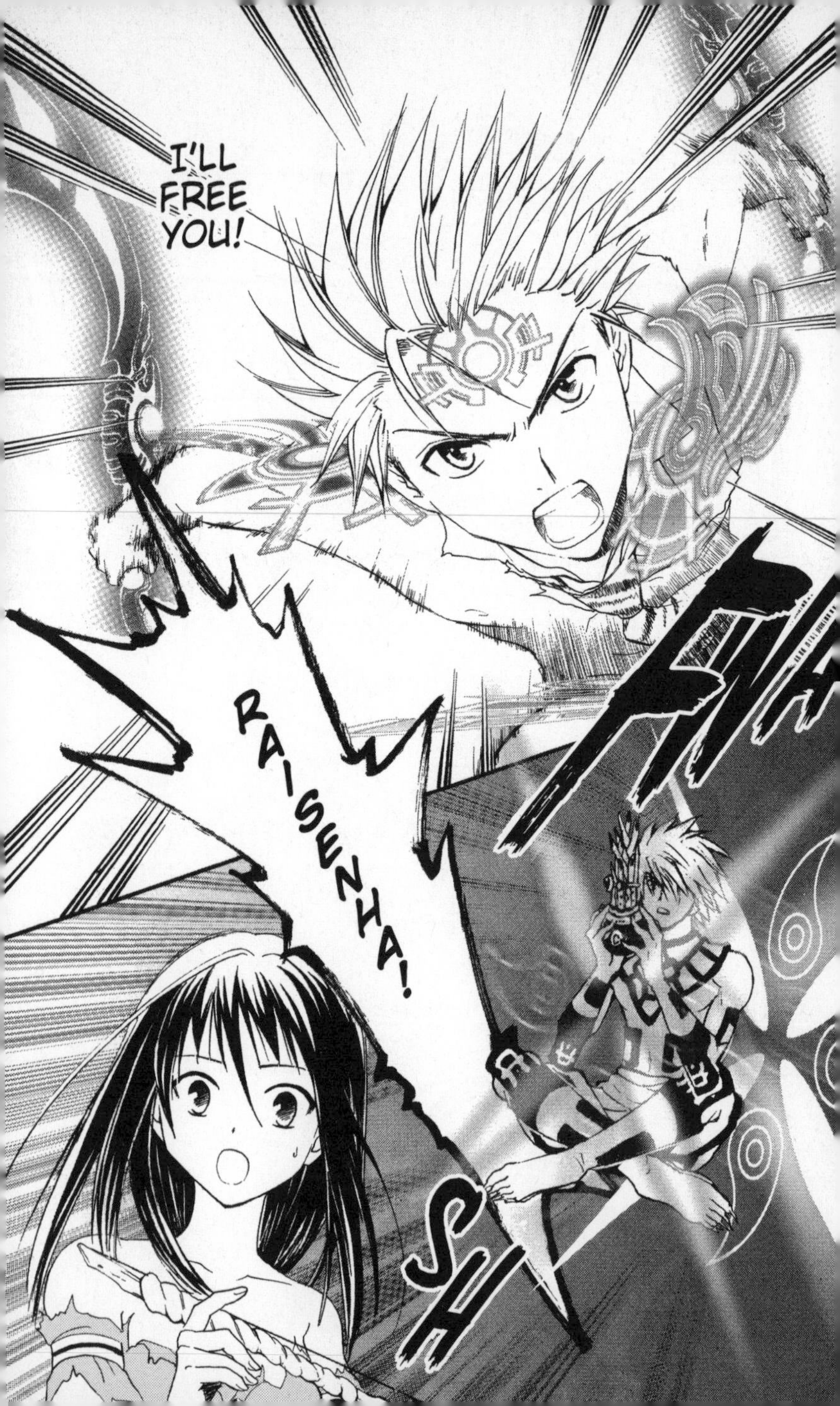
I'LL FREE YOU!
RAISENHA!
SH

CHAPTER 155: TAGIRI'S ROAR

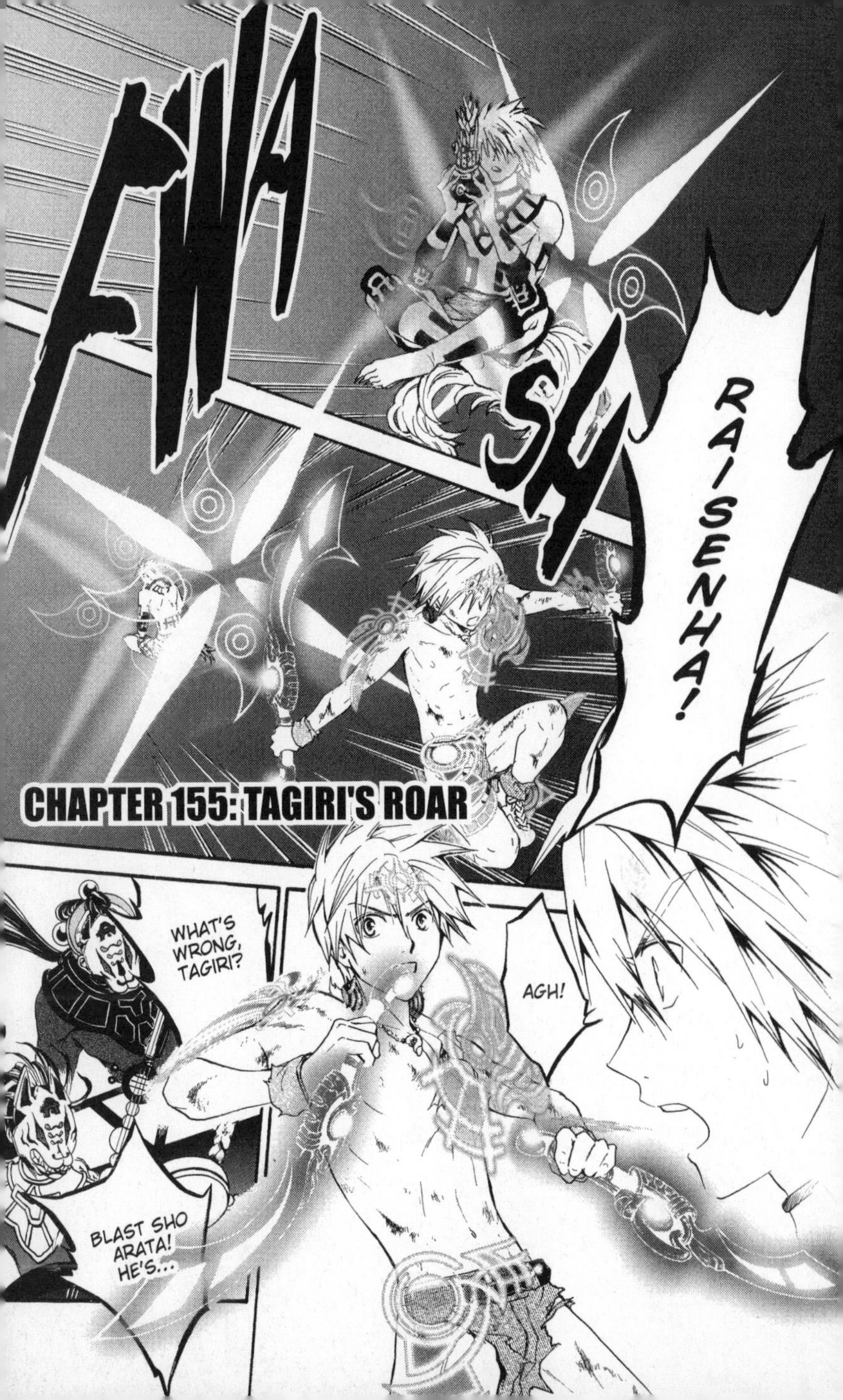
RAISENHA!
FWA
SHA
AGH!
WHAT'S WRONG, TAGIRI?
BLAST SHO ARATA! HE'S...

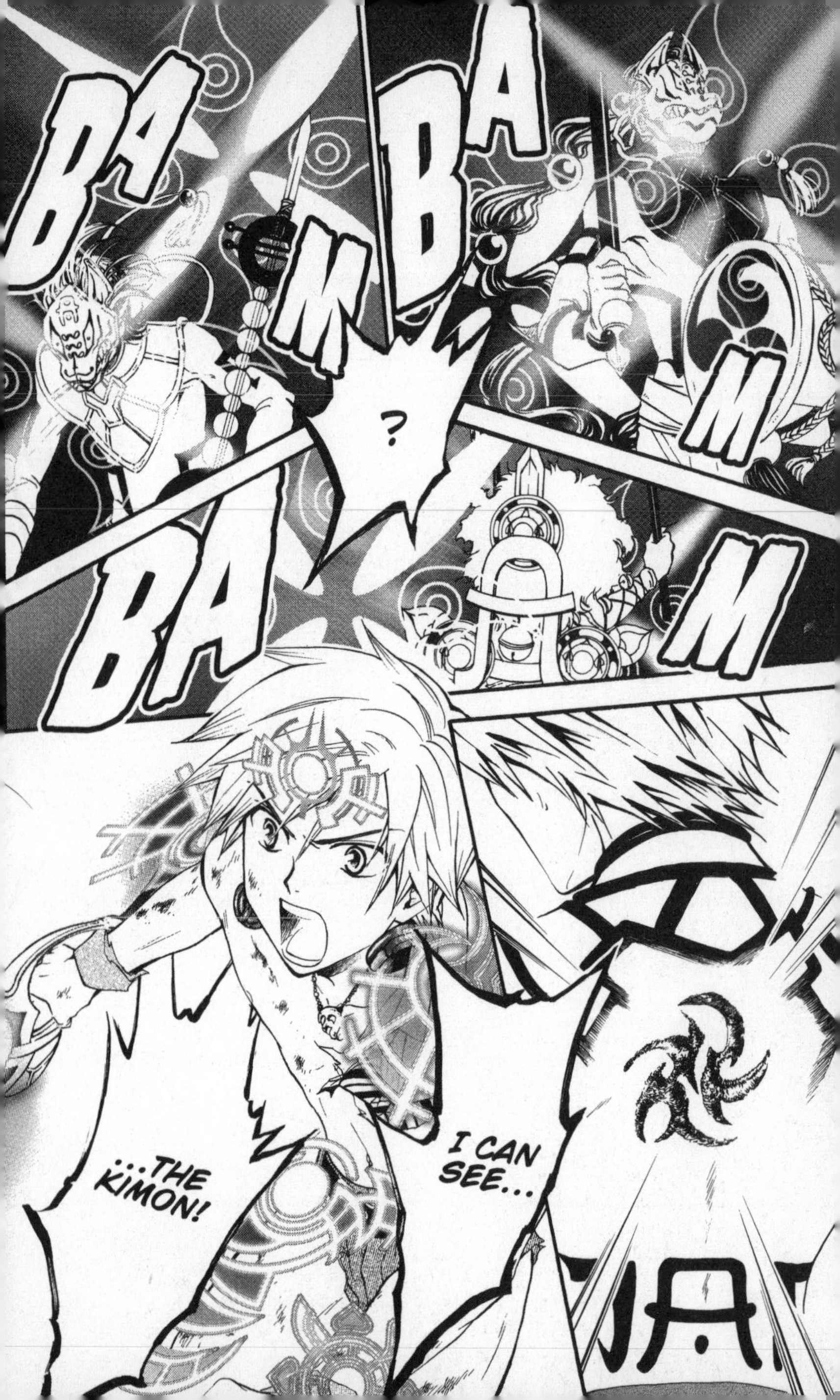
BADAM
?
BAM
BAM
I CAN SEE...
...THE KIMON!

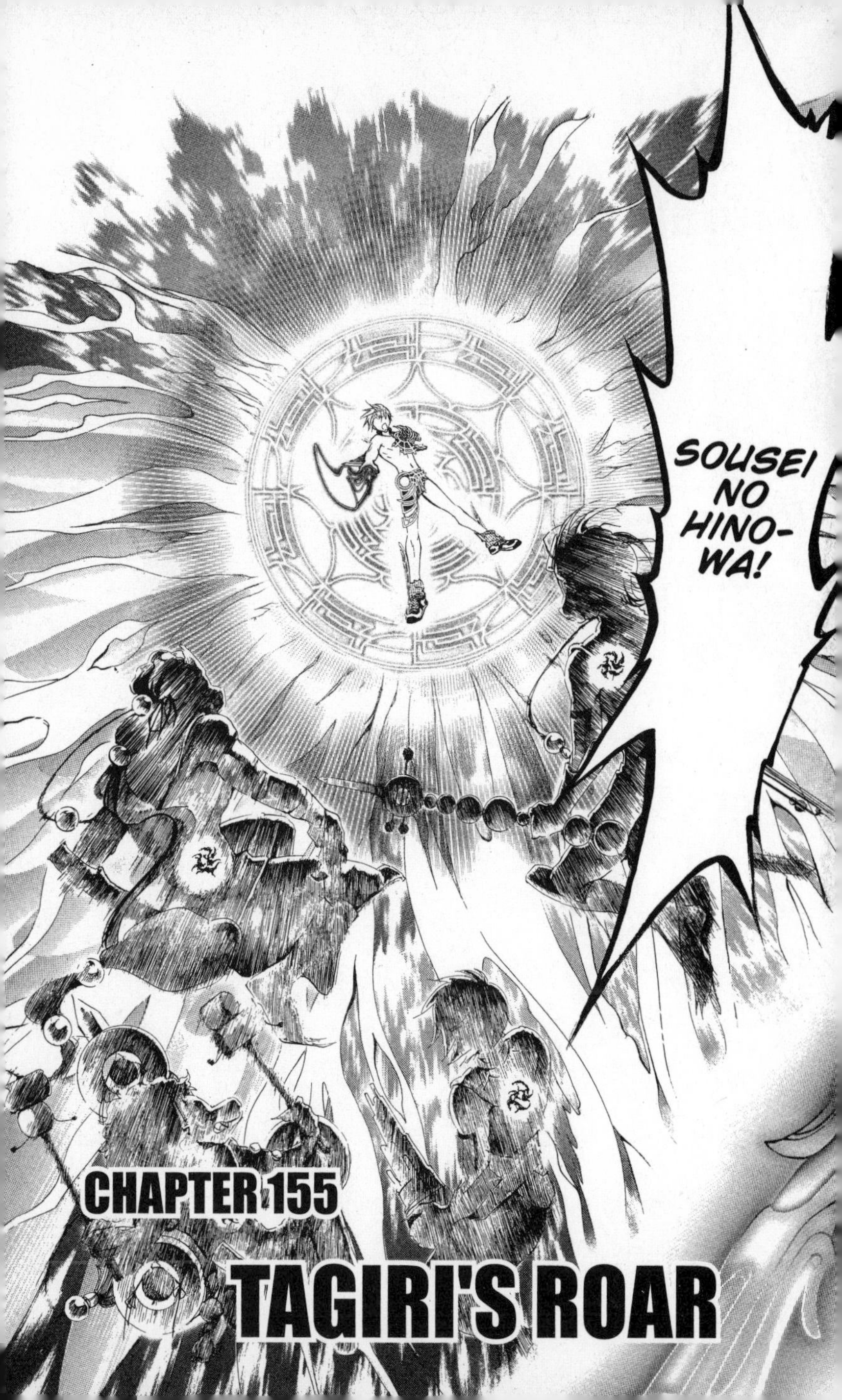
SOUSEI NO HINO-WA!
CHAPTER 155
TAGIRI'S ROAR

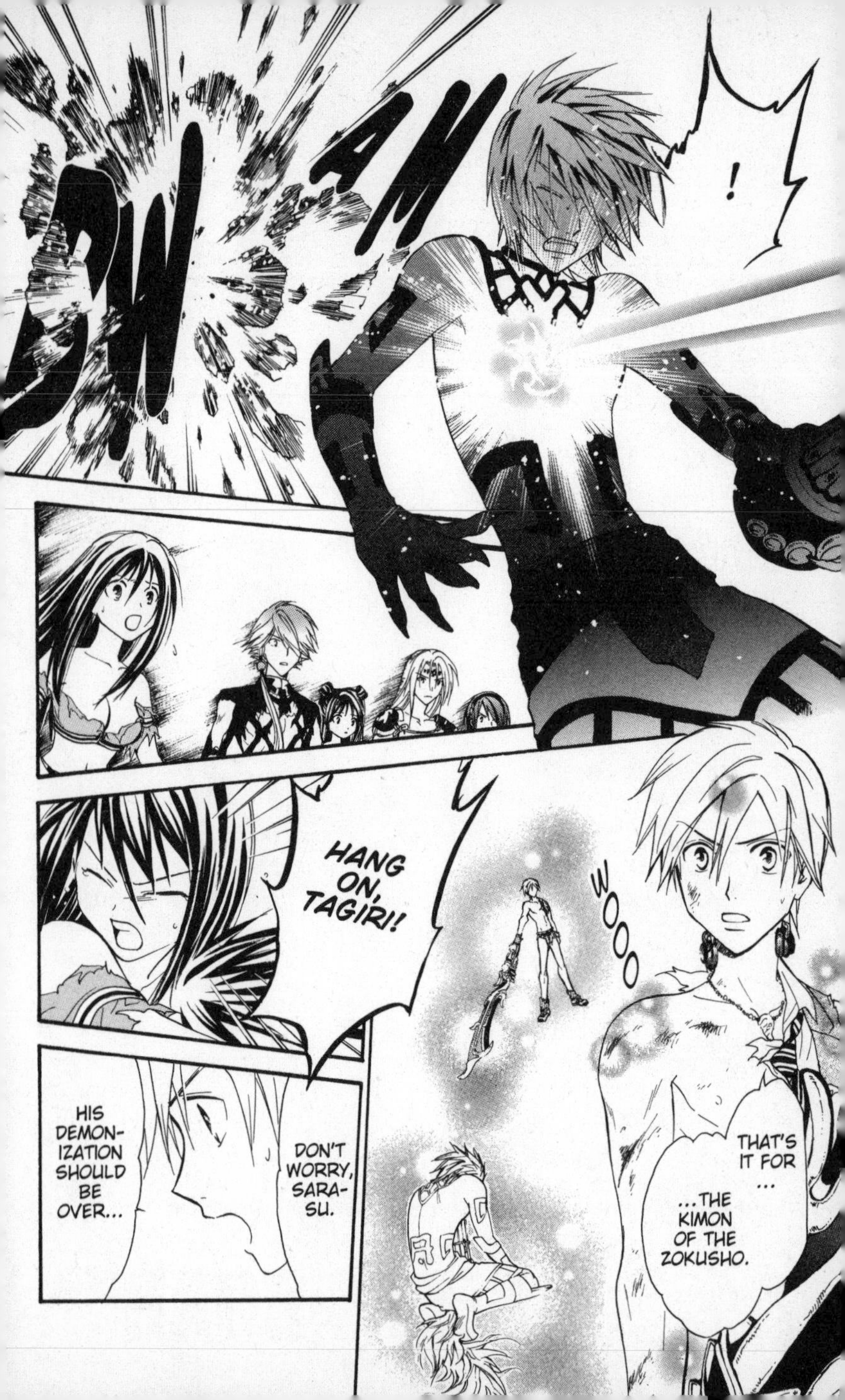
!
DWAM
WOOO
THAT'S IT FOR...
...THE KIMON OF THE ZOKUSHO.
HANG ON, TAGIRI!
DON'T WORRY, SARA-SU.
HIS DEMON-IZATION SHOULD BE OVER...

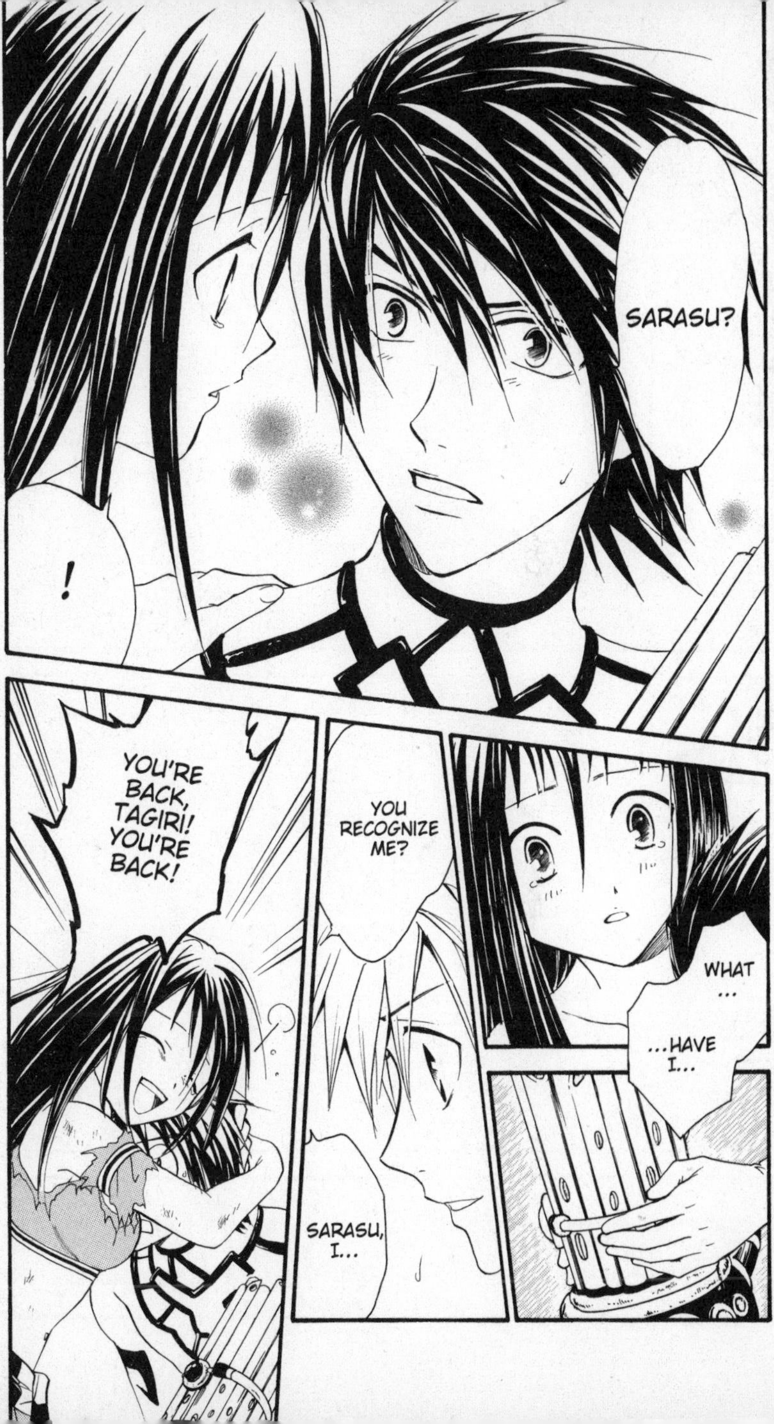
SARASU?
!
WHAT ...
...HAVE I...
YOU RECOGNIZE ME?
SARASU, I...
YOU'RE BACK, TAGIRI! YOU'RE BACK!

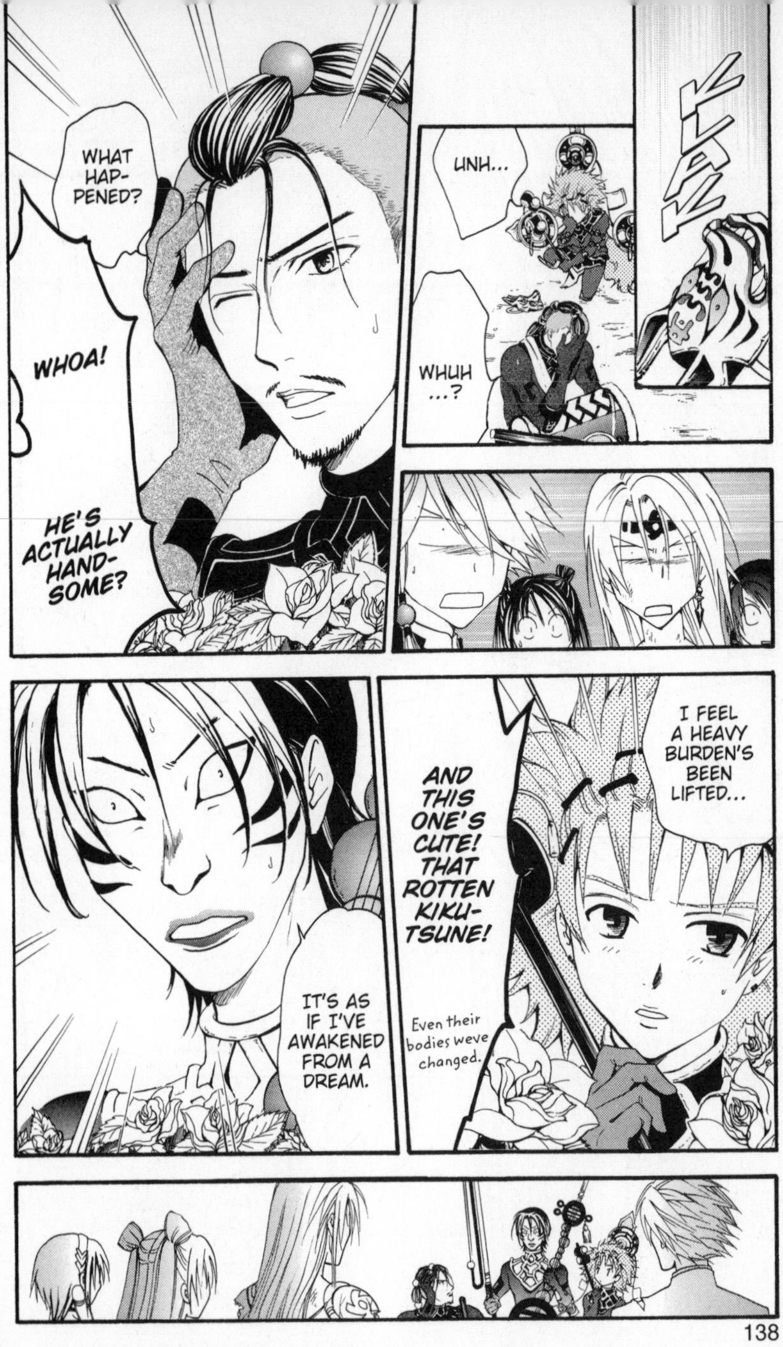
UNH...
WHUH ...?
WHAT HAP-PENED?
WHOA!
HE'S ACTUALLY HAND-SOME?
I FEEL A HEAVY BURDEN'S BEEN LIFTED...
AND THIS ONE'S CUTE! THAT ROTTEN KIKU-TSUNE!
Even their bodies weve changed.
IT'S AS IF I'VE AWAKENED FROM A DREAM.

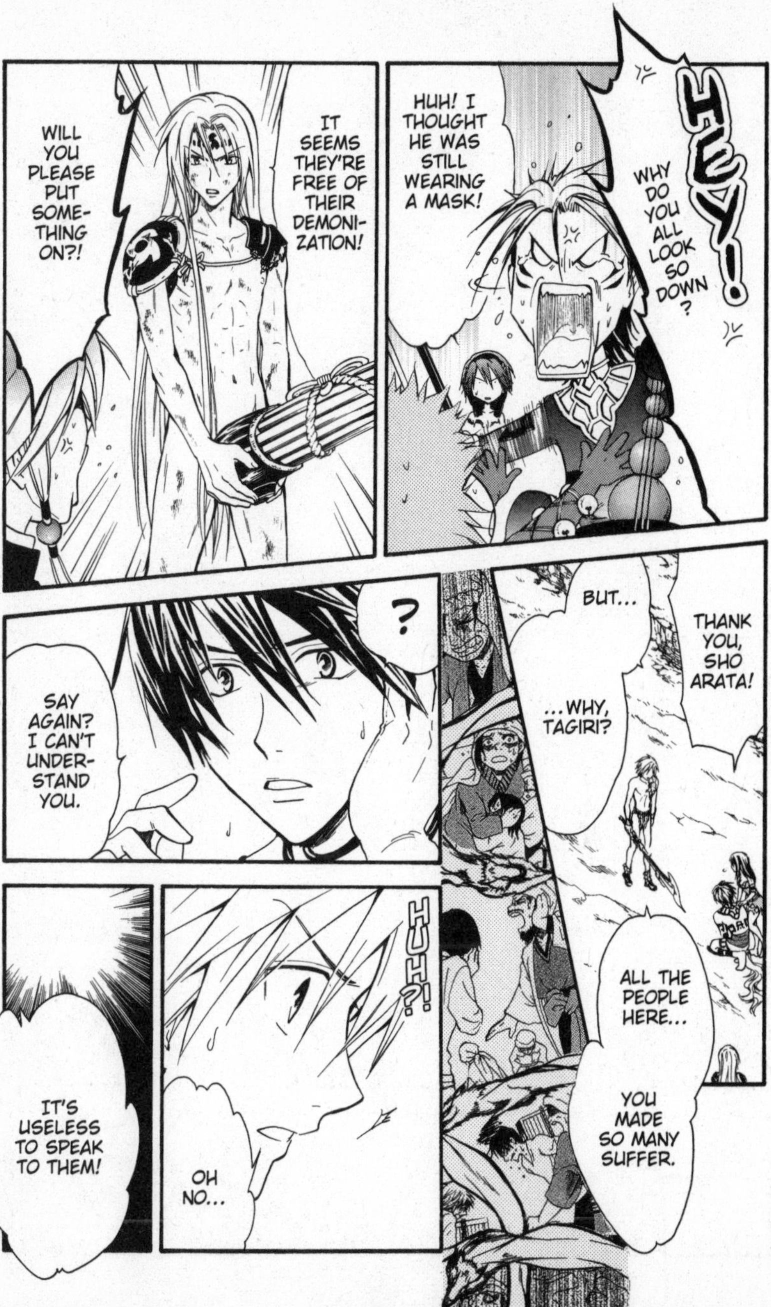
HEY!
WHY DO YOU ALL LOOK SO DOWN?
HUH! I THOUGHT HE WAS STILL WEARING A MASK!
IT SEEMS THEY'RE FREE OF THEIR DEMONIZATION!
WILL YOU PLEASE PUT SOME-THING ON?!
THANK YOU, SHO ARATA!
BUT...
...WHY, TAGIRI?
ALL THE PEOPLE HERE...
YOU MADE SO MANY SUFFER.
?
SAY AGAIN? I CAN'T UNDER-STAND YOU.
HUH?!
OH NO...
IT'S USELESS TO SPEAK TO THEM!

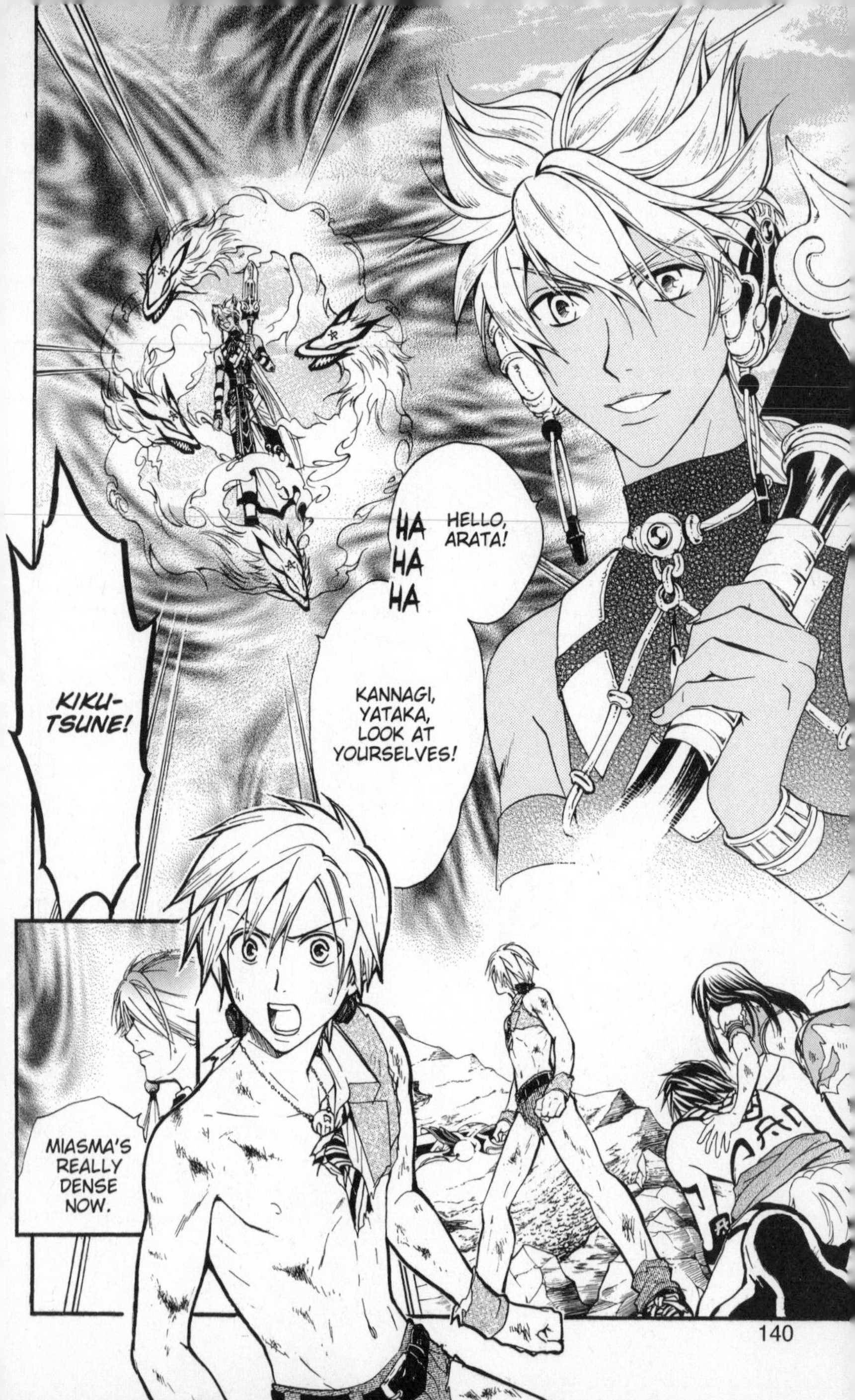
HELLO, ARATA!
HA HA HA
KANNAGI, YATAKA, LOOK AT YOURSELVES!
KIKU-TSUNE!
MIASMA'S REALLY DENSE NOW.

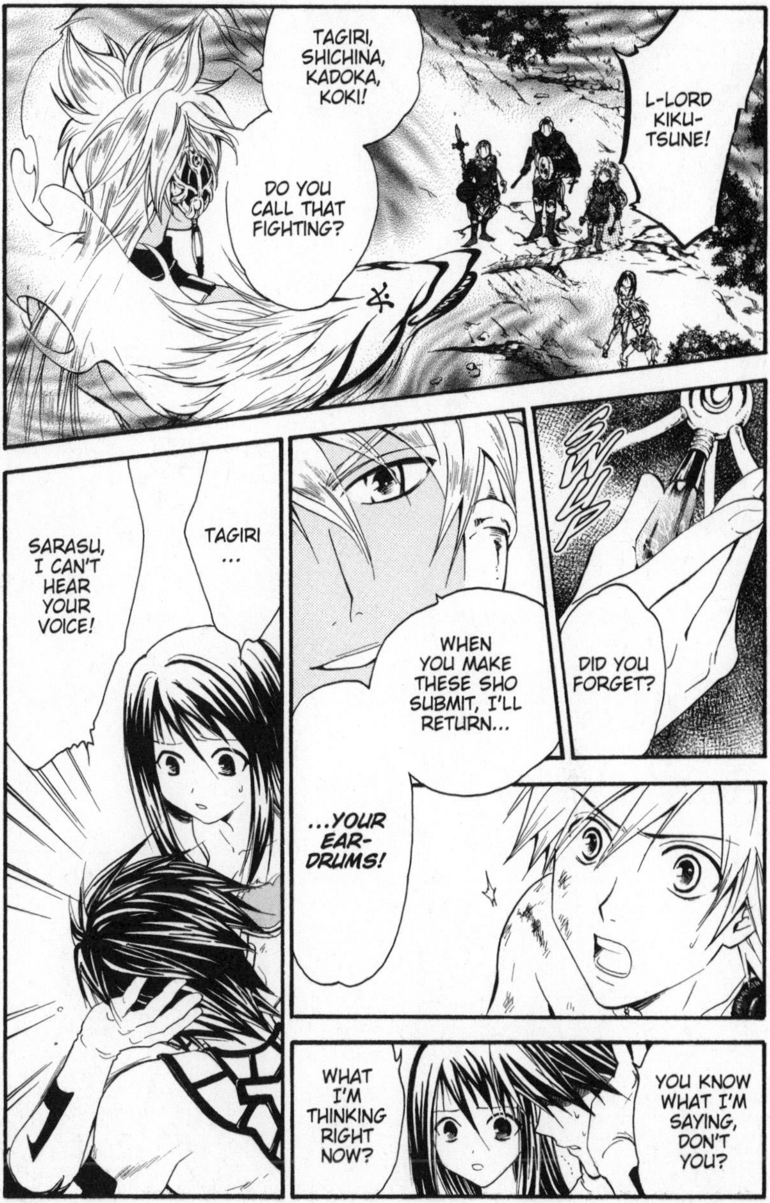
L-LORD KIKU-TSUNE!
TAGIRI, SHICHINA, KADOKA, KOKI!
DO YOU CALL THAT FIGHTING?
DID YOU FORGET?
WHEN YOU MAKE THESE SHO SUBMIT, I'LL RETURN...
...YOUR EAR-DRUMS!
YOU KNOW WHAT I'M SAYING, DON'T YOU?
WHAT I'M THINKING RIGHT NOW?
TAGIRI...
SARASU, I CAN'T HEAR YOUR VOICE!

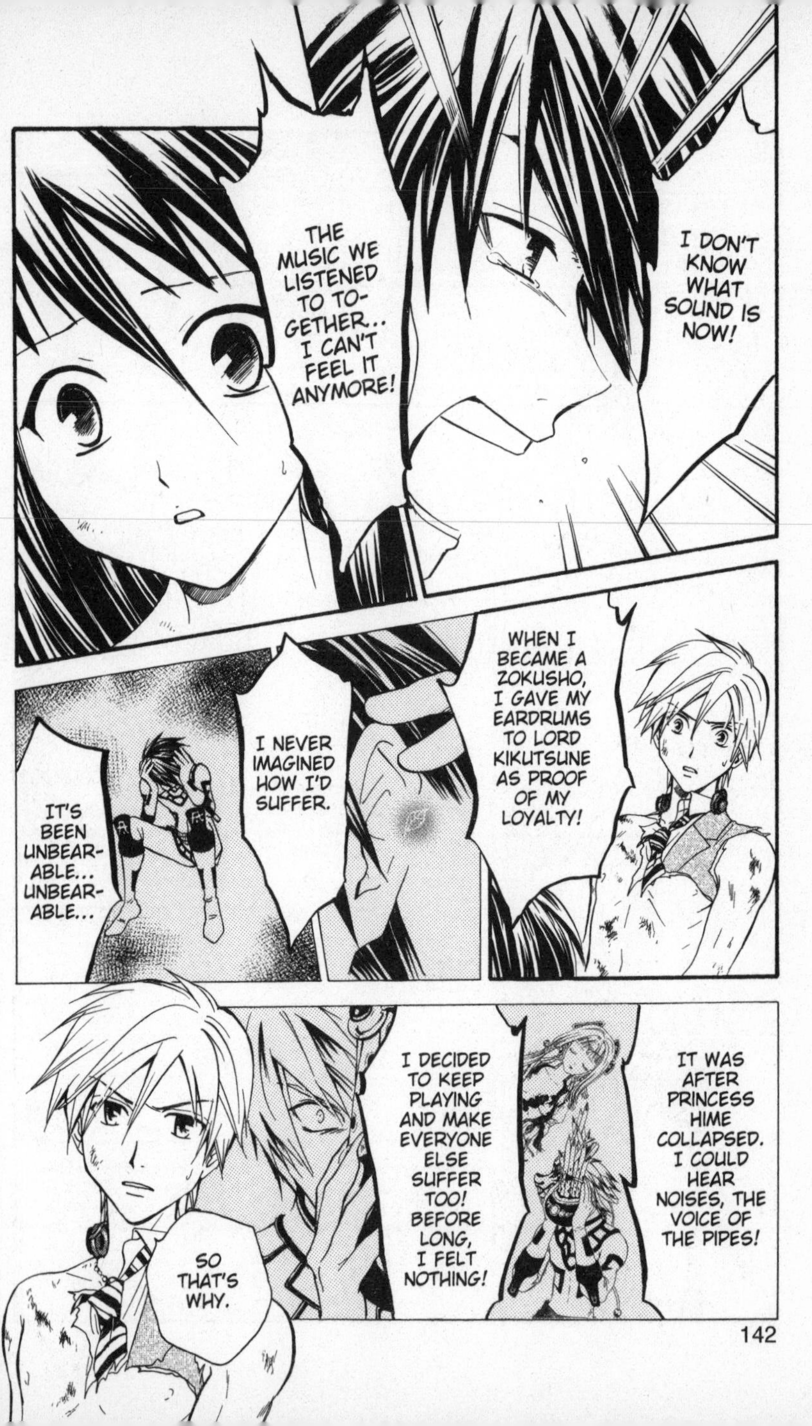
I DON'T KNOW WHAT SOUND IS NOW!
THE MUSIC WE LISTENED TO TO-GETHER... I CAN'T FEEL IT ANYMORE!
WHEN I BECAME A ZOKUSHO, I GAVE MY EARDRUMS TO LORD KIKUTSUNE AS PROOF OF MY LOYALTY!
I NEVER IMAGINED HOW I'D SUFFER.
IT'S BEEN UNBEAR-ABLE... UNBEAR-ABLE...
IT WAS AFTER PRINCESS HIME COLLAPSED. I COULD HEAR NOISES, THE VOICE OF THE PIPES!
I DECIDED TO KEEP PLAYING AND MAKE EVERYONE ELSE SUFFER TOO! BEFORE LONG, I FELT NOTHING!
SO THAT'S WHY.

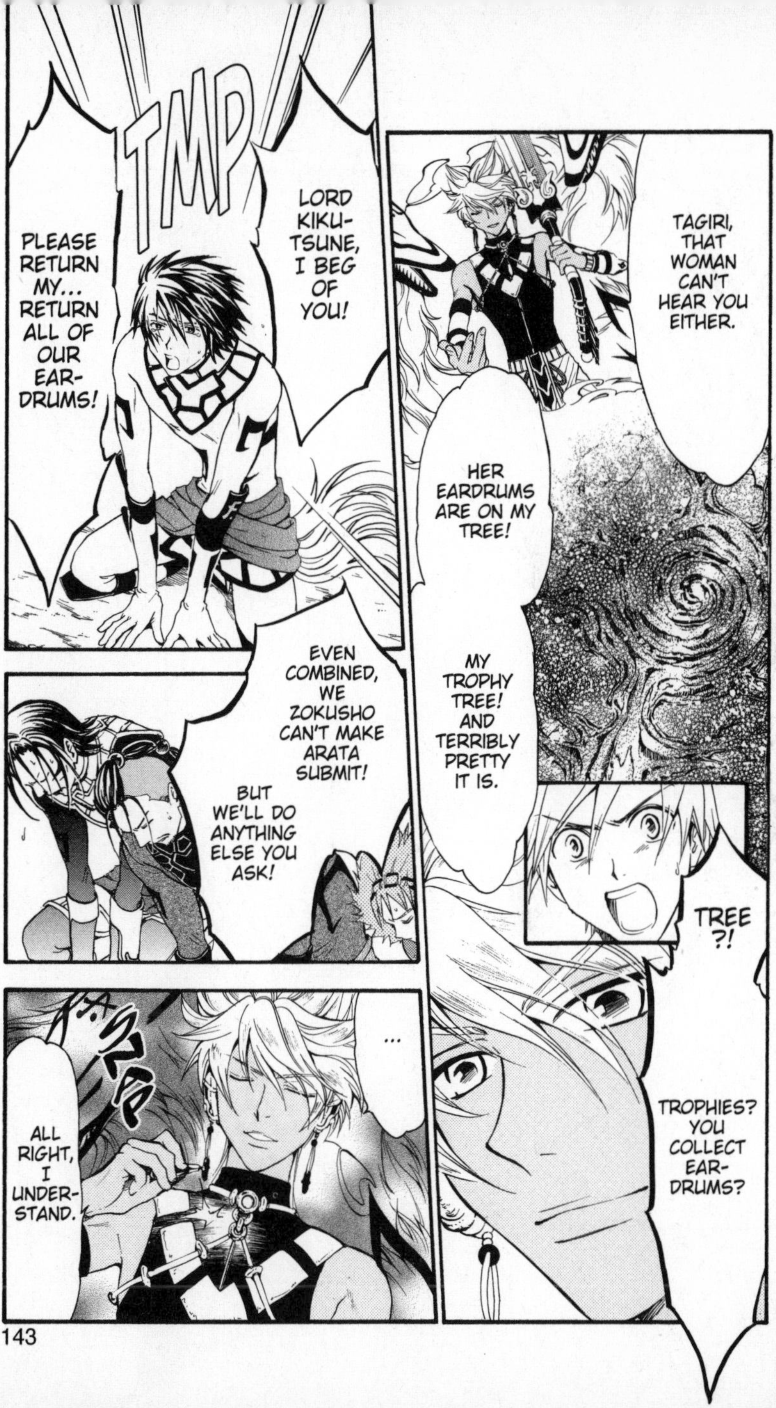
TAGIRI, THAT WOMAN CAN'T HEAR YOU EITHER.
HER EARDRUMS ARE ON MY TREE!
MY TROPHY TREE! AND TERRIBLY PRETTY IT IS.
TREE ?!
TROPHIES? YOU COLLECT EAR-DRUMS?
TMP
LORD KIKU-TSUNE, I BEG OF YOU!
PLEASE RETURN MY... RETURN ALL OF OUR EAR-DRUMS!
EVEN COMBINED, WE ZOKUSHO CAN'T MAKE ARATA SUBMIT!
BUT WE'LL DO ANYTHING ELSE YOU ASK!
...
SNAP
ALL RIGHT, I UNDERSTAND.

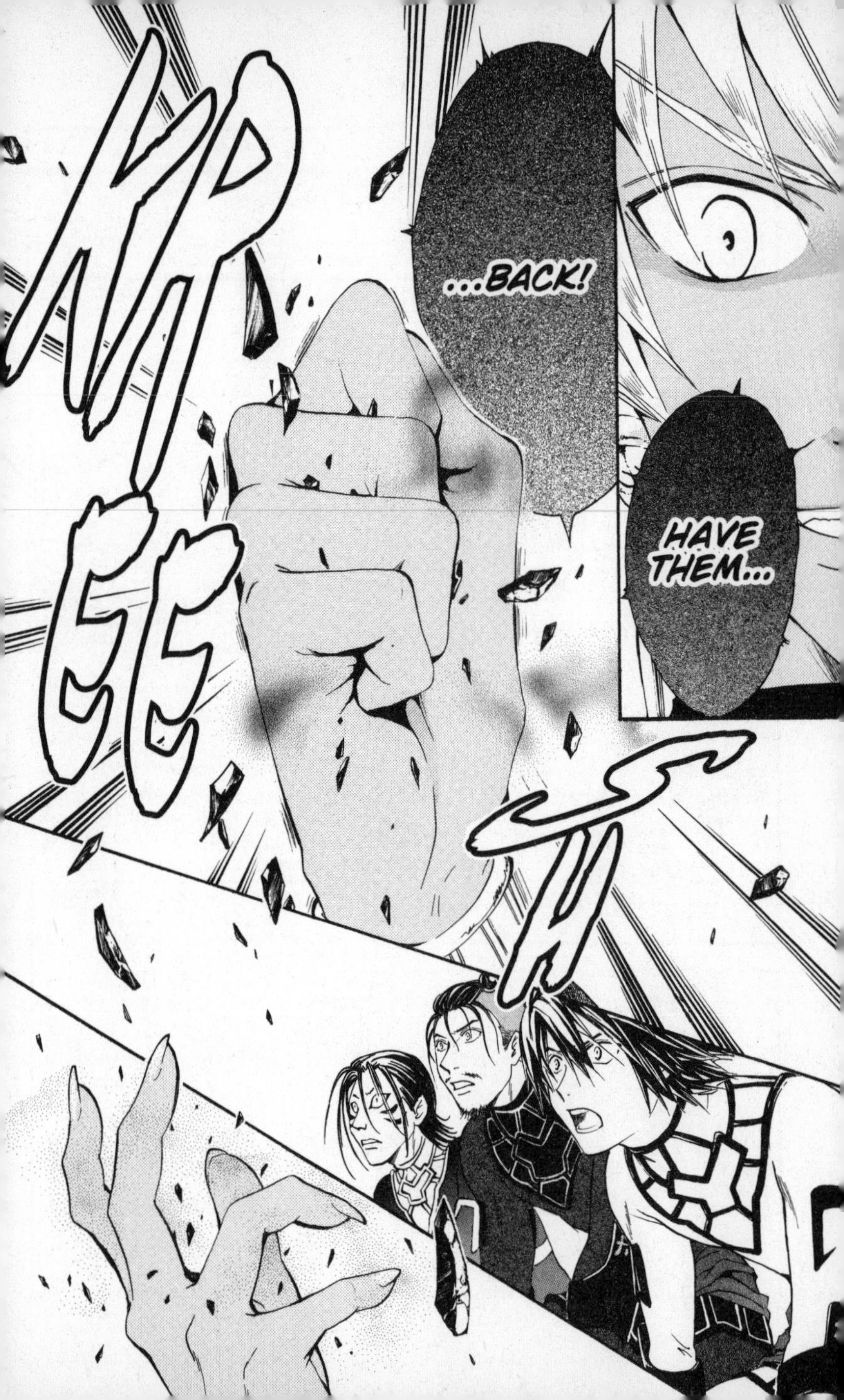
HAVE THEM...
...BACK!

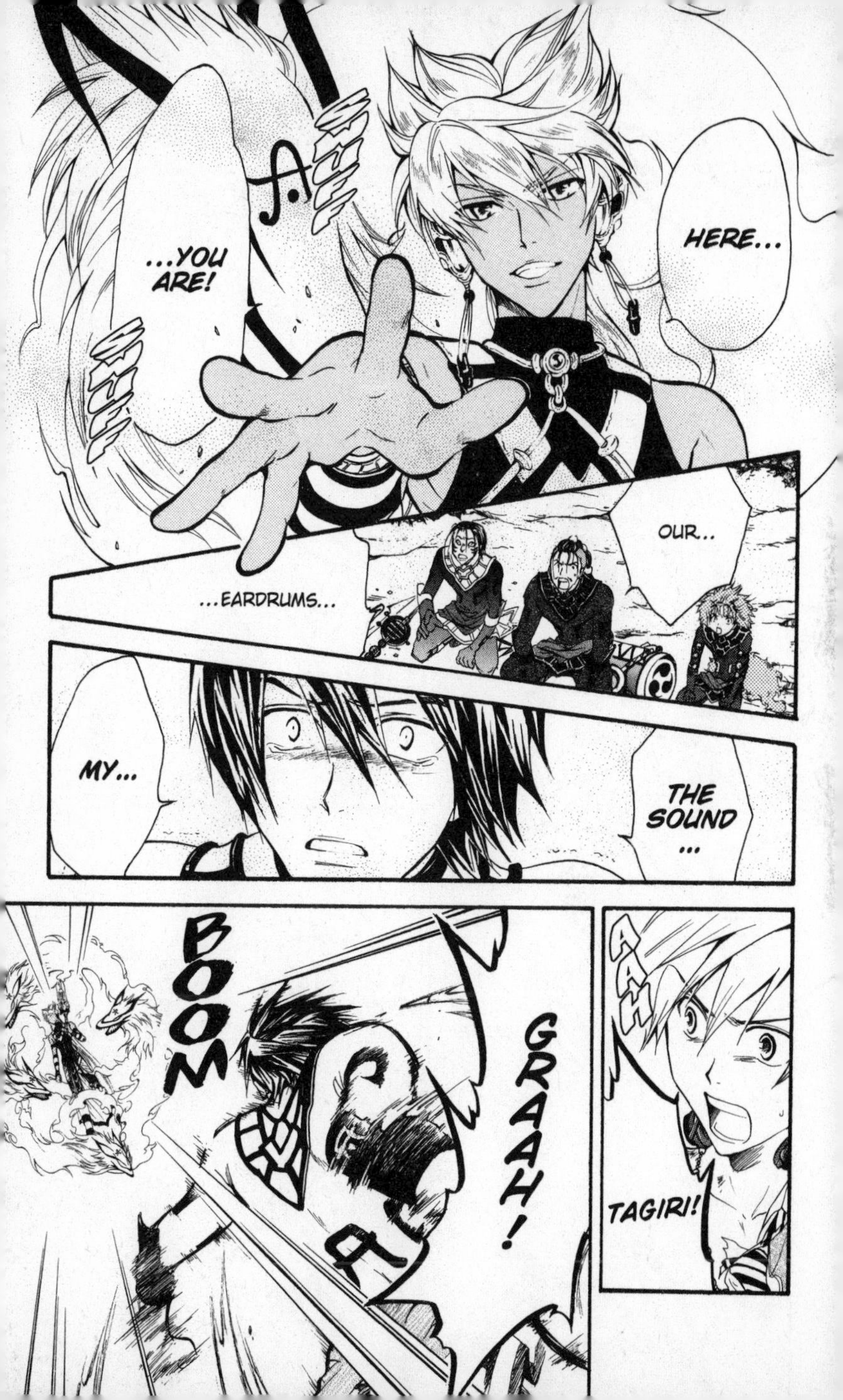
HERE...
...YOU ARE!
OUR...
...EARDRUMS...
THE SOUND ...
MY...
AAH
TAGIRI!
GRAAH!
BOOM

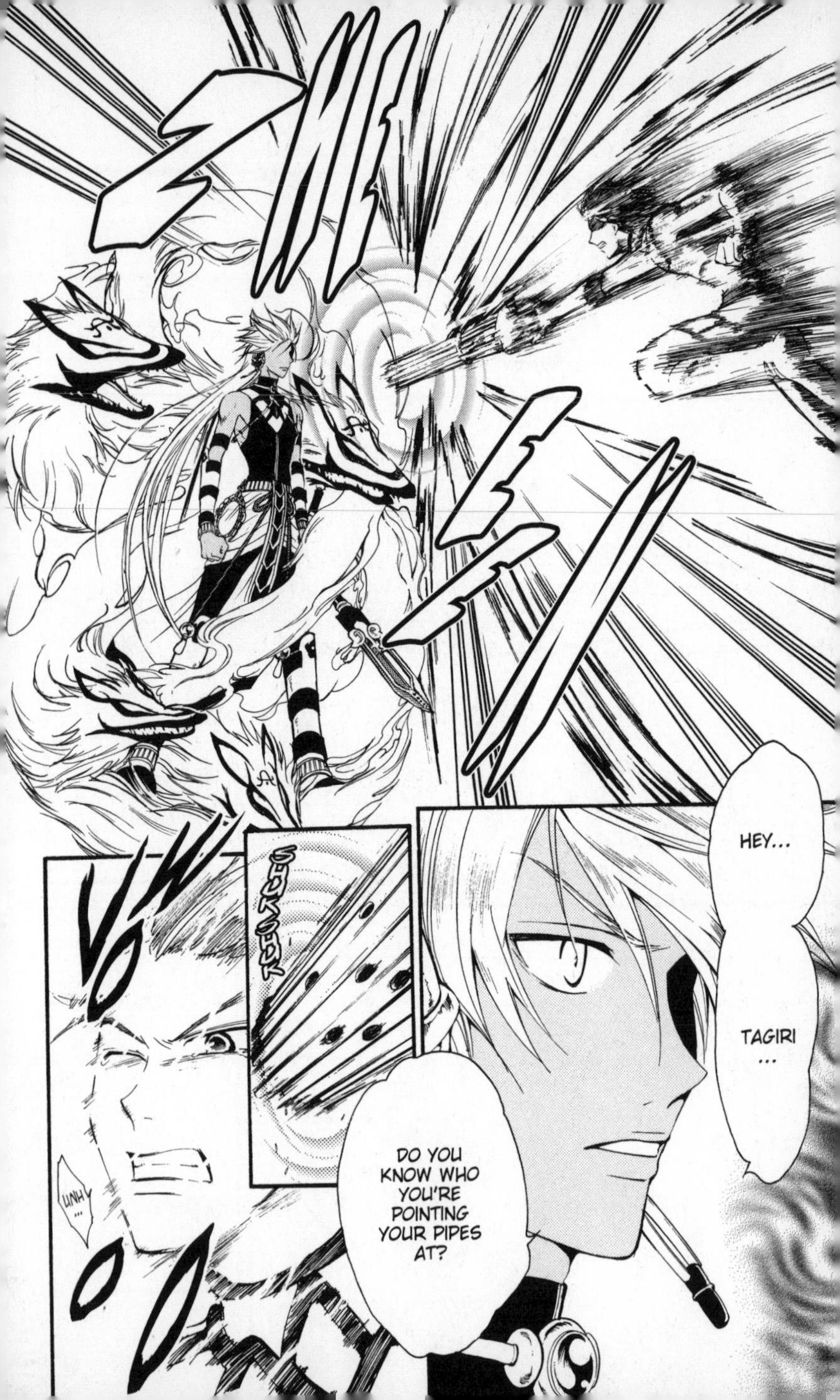
HEY...
TAGIRI ...
DO YOU KNOW WHO YOU'RE POINTING YOUR PIPES AT?
UNH ...

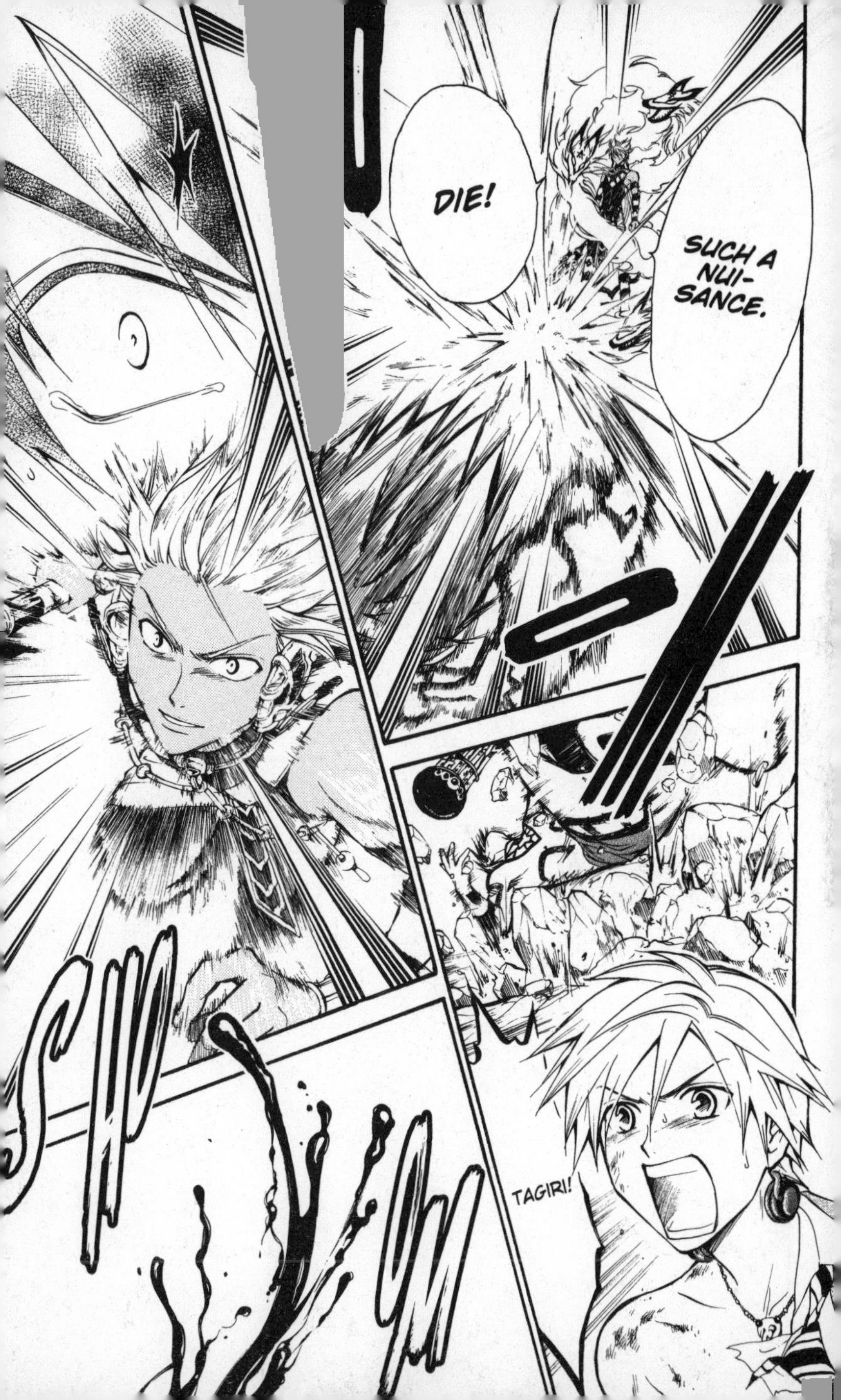
SUCH A NUI-SANCE.
DIE!
TAGIRI!

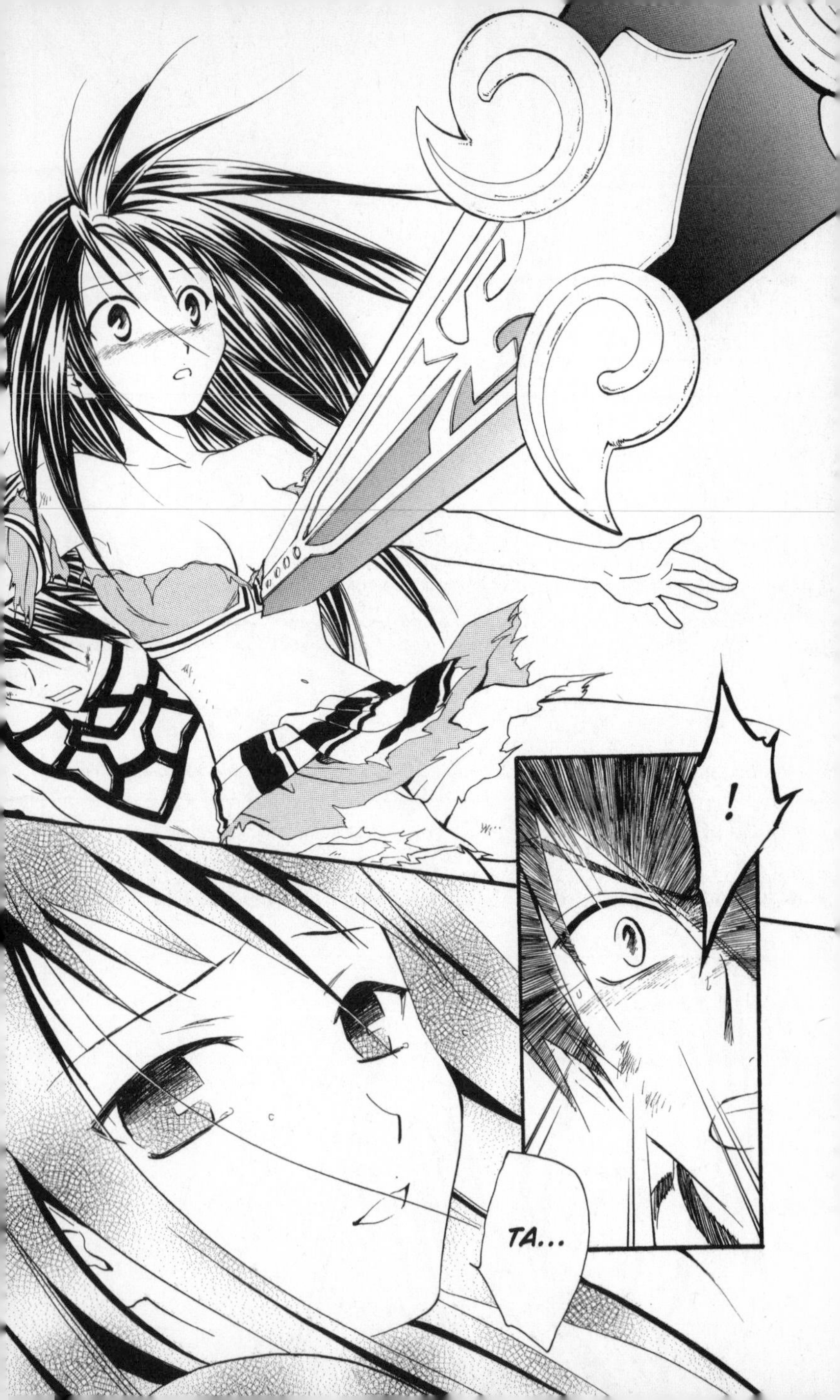
!
TA...

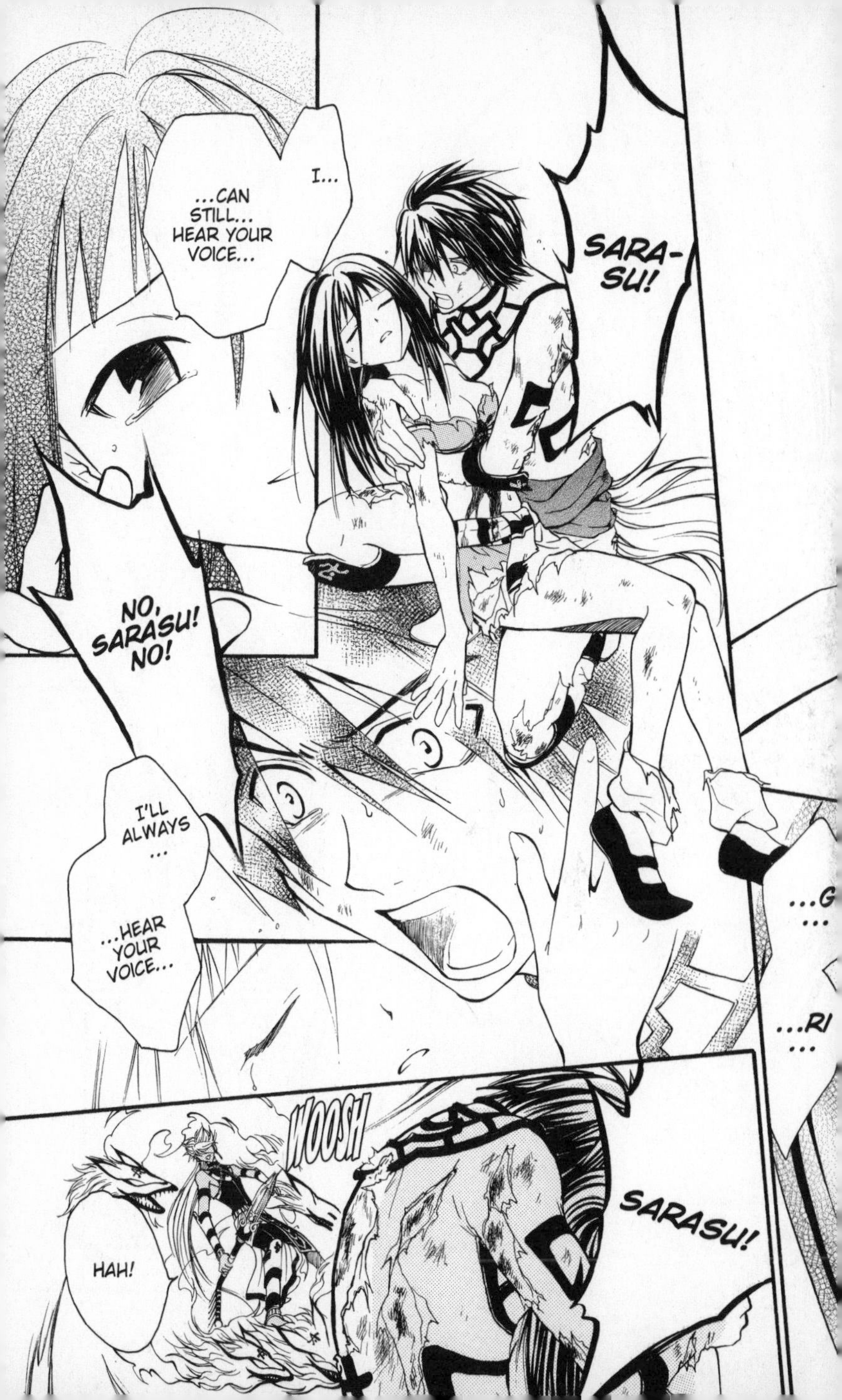
SARA-SU!
I...
...CAN STILL... HEAR YOUR VOICE...
NO, SARASU! NO!
...G...
...RI...
I'LL ALWAYS...
...HEAR YOUR VOICE...
SARASU!
WOOSH
HAH!

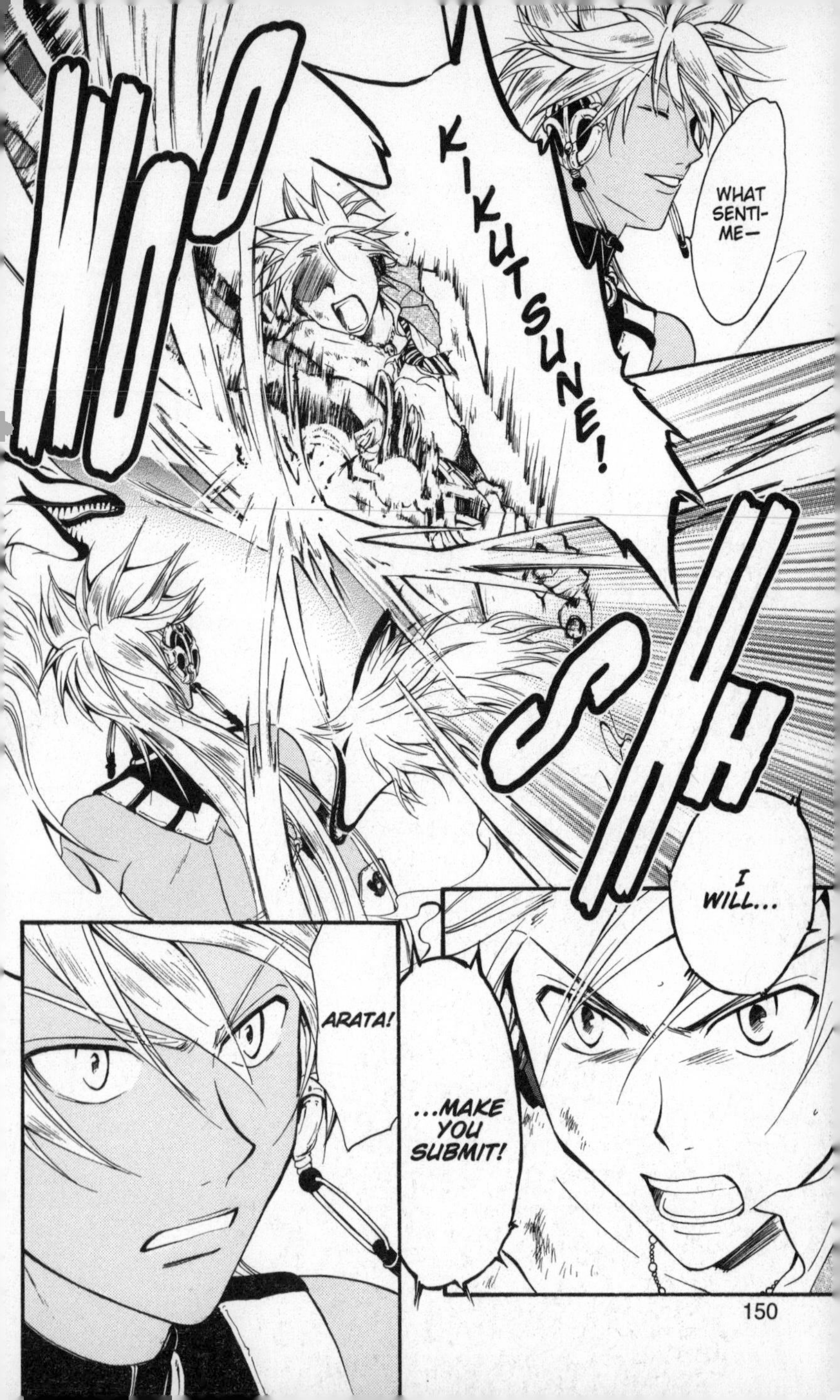
WHAT SENTI-ME—
KIKUTSUNE!
I WILL...
...MAKE YOU SUBMIT!
ARATA!

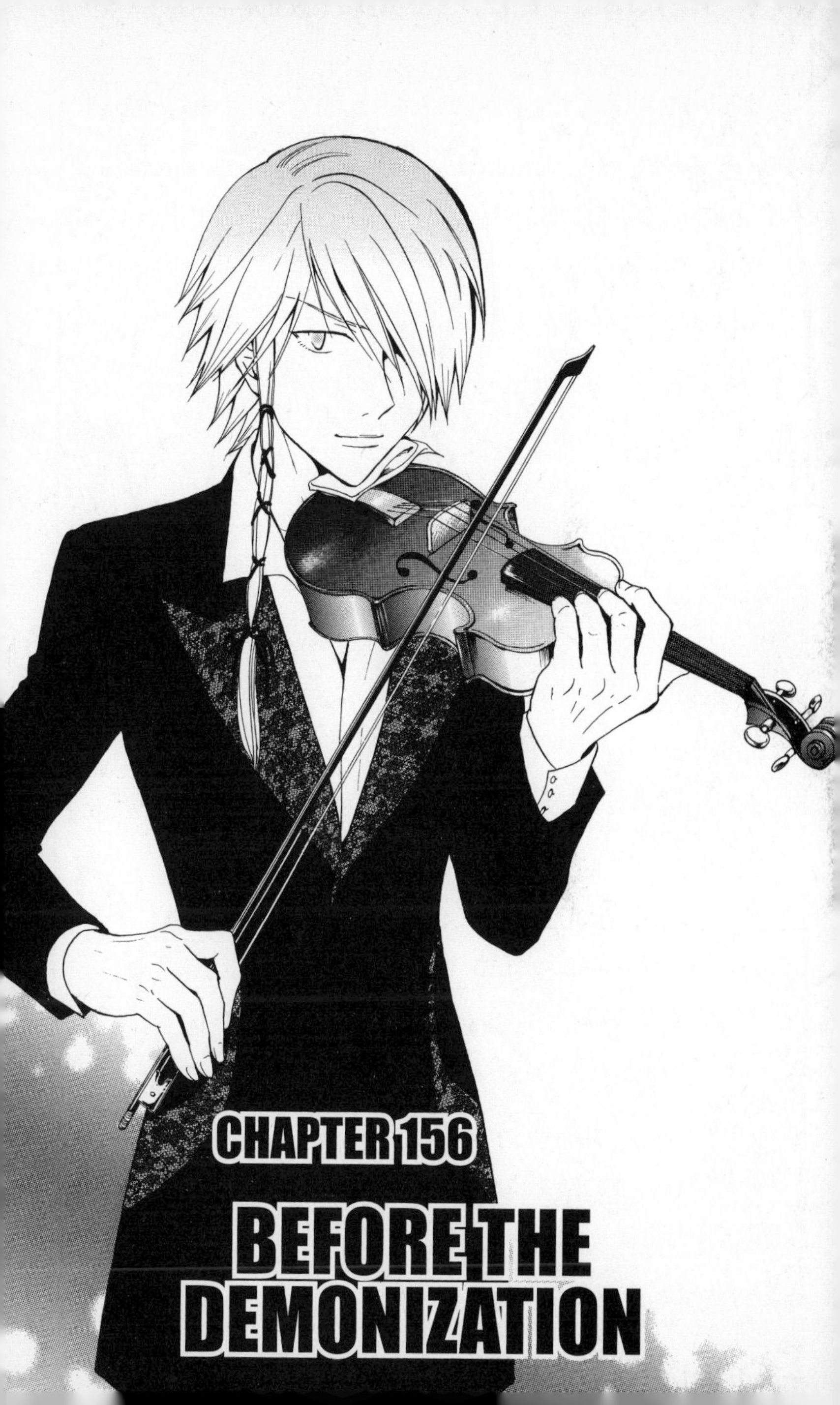
CHAPTER 156
BEFORE THE DEMONIZATION

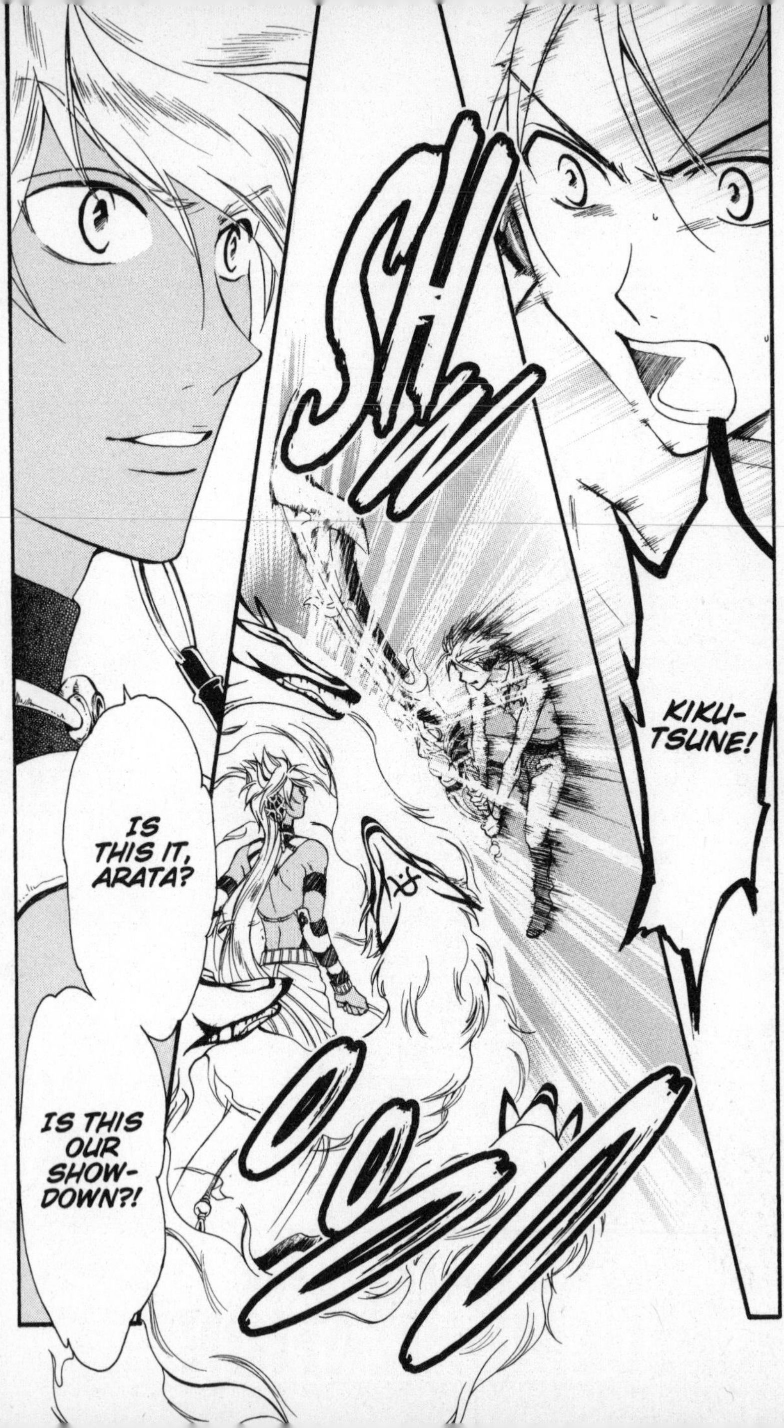
KIKU-TSUNE!
SH
IS THIS IT, ARATA?
IS THIS OUR SHOW-DOWN?!

Gift Order Card

Title: Arata The Legend #16

Agency: LV

☐ Adult ☐ Juv ☒ YA ☐ Ref

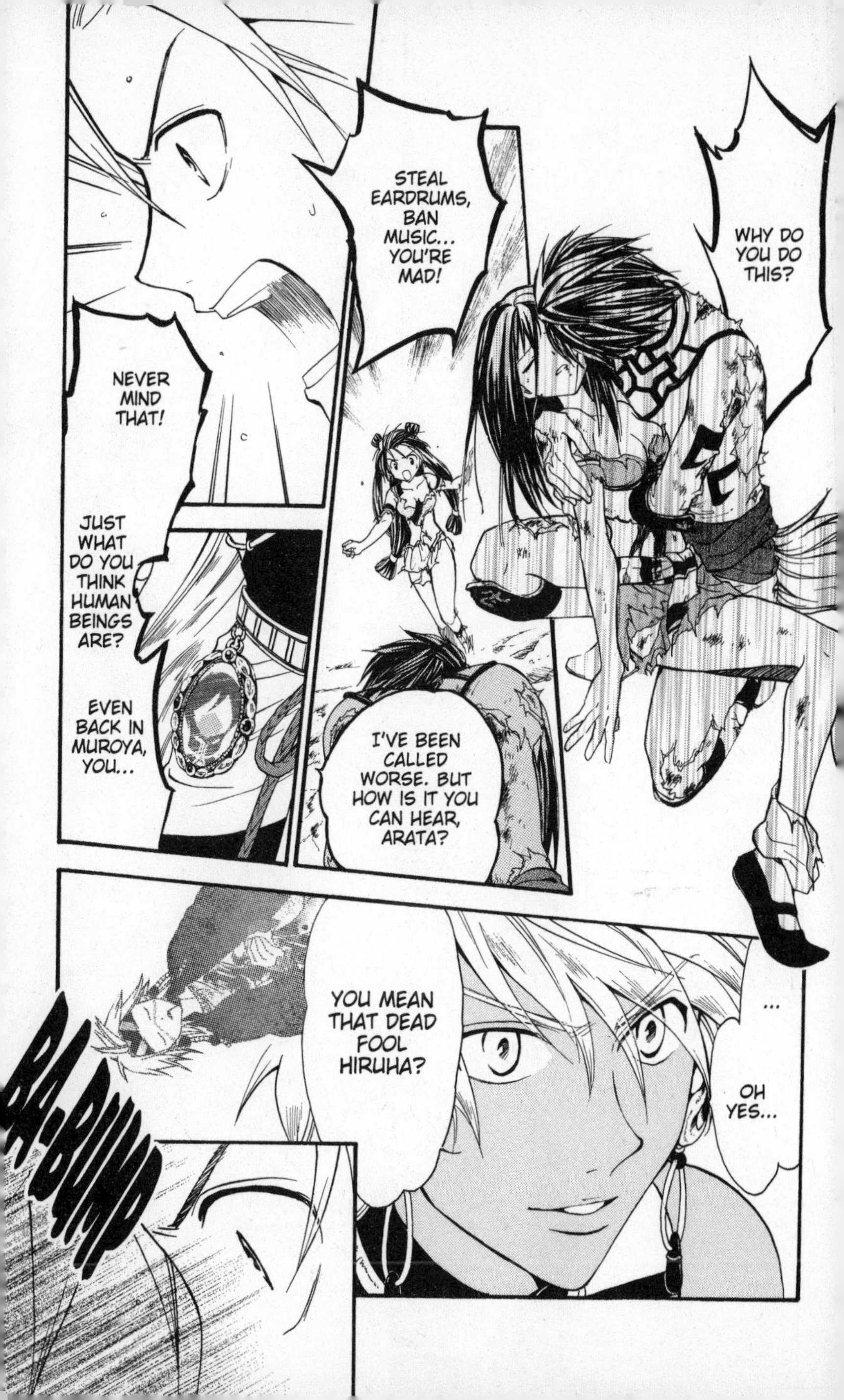
WHY DO YOU DO THIS?
STEAL EARDRUMS, BAN MUSIC... YOU'RE MAD!
I'VE BEEN CALLED WORSE. BUT HOW IS IT YOU CAN HEAR, ARATA?
NEVER MIND THAT!
JUST WHAT DO YOU THINK HUMAN BEINGS ARE?
EVEN BACK IN MUROYA, YOU...
...
OH YES...
YOU MEAN THAT DEAD FOOL HIRUHA?
BA-BUMP

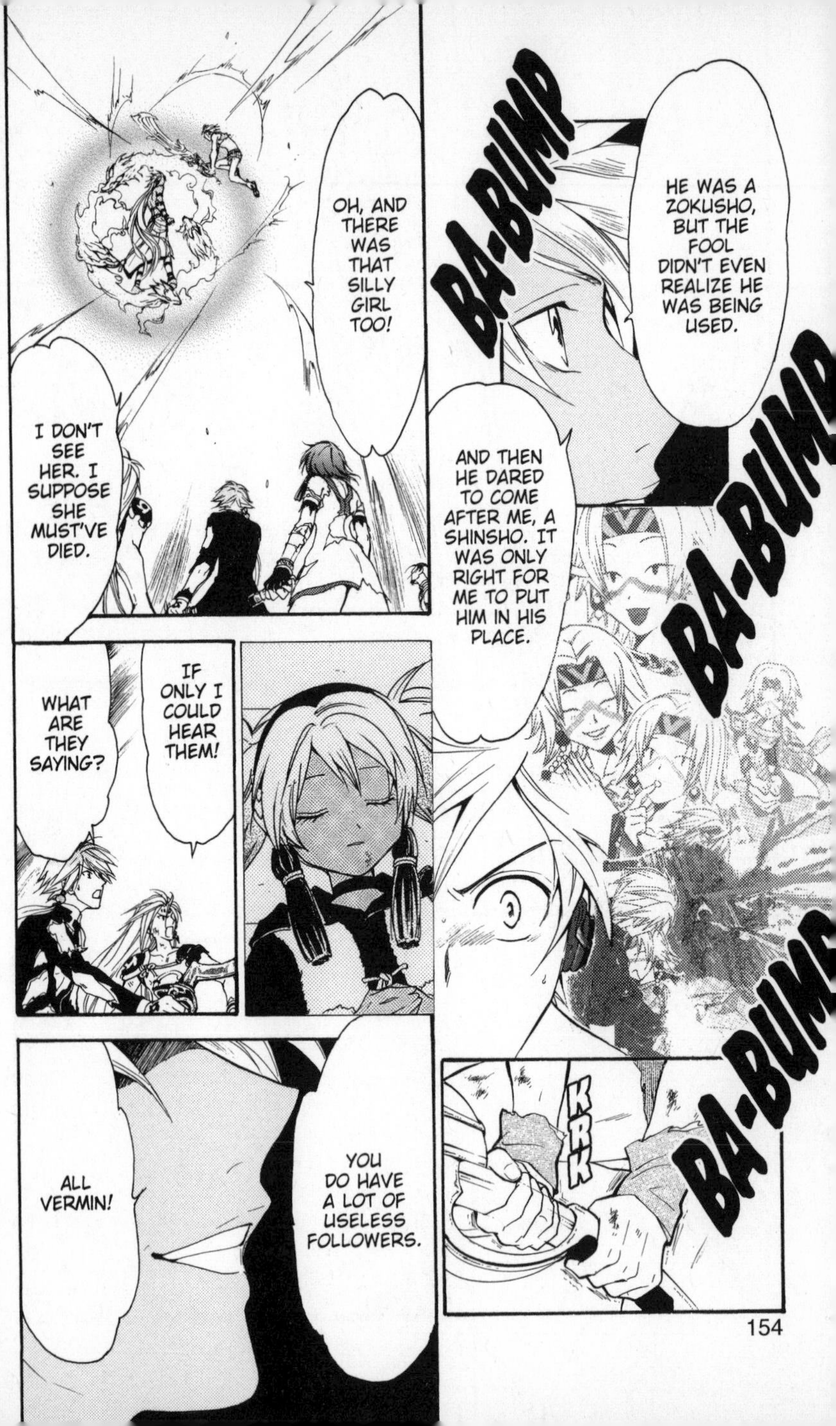
BA-BUMP
HE WAS A ZOKUSHO, BUT THE FOOL DIDN'T EVEN REALIZE HE WAS BEING USED.
AND THEN HE DARED TO COME AFTER ME, A SHINSHO. IT WAS ONLY RIGHT FOR ME TO PUT HIM IN HIS PLACE.
BA-BUMP
BA-BUMP
OH, AND THERE WAS THAT SILLY GIRL TOO!
I DON'T SEE HER. I SUPPOSE SHE MUST'VE DIED.
IF ONLY I COULD HEAR THEM!
WHAT ARE THEY SAYING?
BA-BUMP
KRK
YOU DO HAVE A LOT OF USELESS FOLLOWERS.
ALL VERMIN!

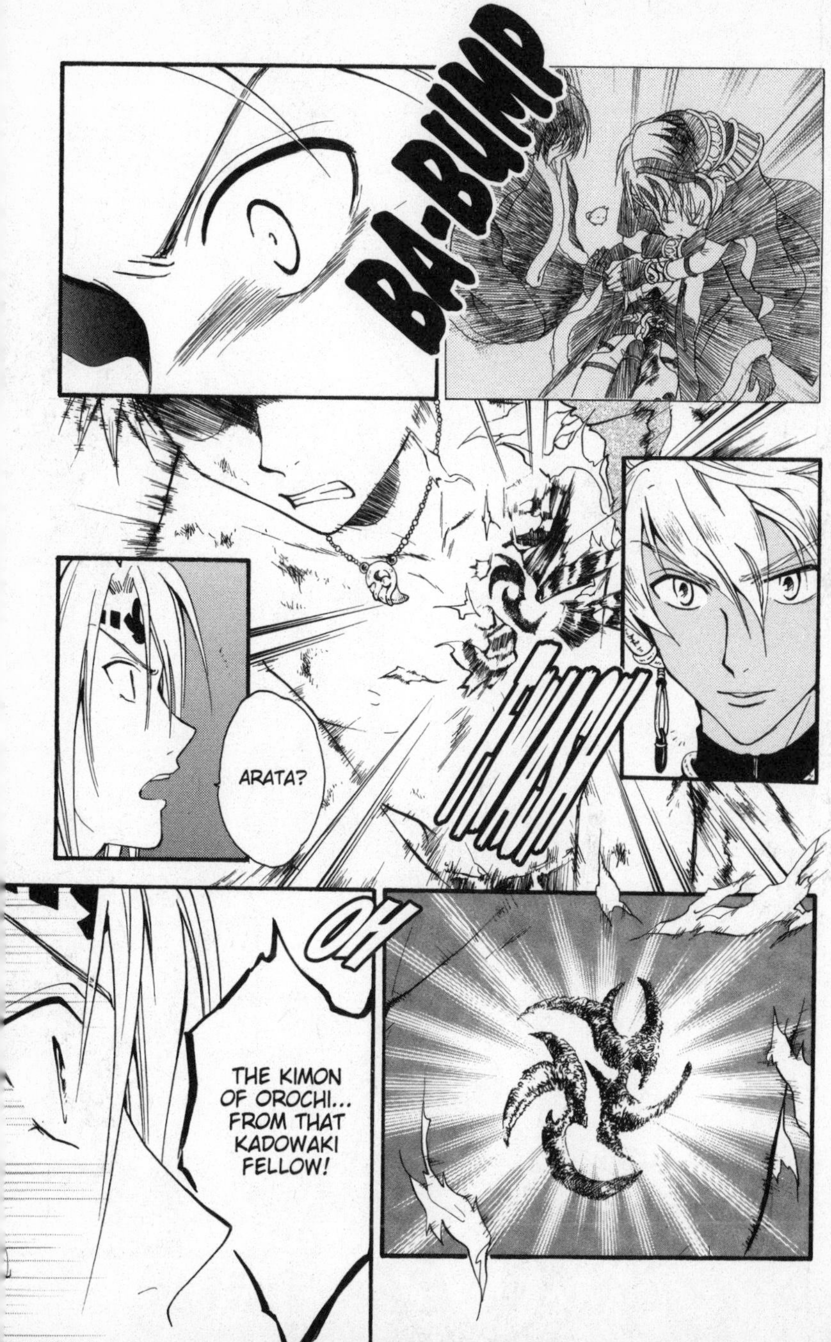
BA-BUMP
ARATA?
OH
THE KIMON OF OROCHI... FROM THAT KADOWAKI FELLOW!

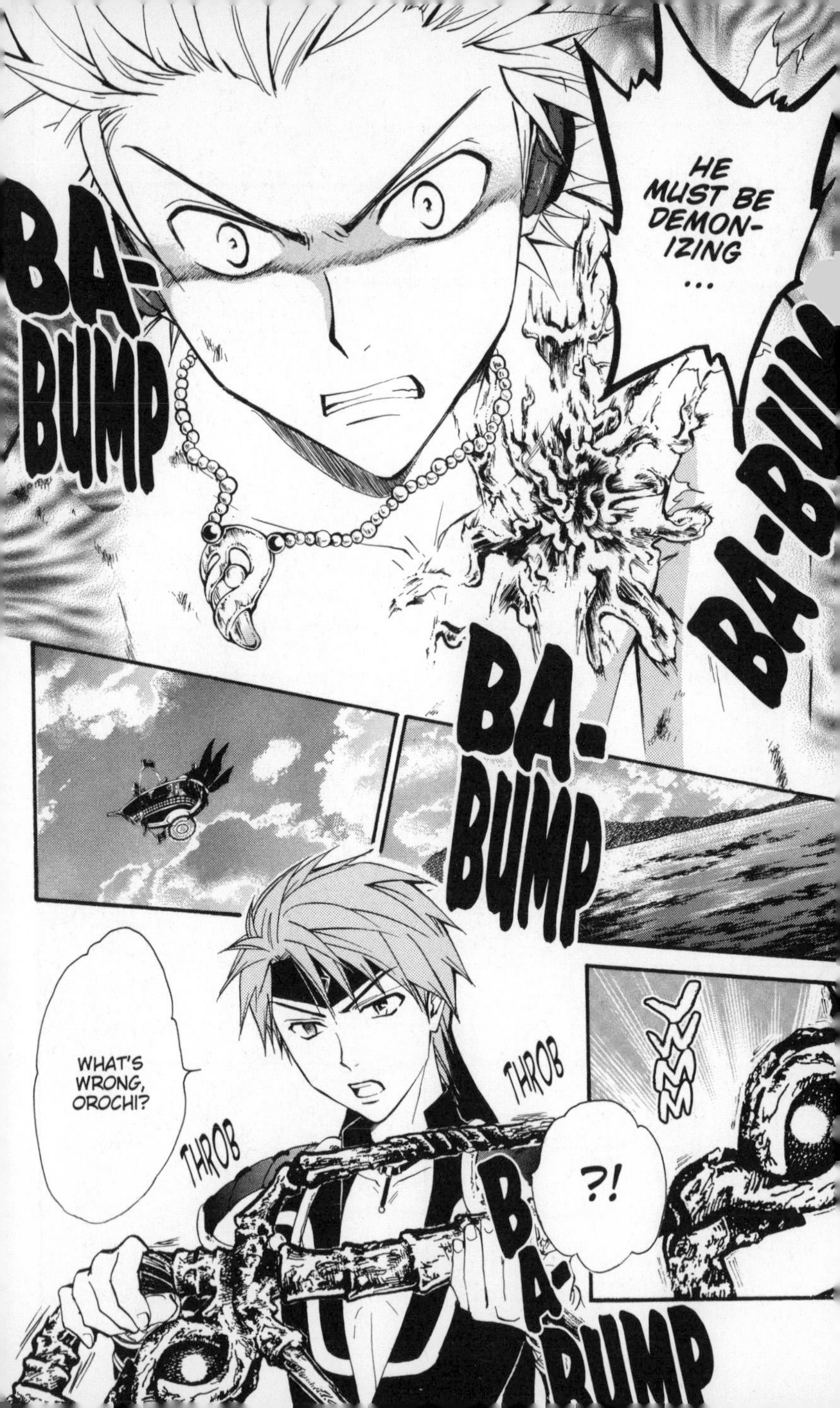

HE MUST BE DEMON-IZING ...
BA-BU
BA-BUMP
BA-BUMP
?!
THROB
WHAT'S WRONG, OROCHI?
THROB
BA-

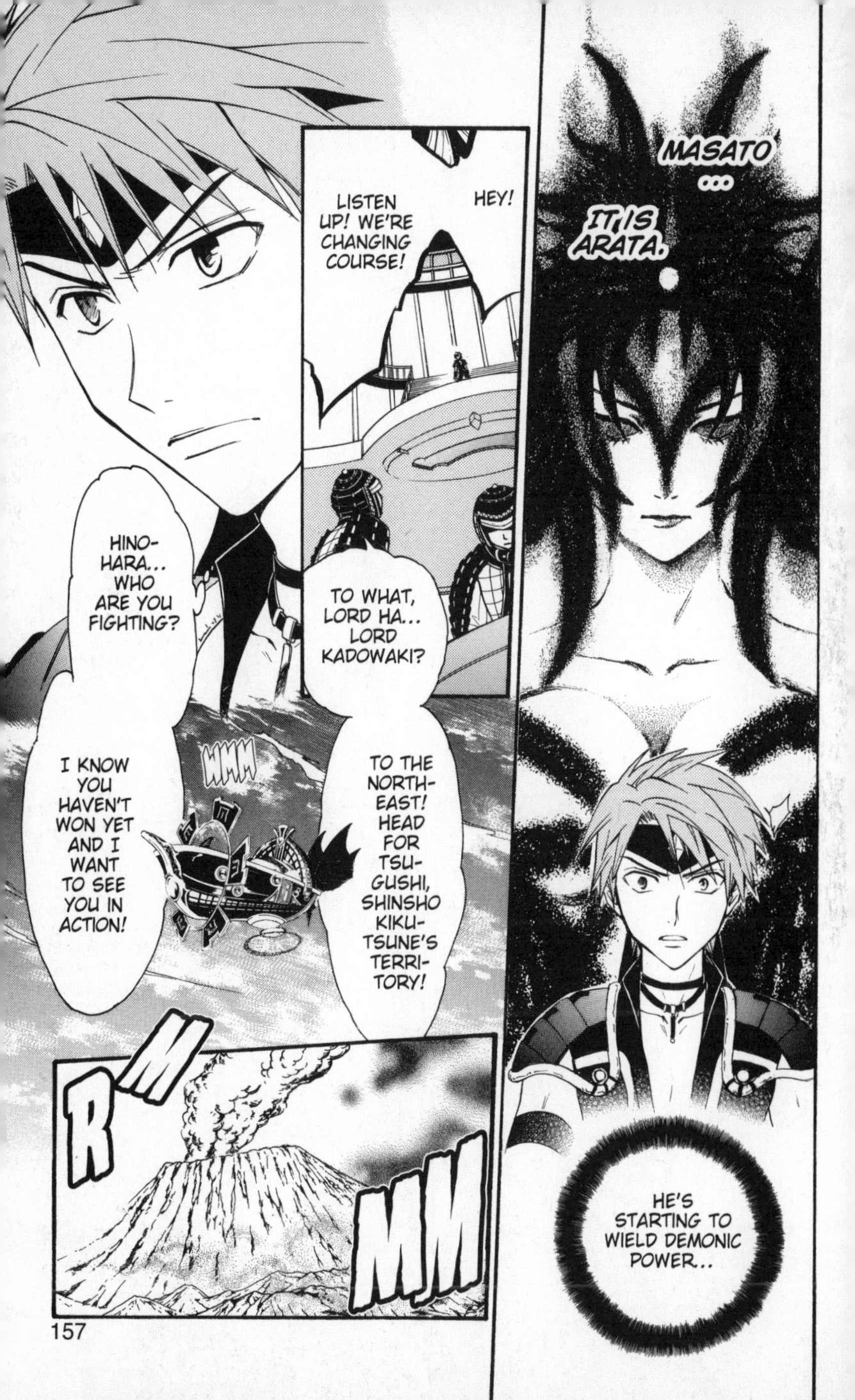
MASATO...
IT IS ARATA.
HE'S STARTING TO WIELD DEMONIC POWER...
HEY!
LISTEN UP! WE'RE CHANGING COURSE!
TO WHAT, LORD HA... LORD KADOWAKI?
HINO-HARA... WHO ARE YOU FIGHTING?
TO THE NORTH-EAST! HEAD FOR TSU-GUSHI, SHINSHO KIKU-TSUNE'S TERRI-TORY!
I KNOW YOU HAVEN'T WON YET AND I WANT TO SEE YOU IN ACTION!
WMM
RMMM

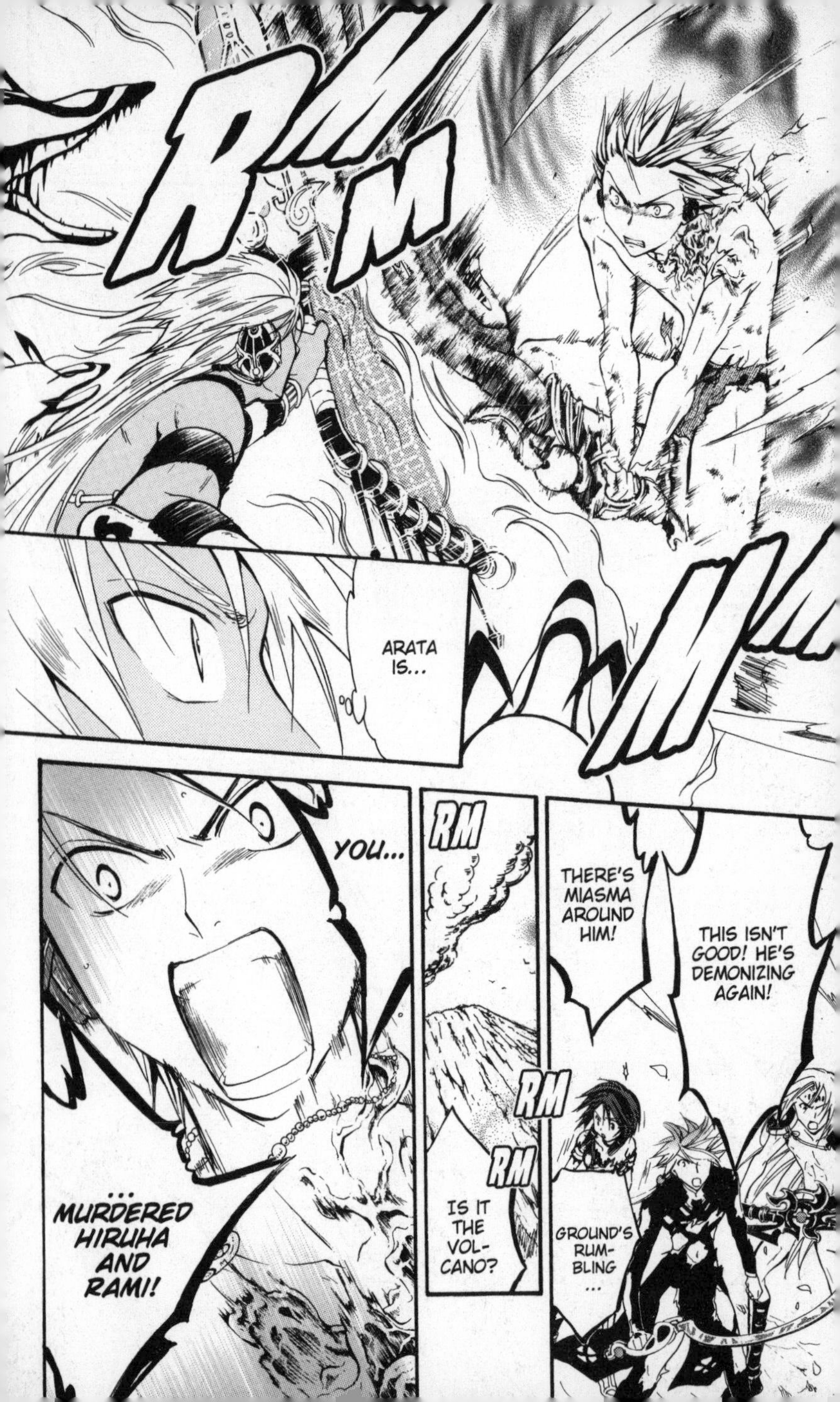
ARATA IS...
THIS ISN'T GOOD! HE'S DEMONIZING AGAIN!
THERE'S MIASMA AROUND HIM!
RM
RM
GROUND'S RUM- BLING ...
RM
IS IT THE VOL- CANO?
YOU...
... MURDERED HIRUHA AND RAMI!

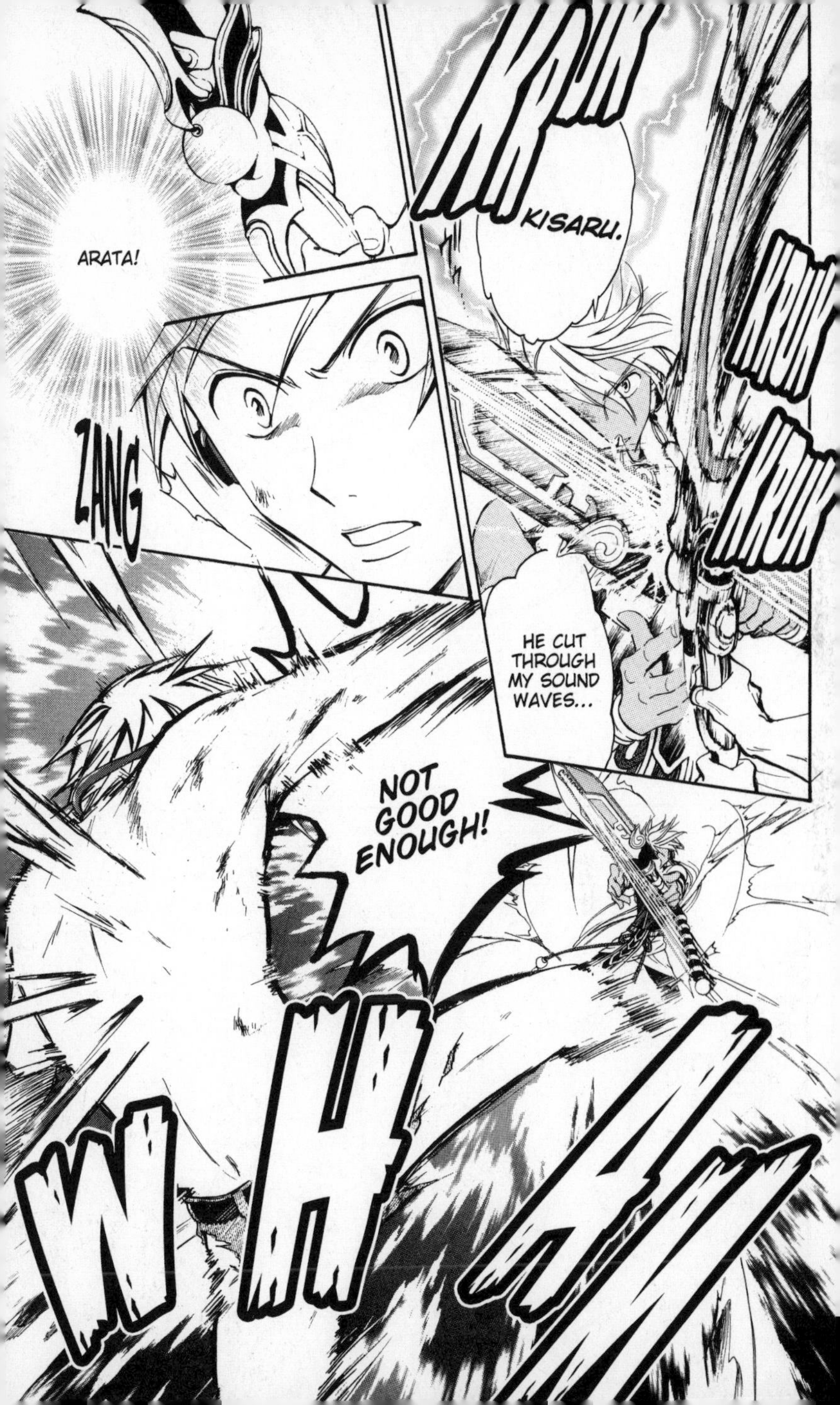
KRUK
KISARU.
KRUK
KRUK
HE CUT THROUGH MY SOUND WAVES...
ARATA!
ZANG
NOT GOOD ENOUGH!
WHAM

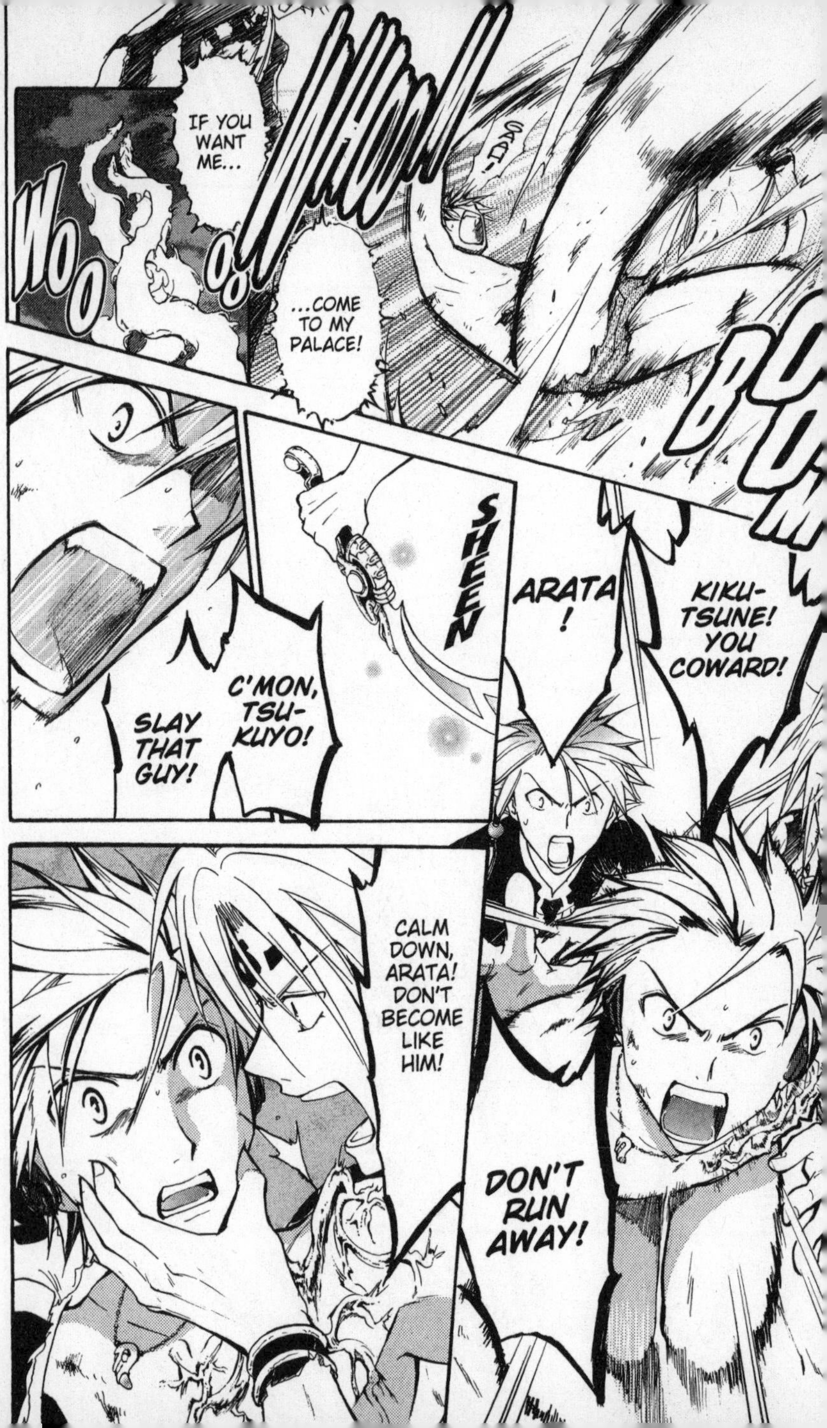
IF YOU WANT ME...
WHOOOO!!
...COME TO MY PALACE!
BOOM
KIKU-TSUNE! YOU COWARD!
ARATA!
SHEEN
C'MON, TSU-KUYO!
SLAY THAT GUY!
DON'T RUN AWAY!
CALM DOWN, ARATA! DON'T BECOME LIKE HIM!

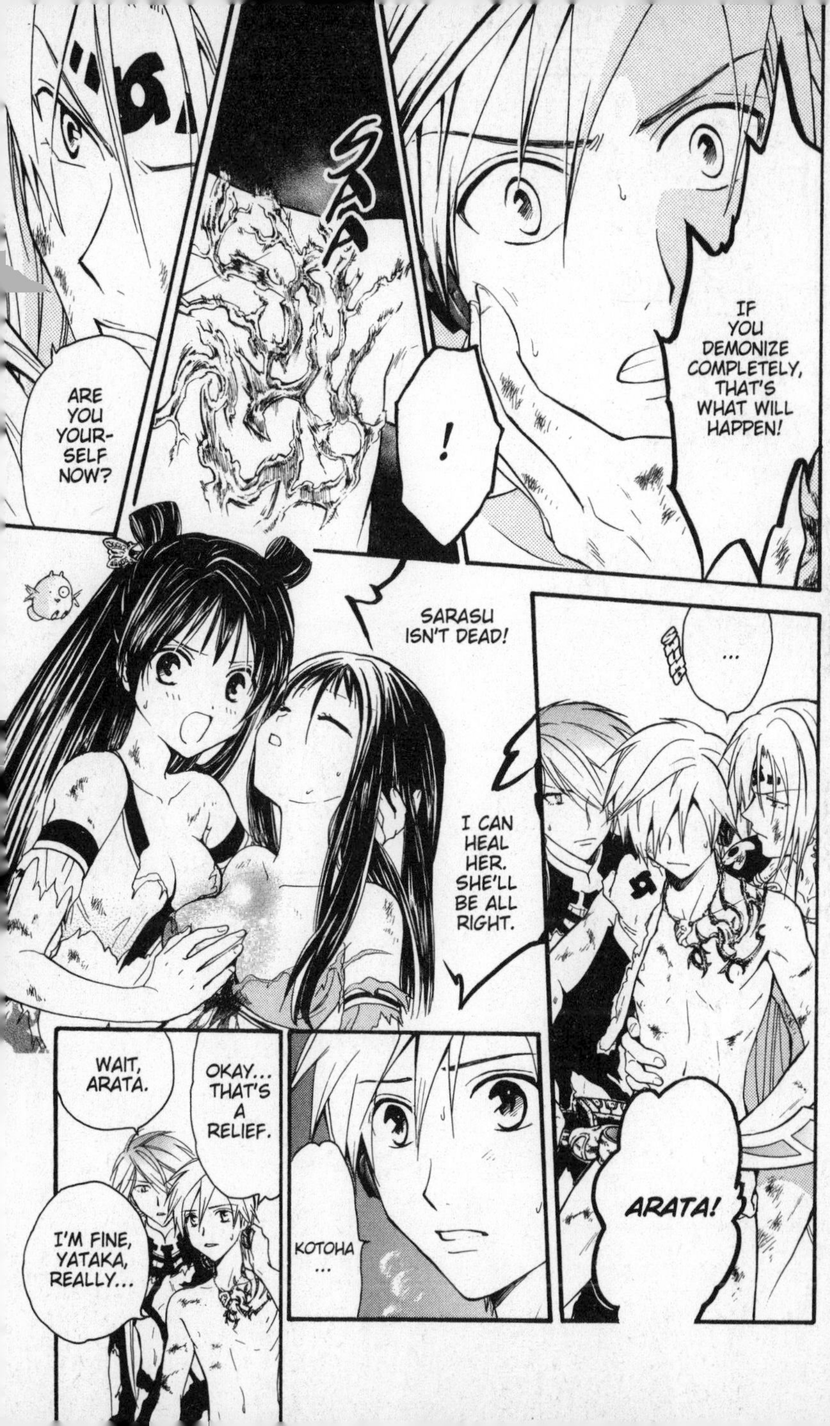
IF YOU DEMONIZE COMPLETELY, THAT'S WHAT WILL HAPPEN!
!
ARE YOU YOURSELF NOW?
...
ARATA!
SARASU ISN'T DEAD!
I CAN HEAL HER. SHE'LL BE ALL RIGHT.
KOTOHA ...
OKAY... THAT'S A RELIEF.
WAIT, ARATA.
I'M FINE, YATAKA, REALLY...

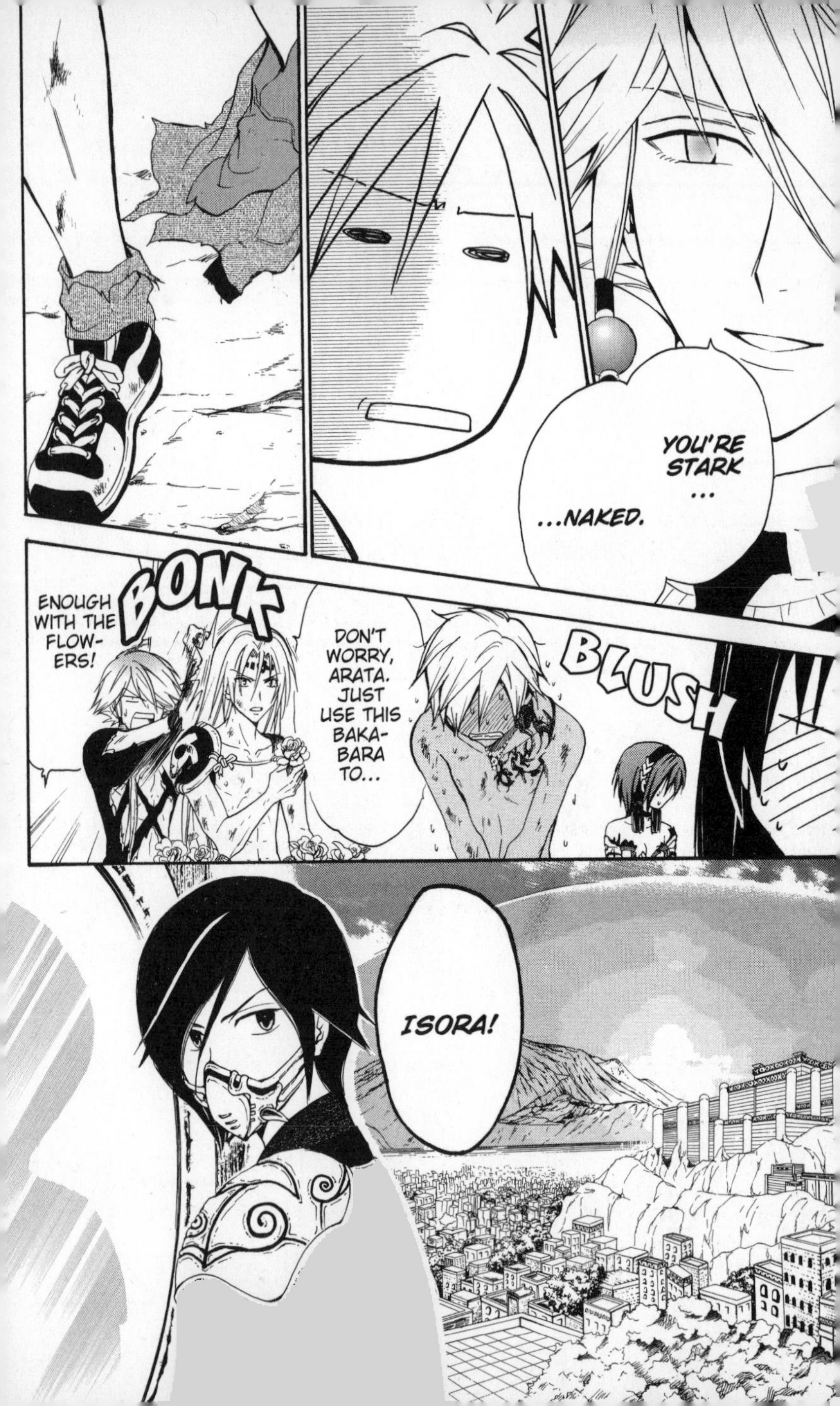

YOU'RE STARK ...
...NAKED.
BLUSH
DON'T WORRY, ARATA. JUST USE THIS BAKA-BARA TO...
BONK
ENOUGH WITH THE FLOW-ERS!
ISORA!

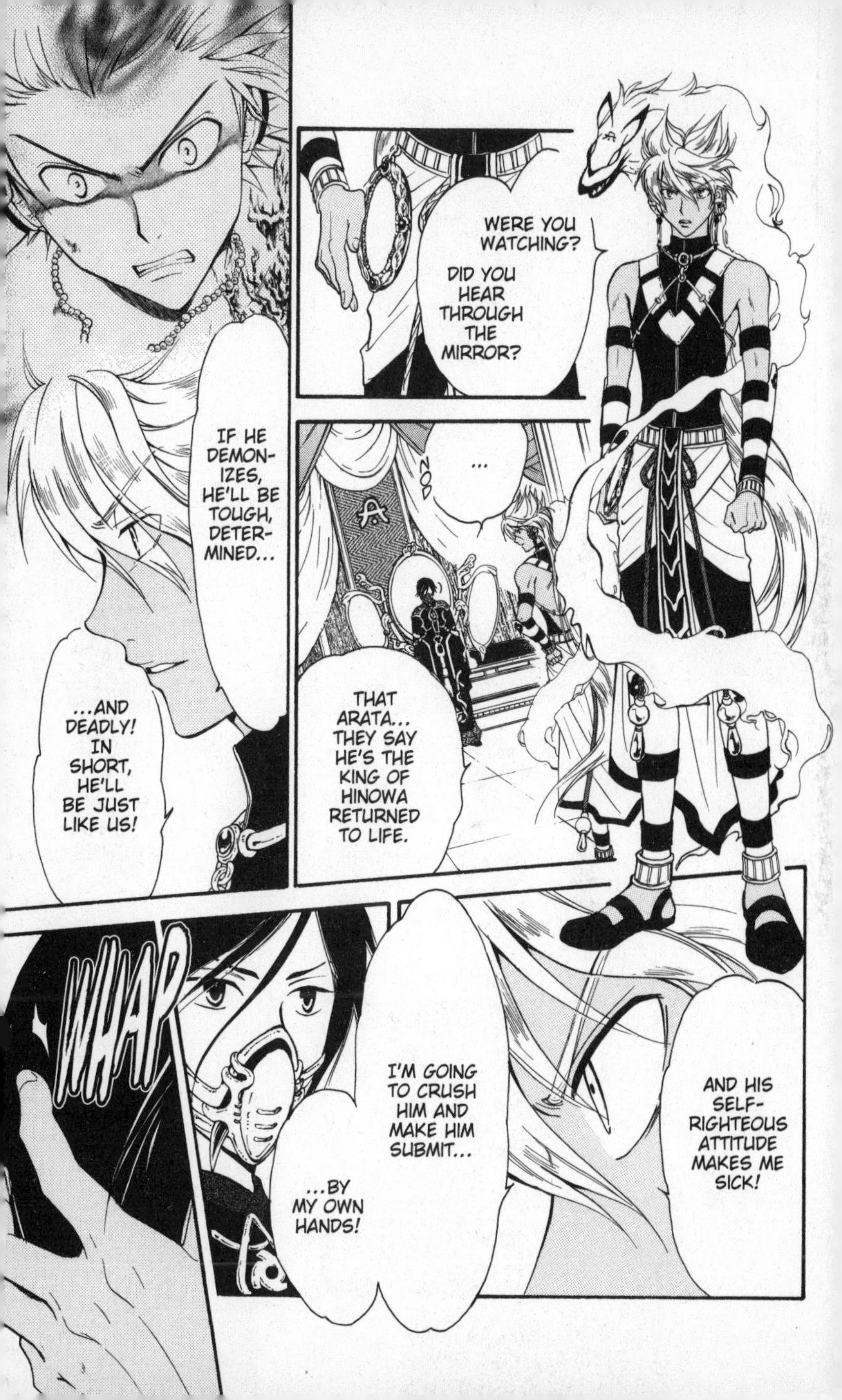
WERE YOU WATCHING?
DID YOU HEAR THROUGH THE MIRROR?
NOD
...
THAT ARATA... THEY SAY HE'S THE KING OF HINOWA RETURNED TO LIFE.
IF HE DEMON-IZES, HE'LL BE TOUGH, DETER-MINED...
...AND DEADLY! IN SHORT, HE'LL BE JUST LIKE US!
AND HIS SELF-RIGHTEOUS ATTITUDE MAKES ME SICK!
I'M GOING TO CRUSH HIM AND MAKE HIM SUBMIT...
...BY MY OWN HANDS!
WHAP

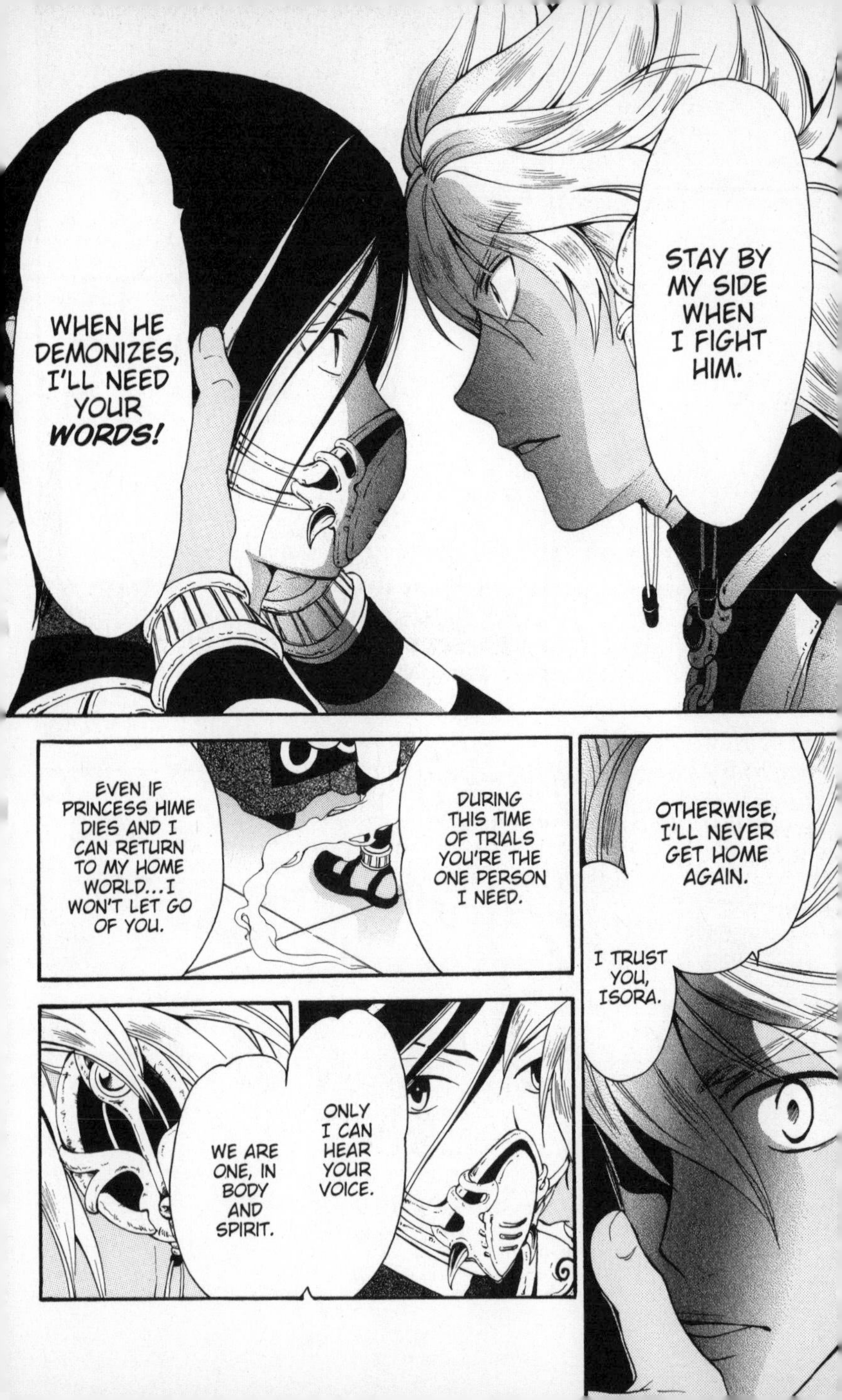
STAY BY MY SIDE WHEN I FIGHT HIM.
WHEN HE DEMONIZES, I'LL NEED YOUR *WORDS!*
OTHERWISE, I'LL NEVER GET HOME AGAIN.
I TRUST YOU, ISORA.
DURING THIS TIME OF TRIALS YOU'RE THE ONE PERSON I NEED.
EVEN IF PRINCESS HIME DIES AND I CAN RETURN TO MY HOME WORLD...I WON'T LET GO OF YOU.
ONLY I CAN HEAR YOUR VOICE.
WE ARE ONE, IN BODY AND SPIRIT.

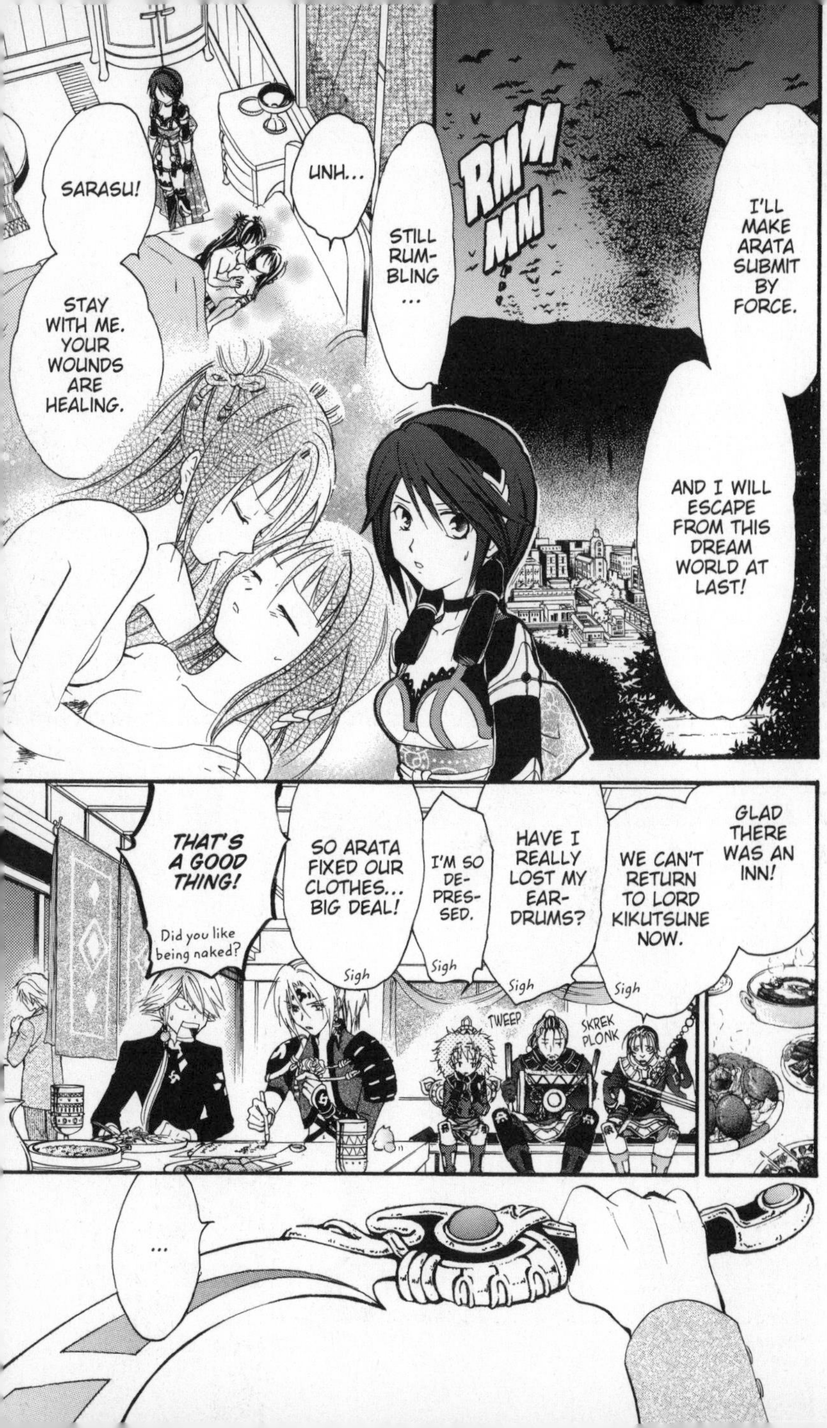
I'LL MAKE ARATA SUBMIT BY FORCE.
AND I WILL ESCAPE FROM THIS DREAM WORLD AT LAST!
RMMM MM
STILL RUMBLING...
UNH...
SARASU!
STAY WITH ME. YOUR WOUNDS ARE HEALING.
GLAD THERE WAS AN INN!
WE CAN'T RETURN TO LORD KIKUTSUNE NOW.
Sigh
SKREK PLONK
HAVE I REALLY LOST MY EAR-DRUMS?
Sigh
TWEEP
I'M SO DE-PRES-SED.
Sigh
SO ARATA FIXED OUR CLOTHES... BIG DEAL!
Sigh
THAT'S A GOOD THING!
Did you like being naked?
...

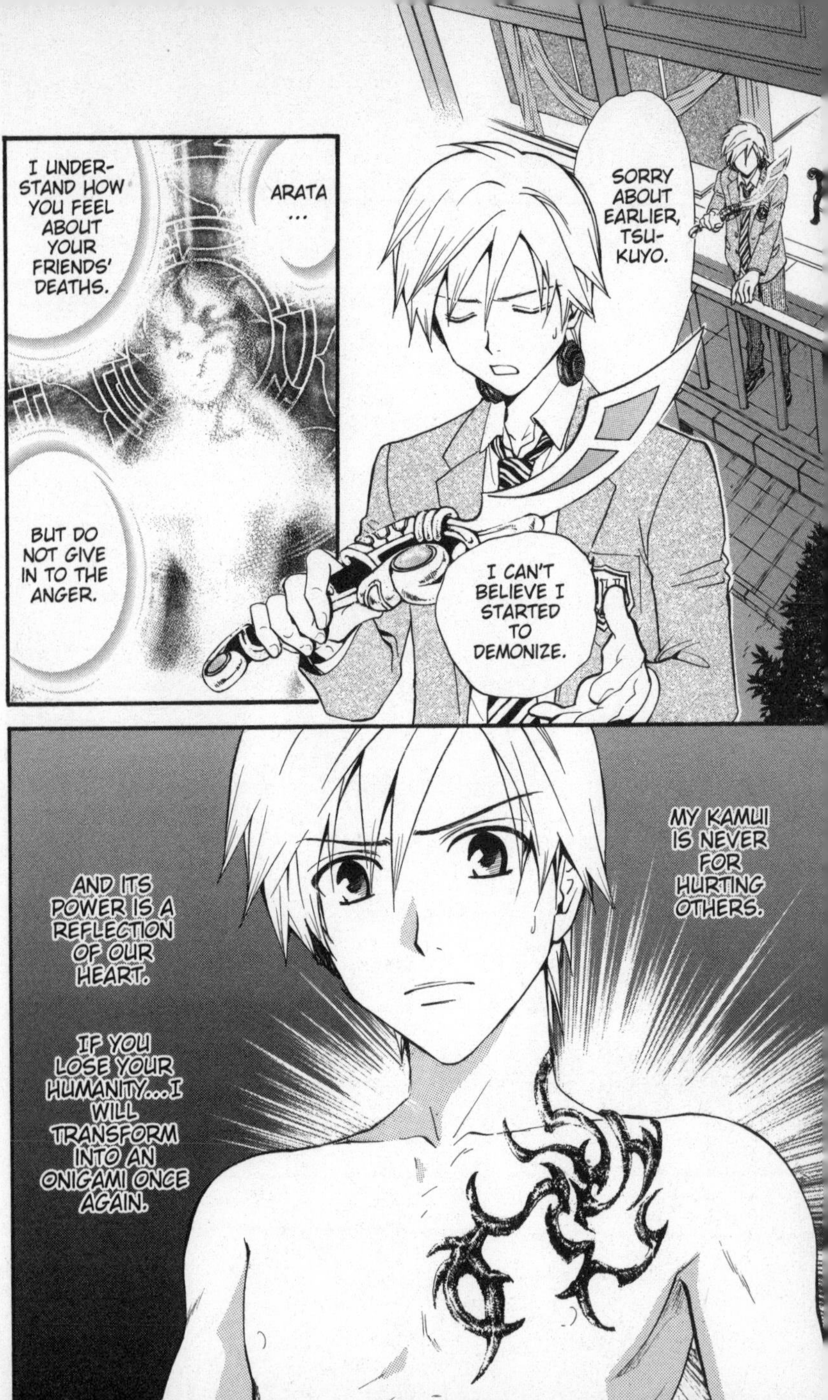
SORRY ABOUT EARLIER, TSU-KUYO.
I CAN'T BELIEVE I STARTED TO DEMONIZE.
ARATA ...
I UNDER-STAND HOW YOU FEEL ABOUT YOUR FRIENDS' DEATHS.
BUT DO NOT GIVE IN TO THE ANGER.
MY KAMUI IS NEVER FOR HURTING OTHERS.
AND ITS POWER IS A REFLECTION OF OUR HEART.
IF YOU LOSE YOUR HUMANITY...I WILL TRANSFORM INTO AN ONIGAMI ONCE AGAIN.

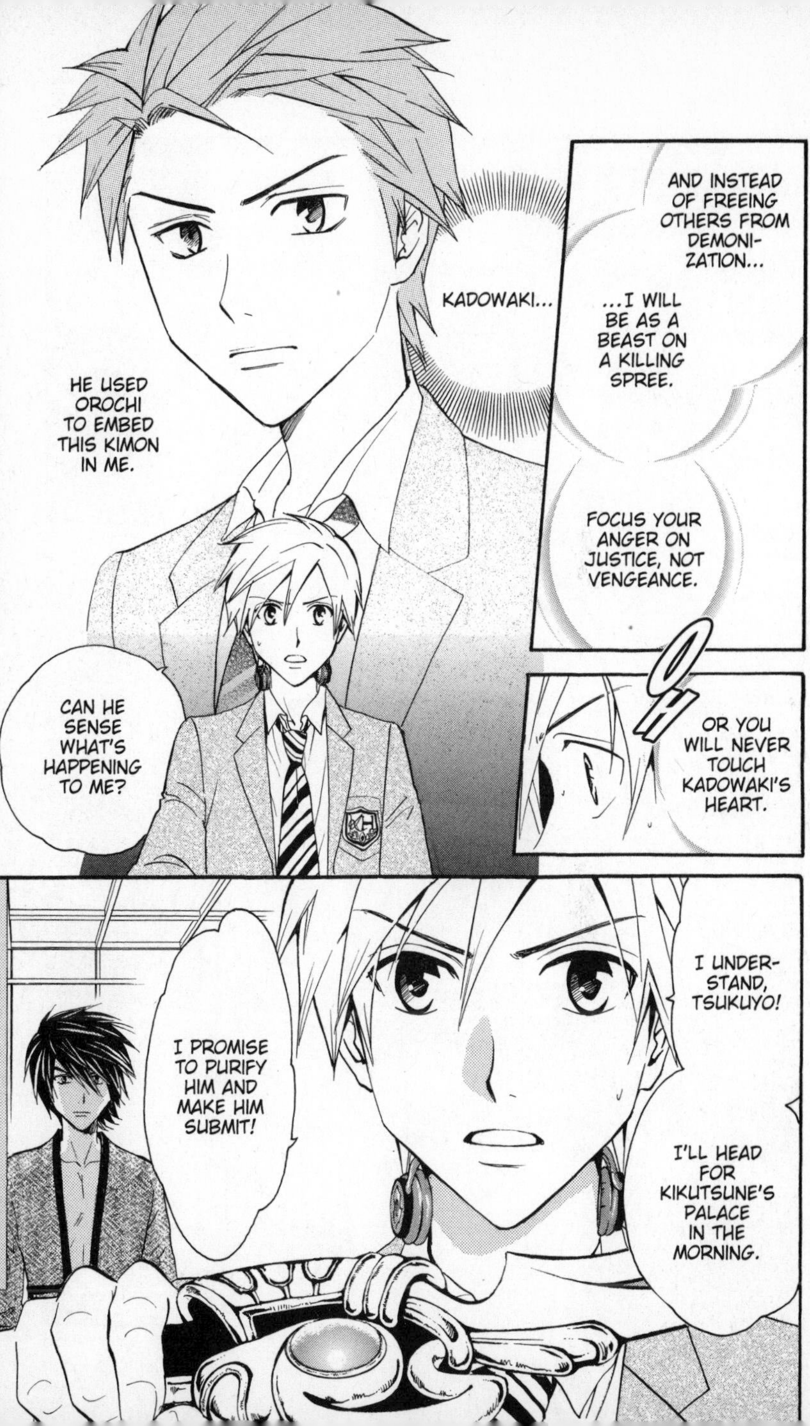
AND INSTEAD OF FREEING OTHERS FROM DEMONIZATION...
...I WILL BE AS A BEAST ON A KILLING SPREE.
FOCUS YOUR ANGER ON JUSTICE, NOT VENGEANCE.
OH
OR YOU WILL NEVER TOUCH KADOWAKI'S HEART.
KADOWAKI...
HE USED OROCHI TO EMBED THIS KIMON IN ME.
CAN HE SENSE WHAT'S HAPPENING TO ME?
I UNDERSTAND, TSUKUYO!
I'LL HEAD FOR KIKUTSUNE'S PALACE IN THE MORNING.
I PROMISE TO PURIFY HIM AND MAKE HIM SUBMIT!

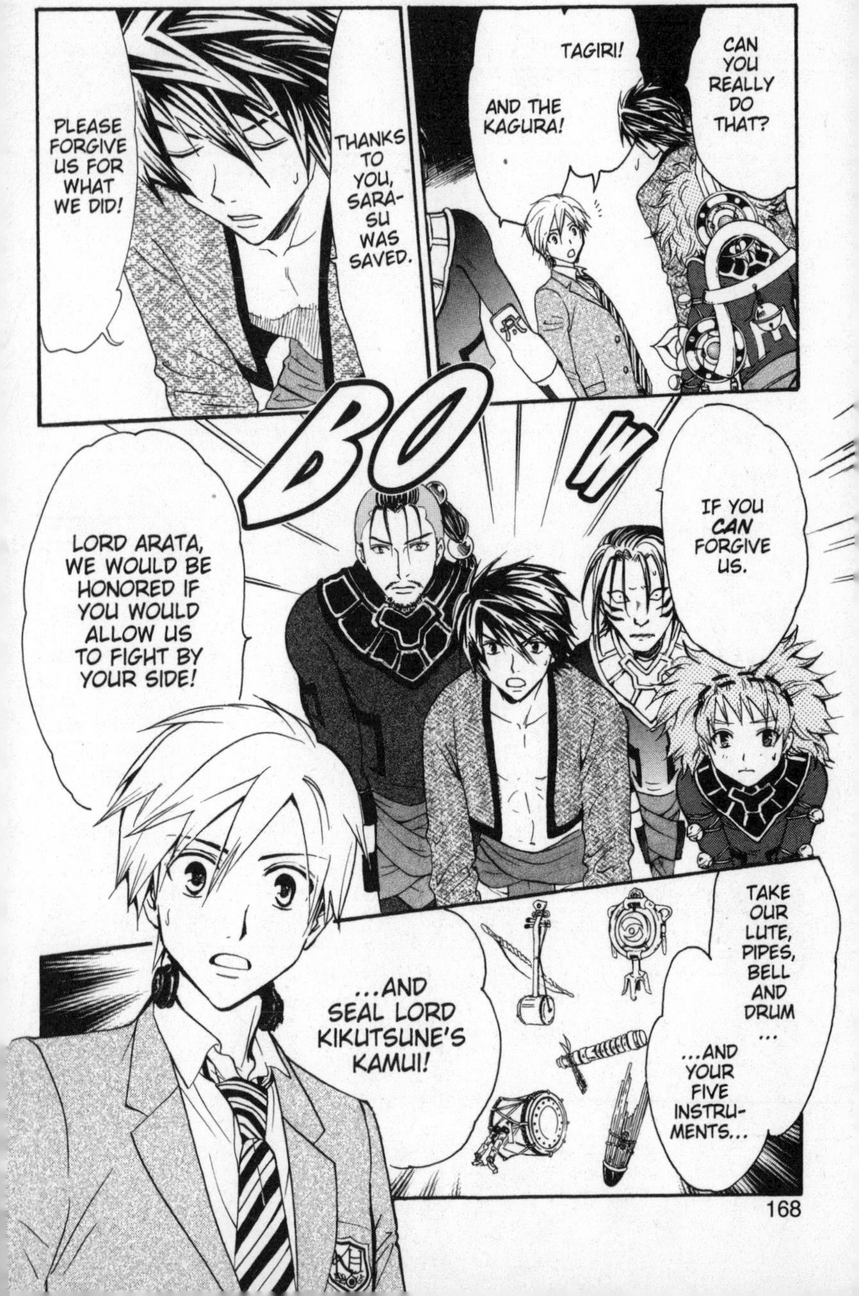
CAN YOU REALLY DO THAT?
TAGIRI!
AND THE KAGURA!
THANKS TO YOU, SARA-SU WAS SAVED.
PLEASE FORGIVE US FOR WHAT WE DID!
BOW
IF YOU *CAN* FORGIVE US.
LORD ARATA, WE WOULD BE HONORED IF YOU WOULD ALLOW US TO FIGHT BY YOUR SIDE!
TAKE OUR LUTE, PIPES, BELL AND DRUM ...
...AND YOUR FIVE INSTRU-MENTS...
...AND SEAL LORD KIKUTSUNE'S KAMUI!

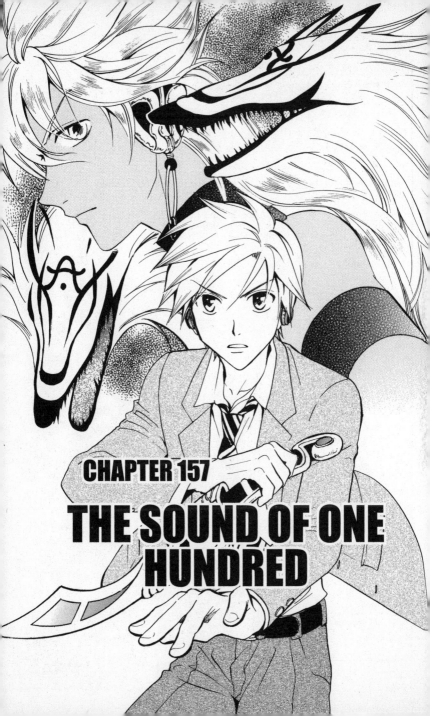

CHAPTER 157

THE SOUND OF ONE HUNDRED

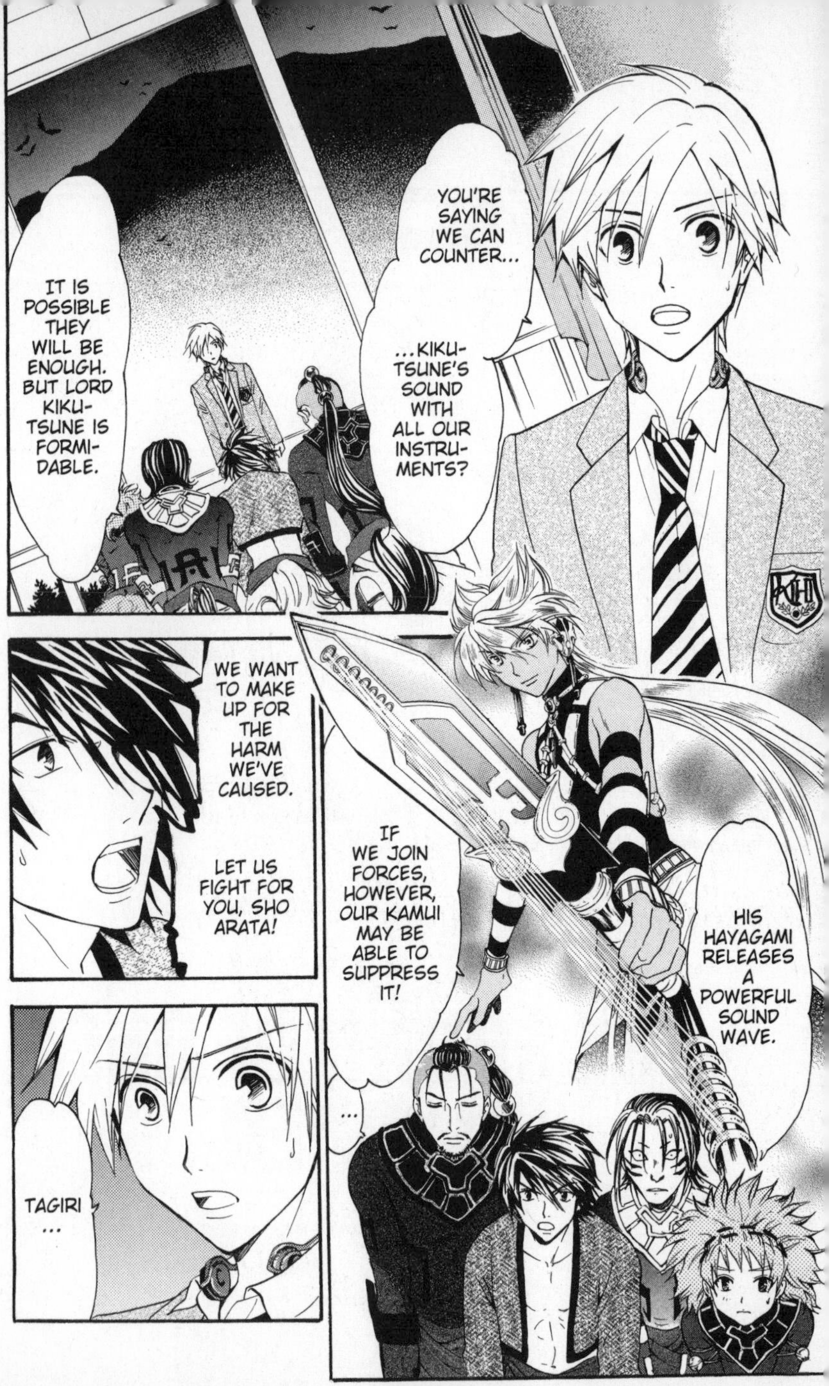
YOU'RE SAYING WE CAN COUNTER...
...KIKUTSUNE'S SOUND WITH ALL OUR INSTRUMENTS?
IT IS POSSIBLE THEY WILL BE ENOUGH. BUT LORD KIKUTSUNE IS FORMIDABLE.
HIS HAYAGAMI RELEASES A POWERFUL SOUND WAVE.
IF WE JOIN FORCES, HOWEVER, OUR KAMUI MAY BE ABLE TO SUPPRESS IT!
...
WE WANT TO MAKE UP FOR THE HARM WE'VE CAUSED.
LET US FIGHT FOR YOU, SHO ARATA!
TAGIRI ...

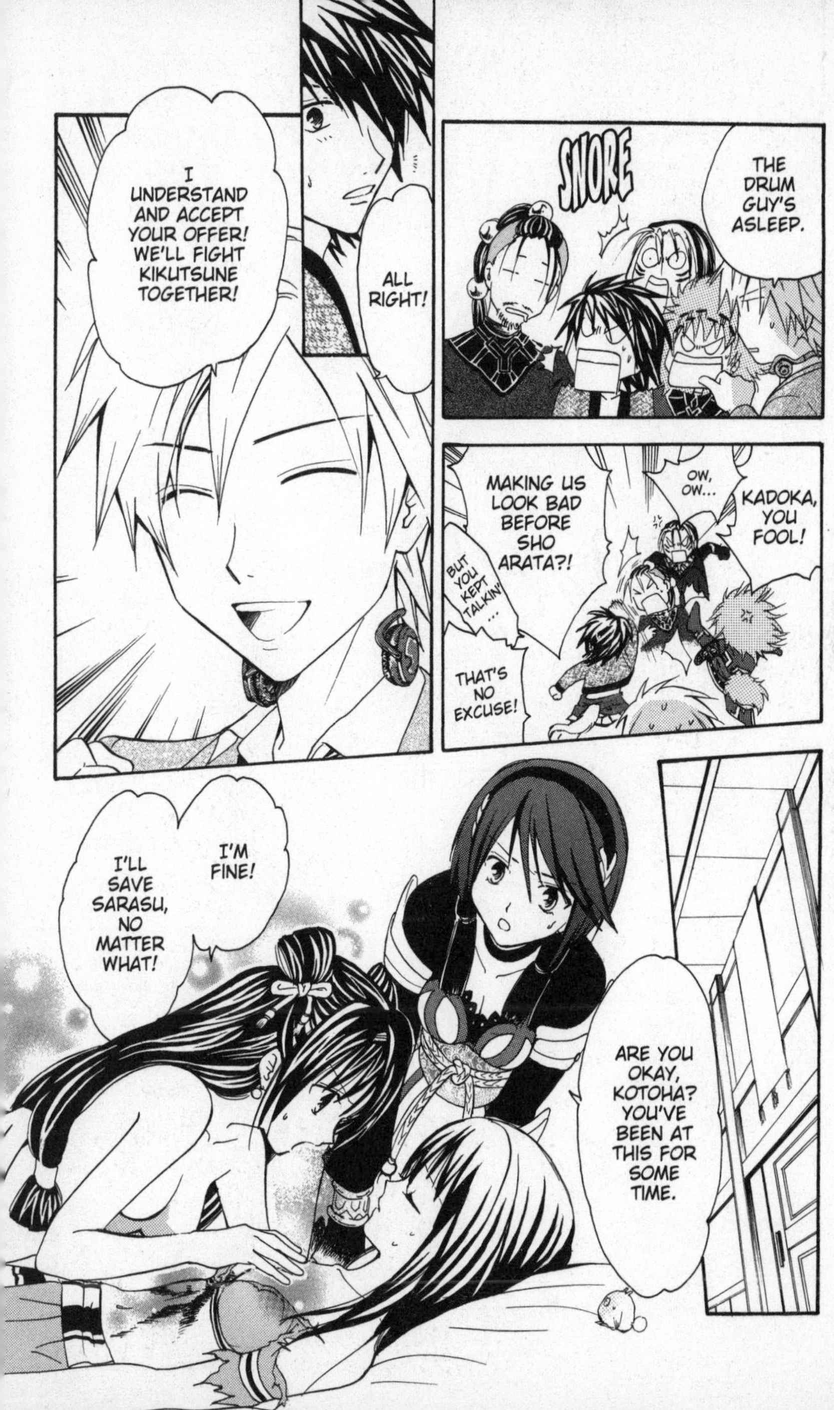
SNORE
THE DRUM GUY'S ASLEEP.
KADOKA, YOU FOOL!
OW, OW...
MAKING US LOOK BAD BEFORE SHO ARATA?!
BUT YOU KEPT TALKIN'...
THAT'S NO EXCUSE!
I UNDERSTAND AND ACCEPT YOUR OFFER! WE'LL FIGHT KIKUTSUNE TOGETHER!
ALL RIGHT!
ARE YOU OKAY, KOTOHA? YOU'VE BEEN AT THIS FOR SOME TIME.
I'M FINE!
I'LL SAVE SARASU, NO MATTER WHAT!

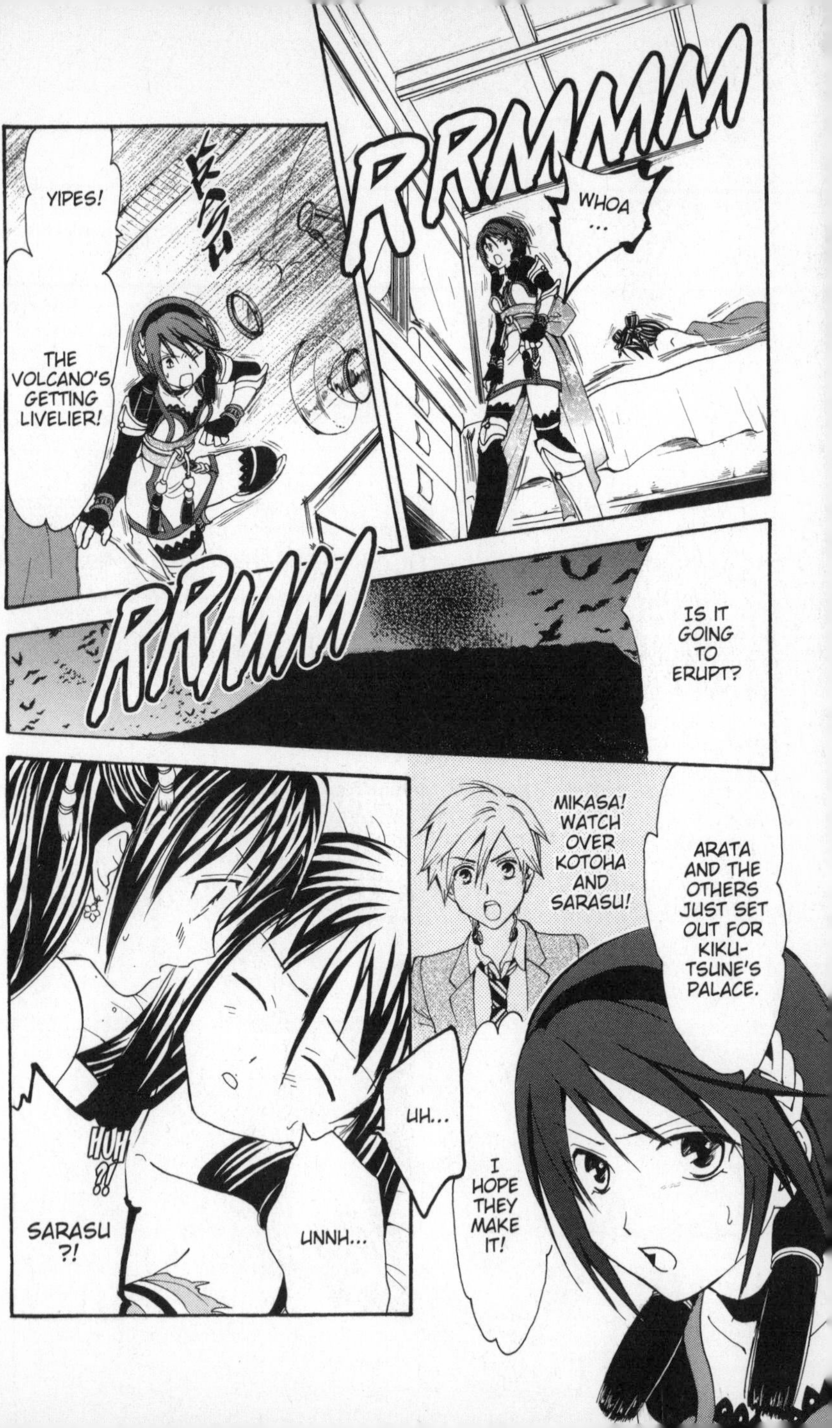
RRMMMM
WHOA ...
YIPES!
THE VOLCANO'S GETTING LIVELIER!
RRMM
IS IT GOING TO ERUPT?
ARATA AND THE OTHERS JUST SET OUT FOR KIKU-TSUNE'S PALACE.
MIKASA! WATCH OVER KOTOHA AND SARASU!
I HOPE THEY MAKE IT!
UH...
UNNH...
HUH ?!
SARASU ?!

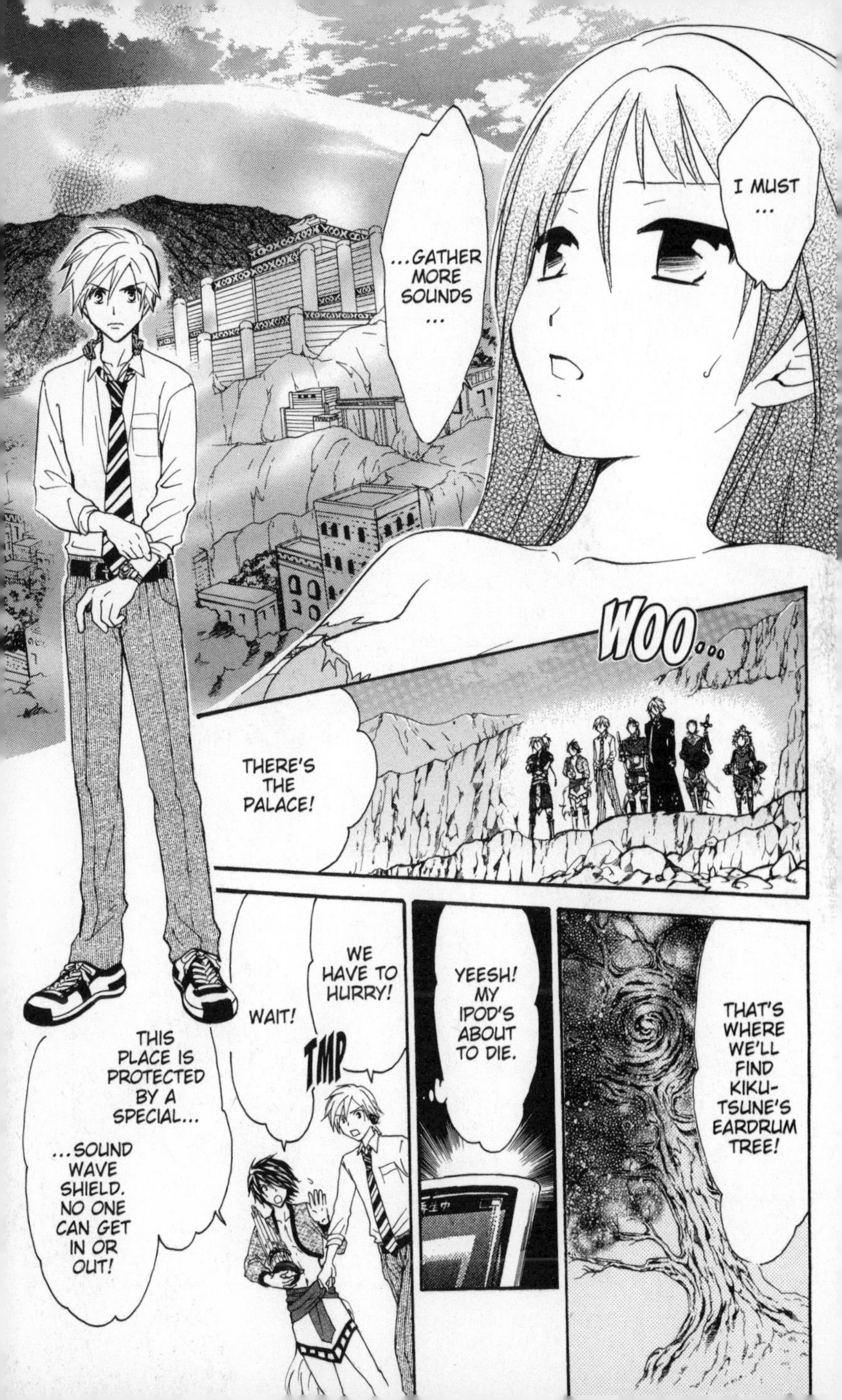
I MUST ...
...GATHER MORE SOUNDS ...
WOO...
THERE'S THE PALACE!
THAT'S WHERE WE'LL FIND KIKU-TSUNE'S EARDRUM TREE!
YEESH! MY IPOD'S ABOUT TO DIE.
WE HAVE TO HURRY!
TMP
WAIT!
THIS PLACE IS PROTECTED BY A SPECIAL...
...SOUND WAVE SHIELD. NO ONE CAN GET IN OR OUT!

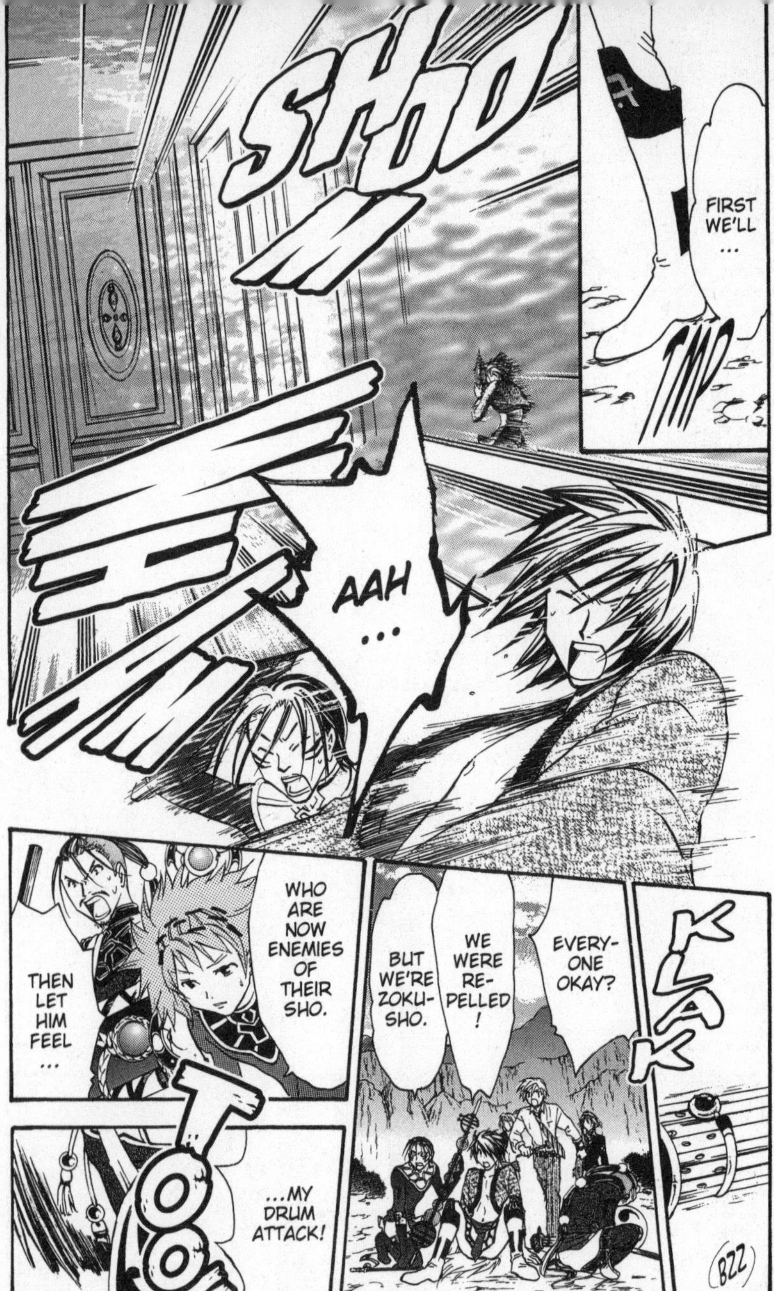
FIRST WE'LL ...
TMP
SHOO
AAH ...
KLAK
(BZZ)
EVERY-ONE OKAY?
WE WERE RE-PELLED!
BUT WE'RE ZOKU-SHO.
WHO ARE NOW ENEMIES OF THEIR SHO.
THEN LET HIM FEEL ...
...MY DRUM ATTACK!
TOOOM

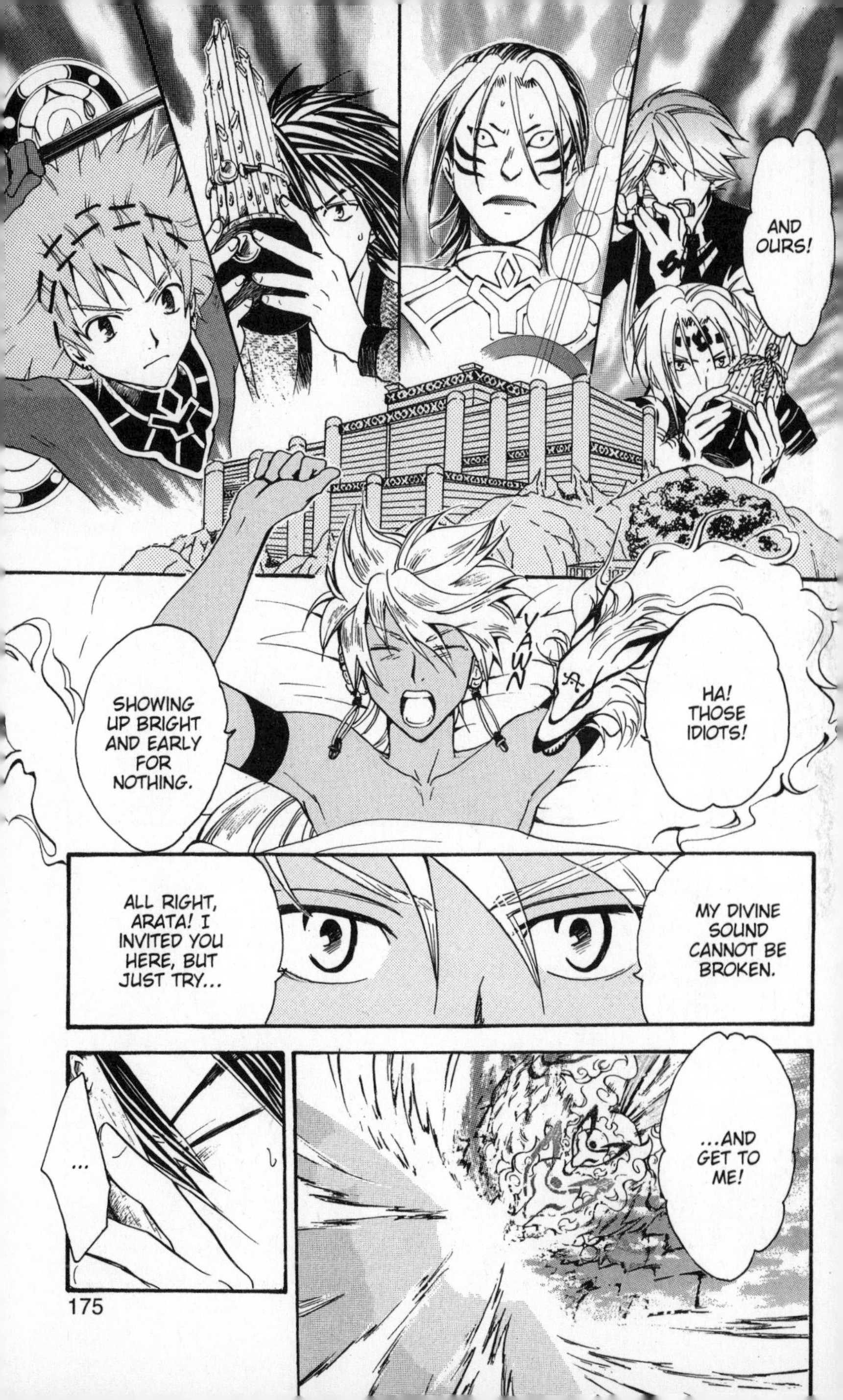
AND OURS!
HA! THOSE IDIOTS!
YAWN
SHOWING UP BRIGHT AND EARLY FOR NOTHING.
MY DIVINE SOUND CANNOT BE BROKEN.
ALL RIGHT, ARATA! I INVITED YOU HERE, BUT JUST TRY...
...AND GET TO ME!
...

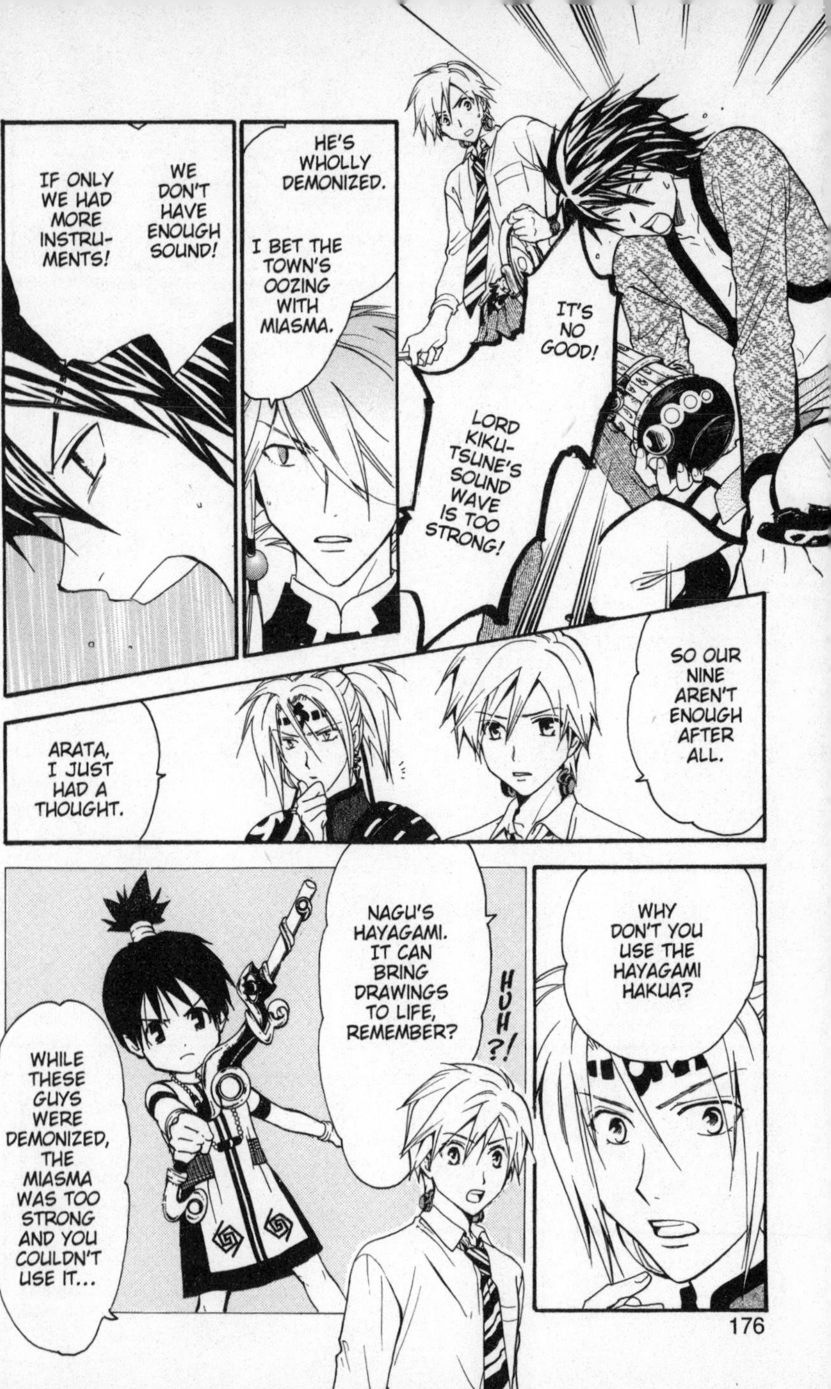
IT'S NO GOOD!
LORD KIKU-TSUNE'S SOUND WAVE IS TOO STRONG!
HE'S WHOLLY DEMONIZED.
I BET THE TOWN'S OOZING WITH MIASMA.
WE DON'T HAVE ENOUGH SOUND!
IF ONLY WE HAD MORE INSTRU-MENTS!
SO OUR NINE AREN'T ENOUGH AFTER ALL.
ARATA, I JUST HAD A THOUGHT.
WHY DON'T YOU USE THE HAYAGAMI HAKUA?
HUH?!
NAGU'S HAYAGAMI. IT CAN BRING DRAWINGS TO LIFE, REMEMBER?
WHILE THESE GUYS WERE DEMONIZED, THE MIASMA WAS TOO STRONG AND YOU COULDN'T USE IT...

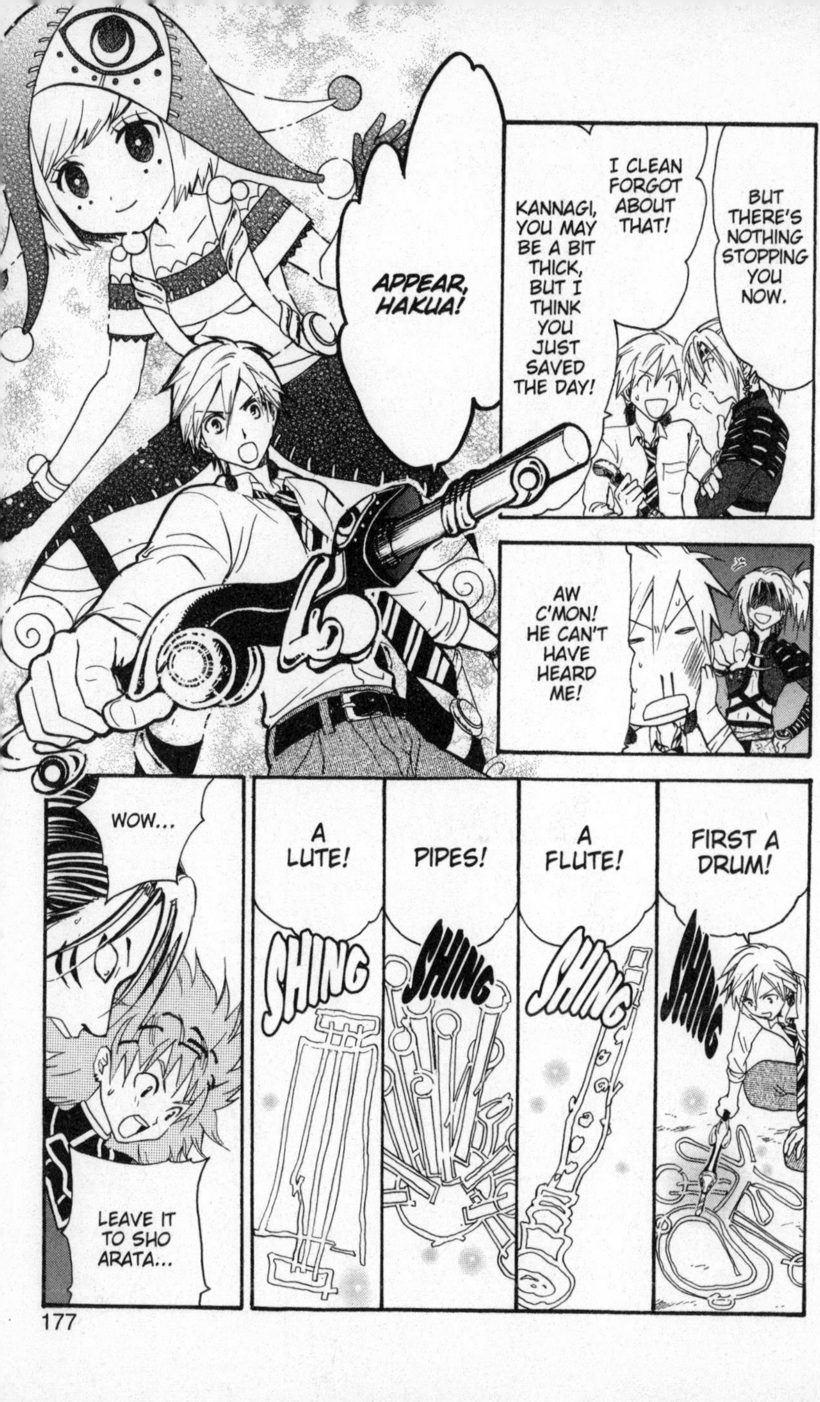
BUT THERE'S NOTHING STOPPING YOU NOW.
I CLEAN FORGOT ABOUT THAT!
KANNAGI, YOU MAY BE A BIT THICK, BUT I THINK YOU JUST SAVED THE DAY!
AW C'MON! HE CAN'T HAVE HEARD ME!
APPEAR, HAKUA!
FIRST A DRUM!
SHING
A FLUTE!
SHING
PIPES!
SHING
A LUTE!
SHING
WOW...
LEAVE IT TO SHO ARATA...

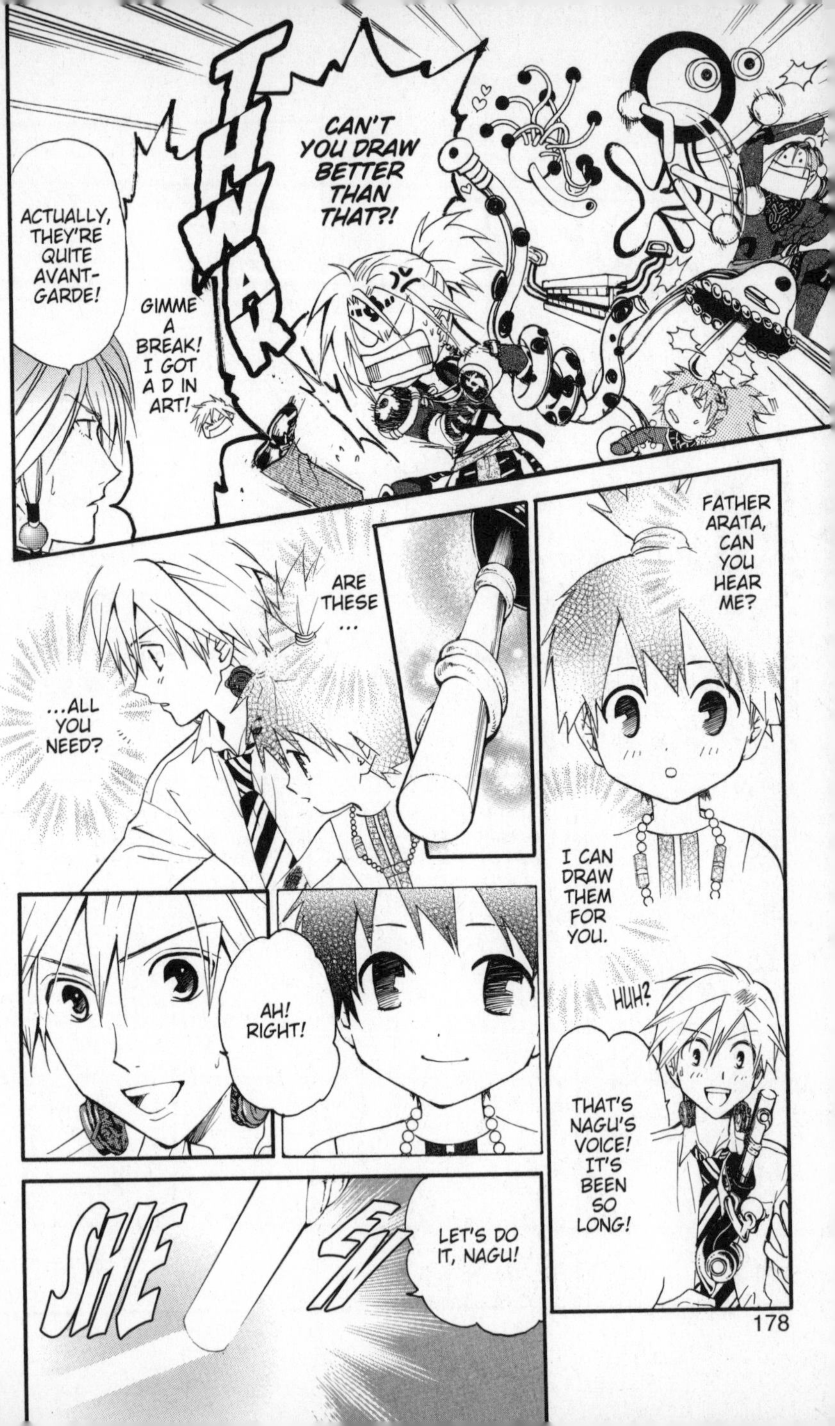
CAN'T YOU DRAW BETTER THAN THAT?!
THWAK
GIMME A BREAK! I GOT A D IN ART!
ACTUALLY, THEY'RE QUITE AVANT-GARDE!
FATHER ARATA, CAN YOU HEAR ME?
I CAN DRAW THEM FOR YOU.
ARE THESE ...
...ALL YOU NEED?
HUH?
THAT'S NAGU'S VOICE! IT'S BEEN SO LONG!
AH! RIGHT!
LET'S DO IT, NAGU!
SHE
EN

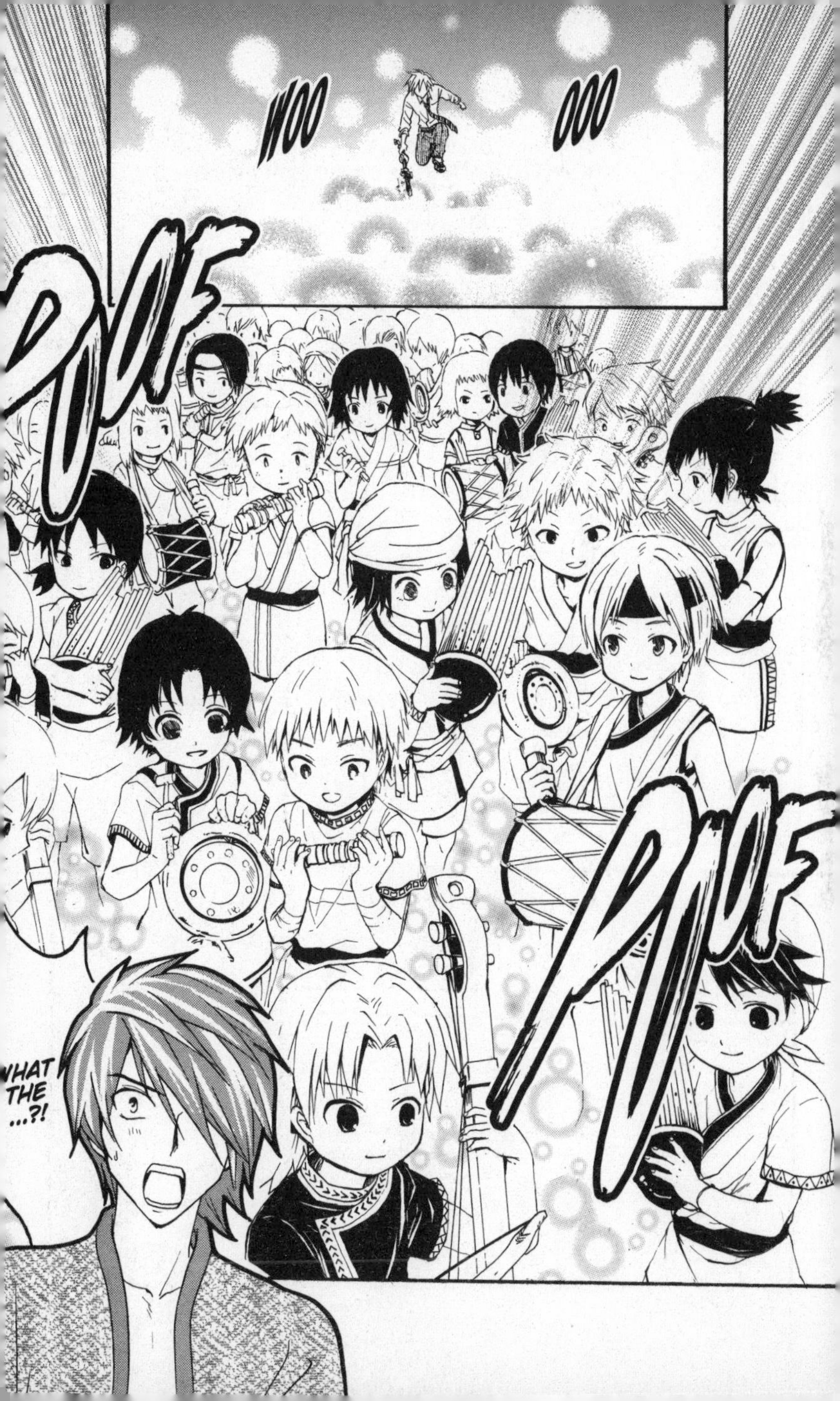
WOO
OOO
POOF
POOF
WHAT THE ...?!

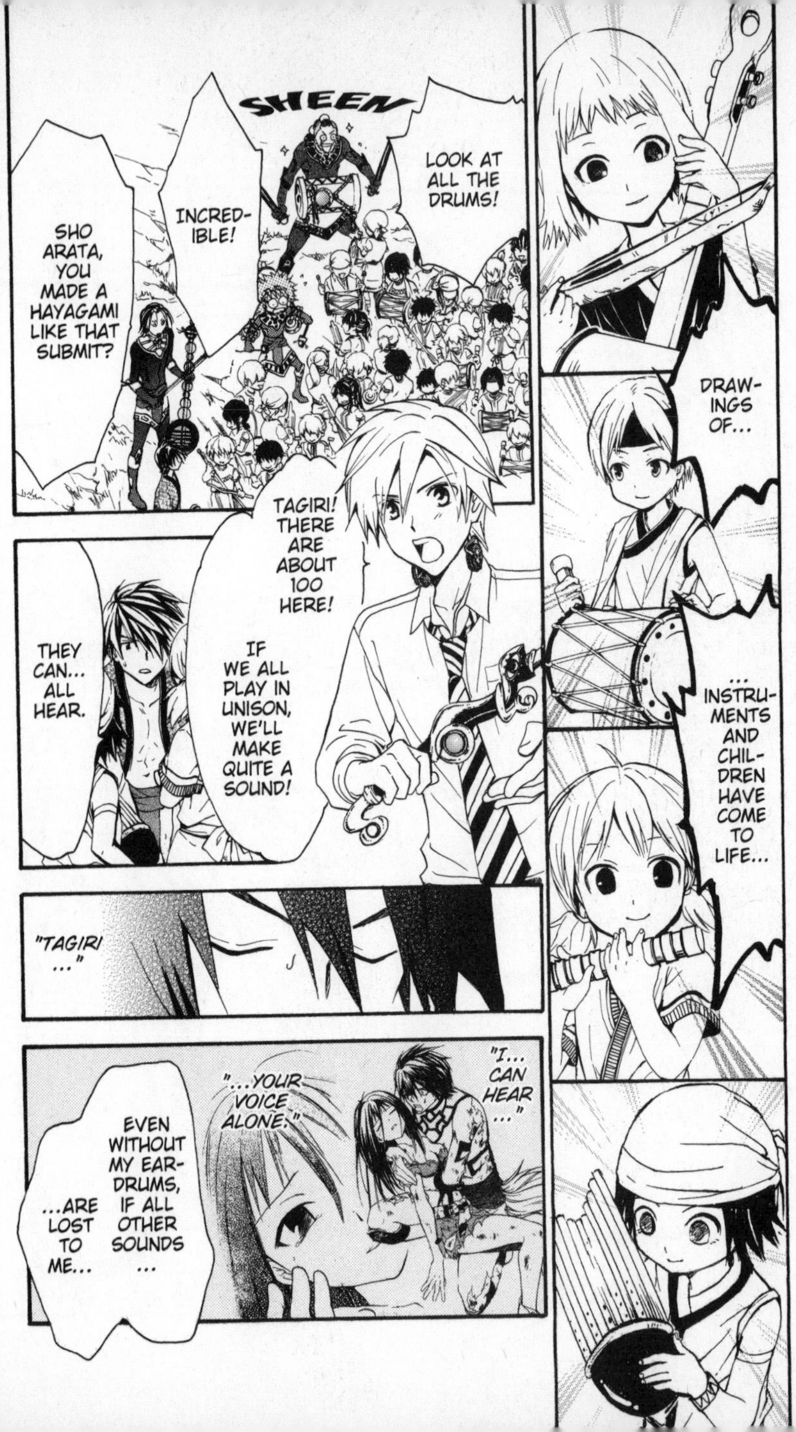
DRAWINGS OF...
...INSTRUMENTS AND CHILDREN HAVE COME TO LIFE...
SHEEN
LOOK AT ALL THE DRUMS!
INCREDIBLE!
SHO ARATA, YOU MADE A HAYAGAMI LIKE THAT SUBMIT?
TAGIRI! THERE ARE ABOUT 100 HERE!
IF WE ALL PLAY IN UNISON, WE'LL MAKE QUITE A SOUND!
THEY CAN... ALL HEAR.
"TAGIRI..."
"I... CAN HEAR..."
"...YOUR VOICE ALONE."
EVEN WITHOUT MY EARDRUMS, IF ALL OTHER SOUNDS...
...ARE LOST TO ME...

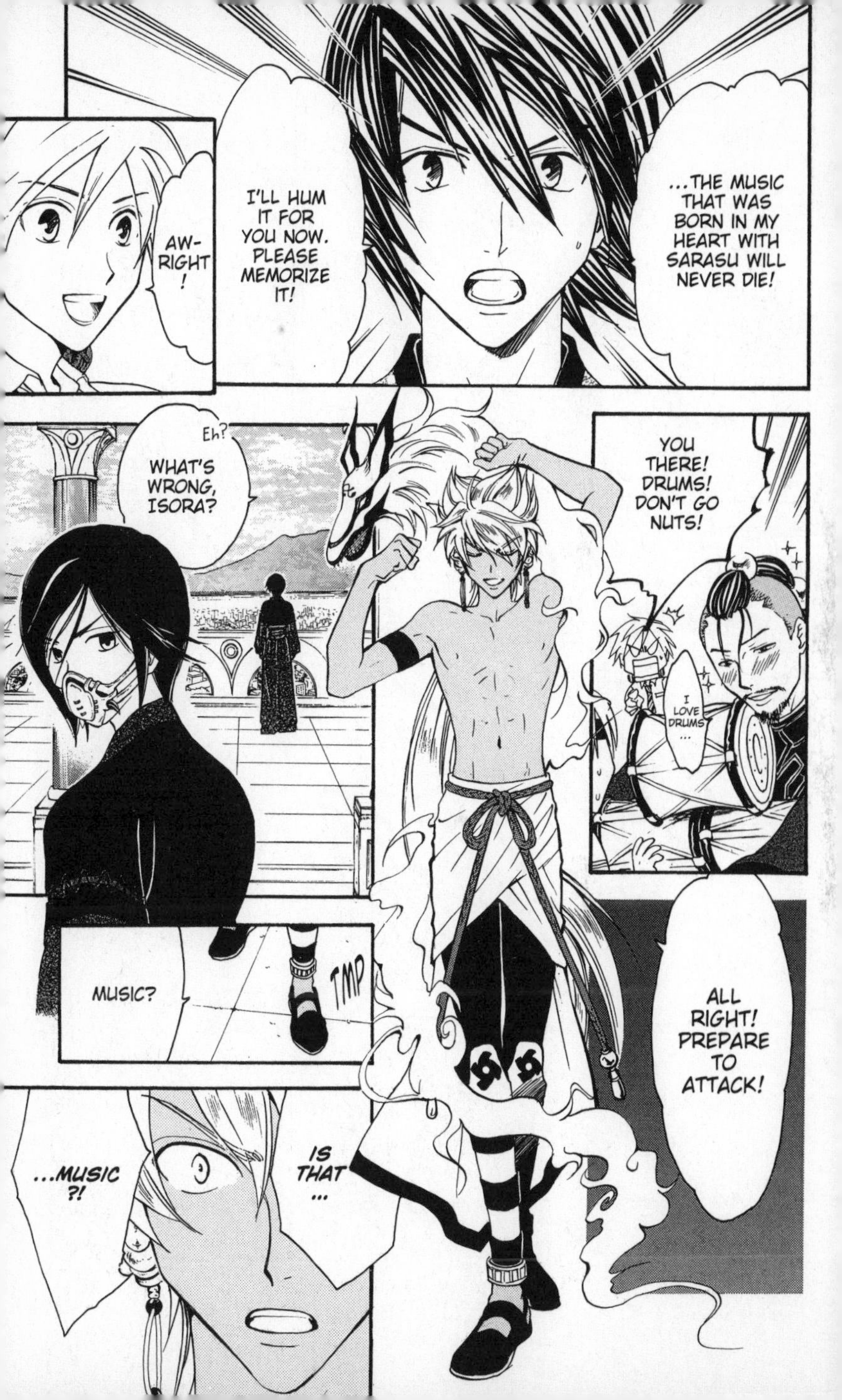
...THE MUSIC THAT WAS BORN IN MY HEART WITH SARASU WILL NEVER DIE!
I'LL HUM IT FOR YOU NOW. PLEASE MEMORIZE IT!
AW-RIGHT!
YOU THERE! DRUMS! DON'T GO NUTS!
I LOVE DRUMS...
ALL RIGHT! PREPARE TO ATTACK!
Eh?
WHAT'S WRONG, ISORA?
TMP
MUSIC?
IS THAT...
...MUSIC?!

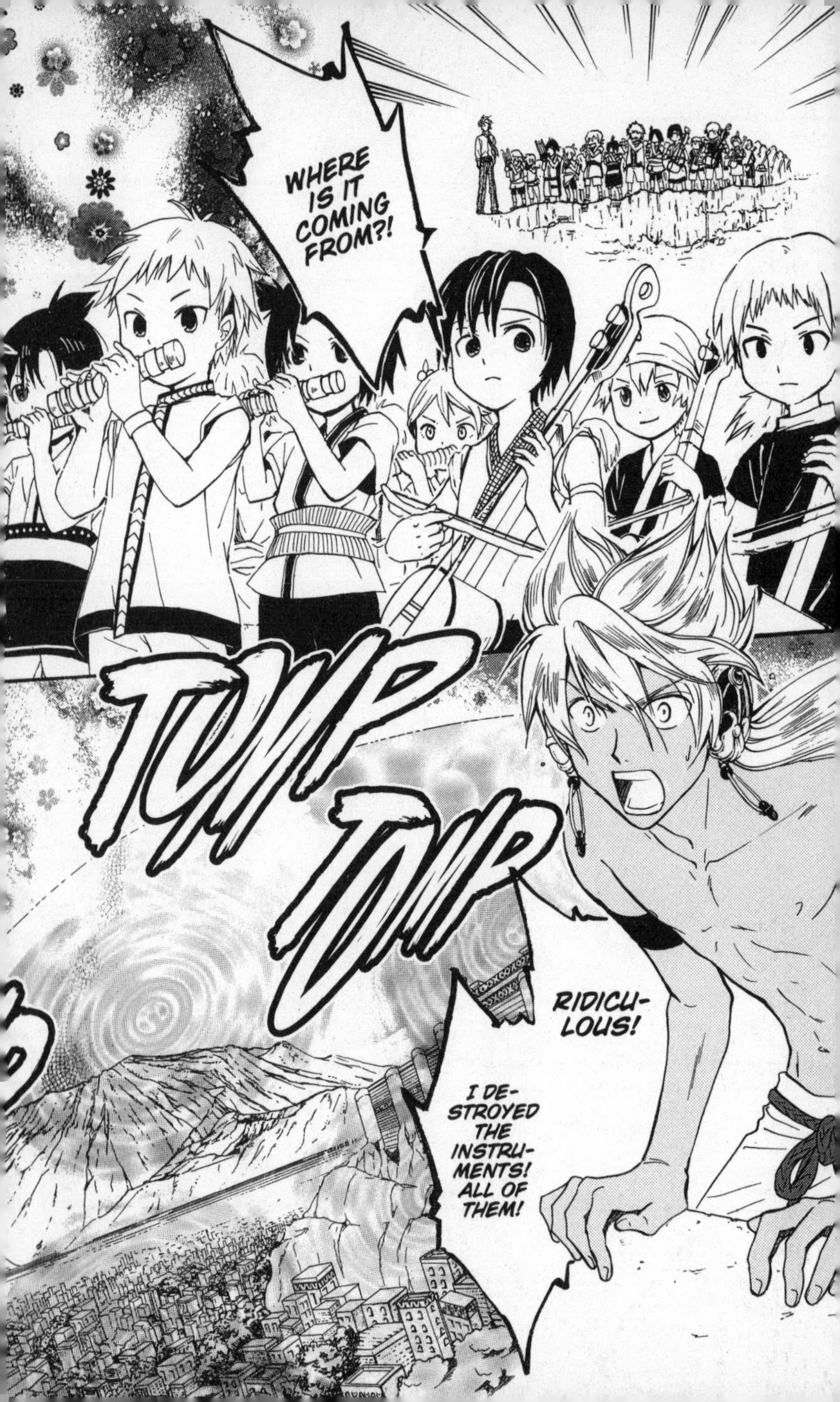
WHERE IS IT COMING FROM?!
TUP TUP
RIDICU-LOUS!
I DE-STROYED THE INSTRU-MENTS! ALL OF THEM!

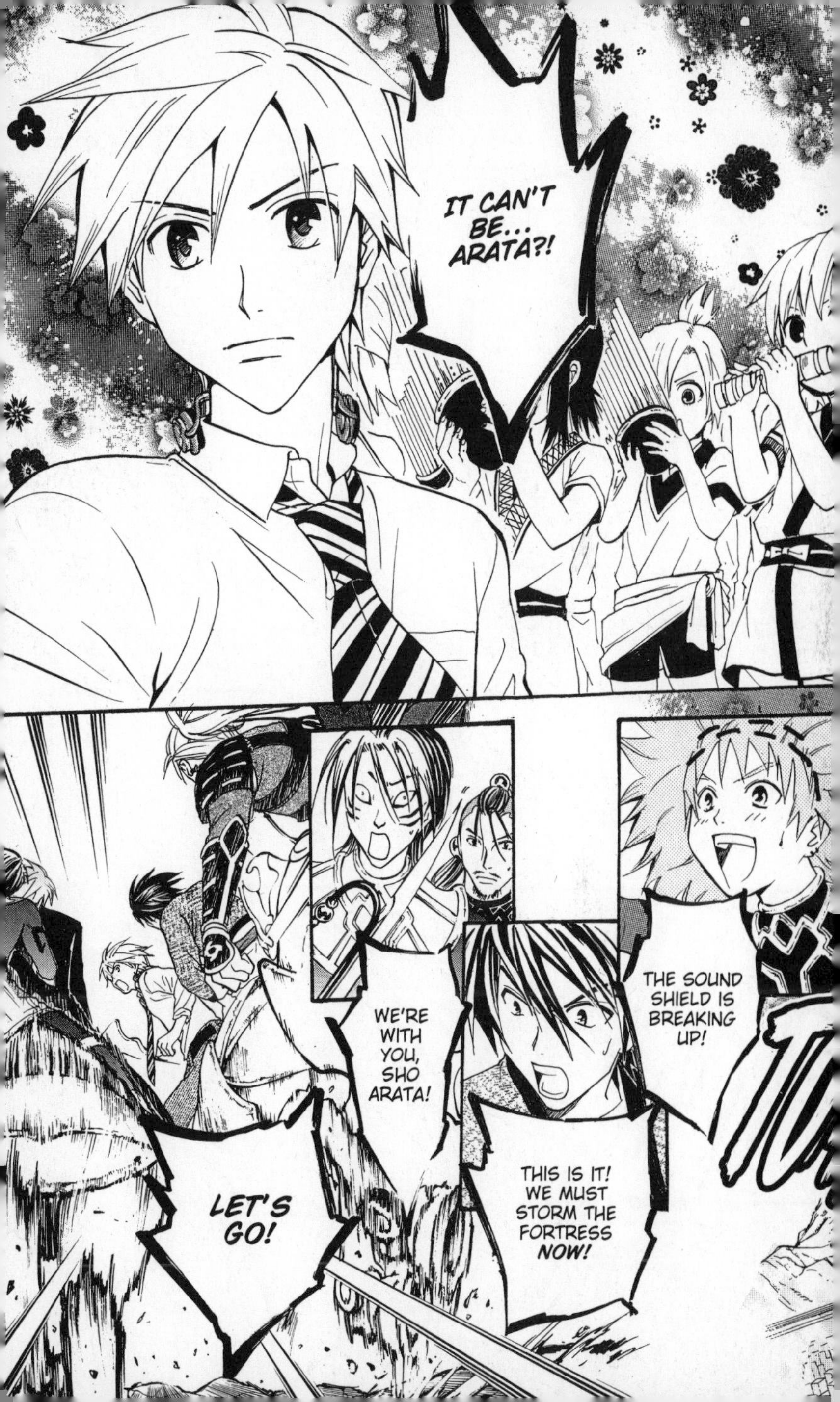
IT CAN'T BE... ARATA?!
THE SOUND SHIELD IS BREAKING UP!
WE'RE WITH YOU, SHO ARATA!
THIS IS IT! WE MUST STORM THE FORTRESS NOW!
LET'S GO!

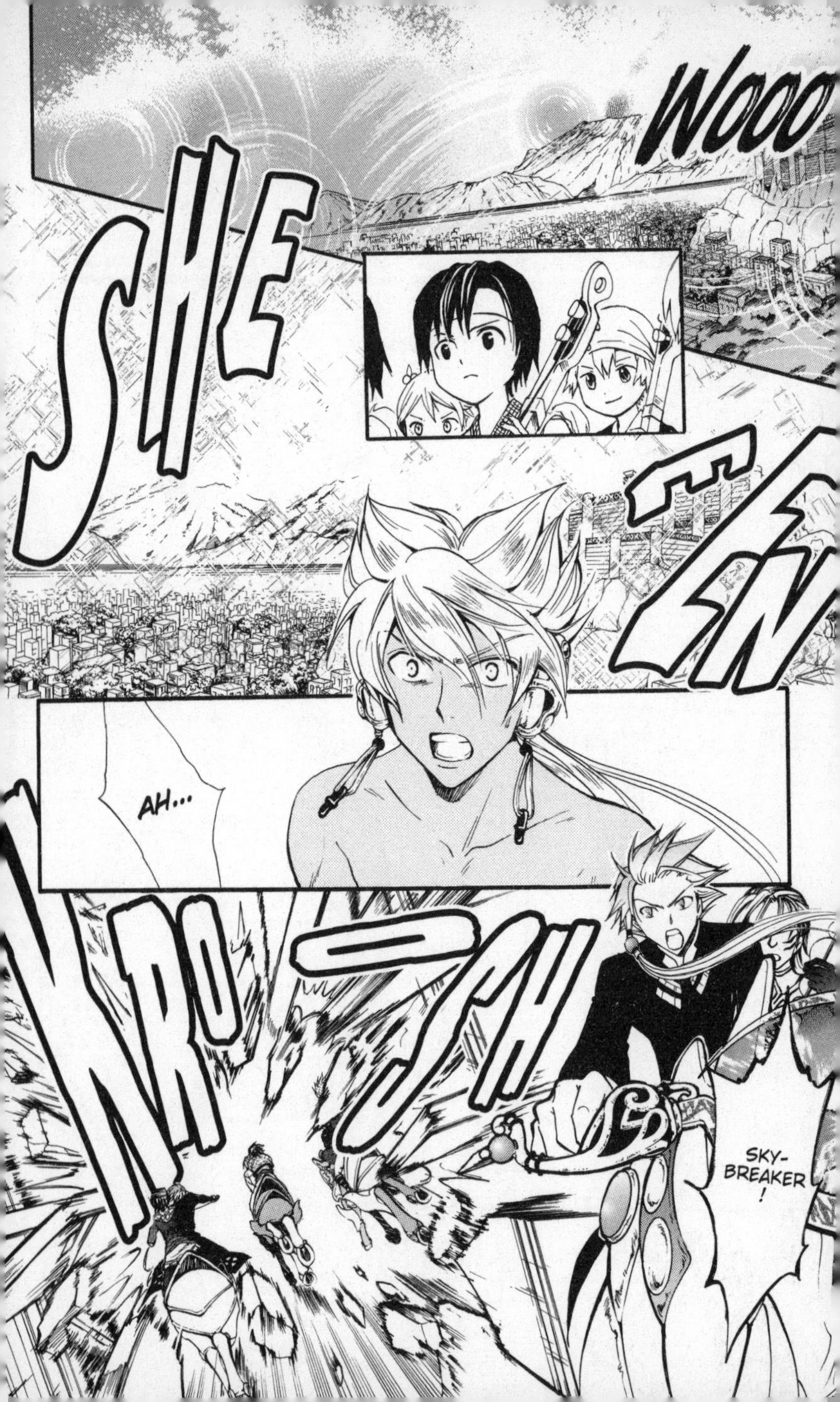
WOOO
SCHE
AH...
SKY-BREAKER!

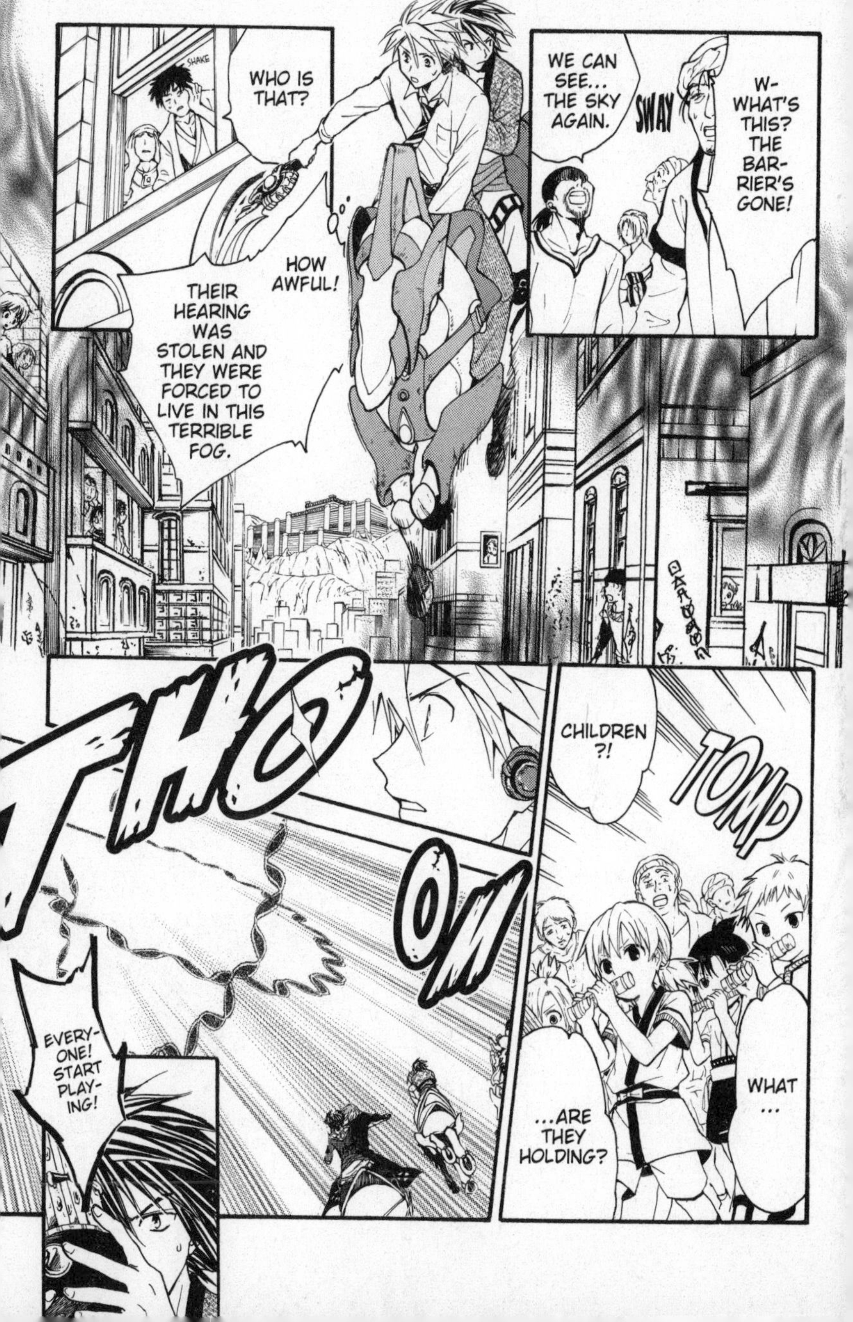
W-WHAT'S THIS? THE BARRIER'S GONE!
SWAY
WE CAN SEE... THE SKY AGAIN.
SHAKE
WHO IS THAT?
HOW AWFUL!
THEIR HEARING WAS STOLEN AND THEY WERE FORCED TO LIVE IN THIS TERRIBLE FOG.
TOMP
CHILDREN?!
WHAT...
...ARE THEY HOLDING?
THOOM
EVERYONE! START PLAYING!

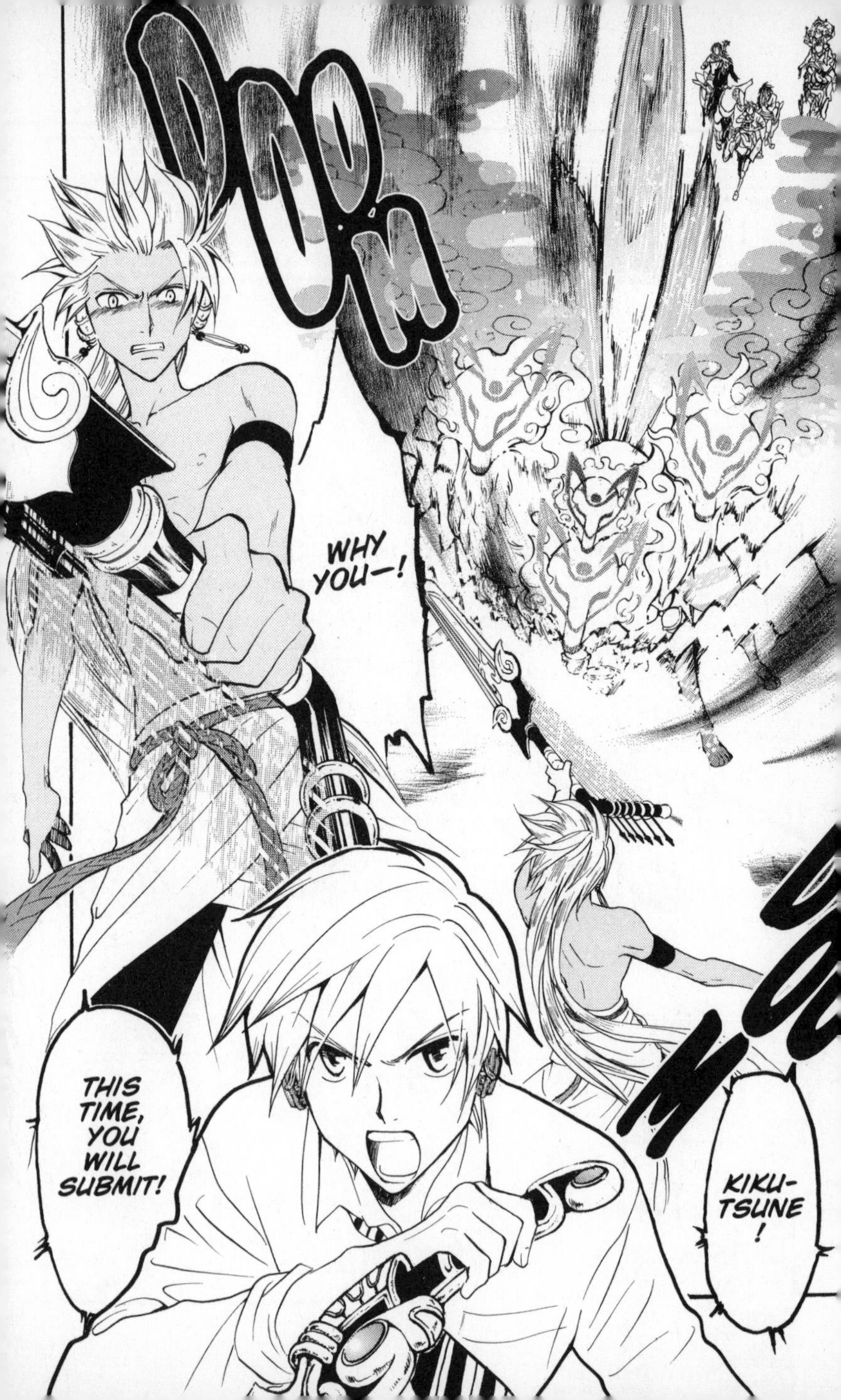
DOOOM
WHY YOU—!
DOOM
KIKU-TSUNE!
THIS TIME, YOU WILL SUBMIT!

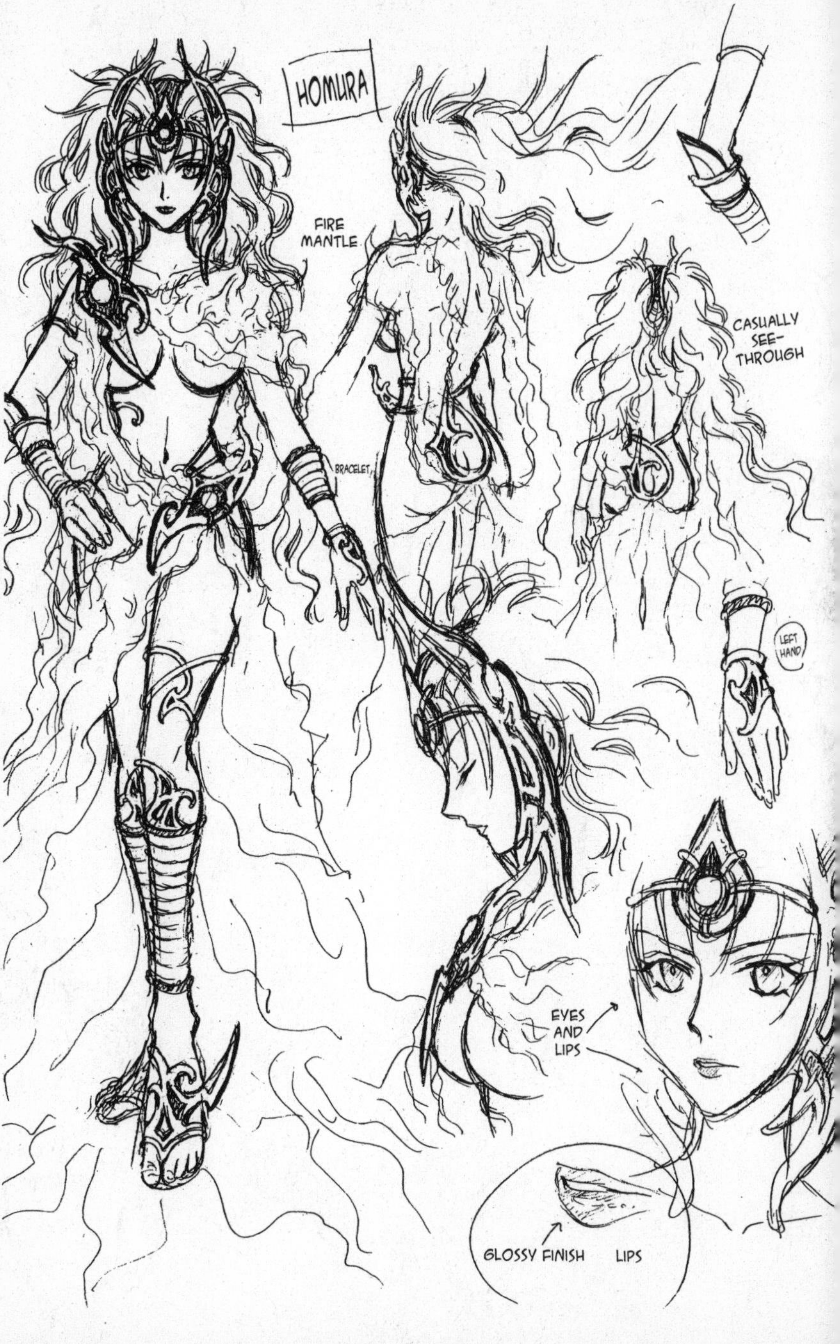
HOMURA
FIRE MANTLE
BRACELET
CASUALLY SEE-THROUGH
LEFT HAND
EYES AND LIPS
GLOSSY FINISH
LIPS

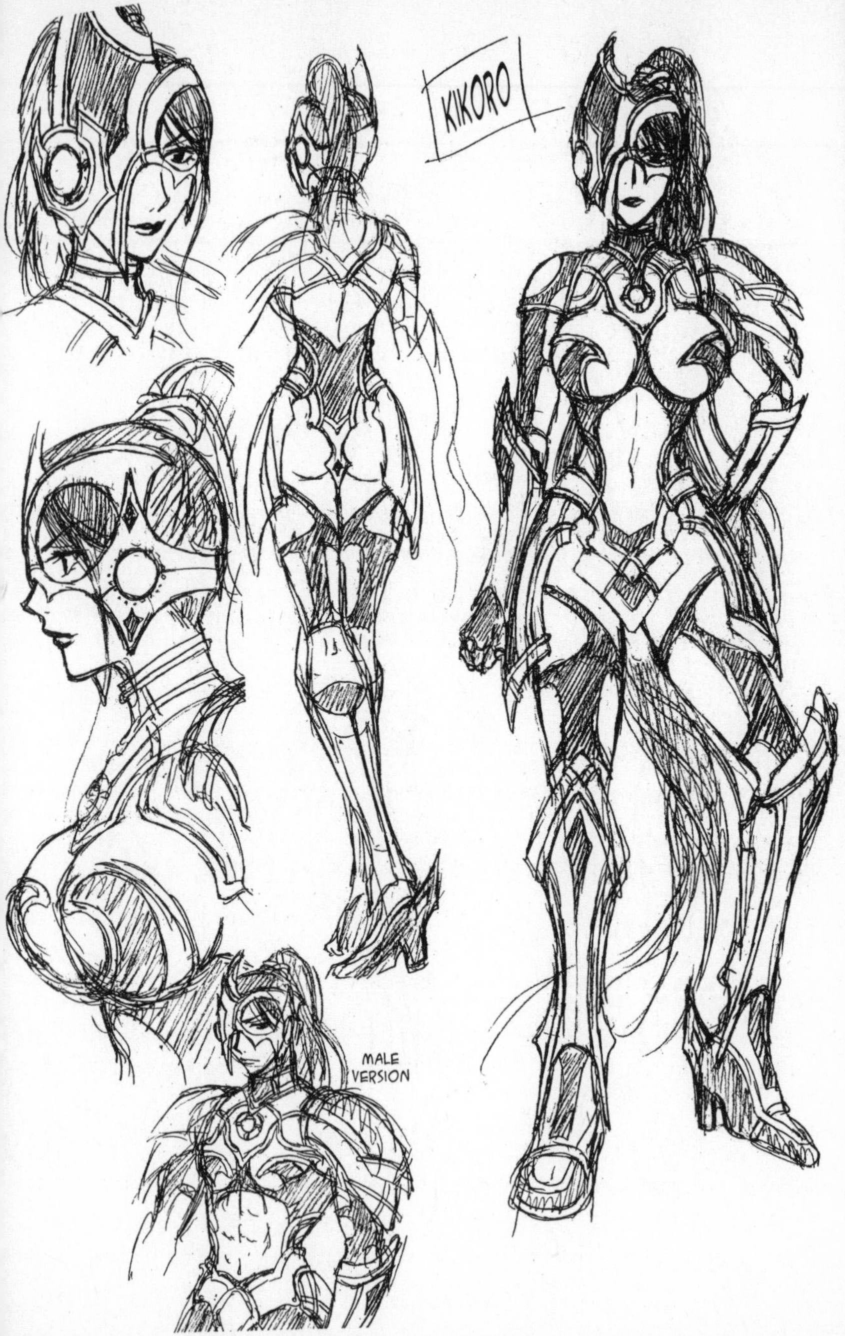
KIKORO
MALE VERSION

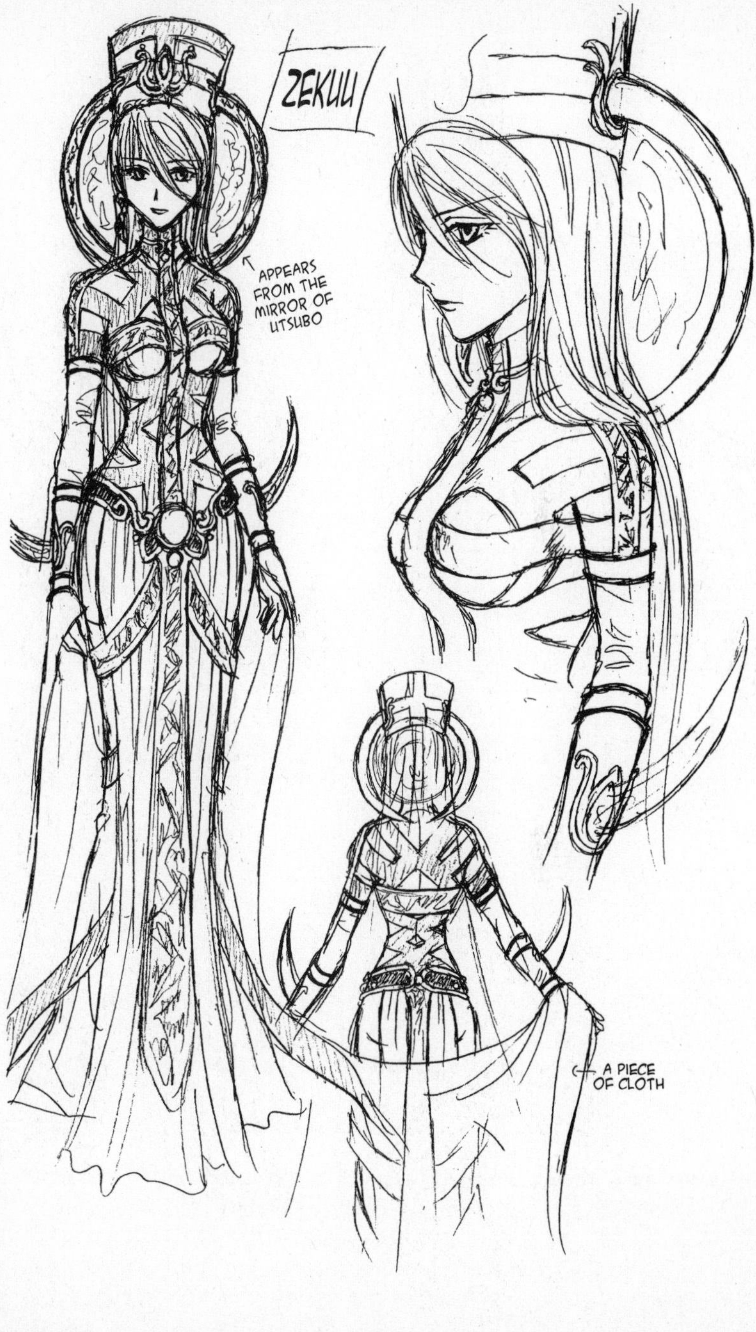
ZEKUU
APPEARS FROM THE MIRROR OF UTSUBO
A PIECE OF CLOTH

This time, we're in Kikutsune's territory.

At first glance, it wasn't obvious how serious this is...

Let me explain. I was able to take a break this month!

I went to bed early and I woke up early, and I stuck to very healthy daily habits! And yet, I lost my appetite, I lost my energy, I began to feel listless and depressed, and I was unable to think clearly. (Am I all right?)

Then I realized something.

The building right in front of my place was being demolished and I had been listening to the din from morning until night for the past month. It turns out this had exhausted my brain. (>.<)

Is this for real?! Since making this discovery, I've been using ear plugs (too late).

It'll be over soon...supposed to be... Please, let it end...

Anyway, Kikutsune's ability is to be feared!!

–YUU WATASE

AUTHOR BIO

Born March 5 in Osaka, Yuu Watase debuted in the *Shôjo Comic* manga anthology in 1989. She won the 43rd Shogakukan Manga Award with *Ceres: Celestial Legend*. One of her most famous works is *Fushigi Yûgi*, a series that has inspired the prequel *Fushigi Yûgi: Genbu Kaiden*. In 2008, *Arata: The Legend* started serialization in *Shonen Sunday*.

ARATA: THE LEGEND

Volume 16
Shonen Sunday Edition

Story and Art by YUU WATASE

ARATA KANGATARI Vol. 16
by Yuu WATASE
© 2009 Yuu WATASE
All rights reserved.
Original Japanese edition published by SHOGAKUKAN.
English translation rights in the United States of America, Canada, the United
Kingdom and Ireland arranged with SHOGAKUKAN.

English Adaptation: Lance Caselman
Translation: JN Productions
Touch-up Art & Lettering: Rina Mapa
Design: Veronica Casson
Editor: Gary Leach

Printed in Canada

Published by VIZ Media, LLC
P.O. Box 77010
San Francisco, CA 94107

10 9 8 7 6 5 4 3 2 1
First printing, December 2013

LV

MARCH 12, 2014

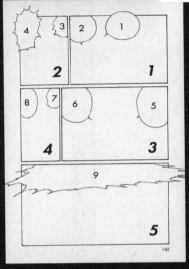

← Follow the action this way.

THIS IS THE LAST PAGE

Arata: The Legend has been printed in the original Japanese format in order to preserve the orientation of the original artwork.

Please turn it around and begin reading from right to left. Unlike English, Japanese is read right to left, so Japanese comics are read in reverse order from the way English comics are typically read. Have fun with it!